WITHDRAWN

Illegal Drugs, Economy, and Society in the Andes

Illegal Drugs, Economy, and Society in the Andes

Francisco E. Thoumi

Woodrow Wilson Center Press
Washington, D.C.

The Johns Hopkins University Press
Baltimore and London

Editorial Offices

Woodrow Wilson Center Press
One Woodrow Wilson Plaza
1300 Pennsylvania Avenue, N.W.
Washington, D.C. 20004-3027
Telephone: 202-691-4010
www.wilsoncenter.org

Order from

The Johns Hopkins University Press
Hampden Station
P.O. Box 50370
Baltimore, Maryland 21211
Telephone: 1-800-537-5487
www.jhupbooks.com

Library of Congress Cataloging-in-Publication Data

Thoumi, Francisco E.
  Illegal drugs, economy, and society in the Andes / Francisco E. Thoumi.
    p. cm.
Includes bibliographical references and index.
  ISBN 0-8018-7849-7 (hardcover : alk. paper)—ISBN 0-8018-7854-3
(pbk. : alk. paper)
1. Drug traffic—Colombia. 2. Drug traffic—Government
policy—Colombia. 3. Narcotics, Control of—Colombia. 4. Drug
traffic—Peru. 5. Drug traffic—Government policy—Peru. 6. Narcotics,
Control of—Peru. 7. Drug traffic—Bolivia. 8. Drug
traffic—Government policy—Bolivia. 9. Narcotics, Control
of—Bolivia. I. Title.
  HV5840.C7T477 2003
  363.45'098—dc21
                                                    2003012400

ABOUT THE CENTER

The Center is the living memorial of the United States of America to the nation's twenty-eighth president, Woodrow Wilson. Congress established the Woodrow Wilson Center in 1968 as an international institute for advanced study, "symbolizing and strengthening the fruitful relationship between the world of learning and the world of public affairs." The Center opened in 1970 under its own board of trustees.

In memory of

Elsa Alvarado
Jesús Antonio ("Chucho") Bejarano
Darío Betancourt
Mario Calderón and
Hernán Henao

Killed because they defended human rights, and thought, taught, and
wrote about Colombian social problems

Contents

List of Tables and Figures   xiii

Preface   xv

1   Introduction and Overview   1

Part I. The Illegal Drug Industry's History and Structure

2   Psychoactive Drug Perceptions and Attitudes in the United States and the Andean Countries   15

3   The Socioeconomic Dimensions of Illegal Drug Production 48

4   The Development and Structure of the Illegal Drug Industry in the Andes   79

Part II. The Effects of the Andean Illegal Drug Industry

5   The Size of the Illegal Drug Industry   141

xi

6   Economic, Environmental, Social, and Political Effects of the
         Illegal Drug Industry   159

7   The Illegal Drug Industry's Effects in Colombia   181

8   The Illegal Drug Industry's Effects in Bolivia and Peru   232

Part III. Country Vulnerability to Illegal Drugs

9   Illegal Drugs, Violence, and Social Differences   265

Part IV. Antidrug Policies

10   The Nature of the Drug Policy Problem   301

11   Policy Case Studies of Alternative Development in Bolivia and
         International Cooperation in Colombia   315

12   A Short Survey of Antidrug Policies in the Andes and Policy
         Conclusions   352

References   373

Index   399

Tables and Figures

Tables

5.1   Illegal Drug Income in Colombia   147

Figures

3.1   The Basic Crime Choice   71

3.2   Crime in a Homogeneous Society   72

3.3   Law Enforcement in a Heterogeneous Society   73

3.4   Changes in Social Constraints and Negative Social Dynamics   74

3.5   Policy Failure in a Stratified Society   75

Preface

In the mid-1970s, trafficking in illegal drugs was evident to a few Andean journalists and academics. However, it took more than a decade for academia and bilateral and multilateral aid agencies to recognize that to explain the social and economic development of the Andean countries, it was necessary to include illegal drugs in their analyses.

I became interested in the issue of illegal drugs in the mid-1980s, when I sensed that Colombia was in a paradoxical situation. On the one hand, Colombia was the only Latin American and Caribbean country that had avoided the external debt crisis of the early 1980s, and it was the only country in the region that had not had a single year of declining gross national product since the end of World War II. Indeed, its economic performance had been noticeably stable and all common social indicators, such as literacy rate, education level, life expectancy, employment rate, female labor force participation rate, nutrition level, housing quality, and presence of public utilities (electricity, water, and sewage) showed remarkable improvement. Furthermore, income inequality was declining. The violent death rate was the only negative social indicator, but it was not reported in most studies. On the other hand, every time one visited the country, one sensed that the quality of life was declining and that something important was hiding behind the good economic performance data.

Since then, I have devoted the largest proportion of my professional efforts to research on the illegal drug industry. During all this time, I have found a significant part of the illegal drug literature to be highly unsatisfactory. Many analyses are partial and make false or half-true statements. These studies have frequently left me confused. The desire to learn and clear up this confusion has been a main motivation for writing this book.

During the 1990s, I had the privilege of participating in several international research projects concerned with illegal drugs. In 1991, the United Nations Research Institute on Social Development offered me the opportunity to participate in a team research project in nine countries. What became the book *Political Economy and Illegal Drugs in Colombia* was my contribution to this project. In 1994, the United Nations Development Program (UNDP) hired me to coordinate a research project in Bolivia, Colombia, and Peru that funded fifteen studies in the three countries. This project produced an edited volume, *Drogas Ilícitas en Colombia*, and manuscripts for the other two countries. During the 1996–97 academic year, I received a fellowship at the Woodrow Wilson International Center for Scholars in Washington, D.C., to write a book that would provide a panoramic view of the illegal drug industry in the Andean countries. My debt to the Woodrow Wilson Center is enormous. Unfortunately, the task proved to be more complex and difficult than what I estimated when I applied for the fellowship, and it took much longer to complete this book, the first version of which was finished in April 2000.

This book thus is the result of more than 15 years of work on illegal drugs. The dynamics of the illegal drug industry are remarkable, and every study is somewhat obsolete when it is finished. The changes in the past few years have been particularly fast, drastic, and difficult to research, and the risks of doing so have increased substantially, especially in Colombia.

The book covers a period that ends sometime in the late 1990s, although an effort has been made to update it to include the most relevant recent developments. Among the most important are the following. The Bolivian government has implemented a highly successful forced eradication program. In Colombia, the nexus between the illegal industry and guerrillas and paramilitary forces has become clearer and stronger. The fall of Alberto Fujimori's regime in Peru has begun to open a window into the role of the armed forces and security agencies in the illegal industry.

Unfortunately, these topics are not covered by the book with the depth one would wish. Despite these limitations, I expect to have contributed more to explaining the nature and structure of the illegal industry and not to the description of specific events. In other words, I expect to contribute more to explaining long-term rather than short-term illegal drug issues.

Many people have contributed ideas and have supported me during the years that this book has been in the making. Their number is so large that I am afraid that any list will miss some.

In Bolivia, Eduardo Gamarra, Clark Joel, and Roberto Laserna participated in the UNDP-funded project, and the UNDP's resident representative, Carlos Felipe Martínez, helped me become familiar with a country and issues that were new to me.

In Colombia, Edgar Garzón, Manuel Hernández, Andrés López, Alejandro Reyes, Ricardo Rocha, and Sergio Uribe participated in the UNDP project and contributed significantly in many working sessions. Alvaro Camacho, Alexandra Guáqueta, Klaus Nyholm, Augusto Pérez, Carlos Pérez, Litza Pérez, Mauricio Rubio, Libardo Sarmiento, Juan G. Tokatlian, and Ricardo Vargas discussed many ideas and relevant topics with me. Gabriel de Vega, Néstor Humberto Martínez, José Antonio Ocampo, Joaquín Polo, and Alfonso Valdivieso provided political support for the UNDP project and facilitated the publication of the project's results.

In Peru, Tito Hernández and UNDP project participants Elena Alvarez, Julio Cotler, and Luis Lamas helped the author understand the relevant drug issues.

In the United States, many Woodrow Wilson Center colleagues contributed to making my fellowship an unforgettable experience. Among them, I owe special thanks to Cynthia Arnson, Joseph Brinley, Dale Eickelman, and Irene Rubin. David Abruzzino was a remarkable research assistant. In Washington, Rensselear W. Lee III, Raphael Perl, and Peter Reuter contributed ideas and read some of my drafts. I owe a particular debt to Laura Garcés, who corrected my deficient English and made innumerable substantive comments on the book.

In Europe, I owe much to Alain Labrousse of the Observatoire Géopolitique des Drogues in Paris, who gave me open access to that institution's library and discussed many drug issues in Bolivia, Peru, and Europe. Héctor Charry-Samper, Colombia's ambassador in Vienna, read and commented on the manuscript. Minister Counselor Ciro Arévalo at the Colombian Embassy in Vienna and Kathleen W. Barmon at the U.S.

Embassy in Vienna were also helpful commentators. While working at the United Nations Office of Drug Control and Crime Prevention in Vienna, I benefited from my interaction with Sandeep Chawla, Alejandra Gómez-Céspedes, Aldo Lale-Demoz, Thomas Pietschmann, Jean-François Thony, Melissa Tullis, and Anthony White.

All quotations from Spanish works cited throughout the book were translated by the author.

It remains to be said that I assume all responsibility for all ideas expressed in this book. They should not be attributed to any of those who discussed them with me and helped me or to any United Nations agency that funded my research in the past. In fact, this book expresses some opinions and ideas that are contrary to official positions of the United Nations Office of Drug Control and Crime Prevention.

Illegal Drugs, Economy, and Society in the Andes

1

Introduction and Overview

Illegal drugs have become a permanent feature of Bolivian, Colombian, and Peruvian societies. Citizens of those countries under 35 years of age do not have a memory of their countries without illicit drugs. Indeed, drugs have been an integral part of their socialization and life experience. They take illicit drugs as a "normal" point of reference that conditions the way they look at the world. Drugs have influenced the Andean countries' social, political, and economic systems; they have determined how people do business, the role these countries play in the international economic and political system, the way domestic politics is practiced, and how people look at themselves.

Earlier Bolivian, Colombian, and Peruvian generations grew up knowing that their countries were renowned for their coffee, tin, fishmeal, sugar, or copper industries and exports and that those industries shaped the national institutions and helped form the national ethos. For the younger generation, particularly in Bolivia and Colombia, illicit drugs have taken the roles of those earlier export commodities. In those Andean countries, the

1

illicit drug industry has had a dramatic impact and has become an important internal and external symbol of their national identity. This has been a burden that many Andean residents have been forced to carry and that many would like to reject or change.[1] Yet many economic, political, and social developments in the Andes have been determined by the illicit drug industry, to the point that the countries' evolution and development since the mid-1970s cannot be understood without incorporating that industry to the analysis.

The study of illegal drugs is intellectually challenging. As is shown below (chapter 2), the discussion of many issues related to illegal drugs is heavily loaded with value judgments and often unspoken fundamental assumptions. For this reason, drug debates many times are proxies for debates about basic social conceptions that determine a priori each debater's position. In other words, every person's ideology and deeply held personal experiences taint his or her analysis and perception of psychoactive drug phenomena. It is the scholar's responsibility to acknowledge this fact and to try to distance himself or herself from his or her own biases. It is necessary to attempt to approach these issues as if one were a Martian anthropologist. The goal should be to explain the situation using a wide-angle lens to evaluate and question all positions.

A further difficulty arises from the nature of the data and information available. The illegality of the drug industry precludes the use of many common research sources and techniques and imposes strong constraints on the interpretation of available information. The complexity of the subject matter and the data limitations make it impossible to draw a complete and accurate picture of the industry. Researching illegal drugs is like painting impressionistic rather than realistic pictures. The painter only hopes that the picture provides an approximate and slightly distorted vision of reality, highlighting the main aspects; he or she does not pretend to draw an exact replica.

This book examines the illicit drug industry in Bolivia, Colombia, and Peru with several goals in mind: to explain the causes for the development

---

[1] "Drug trafficking has determined how Colombia is participating in the so-called world economy, has become an enormous stigma that accompanies us, its effects have influenced our behavior and it has defined our national identity in the contemporary world" (Camacho and López 1999, 4). The importance of illicit drugs in shaping national identities distresses many Andean citizens. Slogans such as "Colombia (or Bolivia or Peru) is a lot more than drugs," and "coca is not cocaine" are in part attempts to reject illicit drugs as national identity symbols.

of and differences in the industry in each country, to describe the industry's evolution, to evaluate its effects on the country's economy and polity, to explain how and why policies have been formulated and implemented, and to evaluate policy effectiveness and the feasibility of policy improvement.

To formulate sensible policies, it is necessary to answer a fundamental question: Why does a country produce illegal drugs? The conventional wisdom responds by asserting that the illegal drug industry is driven by profits. This is a truism in the sense that a main goal of any industry, with the exception of those in the relatively small nonprofit sector, is to obtain profits.

The illegal drug industry is, however, very different from common industries. As is elaborated on in chapter 3, it presents an intriguing paradox. Profits can explain why a particular individual decides to participate in the illegal industry in one country, but they cannot explain the international division of labor of the industry. In other words, most individual industry actors are in it for the money. But despite the very large profits involved, contrary to what economics would predict, most countries that could grow coca or poppies or produce cocaine and heroin do not. This pattern contrasts with all legal crops and footloose industries similar to cocaine and heroin refining that are less profitable but are present in every country that can produce them.[2] This paradox highlights the fact that economic analyses can contribute to an explanation of the illegal drug industry but leave key questions unanswered, and it shows that a multidisciplinary approach is necessary to answer basic questions about the illegal drug economy.

During the past 50 years, mainstream economic analysis has been applied to an increasing number of problems and issues. Indeed, economists have become somewhat imperialistic in their efforts, as they have applied their discipline's more rigorous methods than those used in other social science branches to fields until recently reserved to other disciplines. Unfortunately, their studies pay little or no attention to what other disciplines have to say about the problem in question. Their works resemble a situation in which someone with powerful modern machines arrives to do a job previously done by artisans and begins from scratch, disregarding what others have done. It does not matter that the new machines

---

[2] As noted in chapter 3, the only exceptions are very small countries where large product diversification is simply not practical.

are narrow in scope, cannot do some of the tasks performed by the artisans, and cannot produce many of their high-quality products.

The current separation of academic disciplines is peculiar and has been a response to particular institutional developments in the United States and Europe.[3] Disciplines also tend to lead people with similar intelligence types and skills to congregate. Economics has attracted individuals with abstraction and mathematical skills, whereas other social science disciplines have attracted more verbal types. This makes interdisciplinary exchanges difficult.

The failure of mainstream economics to explain the international division of labor of the illegal drug industry compels the present author to listen to what other disciplines have to say about illegal drugs. This does not mean discarding economic analysis, but only acknowledging that other disciplines can complement and enrich the analysis and debate. The author is well aware that by doing so he incurs the risk of appearing to be confused or fooled in the eyes of economists and naive to those trained in other disciplines.

A multidisciplinary approach requires the study of the institutions that play a role in all illegal drug issues. As expected, institutional analyses advance the understanding of the phenomenon but are short on policy recommendations.[4] This could be considered an important limitation of this study; however, it is a lot healthier and realistic to understand the complexity of drug phenomena and drug policy limitations than to recommend ineffective policies and afterward blame their failure on "lack of political will," the "double standards" of other countries, or similar reasons.

---

[3] E.g., many American universities have agricultural economics departments but they do not have industrial economics or service economics departments. Agricultural economics developed as a discipline only because of the establishment of the federal government's land grant program in the late nineteenth century to serve farming communities. Because of its origin, it had to be an applied discipline, in contrast to the theoretical "pure" economics of the economics departments. It is no coincidence that as agriculture declined in importance within the American economy, some of these departments evolved into applied economics departments. European economics followed a different course of development, focusing more on political economy, and lagged the American economics departments' concentration on economic theory and mathematical approaches to economic problems.

[4] This may disappoint the reader who expects solutions to complex problems. The author is satisfied if this work only contributes to a better understanding of the problem.

The Plan of the Book

The first part of the book focuses on three issues. The first is how the United States and the Andean countries perceive psychoactive drugs' issues, highlighting their differences and the difficulties of establishing a fruitful dialogue. In fact, it is argued that academic and policy discussions about illegal drugs among those holding different views are confusing and fruitless.

Chapter 2 contrasts the way psychoactive drugs are looked at in the United States and in the Andean countries by showing how the attitudes toward and perceptions of the "drug problem" are based on some of the basic values of each society. Many supporters of U.S. policies and many of their Latin American critics argue from the vantage of closed logical systems, within which the interpretation of empirical evidence is predetermined. The American moralistic model demonizes drugs and those who advocate liberalization, whereas the Latin American advocates of the dependency-theory model demonize the United States and its repressive polices. These views collide, producing high levels of distrust and a dialogue of the deft that prevents sensible policy debate and evaluation.

The great power inequality between the main actors compounds the dialogue short-circuit and has allowed the United States, on the one hand, to pressure the international community to adapt its repressive drug policies. On the other hand, Andean countries have been reluctant to aggressively implement those policies, which are perceived as imposed on them by an arrogant power.

The second issue tackled in the book's first part is the question of why the illegal drug industry develops in some countries and not in others. Empirical evidence shows that profits are a necessary but not a sufficient condition for the development of the illegal drug industry because noneconomic factors play key roles determining why a country produces and traffics in drugs. Besides, there is no statistical relationship between the presence and development of the illegal drug industry and poverty, inequality, economic crises, or corruption.

These factors can play the role of a latent cause that may trigger the development of the illegal industry only when the social institutions and values have evolved to a point at which governmental, social, and internalized constraints on individual behavior have weakened. In chapter 3, a model based on the economic theory of crime is developed and expanded to take relevant noneconomic variables into account. This model shows that illegal drugs flourish in environments characterized by weak states and communities, a lack of an individual sense of belonging, the destruction of social institutions, and other factors that result in little "bridging" social capital across social groups.

One important conclusion developed in chapter 3 is that illegal drug production and trafficking depend on institutional and social characteristics that are not easily influenced by traditional policies. Another conclusion is that many antidrug policies are formulated without an understanding or knowledge of the institutional constraints that make policy goals unviable. Furthermore, those policies are formulated without empirical knowledge about their effectiveness; it is simply assumed that they are needed and appropriate to the task at hand. It is not surprising that these polices cannot achieve their goals.

Chapter 4 covers history, evolution, and structure of the illegal drug industry in the Andean countries, which are examined by highlighting country differences. Special attention is paid to the historical, social, and cultural roots of illegal crops, the roles of native cultures, violence, the way in which each country has participated in the illegal industry, and the response of the illegal industry to various policies and its evolution in search of new trafficking systems, routes, markets, and products.

The illegal drug industry has proven to be flexible and able to adapt to changing government policies. The industry in Bolivia and Peru exploited the natives' traditional cultivation and consumption, but it did not succeed in developing very sophisticated international marketing networks or "cartels."[5] It was in Colombia where this happened. The Medellín and Cali cartels developed during the 1970s and controlled the business during the 1980s. In the 1990s, the cocaine industry became more integrated in the three countries as Bolivia and Peru increased their refining and trafficking and Colombia became a primary coca producer. Simultaneously, the industry diversified markets and products. As the American cocaine market stagnated from the late 1980s on, it sought new markets in Europe, the former Soviet Union, and South America. At the same time, Colombia became a principal supplier of heroin in the United States.

During the 1990s, new actors appeared on the scene. A myriad of small trafficking syndicates appeared in Colombia; Mexicans began to substitute

---

[5] The "cartels" referred to in this book are not cartels in the traditional economic sense because they do not control raw material production and most distribution systems in their main markets. Throughout the book, "cartels" is put in quotation marks at its first use in a chapter to remind the reader of this.

for some of the Colombian smuggling organizations into the United States, where Colombia lost market share; Colombian guerrillas and paramilitary groups became principal participants in the illegal business, which has become a main funding source for the country's armed conflict; and Andean exporting syndicates developed links to European criminal organizations.

The illegal industry's need to have a social support network has led its members to simultaneously influence and conflict with the Andean states. This conflict has been particularly violent in Colombia, where it is motivated to a significant degree by the need of the illegal actors to avoid extradition to the United States. The Colombian government has led successful campaigns against the main cartels, but the illegal industry has adapted to those efforts, changing its structure and strategies. The illegal drug industry has weakened in some places, but on the whole it has not declined.

In Bolivia and Peru, coca production declined sharply during the 1990s. This was caused by a combination of factors. The destruction of the Cali and Medellín cartels weakened coca paste demand in Peru because the smaller syndicates that replaced the large cartels had a strong preference to buy paste in Colombia. This was accompanied by the Peruvian government's campaign to seal off coca-producing areas, mainly though an aggressive policy to shoot down illegal planes and manually eradicate coca bushes. However, the coca production decline in Peru was due mainly to the abandonment of coca fields in response to a sharp price decline, which was accompanied by a dramatic expansion in coca plantings in Colombia. Coca hectareage remained stable in Bolivia throughout the 1990s until 1998, when the newly elected government started an aggressive and remarkably successful forcible manual eradication campaign that did away with about 85 percent of the illegal coca plantings.

The second part of the book focuses on the illegal industry's effects on the region. It includes chapters on the size of the industry and its economic, social, political, and environmental effects in each country. Chapter 5 discusses the industry's size in each country; shows the myriad problems associated with the quantification of the industry's revenues, value added, and distribution of its income; and questions many common beliefs about the large size of the illegal industry in each country's economy. It also shows that during the 1970s and 1980s the drug industry generated a higher share of gross national product in Bolivia and Peru than in Colombia and that from then on, this share has declined substantially in the three countries.

Chapter 6 surveys the possible effects of the illegal industry. Chapters 7 and 8 describe the industry's effects in each country. Chapter 8 presents evidence that the Bolivian and Peruvian economies benefited from the industry, particularly during the 1980s, when both countries suffered foreign debt crises. In both countries, the illegal industry was an important employer in rural areas, and illegal income was widely distributed and facilitated structural macroeconomic adjustment. In Colombia—which has had a history of stable macroeconomic management and has a more diversified economy—the positive economic effects of the industry have been less clear. These effects are examined in chapter 7. Illegal income has been highly concentrated in Colombia, which has led to the concentration of land tenancy in the hands of drug traffickers and their associates.

More important, during the past few years in Colombia, illegal drug revenues have become an important funding source for guerrilla and paramilitary groups, the main actors in the country's ambiguous war. Drugs in the country generated illegal regional economic booms in the 1970s and 1980s that were condoned by most (and applauded by some), but in the long run they acted as a catalyst for a great national crisis. It is no wonder that today most Colombians agree that the long-term effects of the illegal drug industry have been disastrous for the country.

The political systems of the Andean countries have been more vulnerable to illegal drug influences than their economies. This is an important lesson from this study. Indeed, the structures and small sizes of the Andean economies present many limitations to money laundering and drug capital investment. In all these countries, it is very risky for entrepreneurs in the modern economic sector to develop a nexus with the illegal industry. Because of this, drug-generated capital tends to be invested in real estate.

In the Andean countries, it is very easy to identify those who have amassed illegal fortunes. Thus, drug traffickers have a pressing need to develop social networks to protect their capital. These networks must involve politicians. The authoritarian traditions of the Andean societies reinforce this tendency. Besides, the traffickers' revenues are too large relative to public-sector salaries, and politicians' income and their bribery or "purchase" is a great threat to the weak Andean democracies. The illicit drug industry's funding of Colombia's internal conflict is another glaring example of the political system's vulnerability to the industry.

The social institutions of each country condition the success or failure of antidrug policies. The third part of the book examines the social characteristics that make some countries more prone than others to develop the illegal industry.

Chapter 9 explores some important variations among Andean societies that explain the differences across countries in the illegal industry's economic geography and other structural characteristics. One key difference to be explained is the concentration until the mid- and late 1990s of coca production in Bolivia and Peru and the predominance of Colombians in cocaine and heroin manufacturing and international trafficking. The chapter shows that the Colombian state has had some modern traits that explain the country's stable economic growth and political continuity. These factors projected an image of a state that was more modern than Bolivia and Peru. However, the Colombian state was the weakest one in terms of territory control, and in its capacity to provide adequate conflict resolution systems and enforce laws.

The rapid modernization process in the mist of weaker social constraints in Colombia resulted in fewer and weaker social restrictions on individual behavior than in the other Andean countries. In Bolivia and Peru, strong native societies had controlled deviant and antisocial behaviors and so did the "white" (*mestizo*) society in which people had to show that they were not Indian. It is not surprising that a significant proportion of Colombians show extreme individualist behaviors when compared with Bolivians and Peruvians. The modernization process in Colombia produced fast urbanization, remarkable increases in education levels, and changes in the role of women in society and in many social relationships. All these changes led to drastic structural shifts that made Colombia more likely to host the illegal drug industry than other Andean countries.

The fourth and last part of the book focuses on antidrug policies in the Andes. Chapter 10 highlights the complex and conflictive nature of antidrug policy formulation in the Andes. It shows that there is no consensus on the nature of the "drug problem" and surveys some of the main difficulties encountered in establishing meaningful dialogues among those espousing different views. It is not surprising that antidrug policies are difficult to evaluate in a way that satisfies those with opposing positions. Policy goals are frequently vague and unclear, and policy implementation is plagued by difficulties.

Chapter 11 illustrates policy implementation problems in detail, using two experiences with international cooperation: alternative de ment programs in Bolivia and the Special Cooperation Pro Colombia funded by the international community after the assa of presidential candidate Luis Carlos Galán in 1989. These experiences highlight the glaring lack of coordination between donor and recipient countries, the lack of participation of beneficiaries in program formulation and implementation, the great differences in expectations between donors and beneficiaries, project implementation difficulties, the frequent political opportunism of project promoters, and the great coordination difficulties among various project agencies.

Chapter 12 surveys the main antidrug policies followed by the three countries: eradication of coca and poppy plantings; crop-substitution and alternative development programs that aimed to provide peasants alternative sources of income; interdiction efforts and controls on chemical inputs ("precursors") used in the refining of cocaine and heroin; laboratory seizure and destruction and domestic interdiction of illegal drugs; interdiction and seizure of the same products outside the Andean countries; extradition of the main Andean traffickers to the United States; strengthening of the Andean justice and law enforcement systems to improve efficiency and to prevent corruption of justice officials and police and military personnel, to change and enact new laws to increase minimum sentences for drug-trafficking crimes, to make money laundering a crime and to facilitate the seizure, confiscation, and expropriation of assets bought with drug money; and training police and armed forces to improve their antidrug performance. The last section of the chapter summarizes the main conclusions about antidrug policies.

Toward Understanding the Illegal Drug Industry

Antidrug policies are formulated from very partial perspectives, mainly in response to moral or public health considerations, and attempt to make illegal drug production and trafficking less profitable in absolute terms or relative to other legal activities. These policies do not deal with the institutional reasons why a country produces and traffics in drugs and frequently counteract each other. Most policies do not take into account economic, social, cultural, political, and environmental factors, and thus it is not surprising that their record of success is very poor.

Following a traditional economic model of crime, polices are geared to make illegal activities less profitable either by increasing costs or reducing revenues. Policies aimed at lowering the profitability of illegal drugs without changing the institutional root causes of production and trafficking confront great economic and political obstacles. Eradication, increased seizures, and similar policies lower profitability in one location but increase it everywhere else. Therefore, to succeed, they have to repress production and traffic globally, a goal that has proven unachievable until now. These policies have also generated significant political backlashes in the three Andean countries, which raise questions about their sustainability. Furthermore, the inability to prevent crop displacement has contributed significantly to environmental deterioration.

Punitive policies frequently produce contradictory economic results because they seek to maximize the price to the final consumer and minimize the revenues to the producer. In fact, some policies tend to neutralize the results sought by other policies. For example, aerial spraying of coca fields acts as a price support for coca, which in turn encourages new plantings. The real policy challenge arises because drug control requires appropriate and well-implemented antidrug policies; more important, it requires institutional changes. This does not mean that all repressive policies are ineffective or have to be eliminated. It only means that expecting current polices to eliminate the "drug problem" is unrealistic.

It is hoped that this book contributes to an understanding of why the illegal drug industry developed in some Andean countries and of how the industry has influenced them. It is obvious to say that only by understanding a problem can one advance in the search for a solution. However, in a field that has been dominated by moral and ideological positions, it is necessary to state the obvious.

Part I

The Illegal Drug Industry's History and Structure

2

Psychoactive Drug Perceptions and Attitudes in the United States and the Andean Countries

Illegal drug trafficking has important peculiarities that make it difficult—and, at times, very frustrating—to study. One of them is the lack of consensus about the effects of drug use and abuse and about what constitutes the "drug problem." Psychoactive drugs have been produced and consumed by all societies, and have always presented a policy challenge. What societies perceive as dangerous drugs vary substantially over time and space. Many drugs considered dangerous today were widely used and thought to have desirable effects in the past. Indeed, "many of the problems associated with drugs and alcohol, significantly, can best be viewed as social constructs" (Heath 1992, 279).[1] For example, alcohol and other psychoactive drugs were thought to increase work productivity when so-

---

[1]Siegel (1989) documented psychoactive drug use throughout history, stressing its presence in all societies, including animal ones! The widespread use of drugs led Siegel to refer to psychoactive drugs as "the fourth need" of all humans. Musto (1999) presented the history of drug use and policies in the United States. Lerner and Ferrando (1989) surveyed drug use in Peru and gave a short summary of the history of drug use

ciety was mainly rural, and drugs were used to relieve the boredom of lonely work in the fields.[2] When society became industrialized, however, the requirements of factory organization and production made drugs an obstacle to productivity.

Simultaneously with industrialization, for the first time in history, most people began to have significant nonwork time available to use as they pleased, and drugs became possible to consume during leisure time. Only then did drugs become a "danger" to society (Husch 1992). In the Andean countries, coca chewing was used extensively during colonial times to increase productivity in the silver mines (Carter and Mamani 1986; Henman 1978; Vidart 1991), and it is still reported to be used to help workers work long shifts.[3]

Psychoactive drug production, trafficking, and consumption are activities based on consensual relations that can generate high social costs, which are exacerbated by the addictive effects of these drugs. The activities that societies have perceived as socially costly or undesirable have varied. They have included premarital and extramarital sex, interracial and interreligious sex and marriage, particular gender roles, migrations, political dissent, religious practices and dissent, gambling, trafficking in small arms and radioactive products, and so on.

These behaviors generate satisfaction or profit for those involved but can also cause social problems, although there has not been a consensus across societies about which of them generate social costs, the size of those social costs, and how to cope with them. Furthermore, social attitudes and policies toward these behaviors have changed significantly over time. For instance, racial segregation, gender roles, and migration restrictions were enforced in many Western countries until a generation or two ago. Indeed, many of the civil rights movements of the twentieth century were organized against social restrictions of this type.

Psychoactive drug production, trafficking, and consumption are particular cases of potentially socially costly behaviors. Societies have developed their own particular ways to cope with them, depending on each so-

---

in the West. Carter and Mamani (1986), Henman (1978), and Vidart (1991) detailed the role of coca and psychoactive drugs in native Bolivian, Colombian, and Amazonian societies, showing how drugs were "domesticated," i.e., how societies developed ways to allow psychoactive drug use under controlled conditions, minimizing social costs.

[2]In the Andean countries, *chicha* and *guarapo*, fermented corn and sugarcane beverages, have been traditionally used for this purpose.

[3]E.g., truck drivers from Bolivia and northern Argentina are known to chew coca to be able to drive long hours in their runs to deliver rural products to the Buenos Aires market.

ciety's perception of the degree of social danger and on its social institutions and values. The way in which each society copes has deep historical roots and a strong cultural component, and coping mechanisms are frequently difficult to understand by outsiders, who may look at them as either charming cultural peculiarities or as signs of cultural or civil backwardness. They might be these things, but they also play important roles because they are instrumental in the ways in which social institutions manage perceived problems.

Psychoactive drug use has been controlled in many ways: by punishing those involved, by controlling drug use through the socialization process, by applying gentle or subtle social pressure, by ritualizing drug use (e.g., religious ceremonies and rites of passage), by allowing only select groups to use drugs (e.g., shamans), and by establishing a period of the year or holiday when they can be used (e.g., carnival).

Policies based on particular social perceptions, institutions, and values can be effective within the social environment in which they are formulated, but they are very difficult to enforce under different conditions. Furthermore, their institutional and cultural specificity makes debate and evaluations very difficult, because doing so requires questioning the ingrained mores that many members of each society take as given and "natural." Psychoactive drug policies fall into the group of those policies that are highly influenced by specific societal characteristics, which account for their great resiliency to change.

In this chapter, an effort is made to sketch the evolution of psychoactive drug policies and the main "models" that determine social perceptions about psychoactive drugs in the United States and Latin America. The aim is, first, to identify those perceptions and, second, to highlight their main differences and to show why it is so difficult to have meaningful drug policy dialogues within the United States, in Latin American societies, and across countries. The next and subsequent sections present short summaries of the development and evolution of U.S. and Latin American attitudes and models. The short final section highlights the conflicts and difficulties in having dialogue among those who espouse the U.S. and Latin American drug visions.

U.S. Attitudes, Perspectives, and Models

Please sir, don't take me wrong, I do demonize drugs.

—Barry McCaffrey at the Woodrow Wilson International Center for Scholars,
January 1997

We must see drugs as the work of the devil.

—Jesse Jackson on CNN's *Both Sides*, January 25, 1998

Illegal drugs are a weapon of mass destruction.

—Brigadier General Keith Huber, director of operations of the U.S. Southern
Command, at the conference "War and Peace in Colombia: Strategy for
Ambiguous Warfare," U.S. Army War College, Carlisle, Pennsylvania,
November 12, 1999

Psychoactive drug consumption has a long history in the United States.
Alcohol and tobacco have been consumed widely throughout the country's history, and some of today's illegal drugs (e.g., opium) were consumed before the nineteenth century (Musto 1999). The use of opiates
was promoted by the discovery of injectable morphine, by Chinese immigration associated with railroad construction in the American West,
and by the Civil War, during which morphine was a main medicine to
treat the wounded.

In the second half of the nineteenth century, medicine's shortcomings
for curing most illnesses encouraged doctors to prescribe drugs that
calmed pain and made patients feel good, and this practice contributed
to the widespread use of morphine, the newly discovered cocaine, and
later on, heroin. Commerce and use of psychoactive drugs were common
at the end of the nineteenth century and beginning of the twentieth. The
patent medicine industry, whose products' ingredients were not revealed
to the public but consisted of alcohol, cocaine, opium, and other addictive drugs, became very successful. The status quo began to change during the last decade of the nineteenth century, when it was perceived that
some of these drugs were addictive and caused costly social problems.
Indeed, at this time the United States experienced its first opium and cocaine epidemic:

At the time, there were an estimated 300,000 opiate addicts in the
United States in a population a third the size of today's. Apart from
Civil War veterans who had become addicted to morphine administered
for pain, most addicts were women, often from the middle and upper
classes. Frustrated by the constraints of Victorian society, they found
solace in opiate use, which at the time was a socially more acceptable
habit for women than drinking. (Falco 1994, 17)

Musto (1999, 42–43) shows that "a national survey indicated that among physicians about 2 percent and among nurses about 1 percent were habitués of some form of opium. Only 0.7 percent of other professional classes and 0.2 percent of the general population were addicted."

From the perspective of the social sciences, one should ask why relatively low addiction levels generated such a strong reaction in American society. A key factor was and has been the association in the American mind of drug consumption with moral decay and foreign threats. It must be remembered that during colonial times many settlers came to the United States escaping religious persecution in Europe.[4] These religious groups maintained strict behavioral controls on their members.[5] Traditional puritanical values have transcended traditional Protestant churches. It is worth noting that the Mormon Church, the most successful indigenous American religion, prohibits consumption of all psychoactive drugs, including caffeine and nicotine (tobacco).

Another factor has been the American belief in unlimited progress and the need to maintain control over the hostile environment and prevent moral decay. Morally based pressure was behind the first incursion by the federal government into drug policies. In the Spanish-American War of 1903, the United States gained control of the Philippines, where there was widespread opium consumption, and American missionaries—motivated mainly by moral considerations—pressured the federal government to formulate and implement anti-opium policies in that country (Musto 1999). Similarly, the opposition to the United Kingdom's opium trade with China was rooted in the large number of American Protestant missionaries who were motivated by religious and moral concerns (Walker 1991). Given this history, it is not surprising that many Americans consider psychoactive drug use first and foremost as something sinful and immoral.

The "moralistic" American model has had a very strong influence on U.S. antidrug policies. It is difficult to find this model spelled out in the illegal drug literature, but the following summary of an off-the-record exposition of a senior United States Senate staff member at a recent colloquium provides a good sketch of it.[6]

---

[4]This is in stark contrast with the conquest south of the border.

[5]This also contrasts with the Catholic tradition in Latin America, which emphasized confession, repentance, and participation in rituals and ceremonies over day-to-day behavior as signs of compliance with the religion's mandates.

[6]This argument was presented at a colloquium sponsored by the National Strategy Information Center, Inc., at Georgetown University, Washington, D.C., October 30–31, 1997.

The moralistic argument begins by asserting a truism. Crime has existed in all societies: democratic, authoritarian, communist, socialist, capitalist, theocratic, and so on. The widespread existence of crime leads the supporters of this model to argue that social characteristics do not determine crime and that criminals are the basic reason why there is crime. The world is divided between good and bad people, criminals and noncriminals, and crime is just an expression of human nature. The reasons that some people are criminals are found within themselves, not in society. To fight crime, we should not blame or try to change society; we should simply fight crime and criminals.

This moralistic approach to crime reflects a conception of life as a continuous struggle between good and evil. Crimes like drug production and trafficking are scourges or cancers that must be extirpated from society. Drugs are simply sinful and/or devilish, and there is no room for alternatives that tolerate controlled forms of drug production and consumption.[7]

This vision of the drug problem concludes that it is imperative to punish drug production, trafficking, and use.[8] Drug producers are demonized, and countries that produce drugs are simply societies dominated by bad guys who should be fought. Because drugs are a scourge and a cancer, failures in the drug fight should simply rekindle the fire needed to fight harder; after all, the conflict between good and evil has dominated the history of humanity, and the struggle should continue until evil is conquered. Drug production and consumption menace American society, foreign drug producers are part of that menace, and illegal drugs are a national security issue.

---

[6]This argument was presented at a colloquium sponsored by the National Strategy Information Center, Inc., at Georgetown University, Washington, D.C., October 30–31, 1997.

[7]MacCoun and Reuter's (2001, chap. 4) book reviews the drug debates in the United States and contrasts the deontological arguments (based on the works of Immanuel Kant), which assert that certain moral obligations hold irrespective of their empirical consequences, with consequentialist arguments (based on the works of Jeremy Bentham and John Stuart Mill), which enjoin us to evaluate acts and rules by their consequences. They find that most people use both types of arguments, that deontological arguments are used by both criminalizers and legalizers, and that "it does seem plausible that legal moralistic sentiments run deep in American opposition to drug law reform" (p. 66).

U.S. drug policies have not been shaped exclusively by moral concerns, however. The health professions have also played an important role. At the beginning of the twentieth century, the health professions were unregulated by the government, there were no national self-regulating professional organizations, and laboratories did not have to list their products' ingredients. In compliance with free trade principles imbedded in the Constitution, federal and state governments had no psychoactive drug regulating policies (Musto 1999). State government attempts to control addictive drugs had been feeble and ineffective.

Drug addiction was concentrated in large cities in a few states, and those states that did not have drug addiction problems were not interested in legislating against it. This presented a dilemma for states with numerous drug users, because it would have not been very useful to have strong antidrug legislation in a particular state if drugs were unregulated in neighboring ones and the state could not prevent interstate trade. Effective drug control would require federal legislation that applied in all states. However, Southern members of Congress—who feared further interference with states' rights and segregation laws—opposed federal legislation of this type.

During the first decades of the twentieth century, the health professions became organized and regulated, and doctors were given a monopoly to practice medicine and prescribe a large number of drugs. These institutional developments facilitated the formulation of drug policies at a time when the role of physicians and pharmacists in promoting drug addiction was a highly debated issue because both groups had strong financial interests in drug distribution and treatment.[9] There were several relevant policy questions: To what extent was drug addiction the result of medical treatment? Should addicts be required to join treatment programs? Should physicians and pharmacists be allowed to treat addicts and to prescribe maintenance doses? Should psychoactive drug consumption be criminalized?

After intense political maneuvering, the Harrison Act, which regulated the psychoactive drug trade, was enacted in 1914. This was the first federal antidrug legislation, and it simultaneously satisfied Southern members of Congress, physicians, and pharmacists. However, some of the

---

[9]As was shown above, the incidence of cocaine and heroin use among those in these professions was significantly higher than in the overall population (Musto 1999), a fact that supports the argument that access to drugs increases the probability of addiction.

act's provisions were appealed to the Supreme Court, which ruled in 1916 that physicians were free to prescribe any drug to their patients (Musto 1992).

These developments coincided with the growth of the prohibition movement, which had a strong moralistic foundation. In 1919, it won the approval of the Eighteenth Amendment to the U.S. Constitution, which prohibited alcohol production, distribution, and consumption. Two months later, the Supreme Court, in a split 5–4 decision, took away physicians' rights to prescribe psychoactive drugs for drug addiction maintenance (Musto 1999), a decision that criminalized drug supply.

Throughout the 1920s and 1930s, drug criminalization advanced. In 1924, opium imports were prohibited. Addiction treatment centers were abolished. In 1933, the Twenty-First Amendment to the U.S. Constitution repealed alcohol prohibition, but in 1937 marijuana trade was heavily taxed, making it de facto illegal.

Throughout the first decades of the twentieth century, there were hot debates about the nature of drug consumption and addiction. On the one hand, the moral-religious position treated drug users as individuals of weak character whose behavior had to be modified.[10] If this was not achieved, they should be punished to prevent the rotten apple from corrupting the rest. On the other hand, health professionals considered drug users as victims and sick individuals who required help. Throughout the twentieth century, these two approaches vied to define U.S. drug policies, which in Falco's (1994) words, were formulated "by the docs and the cops."

Xenophobia (the invasion of the corrupt outside world) has also played a role in drug policies (Musto 1999; Falco 1994). Immigration of non-European racial and ethnic groups has been perceived as a threat to the American mainstream that associated opium consumption with Chinese immigration, cocaine with blacks, and marijuana with Mexicans:

> Fears that respectable white women were being seduced [in the opium dens],...[and of] cocaine, moreover [were] linked in popular perception with blacks—another "alien" race in the white American consciousness. Black stevedores in New Orleans had first used cocaine in the early

---

[10]These groups today also assert, using similar arguments, that homosexual behavior should be modified.

1890s to help endure their grueling work. ... Cocaine use soon spread to black laborers in the other parts of the South ... [and the] link between Mexican immigrants and marijuana was amplified by groups like the American Coalition, whose goal was to keep America "American." (Falco 1994, 19–20)[11]

The link between "aliens" and drugs led to several incidents of collective hysteria and was used to justify segregation policies, many of which intended to protect white women from evil aliens.

Rooted as it is in the traditional core of American beliefs, the xenophobic element in antidrug policies has not gone away:

Once these drugs were linked in the public mind with dangerous foreigners and racial minorities, popular attitudes formed that persist today. Drug users were no longer viewed as victims of careless doctors or overenthusiastic American drug companies, but rather as suspicious deviants who undermined the nation's stability. Because of this early history, heroin, cocaine, and marijuana have been perceived as "un-American" in a way that alcohol, tobacco, and prescription drugs have not. The xenophobia and racial fear that informed the original drug laws still influence our drug policies. (Falco 1994, 21).

One important question raised by the repeal of prohibition is why alcohol prohibition was abolished while prohibition against cocaine and opiates was maintained and that against marijuana was established later on. An answer can be based on xenophobia, but other factors appear to have played more important roles. Alcohol consumption was more widespread, particularly within the country's mainstream, than that of other psychoactive drugs, and the alcohol supply came mainly from domestic sources. These two factors concentrated the costs of alcohol prohibition (i.e., the growth of organized crime; violence within criminal organizations; consumer deaths due to a lack of product quality control; and corruption in police forces, local governments, and other institutions) within the United States and directly affected the country's mainstream.

[11]The use of cocaine by stevedores parallels South American Indians' coca use in the old silver mines of Potosí and the Andean haciendas.

In spite of the social support for the repeal of prohibition, some argue that repressive drug policies were successful. Alcohol consumption fell during prohibition, and heroin and cocaine consumption declined significantly during the 1930s. Other forces also contributed to drug consumption decline because World War II made trade in illicit drugs more difficult and contributed to a drop in the number of addicts. As a result of these developments, during the early postwar period cocaine and heroin consumption was not perceived as a social problem in the United States.

Illegal psychoactive drug consumption in the United States surged back during the 1960s, a transcendental decade in the country's history. The United States became involved in a war in Vietnam that changed the country. The Vietnam War generated stronger domestic opposition than any other foreign war. Simultaneously, the growth of the civil rights movement forced an expansion of domestic democracy and increased human rights protection for ethnic and racial minorities that had been officially segregated in parts of the country. The decade also saw drastic changes in women's social roles and the development of the feminist movement. And for the first time, homosexuals came "out of the closet" and sought to protect their civil rights. The role of the federal government as protector and guarantor of civil rights expanded to include economic rights.

The great institutional changes experienced by American society during the 1960s altered the relation between the individual and social institutions. Social controls on drug use and other behaviors related to sex, interracial relations, and respect for authority weakened. This loosened social cohesion and the sense of belonging and also changed the meaning of patriotism and the ways of expressing it.

Given these changes, it is not surprising that psychoactive drug consumption increased substantially. Indeed, drug use became a symbol and an expression of social protest and an affirmation of the individuality and identity of many Americans. During the 1960s, Americans questioned many traditions and mores, and many accepted and adopted behaviors previously considered deviant. Moreover, many Americans grew cautious about the universality of their own principles and values. All these changes made society more tolerant toward drugs at a time when drug use was growing.

The Vietnam War contributed directly to increased drug use, particularly of heroin, and created the expectation of a heroin epidemic among returning soldiers (Clague 1973). This fear led to the reestablishment of treatment programs, especially those based on methadone, a synthetic substitute for heroin.

By the end of the decade, drug addiction was perceived as a social problem. Marijuana consumption had spread, and other drugs, including synthetic ones like LSD, had appeared. In 1971, President Richard Nixon appointed a National Commission on Marijuana and Drug Abuse. The commission, which was composed of fairly conservative citizens, concluded that marijuana should be decriminalized, although it cautioned against excessive liberalization. The commission also evaluated the consumption effects of other drugs and questioned several widespread beliefs about them. Still, in 1972 President Nixon declared the "war on drugs."

During the 1970s, a few states decriminalized marijuana consumption and tolerated the possession of "personal doses." Consumption of other drugs became glamorous among the "beautiful people," for whom cocaine became the drug of choice. Cocaine consumption increased substantially among middle- and upper-class consumers, who were mainly professionals and school-age youth. Violence, family breakdown, and other social disruptions associated with drug consumption became obvious to many people.

By the early 1980s, the drug consumer profile had changed: Cocaine consumption declined among the upper-middle and upper classes, which had reacted favorably to educational campaigns and to their own negative experiences with drug consumption. Simultaneously, the introduction of "crack" cocaine led to the development of a large low-income market, mainly among African and Hispanic-Americans. These changes led to a reversal of the tolerant trend of the 1970s and to strengthened support for repressive policies that toughened antidrug measures and produced an unprecedented increase in the number of people incarcerated—which reached 1,350,000 in 1992, two-thirds of whom were addicted to some drug (Falco 1994, xxii).[12]

One persistent problem in American society is its need

to target an enemy. An old pattern, this is evident today in the public opposition to Japan that emerged just as tensions with the former Soviet Union were ending. Looking at the past forty years, the Cold War itself immediately followed World War II. Iran was considered a valued ally under the Shah, but became an archenemy after the revolution; similar

---

[12]Recent newspaper reports show a continuous increase in incarceration levels in the United States. By 2000, the number had reached 2 million.

reversals took place with respect to Cuba and Nicaragua. Even non-threatening Grenada and Panama held center stage briefly in recent confrontations, and Iraq's Saddam Hussein has eclipsed even Lybia's Moammar el-Qaddafi as a personalized villain. (Heath 1992, 269–70)

Other analysts of American culture argue that Americans perceive the United States as a crusader with special responsibilities in the world (Robertson 1980). The revisionist school of U.S. history argues that the American ethos requires the country to have a foreign enemy (Dalleck 1983).[13]

Before 1990, the fight against communism primarily drove American policies toward Latin America, and the war on drugs was frequently sacrificed to the war on communism. Since the collapse of communism, antidrug policies have become central to the country's international policy agenda in the Andean countries.[14] In the 1990s, illegal drugs and international organized crime substituted, at least partially, for communism as a national security threat.

The American perception of the "drug problem" and drug policies has been strongly influenced by a combination of factors—including moral concerns that demonize drugs; such institutional developments as the organization of the medical profession, which led to government regulation and the establishment of a monopoly for prescribing many drugs; and xenophobic prejudices. The resulting domestic policies always have categorized psychoactive drug consumption as a mix between a public health and a criminal problem. The importance of these two elements has appeared to shift cyclically over time (Musto 1992). This has led to an ambivalence in the way society looks at addicts, who have been perceived on the one hand as victims or sick persons and on the other hand as criminals or morally deficient individuals.

Under the moralistic approach, those in the drug industry play an evil role. Under the public health one, they are not demons but their behavior is not condoned either because they are important contributors to a grave problem. From the moralistic point of view, policies must be repressive. From the public health one, the policy emphasis should be on prevention,

---

[13]Foreign observers such as Verdú (1996) and Heale (1990) have expanded this point.

[14]Tokatlian (1995, 1997) and Gamarra (1994) respectively studied the effects of this change on Colombian–American and Bolivian–American relations.

education, and treatment, but if repressive polices diminish illegal drug supply, they are also welcome.

It is remarkable how little the social sciences have influenced U.S. drug policies. Studies of the influence of social changes on the demand for psychoactive drugs, of the relation between social marginalization and drug use, and of the relations among drug illegality, high profits, and violence within the industry at best have had a marginal influence on the shaping of policies. As will be shown below, the disregard for social and economic analysis in drug policy formulation has extended to those implemented in the Andean countries, such as crop substitution and alternative development, interdiction, and extradition.

In the Western world, analytical studies are normally precursors of policy changes. Drug policies are a prominent exception to this rule. The list of books and articles that criticize the predominant views on drugs in the United States and the policies derived from them is very large and grows by the day.[15] Criticisms of predominant views and policies come from several angles. Some argue that people have a right to consume psychoactive drugs and get high, and that the government has no business regulating drugs. Others argue on practical grounds that current repressive policies have failed to control drug consumption and that drastic changes are required to minimize the damage of addiction and trafficking, including the possibility of legalization and decriminalization. Still others use similar arguments but, short of recommending a drastic policy change, suggest a change in emphasis from supply reduction to demand control.

Because of the large numbers of minorities incarcerated, some criticize current policies as racially motivated and as part of a conspiracy against minorities. Others point out that when antidrug policies take the form of a crusade or "jihad" all other policy goals and civil rights protection become subordinate to it and warn of an increasingly dangerous crippling of those rights. In spite of all these studies and arguments, the main perceptions, principles, and prejudices that shape American drug views have persisted, and policies continue to be driven by them.

It must be noted that social and political support for current U.S. drug

---

[15]E.g., see (among others) Balakar and Grinspoon (1984); Baum (1996); Bertram et al. (1996); Evans and Berent (1992); Falco et al. (1997); Husak (1992); Hyde (1995); Lusane (1991); MacCoun and Reuter (2001); McWilliams (1996); Meier (1994); Nadelmann (1993); Peele (1989); Rasmussen and Benson (1994); Siegel (1989); Szasz (1992), Thorton (1991); Trebach (1982); and Trebach and Inciardi (1993).

policies is high but that support among academics and analysts who have studied the issue is quite weak. A recent study of drug policy views among congressional staff, academics, think-tank professionals, and consultants in Washington (Thoumi 1999) found a consensus both on the need to change policies and on the impossibility of doing so in the near and medium terms. Everyone interviewed for that study agreed that no possible political gain would be associated with promoting policy change.[16]

Andean Attitudes, Perspectives, and Models

North Americans invented [sic] consumption, promoted production and then prohibited drugs to keep for themselves its fantastic profits.

—Antonio Caballero (1999a, 147)

Cocaine is a political blackmailing instrument used by the United States to control the Bolivian state.

—Hugo Rodas (1996, 49)

The United States does not want to eliminate drug trafficking. It wants to use it as part of its geopolitical strategy towards Latin America.

—Hugo Rodas (1996, 204)

[16]Perhaps the most disturbing finding was the subtle pressure that everyone feels to project a hawkish image and the perceived extremely high cost associated with any decriminalization suggestion. Many analysts believe that drugs should be decriminalized, and that eventually that will happen. However, they feel that open support for those views would be very harmful to their careers. Many policy critics feel that they have to begin their comments by stating that they do not condone drug consumption and that they do not advocate decriminalization. Only after making this point clear, they proceed with their criticism. In several large studies (e.g., Falco et al. 1997 and Riley 1995), the argument developed through several chapters points in the direction of at least a discussion of decriminalization possibilities. However, in the concluding chapter, there is a logical turn around and this possibility is never mentioned. A more disturbing situation arises when political pressure is exerted to limit freedom of expression. E.g., in 1994 I collaborated with the World Bank in organizing a seminar on illegal drugs. The U.S. Department of State requested that the World Bank cancel the invitations of a Colombian and an American who were well-known "legalizers." The bank refused to do so, and the Department of State threatened not to let the Colombian into the country. At that point, the bank canceled the seminar 48 hours before it was supposed to begin.

The "War on Drugs" is the perfect substitute for the Cold War and the United States, starting with Latin America, will use it as an ideal means to consolidate its domination.

—Róger Cortez (1992, 169)

The perceptions of the "drug problem" in the Andean countries, which are very different from those in the United States, reflect the region's history, social structure, and values. Many plants that grow in the Andean countries contain psychoactive drugs that have been widely used since before the Spanish conquest. The main drugs used by the ancient Andean cultures were alcohol and those contained in coca leaves. Alcohol and coca have been used continuously in the Andes, although their use has not been constant throughout time and space.

Coca has received the most attention among all Andean plants used to produce psychoactive drugs. Coca has a long and conflictive history in the region, and it has always played an important role in South American Indian communities. Coca chewing abates hunger, makes the chewer feel stronger, and allows him or her to work harder.[17] Coca was also used in native rituals and ceremonies and was an integral part of Indian culture: "As the Mediterranean civilization was based on the trinity of grape vines, wheat, and olives, the Andean was based on the trinity of potatoes, maize, and coca" (Vidart 1991, 23).[18] Coca also contains important vitamins and is considered a food by many (Carter and Mamani 1986, 134).

At the time of the Spanish conquest, coca was used in the Inca Empire from Bolivia to southern Colombia and by the Muiscas or Chibchas and other minor Colombian tribes. There is no doubt that coca has been present in the Andes for at least a couple of millennia (Carter and Mamani 1986, 69), but the history and social role of coca before the conquest are not clear. According to a well-known version, in the Inca Empire coca consumption was limited and highly regulated. "The Incas...reserved the use of coca for the nobility and may have feuded over the status and use of

---

[17]The literature always refers to coca chewing, although the practice is more like sucking than chewing.

[18]The integral relationship between coca and Indian cultures has been extensively studied. E.g., see Carter and Mamani (1986), Henman (1978), Vidart (1991), Soux (1993), Canelas and Canelas (1983), Medina (1995), Morales (1989), Sanabria (1993), and Fajardo (1993).

coca with other groups that may have looked at coca leaves in other ways" (Morales 1989, 18). Carter and Mamani (1986, 69–71) argued that this theory has become almost universally accepted without sufficient evidence because many of the chronicles of the conquest are contradictory and, as new evidence has emerged, the resulting picture has become more complex than the "Inca coca monopoly" posited. Their evidence indicated the existence of many coca plantings and a widespread coca distribution system in the Inca Empire, which led them to conclude that coca use was common across social classes.[19]

According to the former version, coca consumption spread among common Indian folk after the conquest, when Spaniards realized that they could use it as a means of exploiting the Indians. The later position does not deny the role of coca in the exploitation of the Indian masses, but rather than seeing the growth in coca consumption as a concerted effort sees it as a convenient use of a prevailing practice.

The role of coca after the Spanish conquest increased in complexity, and coca use became a contentious issue. The early Catholic missionaries realized the ceremonial value of coca in the religious practices of the Indians and considered it an obstacle to converting them to Catholicism. This led to the condemnation of coca by a Catholic council that met in Lima in 1567 as "something useless and pernicious that leads to superstition because it is a talisman of the devil" (Vidart 1991, 88).[20] Strong Indian opposition—coupled with the Spaniards' realization that they actually benefited from Indian coca chewing, which allowed workers to toil long hours without food—conspired against the ban. In spite of protests by some religious authorities, coca use increased in the Spanish colony, and coca became a staple of the Indian diet.

The anti-coca forces failed in most of the Andes, but in Quito they succeeded in eradicating coca use, and that city's bishops even outlawed its medicinal use. Carter and Mamani (1986, 133) acknowledge that the reasons why coca use stopped in the areas under Quito's jurisdiction are not

---

[19]Camino's (1989) study of Peru also supports this view.

[20]References to the demonization of coca by the Spaniards are frequent in the Latin American literature on coca. It needs to be noted that coca chewing was not the only demonized native practice. In sixteenth-century Latin America, the Spaniards demonized many aspects of Indian culture, to the point that it became anathema to study the history and culture of the Indians (see González 1997, 51–55).

clear, and they suggest that the practice simply was not as ingrained in that region as in the rest of the Andes. Bonilla (1991) argued that the success in Quito was due to the lack of mines in Ecuador, where coca would have been used to facilitate their exploitation. However, this fails to explain why coca chewing remained a common practice in southern Colombia in the jurisdiction of Popayán, a region very similar to Ecuador.[21] The reasons for the anti-coca campaign's success in Quito remain a question mark in Andean coca history.

The social role of coca transcended its use as a hunger and exhaustion palliative and became a symbol of Indian identity. The use of coca in Indian religious ceremonies has led to a debate about whether the coca leaf was sacred in Indian culture. According to Indian mythology, coca was a gift from Pachamama (Mother Earth), and "the Andean Indian chews coca because that way he affirms its identity as son and owner of the land that yesterday the Spaniard took away and today the landowner keeps away from him. To chew coca is to be Indian...and to quietly and obstinately challenge the contemporary lords that descend from the old *encomenderos* and the older conquistadors" (Vidart 1991, 61). Coca chewing was also part of religious ceremonies, witchcraft, rites of passage, and a facilitator of social relations, and it was practiced collectively during work breaks.

Carter and Mamani (1986, 75) cited several earlier anthropological studies and argue that "the belief in the divine origin of coca and its association with religious rituals comes from remote times, as it is attested by the ceramic statues from the classical Mochica period." However, these researchers accepted the fact that there are no satisfactory explanations for why coca was associated with the divine, except because of its ability to abate hunger and exhaustion and give a feeling of strength. Camino (1989) argued that Indians approach the coca leaf with reverence, and that it indeed is sacred.

The "coca is sacred" argument is widely used today in Peru and Bolivia to defend coca cultivation and use.[22] Some have even argued for the existence of an Indian legend, according to which for the Indians the coca leaf is

---

[21]Gold was produced in the Province of Popayán, but it came from alluvial mines that did not require the extraneous work of Bolivian and Peruvian mines.

[22]Some of the publications that defend coca are put out by Ediciones Hoja Sagrada (Sacred Leaf Editors).

sacred and a gift of God and Pachamama, but for white foreigners it is a damned leaf. The centuries' old legend affirms in its wisdom, the contradiction of the meaning of coca in both cultures: when white men dare to attempt to use the leaf as you do, he will have opposite results. Its juice will give you life and strength; it will be a repugnant and degenerating vice for your lords to whom will turn stupid and crazy. (Comité Coordinador de las Cinco Federaciones del Trópico de Cochabamba 1996, 5)[23]

A similar legend was promoted by drug traffickers during the dictatorship of Luis García-Meza in Bolivia (1980–81) and another one spread by word-of-mouth in the Peruvian coca fields where it was known as "the Inca's revenge" (Bedregal and Viscarra 1989, 124–25).

Other anthropologists argue that "no scientific evidence exists to prove that the Incas considered coca to be a sacred leaf. The Quechua term 'mama' does not mean god or sacred. ... The alleged fact the Incas worshipped the sun and called the moon 'Mama Killa or Quilla' should not be enough reason to argue that 'mama coca' has ever had a sacred meaning in the Andean culture" (Morales 1989, 17). Independent of the sacredness of coca leaves in the Indian cultures of the Andes, anthropologists concur on the social importance of coca and its role in Andean religious rituals. For instance, work by Spedding (1997a, 47) on the Yungas traditional coca-growing area in Bolivia concluded that "the cultivation, harvest, and marketing of coca leaves is a simultaneous economic, social and cultural undertaking central to everyday life" and that coca "unites all the aspects of Yungas peasant life and forms a transcendent symbol of social values" (p. 48).

The confrontation between Spanish and Indian cultures in the Andes has gone on for five centuries. At times it has been overt, but most of the time it has simmered covertly. This confrontation underlies many of the values and cultural characteristics of Bolivia, Colombia, Ecuador, and Peru, and has not yet been resolved. Indeed, in the Andes the process of

---

[23]This is an old legend of recent vintage. It only appears in a book that details the protests of coca-growing women published by the federations of coca growers of Chapare and at the time when coca was supposed to have been given by Pachamama to the Indians and they did not have a concept of "white" men. Besides, it is not mentioned in the main reference works of Carter and Mamani (1986), Quiroga (1990), Sanabria (1993), Medina (1995), Morales (1989), and Mansilla (1991).

"the conquest of 'the other' has not finished" (De Roux 1990, 11), and abuse of the Indians has been a constant in the region's history.[24] As a symbol of Indian identity, coca use and policies became an integral part of the confrontation between the two cultures.

Spanish and mestizo society shunned coca chewing but benefited from that habit among Indians. Coca chewing allowed miners to work long hours in the depths of the silver mines in Bolivia without other food. Coca became a main source of revenue for the haciendas of Peru and Bolivia that supplied the silver mines, and coca chewing also became widespread among hacienda labor forces, which were partially paid in coca leaves.

Financial benefits from psychoactive drugs also reached the state. Indeed, during colonial times, taxes on coca, tobacco, and alcohol were one of the main sources of government income.[25] The fiscal importance of these taxes persisted throughout the twentieth century, for they are one of the main taxes collected by regional (departmental, provincial, or state) governments.

During colonial times, coca food consumption (tea) and medicinal uses spread to mestizo and white societies. In exceptional situations, such as when Spanish foremen went down into the mines, they also chewed coca. During the sixteenth century, Spanish physicians incorporated coca to their pharmacopoeia. Carter and Mamani (1986, 80) found references of increased mestizo and Spanish coca chewing by the end of the eighteenth century. They claim, however, that it never became a fully accepted practice in white society and was rejected by the upper class. Furthermore, a negative perception of coca chewing still persists among the Bolivian elite. In Colombia and Peru, the situation was similar (Henman 1978, chap. 2; Camino 1989).

Although economic interests backed the production and use of coca, there was always a group that opposed them. As was noted above, in the sixteenth century there was an attempt to eliminate coca chewing on religious grounds that succeeded only in Quito. In the rest of the Andes, coca was grown and consumed mainly by the Indians. Coca leaves were often

---

[24]This has been the case not only in high Indian-population density countries like Bolivia, Ecuador, and Peru, but also in Colombia. As an example, De Roux (1990, 11–12) recounted an incident in 1967 in which seven Colombian settlers killed sixteen Indians and were exonerated because "they did not know that killing Indians was a crime."

[25]Carter and Mamani (1986) documented the Bolivian coca and Mora de Tovar (1988) the Colombian alcohol cases.

used as partial or whole payment of wages for peons and other farmworkers. This custom was widespread in Bolivia (Carter and Mamani 1986), Peru (Morales 1989), and Colombia (Henman 1978) until the 1940s.

On balance, from the Spanish point of view, coca profits were more important than saving Indians' souls (Carter and Mamani 1986, 133). For several centuries, coca consumption remained a relatively minor domestic policy issue in the Andes. In the 1920s, the prohibitionist movement in the world, supported mainly by the United States, led to several international conventions and agreements that attempted to ban psychoactive drugs. One of the issues faced at the time was the effects of coca chewing. These were particularly relevant in Bolivia and Peru and less so in Colombia, where most Indians had disappeared or been assimilated into mestizo society and coca-chewing Indian communities were small.

By the 1940s, there was a widespread anti-coca movement in all Andean countries, which was led by the medical profession on the grounds that coca chewing had very negative effects on the Indian population.[26] This was a paternalistic movement, tainted with racial overtones. Coca chewing was frequently referred as a "vice that caused racial degeneration" of the Indians,[27] and the movement also targeted other Indian traditional consumer goods like *"chicha,"* a popular alcoholic drink derived from corn.

This anti-coca movement succeeded in restricting some practices, such as the use of coca leaves to pay a portion of peasants' salaries in part of Colombia (Thoumi 1995d, 124). It was also instrumental in obtaining the support of the Andean governments for international anti-coca efforts, which led to a 1961 United Nations convention that included coca in its list of illicit drugs and categorized coca chewing as an improper drug use. The 1961 convention defined coca chewing as drug abuse and committed the governments of the Andean countries, particularly Bolivia and Peru, to prohibit that practice within 25 years. The 1988 Vienna Convention changed the treatment of coca, allowing its production and accepting traditional coca uses. But the 1961 international coca ban has remained a sore

---

[26]Thoumi (1995d, chap. 3) presented a short survey of the role of coca, tobacco, and *chicha* in Colombian history, including the 1940s campaign against coca and *chicha*.

[27]These arguments have been documented in Bolivia by Carter and Mamani (1986, 135), in Peru by Yrigoyen and Soberón (1994), and in Colombia by Bejarano (1947) and Thoumi (1995d, 124–25).

social and political issue in Bolivia and Peru, where it is still exploited by coca advocates.

The anti-coca movement of the 1940s that was led by the medical profession evolved into a public health approach movement in the 1980s and 1990s. In every Andean country, there are groups that focus on illegal drug consumption problems, but this is not a high-priority policy issue in the region.[28] The Andean countries have a great problem with psychoactive drug consumption caused by alcohol, but illegal drugs are not perceived to be a great problem.[29] The public health approach to illicit drug use in Latin America does not have to be on the shadow of a dominant moralistic model, and it can take more liberal positions than its counterpart in the United States. Thus, it has sought support for prevention, education, and treatment programs, and in some cases it has even supported decriminalizing possession of personal drug doses. The Latin American public health approach is sufficiently different from that of the United States that for about two decades the U.S. government has tried to convince Latin Americans that they are on the verge of a drug epidemic, hoping to drum up more Latin American support for repressive policies.[30]

Significant groups in Latin America see illegal drugs as an expression of the dependency relations between the industrial and developing worlds. According to these adherents of what is know as "dependency theory," the

---

[28]Some of these—e.g., SEAMOS in Bolivia, CEDRO in Peru, and La Casa at the Universidad de Los Andes in Colombia—have active treatment programs and do significant applied addiction research.

[29]Alcohol consumption is a very important cause of violence, gender and child abuse, traffic accidents, and productivity losses. Guerrero (1996) reported several studies in Cali, Medellín, and other Colombian cities that showed at least 25 percent of the corpses of victims of violent deaths had very high alcohol levels in their blood. He also showed a concentration of violent deaths in days when alcohol consumption is high (weekends and holidays. One peculiarly Colombian violent day is Mother's Day, when relatives get together and end up fighting about mother-related issues). As mayor of Cali, Guerrero ordered all bars to shut down (a legally questionable act) after a famous 5–0 Colombian soccer victory over Argentina in 1993. That night, there were about eighty violent deaths in Bogotá, where bars remained open, and only three in Cali. Augusto Pérez, a former Colombian drug czar, estimates that three-quarters of the corpses processed by large city morgues have a blood alcohol content of 0.20 or higher (interview with the author, Vienna, March 2000).

[30]The Department of State has funded several drug treatment and research projects on drug consumption problems in the region. Kirsch (1995) surveyed and evaluated these programs in several Latin American countries.

production of illegal drugs is the result of the nature and characteristics of the world capitalist system and reflect a profound inequity in international relations that victimizes coca-producing countries. The wealth of industrial countries has been achieved through exploitation and it is a reflection of the developing world's poverty. With regard to drugs, the United States imposes its own policies on the dependent countries in the developing world to achieve its own economic goals.

Within this dependency-theory framework, capitalism and imperialism are the real issues, not drugs (Bascopé 1993), and the main (perhaps the only) driving force behind U.S. drug policies is economic benefit. U.S. policies identify the Andean countries with drug trafficking and legitimize repressive mechanisms against groups of people and countries. The moral and public health aspects used to justify and explain U.S. policies that were discussed above are just a smokescreen to hide the real reasons, which are economic and political. The real (hidden) policy goals are to assure profits and U.S. hegemony (Rojas, Burgos, and Sanabria 1993, 70–71). These theorists also see United States–inspired antidrug policies as direct attacks on the sovereignty of Andean countries.

This perception of the drug issue has widespread support among many intellectuals, particularly in Bolivia, where coca growers are seen as the weakest link and as the victims of an international money-making machine whose benefits are concentrated in the United States and where antidrug policies formulated by the United States are perceived as threats to Bolivian sovereignty (Aguiló 1992; Rodas 1996; Bascopé 1993; CEDIB 1993). Even some who cannot be considered left-of-center analysts (e.g., Doria-Medina 1986, 34–35) argue that the Bolivian economy is "deformed" due to "having been assigned the production of primary products" in the international division of labor and stress that Bolivia is left only with a small share of the economic surplus generated by the illegal industry (p. 60).[31]

It is worth noting that these dependency theorists demonize the United

---

[31]Samuel Doria-Medina, an economist trained in England, is an heir of a wealthy cement business family. He has been planning minister and the president of the cement factory's directorate. Unfortunately, in 1995 left-wing guerrillas kidnapped and held him for several months. Since his release, he has continued to play an active political role in Bolivia.

States as the common enemy that is benefiting from drug trafficking and repressive antidrug policies. Moreover, an opinion survey study by Blanes and Mansilla (1994) of social and political leaders and journalists found that their discourses argued for the innocence of coca cultivation and attributed the increase in coca plantings to the country's major problems, such as imperialism and neoliberal economic policies. Curiously, the increase in coca plantings and the illegal cocaine industry in Bolivia was attributed to the structural adjustment policies implemented following the deep economic crisis of the statist government in the early 1980s.

This economic crisis was attributed to the injustices of the international system: a sharp increase in international interest rates, unfair prices for primary products, international lenders eager to lend to corrupt local entrepreneurs, and so on. The fact that the largest expansion in coca cultivation took place during the 1970s and early 1980s, before the economic crisis and the implementation of neoliberal economic policies, is simply dismissed as irrelevant because the development of the illegal industry is justified as the only sensible response to the inequities of the international system. These exculpatory discourses reflect a profound distrust for the market as a mechanism for allocating resources and distributing income and wealth that is pervasive within Andean societies. Indeed, market prices are frequently perceived as determined by political forces, and as arbitrary and exploitative of the masses. In other cases, markets are perceived as foreign intrusions on local culture.[32]

Dependency theory is also used to assign responsibility to the United States for the growth of the illegal industry: "What is it with American society that so many of its citizens must appeal to drugs to survive? This is a crucial question frequently heard around the world. The answer must respond for the price that unjustly is being paid by a society dominated by the insensitive capitalist power" (Bedregal and Viscarra 1989, 348). This type of argument is used to require "shared responsibility" from the United

---

[32]E.g., in an interview with a coca grower from Yungas in La Paz in April 1999, he expressed his frustration with government plans to privatize the water supply. His argument was simple: Water is to earth what blood and milk are to the human body. Having to pay for water is similar to forcing a man to pay his wife to breast-feed his baby. I am afraid I was left with no response to his argument simply because there was no common ground on which to base an exchange of ideas.

States and the rest of the industrial world that should be expressed in large foreign assistance flows.

In Colombia, dependency-theory analysis has also been popular. Tovar (1994) rejected the moralistic American model and adhered to a dependency version of the problem:

> The issue cannot be reduced to a moral debate, as it has been defined by the United States and its allied countries. This issue has to do with other stark realities faced by Latin Americans: the defense of their incomes and the improvement of their precarious living conditions. It also has to do with the logic of capital and the market, which contributes to the consolidation of high-benefit economies. The decision to cultivate coca by poor and pauperized sectors of Andean society is not a product of their own free will, but of factors inherent in their development and of the opportunities offered by capitalist society. Their biological and social needs propel these marginalized sectors of the economy into illegality, where they can satisfy quickly all that the market has denied them. (Tovar 1994, 88)

Other researchers have blamed the unjust trade conditions faced by the Latin American countries for the development of the coca industry. Their basic argument (Bascopé 1993; Del Olmo 1988; De Rementería 1995) is that protectionism in industrial countries closes down other opportunities for developing countries to export agricultural products and forces those countries into the illegal drug industry. These researchers clamor for the opening of industrial countries' markets to agricultural products of the coca-producing countries.

Until the late 1990s, the main actors in the Colombian illegal drug industry were manufacturers and traffickers as opposed to peasants. The country grows marijuana, poppies, and coca, but its main source of illegal drug income is cocaine and heroin manufacturing and exporting. Furthermore, its illegal drug industry is relatively new and does not have local roots. These facts weaken the appeal of indigenist and rural-exploitation interpretations of the country's participation in the industry. Perhaps because of the need to explain the country's industry on other grounds that require greater criticisms of its society, most of these interpretations are less elaborate.

There are several frequently mentioned explanations for the development of the illegal drug industry. One of the most popular ones, adhered to by analysts from across the political spectrum, places the responsibility on U.S. drug demand and on the poverty of Latin American peasants. For many of these analysts, illegal drugs are also a scourge. The sentence "when there is demand, there is supply" is cited as definite proof that the problem is not caused by the "poor miserable settlers" who seek to make a living satisfying the international demand for drugs (e.g., see Santos-Calderón 1989, 105;[33] Cano-Isaza 1997; A. Caballero 1996, 139).

Two variations of this position can be detected. A mild one simply states that poor peasants who do not have alternatives take advantage of the existence of U.S. demand and see the Latin American countries as small players and victims in a large international business (Santos-Calderón 1989; Cano-Isaza 1997).[34]

Cano-Isaza's (1997) condemnation of the United States' "decertification" of Colombia in March 1997 in El Espectador is particularly revealing:[35]

The U.S. government, with its characteristic arrogance, proclaims itself as having a universal veto over cocaine- and heroin-producing countries, whose only sin has been the unfortunate fact that some of its citizens decided to turn its lands into immense plantings of coca and poppies, with its industrial complexes to process, refine, and distribute wholesale the drugs derived from those plants, to supply the growing

---

[33]Enrique Santos-Calderón has been the most read columnist in Colombia during the past 20 years and is currently a director of *El Tiempo*, the country's main newspaper, which is owned by his family and was founded by Eduardo Santos, his grandfather's brother and the country's former president (1938–42). His younger brother, Juan Manuel, has been foreign trade minister, minister of finance, and first presidential designate. He ran for the presidency in 1998 and will likely run again in the future.

[34]Poverty has also been a popular explanatory argument in Bolivia and Peru: "The international community has progressively come to understand the link between the coca-cocaine phenomenon and extreme poverty in our country" (Quiroga 1990, 3). See also Fajardo (1993).

[35]This is true because of the strong antidrug industry tradition of that newspaper and because the author is the brother of Guillermo Cano, the *El Espectador* editor assassinated by the Medellín "cartel" on December 17, 1986.

[36]Antonio Caballero is also an important opinion maker with elitist ancestors. His widely read column appears in *Semana*, the country's most important weekly magazine, which is owned by the family of former president Alfonso López-Michelsen.

number of psychoactive drug consumers in the world, who paradoxically, are mainly young Americans. (Cano-Isaza 1997, 2-A)

A more complex position is expressed by A. Caballero,[36] who argued that drug demand creates its own supply and that most of the value added and profits of the drug industry occur in industrial nations.

> When would the United States recognize the self-evident fact that prohibition *is* the business? Its policy could be immoral, but drugs are a great business because of it, and that business is in the United States. On the other hand, the policies of [Harold] Bedoya or the Sampers and all their predecessors during the last thirty years are not only immoral, but in practice also counterproductive: far from generating any wealth for Colombia, they have drowned it in corruption and violence. In the United States, the drug business increases its gross domestic product. In Colombia, it destroys it. (A. Caballero 1996, 139)[37]

In a more recent and vitriolic column titled "The True Criminals" (A. Caballero 1999a, 147), Caballero argued that Americans invented [sic] massive drug consumption, that individual Americans promoted illegal crops in Colombia, and that the U.S. government could not enforce its laws in its own territory and thus decided to export them to enforce them abroad. These developments have produced a great business for the United States. American banks keep 95 percent of the fantastically large illegal industry's profits. The U.S. government gets the producing countries' governments to provide aerial space for U.S. planes, to confiscate assets abroad, and to sell arms and herbicides, and it would likely use the illegal drug

---

[37]As used in this quotation in the plural, "Sampers" refers not only to President Ernesto Samper but presumably also to his wife and his brother, a well-known newspaper columnist. General Bedoya was at the time the army chief. Caballero periodically repeats his legalizing and anti-American position. In another remarkable column, he supported both Julio Mario Santodomingo (the head of the country's largest financial conglomerate) and Tirofijo (Sure-Shot, the main guerrilla leader) in claiming compensation from the United States for the Colombian social costs generated by mistaken American drug policies (A. Caballero 1999b). He fails to recognize, however, that FARC guerrillas do not tolerate cocaine consumption and that after warning drug users a couple of times, they simply apply a death sentence to them! In other words, the guerrillas' policies toward drug consumption are much more repressive than those of the United States.

[38]Of course, Caballero does not explain why the United States does not declare more products illegal to increase profits.

issue to keep the Panama Canal (p. 147).[38]

Not all dependency theorists support coca. In Bolivia and Peru, there is a small group of politicians and intellectuals who adhere to dependency theory yet argue against coca chewing on the grounds that it has always been used to exploit the peasants and mine workers. This argument has led some Bolivian and Peruvian Marxists to the abolitionist camp (Carter and Mamani 1986, 131).

Fajardo (1993, chap. 2) presented one of the most articulate and comprehensive dependency-theory positions about drugs and argued that, indeed, coca leads to racial degeneration and that contrary to the common coca-grower slogan, in reality "coca is cocaine." One of his main points was that accepted coca-chewing practices result in an actual cocaine intake "of 0.24 grams per day, a significant amount compared to medical doses and those obtained in the vice markets. The U.S. Dispensary assigns a tolerable daily dose of 8 to 16 milligrams for pharmacological uses, which is 15 to 30 times smaller than what a Bolivian coca chewer receives" (Fajardo 1993, 67).

Fajardo's (1993) elaborate argument evolves as follows. (1) Coca growing countries are the "poorest and least developed on the earth, in spite of having very valuable natural resources" (p. 145). (2) "The commercial success of the industry is due to the dozens of thousands of consumers who use drugs in the super-developed countries" (pp. 147–48). (3) "The super-developed countries headed by the colossus of the north control the Western world's economy, including all the countries of the hemisphere, some of them as primary product producers and the rest as beginning or advanced industrial economies that in any case are dependent on a borderless economic system. The poorest countries and the rest of those whose economies depend on the super-developed countries' economy are the key elements of the system: the most developed countries absorb the natural resources of the producing countries and transform them into manufactured products that they sell at prices they fix themselves" (pp. 148–49). (4) As a result of the first three points, "it is inferred that the problem should be solved by the United States...which should correct the errors of its economic system, which, even though it generated greatness and prosperity to its people, sunk others in degrading misery" (p. 149). (5) "The drug and cocaine problem is rooted in a dehumanizing economic system to which the youth of the rich and developed countries are paying tribute" (p. 149). (6) "The poverty of the underdeveloped countries of South America is the main cause why they grow coca, manufacture cocaine and traffic it around the world" (p. 160). (7) "Summing up, the material misery of the largest number is a consequence of the material abundance of the few" (p. 161).

The above arguments focus on peasants' poverty and coca plantings. In Colombia, it was clear after the late 1970s that this country's involvement in the illicit drug industry was very different from that of Bolivia and Peru. Indeed, in Colombia the agricultural side of the industry was marginal, and the main business was drug manufacturing and export smuggling to U.S. and European markets.

A few Colombian analysts have sought to explain why their fellow citizens became the main actors in the cocaine business during the 1980s. As discussed in Thoumi (1992) and (1995d), one of the first explanations provided by a few prominent Colombian politicians was based on the country's location halfway between the main producing regions and the largest market.[39] The importance of being midway between the traditional coca-growing regions and the United States has also been stressed by some foreign researchers (Whynes 1992; MacDonald 1988, 28). MacDonald considered Colombia's advantage to be based on several factors, among which its location is "first and foremost." Other reasons are Colombia's vast, sparsely populated jungle, which makes it easy to conceal laboratories and landing strips, the stronger entrepreneurial skills of Colombians as compared with natives of other Andean countries, and the willingness of part of the Colombian community in the United States to function as a distribution network. MacDonald (1988, 29) also argued that these factors interact as a package, but he maintains the predominance of geopolitical location as the main factor.

Arango and Child (1987) and Arango (1988) argued that a set of factors induced Antioqueño entrepreneurs to get involved in the cocaine business.[40] The growth of unemployment in Medellín was caused mostly by

[39]In 1989, the Colombian ambassador to the United States argued that "because its location in the north-west corner of South America, Colombia has been chosen by the narco-trafficking gangs as one of the main crossroads from where cocaine is brought to the United States" (Mosquera-Chaux 1989, 3).

[40]Medellín is the capital of Antioquia Department, which has the reputation of producing the most entrepreneurial Colombians, and in the first half of the twentieth century became the cradle of Colombian industrialization. A well-known body of literature has studied why the Antioqueños have developed those entrepreneurial skills (see, e.g., López-Toro 1970 and Twinam 1980).

the decline of the textile industry, which grew from the 1940s to the early 1970s but which by the mid-1970s could not compete with an increased level of contraband. There was an old tradition of contraband in Antioquia. The Antioqueño values an individual's social worth by his or her wealth, independent of its origin. And finally, there was a fortuitous event: The frequent confusion among many North Americans between Bolivia and Colombia led to frequent inquiries from U.S. dealers to Colombian smugglers in Panama about cocaine sources, inducing the Colombians to look for ways to supply cocaine.[41]

Santos-Calderón (1989, 381) also emphasized the cultural characteristics of the Antioqueño:

The interaction between the patriarchal Antioqueño and the modern gringo is a key characteristic of this subculture. But the link between the new and old Antioqueño societies is money that Arango points out as the strongest Antioqueño value. This circumstance, joined to the well-known entrepreneurial ability of the *paisa* and his business acumen, explains his predominance in the international drug trade.[42]

Dombois (1990) argued that the negligible presence of the state in many areas of the country, the widespread corruption of the state's bureaucracies (promoted at least partially by a clientelist political system), and the existence of an active guerrilla movement created a very auspicious environment for the industry's growth. Craig (1981) argued that the Colombian environment was particularly conducive to the growth of the illegal drug industry because of the prevalence and social acceptance of contraband, the large growth of the underground economy during the 1970s, and the willingness of Colombian illegal drug dealers to use violence.

---

[41]U.S. president Ronald Reagan, who made this mistake during his visit to Colombia in the early 1980s, reinforced the belief that North Americans confuse the two countries. Although this cause may seem trivial to most researchers, Arango and Child (1987, 128) and Arango (1988), two influential Antioqueño journalists and academics, have seriously advanced it. For this reason it should be mentioned, if only to dismiss it. Their statement was based on an interview with a former smuggler who claimed to have been a link between the Colon Free Zone smugglers in Panama and the Antioqueños during the late 1960s.

[42]"*Paisa*" is a common nickname given to the descendants of the Antioqueños who settled Antioquia, Caldas, Risaralda, and Quindío Departments, the hub of Colombia's coffee industry.

Sarmiento (1990, 33) argued that Colombians developed a comparative advantage in illegal drugs by mastering the appropriate technology to successfully break anti-narcotics laws and thwart the enforcement efforts of producing and consuming countries' governments. According to Sarmiento, the main learned technologies are in "transportation, commercialization, the capacity to bribe and intimidate, and above all, to mobilize the (economic) surplus" (Thoumi 1995d).

Thoumi (1992, 1995d) argued that Colombia was the lowest-risk location for the industry because it had the most propitious conditions among Latin American countries. These included a growing gap between de jure and de facto behaviors that condoned illegal economic activities and an extremely violent society in which people were quite comfortable using violence to solve conflicts; unique experience exporting black-market, illegally mined emeralds to industrial-country markets and exporting legally produced coffee illegally, contravening the International Coffee Agreement limits; and exchange controls enforced during a period of 60 years (1931–91).

These factors encouraged the development of money-laundering skills. Moreover, there were many totally isolated regions, where the state had virtually no presence and organized crime and guerrillas could substitute for the state. A clientelistic political system and decentralized political parties without strong ideologies or policy agendas granted a great deal of autonomy to local leaders; and the large number of Andean country immigrants in the United States facilitated the development of drug distribution networks in that country. These characteristics, which were the result of the country's institutional development and evolution, attracted the illegal industry, which in turn became a catalyst that accelerated a process of social decomposition.

Many Colombians felt uncomfortable with Thoumi's interpretation. The Colombian Financial Institutions Association (Asociación Nacional de Instituciones Financieras; ANIF 1995)[43] dismissed it as "farfetched" and as Thoumi's attempt to differentiate his product from Sarmiento's (1990). ANIF implicitly assumed that Colombia's structural, institutional, and historical differences with the rest of the Andean nations were not important determinants of the illegal industry's location. It concluded that the

---

[43]This is an official ANIF document. However, Reina (1996) cited it as written by Javier Fernández, ANIF's chief executive. Steiner (1997) also cited this article as written by Fernández.

only possible explanation for the concentration of the Andean cocaine industry in Colombia was its weaker law enforcement and greater corruption relative to the rest of the region.

Betancourt and García (1994) argued that Colombian sociocultural and political environments have played a key role in the development of international organized crime in that country. This has been stimulated by "four important historical constants in Colombian society: the persistence of *caciquismo, gamonalismo*, and clientelisim; a great level of corruption at all (social) levels; contraband; and finally, the existence of illegal economic activities" (Betancourt and García 1994, xx).

They also argued that during the 1980s, the economic crises experienced by "five large regions: Atlantic Coast (cotton), Antioquia (textiles), Valle (sugar), central (emerald zones of Boyacá and Cundinamarca), and eastern (bordering Venezuela), whose currency suffered a large devaluation at that time" (Betancourt and García 1994, xxii) were the immediate causes for the development of the cocaine industry. Criminal organizations grew "supported by the process of impoverishment of wide sectors of the middle and lower classes, which, faced with blocked social mobility channels, appeal to and seek other means to improve their standard of living and their social and political expression" (p. xxii). The distinction of structural and immediate causes of the illegal industry growth is very useful, as will be shown in chapter 3.

Alvarez and Cervantes (1996, 151) explained the development of the large illegal drug industry in Peru as caused by

the significant external demand for coca by-products and the comparative advantage of producing coca in Peru combined to bring about a massive expansion in the export of these products. In sum, these two factors were aided by the following conditions:

1. The low income levels in the Andes and the high profits associated with coca/cocaine production;
2. Institutional corruption;
3. The gradual loss of domestic urban food markets;[44]
4. The effective exclusion of Andean peasants from the 1969 agrarian reform program;

[44]This occurred as urban food tastes shifted toward "modern" imported and manufactured products.

5. The low profitability of agricultural activity;
6. Government inefficiency in serving agricultural producers in the jungle: and
7. A change in the pattern of internal migration.

This explanation is interesting, but it does not clarify why the comparative advantage of Peru is in coca production and not in cocaine manufacturing, in spite of the high profits in both activities (indeed, the annualized rate of return for cocaine manufacturing is much higher than that for coca). It also fails to explain why Peruvians did not have a comparative advantage in exporting cocaine but Colombians did have one. Alvarez and Cervantes's (1996) explanation was similar to Betancourt and García's (1994) for Colombia and hinted at a difference between institutional and triggering or immediate causes.

By Way of Conclusions

This short survey of American and Andean views on psychoactive drugs has highlighted the differences in the approaches used to interpret drug problems in the United States and Andean countries. These are so deep that they make it very difficult to debate drug issues, evaluate policies, and arrive at a consensus within and among countries. Some of the more elaborate models, such as the American moralistic and the dependency-theory ones, are closed systems, within which the interpretation of empirical evidence is predetermined. In both these models, there is a demonization of those who support different views.

The American moralistic model demonizes drugs and those who advocate legalization, whereas the dependency-theory model demonizes the United States and its repressive polices. Supporters of both conclude that their own societies are victimized. In the moralistic model, society is victimized by criminals; in the dependency model, poor countries are victimized by rich ones, and within poor countries the lower classes are victimized by the rich elite. It is not surprising that supporters of both models look at themselves as defenders of fundamental moral or ethical principles. At best, their opponents are judged as mistaken souls who fail to see the light; at worst, they are seen as people who act in bad faith.

From the American moralistic perspective, the Andean countries' failure to wipe out the drug industry is seen as a reflection of their lack of zeal and commitment to the war on drugs and as a sign of their moral turpitude and inferiority. From the dependency-theory perspective, the failure by the United States to control consumption reflects the U.S. interest in profiting from the illegal business. In either case, adherents reject, dismiss, or simply do not respond to alternative interpretations and arguments.

From the American moralistic viewpoint, arguments such as the impossibility of the government of a country with a weak state actually waging a "war on drugs," which is perceived by most of the country's population as foreign, or the impossibility of some antidrug policies achieving their promised results without sacrificing significant individual rights and risking a general uprising, are dismissed as a confirmation of the moral weakness of the Andean societies and reinforce the need to continue the fight.

From the dependency-theory viewpoint, explanations of moral reasons why the United States promotes its drug policies are also dismissed as naive or disingenuous because "we all know" that the only real force behind U.S. policies is greed and profit maximization. Thus, to explain antidrug policies, one only needs to figure out who makes money as a result of them. Those who argue that noneconomic factors are important determinants of drug policy are at best useful idiots who fail to see the truth but who are to be distrusted.

Other, less elaborate positions toward drugs are also influenced by feelings of fear and helplessness. In the United States, many parents, teachers, and politicians fear the effects of drug addiction, but they either consciously or subconsciously realize their own difficulties in preventing drug use and find solace and comfort in defining drug use as a supply-caused phenomenon. In the Andean countries, policymakers and intellectuals are aware of the state's limitations in fighting drugs successfully, and they consciously or subconsciously conclude that the "drug problem" is demand driven.

At the end of the day, the United States and the Andean countries' different perceptions of the drug "problem" result in attempts to export the responsibility for drug production and consumption. It is not surprising that those on both sides of the argument end with feelings of self-righteousness and victimization. In the end, many discussions about illegal drugs are just dialogues among the deaf, and current policies are maintained independent of their effectiveness. As will be argued in the last section of this book, achieving success in antidrug policymaking requires resolving the perceptual conflict that prevents any meaningful dialogue.

3

The Socioeconomic Dimensions of Illegal Drug Production

To explain the development of the illegal drug industry in the Andes, to evaluate current policies, and to determine whether it is possible to formulate and implement successful policies, two key questions must be answered. First, why do some countries produce illegal drugs and why others not do so? Second, why does a country produce illegal drugs at some periods in time and not at others? Most analysts do not develop formal models to answer these two questions directly—although, as was discussed in the previous chapter, many have posited answers that unfortunately have been at best partially satisfactory and have left too many loose issues.

Among the most frequently mentioned causes for the development of the illegal drug industry are poverty, inequality, economic crises, and state corruption. The relationship between poverty and the illegal industry is, however, very difficult to determine. To begin with, none of the proponents of this hypothesis surveyed in the previous chapter provided statistical evidence to support their claims. They simply assumed that this is the case. It is true that all laborers and most farmers in the coca fields are quite poor, but many poor farmworkers do not participate in illegal crop cultivation. It is also true that coca grows in poor countries, but most such countries do not grow illegal crops. In the Andes, Colombia is richer than Bolivia, Ecuador, and Peru and it is the main illegal drug actor. Ecuador is significantly poorer than Colombia and Peru, and has not been a main industry player.

Furthermore, in Colombia there is no correlation between peasant poverty levels and illegal crops.[1] Besides, it is also true that some large coca farmers are relatively rich (S. Uribe 1997), and most participants in illegal manufacturing and smuggling have relatively high levels of education and employment alternatives in the legal economy and cannot plead poverty (Hernández 1997). In Bolivia, most migrants to Chapare did not come from the poorest rural regions of the country in Oruro, Chiquisaca, Potosí, and Tarija, but rather from nearby highlands "where coca growers maintain high altitude traditional crops" (Blanes and Mansilla 1994, 53).

A further difficulty arises because illegal drug activity does not vary over time with poverty levels and inequality. The record of Colombia is also quite clear in this respect. During the 1980s, a decade when illegal drugs grew at a fast pace in Colombia, the measures of inequality and poverty actually declined in the country and the standard of living of most Colombians increased. This does not mean that poverty and extreme misery do not play causal roles in the development of the illegal drug industry, but rather that the relationship is indirect and quite complex. Poverty and inequality are likely to contribute to the growth of the illegal industry, but they are not per se determining factors.

Let us also look at the role of economic crises. In Colombia, Betancourt and García (1994), Tovar (1994), Vargas and Barragán (1995), and others associated regional crises during the 1980s with the development of trafficking organizations in Colombia. During the 1980s, Colombia was the only country in Latin America and the Caribbean that avoided the external debt crisis faced by the region, and the only one in which the gross

---

[1]There is no correlation either between poverty and violent deaths (Gaitán Daza 1996; Bejarano et al. 1997; Rubio 1999). Rubio (1999) is the most important recent contribution to understanding Colombian violence.

national product did not decline in a single calendar year.[2] The crises experienced by Colombian regions were a great deal milder than those faced by other Andean countries, yet still Colombia was where international trafficking organizations developed. This is an important phenomenon that needs to be explained.

Outside Colombia, others also link economic crises to illicit drugs. Every analyst of the Bolivian experience has associated that country's macroeconomic and tin mining crisis of the early 1980s with miners' and peasants' migration to Chapare and the expansion of coca plantings.[3] In Peru, Alvarez (1992) and Cotler (1999) associated the international debt crisis of the early and mid-1980s and the gross mismanagement of the economy during the Alan García administration with the growth of coca in the Upper Huallaga Valley. Still, many countries experienced similar crises before the 1980s, including Bolivia and Peru, and they did not result in the growth of the illegal economy. As with poverty, it cannot be denied that economic crises have played a role in the development of the illegal drug industry, but as in that case, the causality relation is also complex, and maybe indirect.

There is no doubt that poverty and crises create incentives for illegal behavior, but there is no one-to-one relation between them and illegal behavior. For example, chronic poverty seems to be a less important cause of crime than sharp declines in income or disappointed rising expectations. In informal conversations in the Andean countries, one frequently hears statements such as "he has to commit a crime to feed his children." Even in cases in which a head of a family commits crimes to avoid family starvation, why is it that in some countries these parents just steal food but in other countries they kidnap, extort, abuse, and even kill their victims?

Corruption is also frequently associated with the illegal drug industry. As will be shown in chapter 4, there are several reasons why the relationship between illegal drugs and corruption is difficult to determine clearly. First, there is no agreement about the definition of corruption, and behaviors considered corrupt in some environments are normal in others.

---

[2]This positive performance of the Colombian economy was the result of good macroeconomic management and not of the growth of the illegal drugs industry as some might think (Thoumi 1995d, chap. 1).

[3]See Quiroga (1990), CEDIB (1993), J. Painter (1994), and Rodas (1996), among others.

Second, corruption and drug trafficking are difficult to measure, and their size, scope, and importance are difficult to establish. Third, corruption is a multidimensional phenomenon, and different types of corruption can have different effects on the drug industry. Fourth, the relationship between illegal drugs and corruption is circular; that is, corruption may attract the illegal industry, but illegal drugs also are a main source of corruption. Fifth, corruption and drug trafficking are generally symptomatic of deeper social problems.

To illustrate the difficulty in relating illegal drugs and corruption, it suffices to look at the 1998 and 1999 country Corruption Perceptions Index calculated by Transparency International.[4] In the 1998 rankings, Colombia was the 6th most corrupt country in the world, Ecuador and Venezuela were tied for 7th, Bolivia was 16th, and Peru 45th. In 1999 Ecuador came out the worst Andean country as the 18th most corrupt country in the world, followed by Bolivia (20th), Venezuela (25th), Colombia (28th), and Peru (59th). It is obvious that this most frequently used corruption index is very unstable and is not directly related to illegal drug activity.

Let us now consider the role of U.S. protectionism in promoting repressive policies, another of the arguments used to explain illegal drug growth, which was discussed in chapter 2. There is no question that economic interests play a role in drug policy formulation and are an obstacle to policy change. However, current U.S. policies are not protectionist with regard to the illegal drug industry in the commonly used meaning of the word. It is true that illegality increases profits and value added in the industry, but policies are not designed with that goal in mind. A true protectionist policy for the industry would not prohibit imports and production but would impose high tariffs, import quotas, and other trade barriers.

Current U.S. policies do benefit those who participate in repressive antidrug activities and in the paternalist "caring industries" (Mishan 1990). The incomes of policemen, detectives, counselors, jail personnel, lawyers, bureaucrats, physicians, paramedics, and so on are protected by current policies and constitute a political barrier to policy change. It is clear that drug traffickers, money launderers, and other crooks also benefit, but it cannot be argued that they have the political clout to influence the federal government to keep current policies.

---

[4]These rankings were found in Transparency International's Web site. These corruption indexes are based on the opinions of large enterprise managers, are subjective, and do not reflect certain types of corruption.

According to the conventional wisdom, profitability is the main motivation behind the production of illegal drugs. A careful look at the
geographical distribution of the world's illegal drug industry leads to an
interesting paradox: Profits can explain why a particular individual participates in the illegal business, but they do not explain why some countries
produce illegal drugs and others do not.

Legal economic activities and the illegal drug industry are similar in
their search for profit, but the illegality of cocaine, heroin, and other psychoactive drugs makes for significant differences from other goods and
services. The remarkable differences between the geographical patterns for
the production, marketing, and consumption of illegal drugs and for those
of legal goods highlight the importance of illegality.

To illustrate this point, let us focus on the case of such legal agricultural products as coffee, banana, tobacco, rice, sugarcane, cocoa, soybeans,
potatoes, wheat, and corn, to name only some of the most important ones.
For these products, the availability of natural resources determines
whether a country can produce them; indeed, the list of countries that have
the capacity to produce overlaps almost perfectly the producer-country list.
Indeed, virtually every country that can produce them does so. Some countries produce higher-quality goods than others, some produce at low and
others at high prices, and some are net exporters and others are net importers, but every country produces some quantity of them. As is shown
by mainstream economic analysis (discussed below), only in exceptional
cases does one find countries that can produce these goods but do not.

Footloose industries—those that require little capital and use well-
known technologies that do not require scarce skills or a location near
demand or input supply sources—show similar patterns. For example,
clothing, wood furniture, leather shoes, soap, and cosmetics, and other
simple manufacturing products are found in virtually every country.
Again, qualities vary, and some countries are net exporters and others net
importers, but all that can produce do so. As in the case of primary
agricultural products, nonproducing cases are exceptional.

In contrast to common goods, virtually all countries can produce and
traffic in illegal drugs, and launder drug profits, but most do not.[5] Official
U.S. data indicated that in 1990 there were only nine opium-producing and

---

[5]On the demand side, there are also great variations across countries and across
time: In some countries, there is a large demand for illegal drugs, in others there is not;
at some points in time the demand for drugs in a country is low, at others it is high.

four coca-producing countries of interest to the United States (U.S. Department of State, Bureau of International Narcotics Matters 1990).[6]

Coca is produced mainly in parts of the Andes Mountains and the Amazon Basin, but it can also be produced many in other places in Africa, Asia, and Latin America, and even in small areas of the United States in Guam, Hawaii, and Puerto Rico.[7] Indeed, a century ago, in the 1890s, the Andes suffered one of its frequent export busts when the Dutch developed large coca plantations in Indonesia and Malaysia and flooded the market. At the time, coca was also grown in India. In the Andes, coca is produced mainly in Bolivia, Colombia, and Peru, whereas Brazil, Ecuador, and Venezuela produce marginal amounts.

The geographical distribution of the opium poppy is even more puzzling because it can grow in more regions of the world than coca. Poppies can grow in parts of Europe, large portions of Africa and Asia, parts of North America, tropical highlands of South America, and other parts of the Southern Hemisphere. Still, relatively few countries grow poppies.

The patterns of coca- and poppy-based drugs are also peculiar. Coca leaves must be processed into coca paste, and opium latex must be produced at or very near the planting sites. Cocaine base, cocaine, morphine, and heroin can be refined anywhere because they are archetypal footloose industries: They require very little capital and few labor skills, the needed technologies are extremely simple and well known, and the chemical inputs used are common and all have possible substitutes.[8]

From a purely economic perspective, the narrow geographical distribution of illegal drugs is quite remarkable because the industry's extremely high profits provide very strong incentives to produce everywhere. Their uncommonly high profits lead to the expectation of a pattern of more dispersed production than that of legal goods.

It must be pointed out that although the production and trafficking patterns of illicit drugs are significantly more concentrated than those of licit

---

[6]More recent world surveys of illegal drugs present a similar picture (Observatoire Géopolitique des Drogues 1996; UNDCP 1997).

[7]The development of coca plantings in the Colombian (Guaviare, Caguán, and Putumayo) and Bolivian (Chapare) Amazonia shows that coca can grow in many non-traditional growing areas. All these are humid, low tropical jungles similar to those of many parts of Africa and Asia.

[8]Descriptions of the production processes and technologies used are frequent in the literature. E.g., see Morales (1989), Thoumi (1995d), Clawson and Lee (1996), and S. Uribe (1997).

goods, they are spreading across the globe. The number of countries mentioned in the U.S. government annual strategy reports (U.S. Department of State, Bureau of International Narcotics Matters 1990; U.S. Department of State, Bureau of International Narcotics and Law Enforcement Affairs 1995) increased from 46 in 1990 to 102 in 1995.

Moreover, the survey of illegal drugs in the world by the Observatoire Géopolitique des Drogues (1996) finds more and more complex patterns: Not only have illegal drug consumption, production, and trafficking expanded to more countries, but new actors are participating, such as guerrillas, paramilitary forces, and international criminal organizations. The illegal drug trade is now related to other international criminal activities, such as money laundering in many fiscal paradises, illegal arms sales, and various types of smuggling.

The differences in geographical distribution between legal products and illegal drugs raise many questions: Why do some countries that produce illegal crops not develop international marketing systems for the finished products? Why do some countries become transshipment sites when other similar ones do not? Why do some countries develop illicit drug manufacturing industries when others do not? To what extent do natural factors such as weather, land, and other natural resources determine whether a country produces illicit drugs? Why are illegal drugs consumed in some countries and not in others? Why does the pattern of illegal drug consumption differ among various cities of the same countries? Why do production and consumption patterns change over time? Given that criminal organizations rely on group loyalty, why do some ethnic and social groups develop criminal organizations or "cartels" when others do not? Why do criminal organizations and gangs tend to be made up of recent immigrants and people with a weak sense of belonging to society at large?

These questions are scientifically intriguing and politically important. Answering them is a prerequisite to explaining the development of the illicit drugs industry and the factors that influence it, and to formulating effective drug control policies.

This chapter develops a theoretical framework to help answer at least some of the questions posited. The very high revenues of the illegal drug industry make it advisable to start with a look at an economic approach. The second section discusses the relevance of the standard comparative and competitive advantage models and the need to focus on the economics of criminal activities. The third section presents a frequently used crime economics model and highlights some of its characteristics and the role that "moral values" play in it. The fourth section focuses on the crime control roles of moral values and behavioral constraints generated by the state and such other institutions as the family, religion, and other nonstate entities. In the fifth section, a modified socioeconomic model is presented. The sixth section illustrates several theoretical applications of the model that show what determines the level of crime in a society. The seventh and final section uses the model developed thus far to discuss the causality of illegal drug activity.

The Competitive Advantage in Illegal Drugs

Standard models used in economics and international trade theory posit a production function—that is, the *physical* relationship between inputs and outputs. Any production process requires a set of factors of production: various types of capital, labor, natural resources, and technology. The relative abundance of these factors determines what products a country will specialize in and export; that is, products for which it has a *comparative advantage*. Recent theoretical advances show that when imperfect competition prevails, market structure and institutions also affect the nature of goods and services a country trades. When a country's advantage is the result of its type of institutions and the way they influence markets and not of the relative abundance of factors of production, it is said that the country has a *competitive advantage*.

The standard model shows that countries specialize in goods and services in which they have comparative and competitive advantages, but specialization is rarely complete. International trade changes the composition of output in a country, increasing that of the goods and services in which the country has comparative and competitive advantages and lowering output in those in which the country does not have advantages. Only in exceptional cases does international trade result in situations in which the production of a particular product is wiped out from a country. This happens only when countries are very small and their internal markets limit the number of goods and services that can be profitably produced or when countries face extremely large comparative and competitive disadvantages; that is, when the difference in production costs in and outside the country is very large.

To explain how the spatial distributions of the coca-cocaine and poppy-opium-heroin industries differ from those of other agriculturally based industries and their changes during the 1990s it is necessary to focus on the differences between licit and illicit industries. Of particular importance are the different tasks required by the two types of industries. Illicit drug industries require the performance of several industry-specific tasks that are not required by licit activities:

1. To trade in illegal inputs, which are frequently controlled substances and have to be smuggled and/or obtained on an underground market.
2. To grow illegal crops.
3. To develop clandestine drug manufacturing systems.
4. To sell illegal products on the domestic market.
5. To smuggle the final products out of the country.
6. To develop illegal marketing networks abroad.
7. To transport illegally obtained currency across international borders and to exchange these funds from one currency to another without revealing their origin.
8. To launder and invest illegally obtained funds, and to manage portfolios of illegally obtained capital.

The successful performance of these tasks requires special "illegal skills" used to develop illegal business organizations, social support networks to protect the industry from law enforcement efforts, and contract enforcement and conflict resolution systems within the criminal organizations, and to have the will to break economic laws and regulations and to use violence if necessary.

Illegal activity skills are necessary to do business in many countries, but they are not productive skills in the sense that (using economics jargon) they are not factors of production and are not independent variables in a firm's production function. Traditional microeconomics started out considering three factors of production: capital, labor, and natural resources (land). Later on, technology and entrepreneurship were added. These may be interpreted in several ways. For example, an entrepreneur can be someone who introduces an innovation (e.g., a new product, an improvement in the way to make things) or can be someone who finds better ways to negotiate with the government to obtain privileges. Technology can be similarly classified. The literature on technology explains that it can be embodied in capital (machines and equipment), or disembodied. The latter can include new ways to manufacture a product or to bribe government officials without risk. From the private point of view, all these actions are productive. From the social point of view, some are not.

Illegal activity skills are needed to operate in many environments, but they are not part of "the recipe" to produce goods and services and are not factors of production. The usefulness of illegal activity skills arises from the institutional environment in which a firm operates ("the rules" imposed by institutions), not from the physical production process itself. They differ from common factors of production in three important ways.

First, illegal skills appear in an environment in which the government cannot enforce its own rules, laws, and regulations, and in which other social institutions condone criminal activities. At their core, these skills are used to break laws and norms that regulate economic activities. It may be argued that many laws create obstacles to economic growth, and that breaking them improves the country's economic welfare, or that these skills can "grease the workings of the economic machine" and allow production that otherwise would not take place (De Soto 1986). Still, they are not productive factors; they are behavioral responses to particular legal and institutional environments.

Second, in many cases the contribution of illegal skills to increased violence, corruption, and other illegal activities is harmful to economic growth because they increase business risks and security expenditures (Rubio 1996a). Violence is used to extort, kidnap, and apply other pressures to individuals. These are equivalent to taxes on economic activities, just to allow them to go on. Violence transfers rents, income, and capital, but it does not increase physical production.

Third, the value of illegal skills can be destroyed or enhanced by legal changes. The establishment and elimination of alcohol prohibition in the United States, the postwar protectionist Latin American policies, and the opening of their economies to international competition since the late 1980s are good examples of how government policies enhanced and destroyed the value of illegal skills.

Explaining why some countries develop and use illegal skills but others do not is a prerequisite to explaining why the illegal drug industry develops in one country and not in others. To do so, it is necessary to focus on the economics of criminal activities.

The Economics of Criminal Activities

The following sections discuss the basic economic model applied to criminal choices, point out its strengths and weaknesses, and build on it to make it more relevant to the case of illegal drugs in the Andes.

A Simple Economic Model

The approach used by economists to explain illegal economic activities is based on the premises that many criminal actions are motivated by expected economic gains and that these crimes can be analyzed in similar ways to other economic activities. From this point of view, the decision to commit a crime is based on the criminal's evaluation of its own costs, benefits, and risks.[9] Following a recent World Bank (1997, 8) study: "The net benefit of committing a crime is equal to the gross payoff (or loot) from the crime, minus the direct costs associated with acquiring the loot, minus the forgone wages from otherwise legitimate activity, minus the product of the probability of conviction multiplied by the value of the punishment associated with the conviction." In simple mathematical terms:

$$NB = l - c - w - (pr \times pu) \tag{1}$$

where "*NB* stands for the benefits (to the criminal) of committing a crime, *l* is the value of the loot (what the criminal can get for it in the market), *c* are the costs associated with planning and executing the crime, *w* is the total value of wages forgone during the period of planning and implementation of the crime, *pr* is the individual's perceived probability of being convicted, and finally, *pu* is the 'value' of the punishment associated with the crime under consideration" (World Bank 1997, 8). In equation 1, *NB* is an expected net benefit of the criminal activity. If the criminal is not caught, his or her benefit will exceed *NB* by the amount $(pr \times pu)$, and if the criminal is caught, his or her benefit will be lower than *NB* by $[(1 - pr) \times pu]$.

The simple economics approach to crime has proven quite useful in many contexts because it can explain variations in crime over time in a particular locality, as long as the social structure and social constraints on crime do not change. This is the model's main strength. But when the underlying social structure changes, it cannot be expected to maintain its explanatory power. Specifically, the model does not explain several important characteristics of the international illegal drug trade and markets. To illustrate this point, let us consider four examples.

[9]This approach was originally developed several decades ago in a seminal paper by Becker (1968) and extended in Becker (1976). *The Journal of Economic Perspectives*, a widely read publication of the American Economic Association devoted to disseminating recent economic research findings to a wide audience, offers an excellent set of articles that summarizes the "state of the art" in this field. See DiIulio (1996), Ehrlich (1996), and Freeman (1996).

First, Colombia is deeply involved in the cocaine industry while Ecuador is not. Following equation 1, because the revenues and costs represented by l, c, and w are similar in both countries, one must conclude that Ecuador is not involved in the illegal drug industry because $pr \times pu$ in Ecuador is much higher than in Colombia. Thus, to accept the model, it is necessary to accept that Ecuador has superior police and justice systems that totally discourage the illegal drug industry but that Colombia's systems are totally corrupted.[10] However, both countries have weak central governments that suffer from widespread corruption. Local governments are controlled by economic and political elites and are very vulnerable to bribes and prone to abuses of power. Economic power is concentrated in a group of economic conglomerates that exerts great influence on the political system and succeeds in bending and manipulating laws and regulations to create and capture economic rents, and politicians and the state apparatus have a reputation for being easily bought.[11]

Second, during the past 20 years, wholesale cocaine prices in Europe have been substantially higher than in the United States.[12] Here again, one must conclude that either $pr \times pu$ is much higher in Europe than in the United States to limit supply and increase prices, or that smuggling cocaine into the United States has been significantly easier than into Europe, in spite of the "war on drugs" pursued by the U.S. government.

Third, curiously, though cocaine prices have been significantly higher in Europe than in the United States, the opposite has happened with heroin. Because both products are imported by similar criminal organizations, if

---

[10]As was noted above, the 1999 Transparency International report ranks Ecuador as the eighteenth most corrupt country in the world and Colombia as a less corrupt twenty-eighth.

[11]For the case of Ecuador, see Hurtado (1986), Roldós-Aguilera (1986), Fierro-Carrión (1992), and Thoumi (1990). For Colombia, see Cepeda (1994a, 1994b, 1997), Thoumi (1995a, 1995d, 1996), Kalmanovitz (1989), and Lee and Thoumi (1999). It should be acknowledged that this position is diametrically different from that expressed by ANIF (1995), which argued that Colombia became the center of the Andean illegal drug industry because of its high impunity level relative to the rest of the region. It was not surprising that ANIF's only policy recommendation was a strong law-and-order program.

[12]Data on European prices are less reliable than on American ones. Still, most estimates indicate that cocaine prices have been significantly higher in Europe than in the United States, at times doubling and even trebling American prices. Recently, the gap has been closing, and in some European cities, current prices are comparable to those in the United States. In Amsterdam, where drug polices are most permissive, cocaine's retail prices can be lower than in the United States.

their price differences would be determined by repressive policies only, both would be expected to be higher in the most repressive country and lower in the least repressive ones.

Fourth, cocaine is distributed in the United States, among others, by ghetto-based gangs like the Crips and the Bloods and by groups of Colombians, Dominicans, Haitians, Jamaicans, and Mexicans. It is true that strong loyalty ties among criminal organizations members' increase the return to crime and lower the risk of punishment, but there are other immigrant and nonimmigrant groups with strong internal loyalty ties that have not developed cocaine distribution networks.

Economists who have recognized the limitations of the simple economic model have altered it to include noneconomic motivations to crime. In these cases, the model is modified to include "moral values" that constrain individual behavior. The net benefits of committing a crime would have to exceed a certain threshold before a person commits a crime. The individual threshold would be determined by his or her moral values. Again, in simple mathematical terms, a new equation is introduced:

$$D = 1 \text{ when } NB > M, \text{ and } D = 0 \text{ when } NB \leq M \qquad (2)$$

where D stands for the decision to commit the crime ($D = 1$ is yes) or not to commit the crime ($D = 0$ is no), and M represents the threshold level of net benefits that determines whether the individual will (or will not) commit the crime. Anytime that $l - c - w - (pr \times pu) > M$, the individual decides to commit a crime. The criminal threshold M reflects the popular dictum "everybody has a price," and indeed, M may be interpreted as each person's "price."

The Role of "Moral Values"

Equation 2 introduces "moral values" to the model as an exogenous restriction on individual behavior, but it does not specify which moral values are relevant, how they are formed, or how they change. That is, as a noneconomic exogenous constraint, moral values simply fall beyond the realm of economics and of what the model is meant to explain.

There are several reasons why it is difficult to incorporate moral values into economic models, except as constraints. First, moral values are not measurable or observable—only actions and behaviors are—and the best that can be done is to find out whether a particular action or behavior is consistent or inconsistent with particular values such as human solidarity, patriotism, compassion, selfishness, and so on.

Second, a particular action or behavior can be consistent with more than one set of values, making it impossible to establish which value or values are the ones that actually determine behavior. For example, charity can be motivated, among other values, by human solidarity, compassion, paternalism, or a person's need to feel good about himself or herself. In the economist's jargon, this presents an "identification" problem that in most cases cannot be solved.

Third, there are many associations between crime and other variables. Strong nuclear families, contact with extended family members, a sense of community and social belonging, participation in social and religious activities, frequency of religious participation, and others, are associated with low crime rates and are factors that contribute to raise the "crime threshold" (M) in the model above. However, there is no rigorous theory about the way in which each of these factors operates and interacts with others or with different individual personalities to lower or increase crime.

Fourth, value changes over time are influenced by the institutions of each society, which creates modeling problems. Many value-change and adaptation theories are based on case studies, are likely to be culture specific, and are difficult to prove and generalize to many societies and social contexts. This is a significant disincentive for academics, who get great pleasure and status from developing models that produce broadly applicable conclusions and results.

Fifth, economists and other academics find explanations that are endogenous to their models a lot more congenial than those provided by non-measurable exogenous variables like values. Furthermore, moral values are not only difficult to incorporate into economic models, but economists are also reluctant to do so because introducing exogenous constraints to explain behavior could open a Pandora's box that could be used to explain away anything.

Because of these difficulties, moral values are assumed to remain constant in economic models, at least for the duration of the periods analyzed, and are not treated as subject to policy-induced changes.

To conclude, economic profitability plays a relevant role in promoting crime, but other important factors also affect it. It is argued below that these include social controls and each individual's internalized constraints on behavior.

Moral Values and Behavioral Constraints

Individual behaviors can have undesirable social effects; however, the definition of deviant and damaging individual behaviors varies among societies and over time. These include behaviors related to political activity; sex and gender relations; religious activity; violence; gambling; private property accumulation and use; the production, commerce in, and consumption of certain goods and services; and so on.

To control and regulate those behaviors, societies rely on norms that are enforced by many institutions, such as the family, religion, the state, peer groups, and schools.[13] Justifications for controlling individual behaviors have been diverse, and they have been based on moral, ethical, political, or practical grounds. These have frequently appealed to God's revealed word, the social and individual good, nationalism, and other sentiments. Ideologies, religions and other institutions have influenced individual behavior control mores, regulations, and legislation in all societies.

The need to control consensual relations that generate negative social externalities presents a particular problem in all societies.[14] In these cases, the question is how should the negative effects of consensual relations be dealt with? Should any of these relations and behaviors be criminalized? If not, which control methods should be used?

There is no consensus on how to proceed to answer those questions. Some religious fundamentalists might argue that they should not even be raised. For them, it is obvious that alcohol, other psychoactive drugs, and sex outside marriage should be either banned or strictly controlled. For extreme libertarians, there is no question that these should not even be regulated.

Psychoactive drug production and use have presented a policy problem for all societies. The facts are simple: All societies have used psychoactive drugs;[15] many psychoactive drugs are addictive, and their consumption can

---

[13]Coleman (1990) studied in detail the demand for norms and the conditions under which norms develop in a society.

[14]E.g., gambling, addictive psychoactive drug consumption, prostitution, and premarital sex can have high social costs.

[15]The only exception found by anthropologists was the traditional Eskimo society, whose members became heavy alcohol users once it came in contact with Western traders.

produce negative social externalities.[16] Every society has confronted the need to develop policies to cope with psychoactive drug consumption.[17] Societies have differed significantly in their response to psychoactive drugs. Some have tried to ban them, to make them illegal, and to punish their production and use; they have controlled their use by taxing them, forbidding underage use, imposing other legal restrictions, or ritualizing their consumption.[18]

Many social institutions have played a role in psychoactive drug control. Religion has many times banned or ritualized their use, and the family and social groups have established conditions and environments in which users can consume them while minimizing negative externalities. For example, alcohol can be consumed in small quantities with meals or as part of a religious ceremony, but its consumption just to get drunk is not tolerated.[19]

In modern democracies where executive, legislative, and judicial powers and state and religion are separated, behavioral controls are imposed by the same institutions as in traditional societies (family, religions, state, etc.). Because legislation is formally separate from religion, there is the appearance that the main controls are the responsibility of laws and regulations enacted and enforced by the state.

As the process of modernization has advanced, extended families have become weaker, people have moved away from native localities where local institutions restricted behaviors, and religion has lost some of its clout. Old social norms become more and more difficult to enforce, and the burden of enforcing deviant behaviors shifts to the state.

---

[16]The consumption of some addictive psychoactive drugs like caffeine generates very mild negative effects, as does coca tea drinking. Others, like nicotine (tobacco smoking), can have lethal long-term effects on users, and still others, like alcohol, pure cocaine, crack cocaine, heroin, LSD, and other synthetic drugs, can cause great short- and long-term harm to users, their families, and other possible victims.

[17]Psychoactive drug consumption is also common among many animal societies that face a similar problem! (Siegel 1989).

[18]The literature on these various types of controls and regulations is extensive. E.g., see Siegel (1989), Morales (1989), Carter and Mamani (1986), Vidart (1991), Del Olmo (1992), and Henman (1978).

[19]Other potentially socially damaging behaviors are tolerated occasionally during unique circumstances like carnivals. In these cases, societies recognize that the attraction of psychoactive drugs is so strong that they had better allow a periodic binge under controlled conditions (Siegel 1989).

There is no doubt that authoritarian regimes can much more success-fully fulfill this task than democratic, pluralistic ones. Behavioral restrictions in such regimes reflect the ideology and values of the authoritarian power, be that a person, a political party, or a religion. Behavioral control legislation in these societies reflects religious beliefs as well as social and party ideologies, and it is the result of the interaction of various institutions that participate in policymaking, a process that varies from country to country.

A Modified Model

The "pure" economic model defines *pr* as the probability of being punished, and *pu* as "value" of the punishment to the criminal. In this model, the state is the only punishing authority and institutions such as the family, religion, groups of peers, and others do not play a role. To expand the model to include behavioral controls imposed by those institutions, equation 1 can be rewritten as

$$NB = l - c - w - (gpr \times gpu) - (spr \times spu) \qquad (3)$$

where $(gpr \times gpu)$ refers to the probability and magnitude of government punishment and $(spr \times spu)$ to social punishment imposed by other institutions.

In both the pure and the modified model, any individual's decision to undertake a criminal (or deviant) action is the result of a comparison between the net benefits of the action (NB) and the individual's internal constraints (M). In other words, the individual faces a set of external conditions and restrictions that make it more or less attractive to undertake a particular action and also some internalized behavioral constraints or "values" that affect the decision.

Humans are social, and their position in society influences their behavior and productivity. During the second half of the twentieth century, the roles of physical capital, human capital, and technology in economic development were emphasized. However, the productivity of these factors of production varied significantly from country to country, and their accumulation alone could not explain economic growth. This led to research that identified social differences that explained the performance differences across countries and that found that "social capital" played an important role (Coleman 1990, 300).

Social capital refers to connections among individuals—social networks and the norms of reciprocity and trustworthiness that arise from them. In that sense social capital is closely related to what some have called "civic virtue." The difference is that "social capital" calls attention to the fact that civic virtue is most powerful when embedded in a dense network of reciprocal social relations. A society of many virtuous but isolated individuals is not necessarily rich in social capital. (Putnam 2000, 19)

The point is simply that the social fabric—that is, the set of relations within the family, neighborhood, school, and other institutions within which every person's life takes place—has a significant influence on the way in which people behave and their attitude toward the social repercussions of their actions. Individuals who grow up in environments with high levels of social capital have a strong sense of belonging to the society, trust other community members, and take into account the socially positive and negative effects of their actions in their decision-making processes and are confident that others would do the same. Trust in social reciprocity generates solidarity and large social benefits (externalities). Social capital influences the capacity of a community to generate behavioral constraints to help achieve social goals (Coleman 1990, chap. 12; Fukuyama 1995).

The concept of social capital is old in the social sciences but its use has only been popularized in recent years. In fact, Putnam (2000, 19) found that it was "invented" on six different occasions during the twentieth century. In other relevant work, Putnam (1993) contrasted the roles of civil society and nonpunishing state activities (i.e., schools) in the north and south of Italy and concluded that social capital was important in shaping internalized and social behavioral constraints. Besides, there are "features of social organization, such as trust, norms, that can improve the efficiency of society by facilitating coordinated actions" (Putnam 1993, 167). That is, social capital is an important explanatory factor for the differences in economic development between the two Italian regions and the development of organized crime in the south.

There is no question that social networks within a particular community generate social capital. Social capital is an asset to society, but when societies are segmented and individuals are strongly loyal and act with solidarity to social subgroups but not to society as a whole, the social capital of some groups can be detrimental to others. In these cases, the social capital that develops belongs within each group and there is a possibility for the social capital of one group to become perverse for society as a whole or for other social groups.[20]

Rubio, inspired by the Colombian experience, defined "perverse social capital" as what is generated when "networks, the contacts, the power relations, the legal system, the informal norms of behavior, the political activities, and the reward systems established in this society inspire rent-seeking, or criminal behavior, to the detriment of productive activities and technological innovation" (Rubio 1997, 815). Rubio (1999) argued that in the United States social capital deficiencies have been used to justify increases in government expenditures, particularly in education, child care, and the like.

In this work, Rubio appears to deemphasize the role of social capital and does not make references to "perverse social capital." This is because he finds that "social capital as an explanation for violence in Colombia presents serious difficulties. Most youth violence foci are not found in the most socially and economically backward regions but in the blue-collar neighborhoods of the most industrialized cities, precisely where there are more education and employment opportunities" (Rubio 1999, 97).

In the social capital discussion, it is important to differentiate the organizations such as the family and schools, that are instrumental in creating and using social capital, from the actual sense of belonging, trust, and respect for other members of the community that is the expression of social capital. Those organizations are easily measured and have been the subject of empirical social capital studies.[21] However, social capital requires that the welfare of others is taken into account in an individual's decision-making process and that increases in such welfare increase that individual's own welfare.

Putnam (2000, 23) argued that there could be several types of social capital and contrasts bonding and bridging social capital. The former generates strong intragroup loyalties. The latter strengthens ties between groups. Putnam argued that both types are needed for a society to function satisfactorily. When there is only one type of social capital in a society, it can easily become perverse. When there is only bonding social capital, it

---

[20]La Violencia of the 1940s and 1950s in Colombia is a good example. Social capital within the Liberal and Conservative parties was sufficiently strong to make people willing to kill in the parties' names, despite the grossly detrimental effects of those actions on Colombia as a whole.

[21]E.g., see Sudarsky's (1999) study on Colombia.

becomes very easy to antagonize other groups or societies and generate conflicts.[22] If a society only has bridging social capital, life within a group would not be pleasant and the group would tend to dissolve.

In segmented societies, personal attitudes toward crime inside and outside a particular community or group can be very different. For example, stealing from the poor can be "bad," but killing the rich can be "good."[23] Coming back to the model, the point is simply that a complex network of social relationships that generates strong social capital within a marginal community can become perverse and produce negative social capital for society at large. In these cases, social constraints and norms within a group can become very detrimental to society at large.

It is important to point out that many recent analyses of Andean societies point to the lack of "civil society" as a cause of violence and other problems. Civil society refers to organizations outside the state that in many instances contribute to the development and strengthening of social capital. However, they are not social capital by themselves, and on occasion they may not contribute to its formation or strengthening. There is no question that many nongovernmental organizations (NGOs) have developed in Colombia and other Andean countries in response to high levels of violence, discrimination, and other social crises. These are very important institutions, many of which have positive social roles and functions, but they do not always contribute to solving social problems. For example, when foreign donors declare their willingness to fund NGOs, there is always the risk that people will use old NGOs or found new ones just to have access to and misuse those funds.

Internalized Constraints

"A norm may be embedded in a social system in a more fundamental way: The norm may be internal to the individual carrying out the action, with sanctions applied by that individual to his own actions" (Coleman 1990, 243). That is, every citizen has his or her own "criminal threshold" level (M), but norm internalization does not succeed equally among all citizens, and in every society there is a distribution of M values among the population

---

[22]The U.S. ghetto gangs and the killers for hire in Medellín's slums are good examples of these situations (Salazar 1990; Salazar and Jaramillo 1992).

[23]E.g., this ethic is expressed explicitly by members of gangs of assassins for hire in Medellín (Salazar and Jaramillo 1992, 129–44).

reflecting the fact that some people are more honest than others. The "criminal threshold" or the "price" of a particular individual's honesty depends on his or her own endowment of natural attributes and the internalized behavioral constraints developed through socialization and life experience.

Every individual is born with certain attributes that makes him or her more or less prone to criminal behavior. Indeed, people with similar family backgrounds and life experiences have different behaviors. One can expect the distribution of endowment attributes to be similar across countries, but all other behavior-shaping factors are specific to each society.

The controls internalized by the individual—mainly during the socialization period, before he or she becomes an adult—are developed by the interaction of the individual with parents, religious organizations, school, peer groups, and so on. Most of those controls are created by institutions other than the state, although it also plays a role as it funds and regulates public education, regulates newspapers, radio, and television stations, and so on. Adults may also adapt their behaviors in response to their own life experiences. People who interact with mostly honest or dishonest people are likely to develop similar habits. Perhaps this adaptability declines with age.

Internalized constraints can also vary depending of the type of action or crime considered. For example, if two crimes have the same *NB*, but one requires the use of violence while the other does not, some would-be criminals will decide to commit the nonviolent crime but will refrain from the violent one. Similarly, crimes that do not have clear-cut personal victims, such as embezzling from the state or large corporations, might be chosen over crimes that have the same payoff (*NB*) and clearly identifiable personal victims.

In the same way, as was noted above, the decision to commit a crime may also vary, depending on whom the victim is. For example, given the same monetary benefits *NB*, a criminal might choose a rich or foreign victim over a poor compatriot.[24]

External Constraints

In the model, *NB* also depends on the value of the loot, the costs of the criminal activity, the opportunity cost of the time used by the criminal and

---

[24]Of course, in this case, economists might argue that the two payoffs are not really equal because the satisfaction that the criminal receives by committing the crime is different in each case.

the punishment that the state and other institutions can give the individual. The state and other institutions can encourage and discourage behaviors, and their policies can lower or raise the costs and punishments faced by would-be criminals. Civil societies can exert peer pressure and can punish individuals in many ways, including praising, granting status, shunning, shaming, and excommunicating. The state can pass and enforce laws regulating, promoting, outlawing, and punishing behaviors, or it can establish market and nonmarket incentives to achieve its goals.

The variables l, c, w, gpr, gpu, spr, and spu vary among individuals and population groups. Individuals with good market connections to distribution networks or fences can obtain higher prices for their loot than others, some people have a higher opportunity cost for their time than others, and expected punishments may vary depending on connections, race, ethnicity, place of residence, and other individual characteristics. These differences partly explain why some social groups are more prone to commit crimes than others.

The opportunity cost of the time devoted to crime can vary substantially depending on the education and skills of each individual. Even though higher crime rates can be associated with people with very low w levels, it is also true that most people in those social groups *do not commit crimes*. Expected punishment can vary with ethnicity, race, and other arbitrary factors, but it also varies inversely with the opportunity cost of the time of the criminal. The value $(gpr \times gpu)$ is lower for unemployed, unemployable, and low-wage people that face incarceration than for those with higher wages and income.

In extreme cases, it can be argued that gpu can actually be negative, so that $[- (gpr \times gpu)]$ is positive. For example, a poor, chronically unemployed Colombian takes a job as a cocaine or heroin "mule" (i.e., an individual who transports cocaine inside his or her body or concealed in luggage) and is captured at a U.S. airport with a kilogram of drugs. The "mule" is then sentenced to a few years in jail, where he or she has a roof, food, medical attention, access to television and radio, educational material, an exercise room, the opportunity to learn a foreign language, and so on. This standard of living is likely to be much higher than the one back in his or her country. The value of the punishment to the criminal would depend on the individual's own comparison and evaluation of the benefits of the increased physical standard of living with the cost of lost freedom. Some people could prefer the punishment to life outside prison.

The expected value of the government punishment also depends on the type of crime, victim, and criminal. Being confronted with innumerable laws, law enforcement officials need to decide which ones to enforce more forcefully, which crimes to tolerate, in which areas of the city or country to concentrate their activity, and so on.

Social punishments ($spr \times spu$) are expected to be positive, although in some cases they may also be negative. For instance, in U.S. ghettos, going to jail can be a "rite of passage" that increases the status of many young males. Thus, instead of a social sanction, there can be a social prize within the community relevant to the criminal. In extreme cases, it is also possible for ($spr \times spu$) to be positive and to exceed ($gpr \times gpu$) in absolute value, turning net crime punishment into a benefit for the criminal. For example, tax evasion in many Latin American countries faces a very low risk of government punishment, is widely condoned by society, and frequently is a source of pride (Guisarri 1988).

Government and social institutions are not monolithic in their attitudes toward crime and punishment. Many government agencies formulate and implement crime-related policies. Frequently, they do not coordinate their actions with other agencies, fight over budgets and jurisdiction and over policy formulation and implementation, and may even work in opposite directions.[25] The same happens with institutions outside government; many may chastise crime, but others may actually encourage it.[26] To take this into account, equation 3 can be modified and written as

$$NB = l - c - w - \Sigma_i\,(gpr \times gpu) - \Sigma_j\,(spr \times spu) \qquad (4)$$

where $i = 1 \ldots n$, the different government agencies and $j = 1 \ldots m$, the different social institutions.

Finally, in the medium and long terms, social and government institutions also have an effect on M. Failure by the government and society to punish deviant behaviors weakens the incentives for the development of strong internalized constraints. The long-term dynamics generated by weakened external behavioral constraints can be devastating. They first

[25]E.g., in the United States, many government levels and agencies are involved in drug policies. The creation of the Office of National Drug Control Policy was an attempt to coordinate the local, state, and federal agencies involved. The conflicts among various government agencies in charge of antidrug policies are legendary and are revealed by the writings of former officials (Levine 1991; Gately and Fernández 1994).

[26]E.g., families of assassins for hire in Colombia and retail drug traffickers in U.S. ghettos condone many of their activities, at least implicitly.

increase the profitability of criminal actions, and as those become widespread and increasingly accepted by society, people realize that honest behavior is more costly, and their own internal constraints weaken. Besides, when criminal behavior is tolerated and accepted, the socialization process ends up producing a generation of individuals with weak internalized constraints. In these cases, it may be argued that a society falls into a "dishonesty trap," from which it is very difficult to escape (Thoumi 1987).

Applications of the Model: The Level of Economic Crime in a Society and Policy Effectiveness

According to the model, the number of economic crimes and criminals in a society is determined by the interaction of NB and M, and these are the result of the interplay of policies that create or destroy incentives to commit crimes, law enforcement efforts, and social and internalized controls. Figure 3.1 illustrates the choice between criminal and noncriminal activities confronted by every citizen in a society. On the positive side of the x-axis, all members of a society are ranked according to their M values, from most to least honest. The y-axis measures their corresponding NB and M values. In this example, NB is assumed to be the same for every citizen. Those to the right of the intersection of M and NB (the least honest

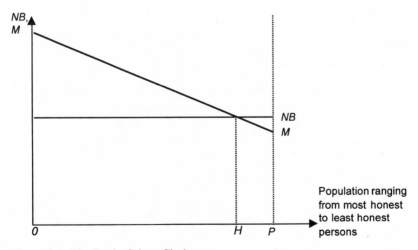

Figure 3.1 The Basic Crime Choice

citizens), for whom *NB* exceeds *M*, decide to become criminals. That is, *0H* is the percentage of honest citizens and *HP* that of dishonest ones.

The model can also be used to show that the distribution of *M* in a society is crucial to determine the success of government anticrime policies. Let us assume a homogeneous society in which people have strong internalized constraints (*M* is high) and everyone has the same values and thus the same *M* level. In this case, if government law enforcement efforts and social controls affect all citizens similarly, there are two possible outcomes: Either there is no crime (when *M* is high), or everyone will be a criminal (when *M* is at *M'*). If the government wants to enforce its laws and lower *NB* to just below the level of *M'*, it can eliminate crime. This result can of course be reinforced if other social institutions also impose their own behavioral controls on people. This case is illustrated in figure 3.2.

Let us also consider the case of a heterogeneous society where values differ substantially among people and *M* has a wide distribution; that is, some people are significantly more prone to crime than others. In this case, government policies consistent with low criminality in the "homogeneous society" will not avoid high criminal levels, even if the average level of *M* is the same in both cases.

Furthermore, in this case there is a "waste" of governmental efforts in the sense that to avoid crime the government will have to lower *NB* to a

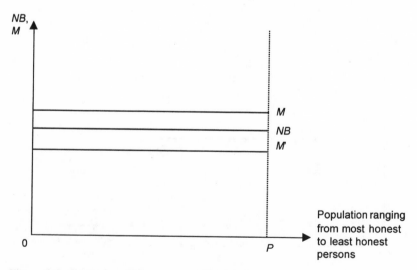

Figure 3.2 Crime in a Homogeneous Society

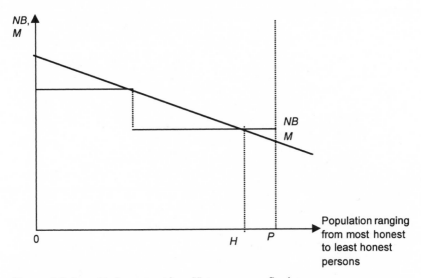

Figure 3.3 Law Enforcement in a Heterogenous Society

level significantly below the M level of many people (figure 3.3). In the heterogeneous society, law enforcement policies can improve their effectiveness by targeting special social groups—that is, by lowering NB for social groups that have low M values and by keeping NB at higher levels for the rest of society. These policies require selective prevention, policing, and enforcement activities. Of course, in many societies some of these policies are considered discriminatory and may be unconstitutional and/or violate human rights.

Changes in social constraints and in the state's ability to enforce its laws can generate a very negative dynamic, which is illustrated in figure 3.4. To begin, let us take a traditional rural society in which M is high and NB is low. In period 1, this society has very low crime rates, as is depicted by the interaction between M_1 and NB_1. Social changes—such as migration, increased education, rapid urbanization, and the growth of urban informal work—weaken government and social constraints (raising NB_1 to NB_2), resulting in higher crime rates.

After a time, continuing social changes push NB_2 higher to NB_3, and socialization fails to generate internal crime constraints, lowering M_1 to M_3. This process can result in a crisis situation, in which the government budgetary effort to achieve a low crime level increases drastically and may simply fail altogether. When this happens, the solution to criminal

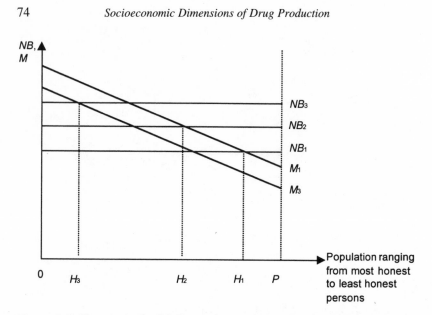

Figure 3.4 Changes in Social Constraints and Negative Social Dynamics

behavior cannot be based on stronger law enforcement alone but also requires institutional and value changes. This does not mean that social scientists and economists know how to make such changes, but it does explain punitive policy failures.

Figure 3.5 illustrates the case of a particular stratified society in which there are two social groups with substantially different M levels. Those who share the values of the dominant group comply with the laws and regulations of the government, but the rest do not. If the difference in M levels is criminal behavior, as is shown in figure 3.5, government policies are ineffective in the sense that they cannot reduce crime through repressive policies that lower NB. Furthermore, if over time some of those who obey the laws decide not to, their M becomes lower and the society is caught in a dishonesty trap, from which government policies alone cannot rescue it. In this case, as in the previous one, government policies are ineffectual, and institutional and structural changes are required to control economic crimes.[27]

[27]Several Colombian authors interpret this as possibly reflecting the Colombian case (Kalmanovitz 1989; Herrán 1987; Thoumi 1987, 1995d; Sarmiento 1996).

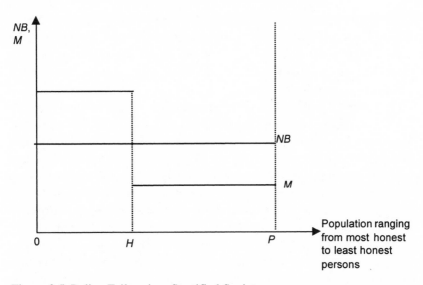

Figure 3.5 Policy Failure in a Stratified Society

The Model and the Causality of Illegal Drugs in the Andes

In the model developed in this chapter, profits are one of the variables that promote crime. But other variables also play important roles: social restrictions and attitudes toward crime, and the strength of internalized controls of the citizenry. Within this framework, the effectiveness of law enforcement efforts, the level of punishment that the state can apply, social punishments, and the effectiveness of social institutions and the state in inculcating internal behavioral constraints on individuals all play causal roles and can be considered institutional causes.

All the examples given highlight a key policy problem: If the shapes of *NB* and *M* are not known, the success of various policies cannot be predicted. Most antidrug policies are designed to lower *NB*, but we do not know the current level and shape of *NB*, or the policy's effect on them. Similarly, the policy effect depends on the shape and level of *M*, but again, there is no real knowledge about them.[28] Policymakers and many analysts that propose policies as "solutions" to a problem do not recognize this fact.

---

[28]E.g., the criminology literature talks about the "deterrent" policy effect. There are, however, few cases in which this factor has been measured, none of them in the Andean countries.

Once policies fail to achieve unrealistic goals, policy failure is the attributed to "lack of commitment or political will," "corruption," and the like, but not to the existence of social and value constraints that makes it impossible for policies to succeed even if government is "committed, has political will, and is not corrupt."

Following the model, the development of the illegal drug industry in a particular country requires an environment characterized by institutions that do not impose behavioral controls and that tolerate or condone deviant behaviors. The model also stresses the role of institutional evolutionary processes. Criminal activity responds not only to illegal profits, but also to changes in the institutions that weaken behavioral controls, including those within the state. When the controls imposed by a particular institution weaken, others have to take up the slack to prevent crime increases. However, these changes are not always smooth or feasible—for example, when the state has to, or attempts to, take over more behavioral control functions because changes in family structure or other institutions weaken social controls. In this case, the state might not be effective because of conflicts with other state functions and goals such as protection of the rights of the individual.

One clear-cut implication of the model is that crime levels reflect social institutions. In this sense, the presence of the illegal drug industry is symptomatic of changes in social constraints on behavior.

The evolutionary processes that generate an environment where crime can thrive take time to develop. Conversely, reversing those processes is also likely to require time. In this sense, one should not expect the possibility of implementing a "silver bullet" type of policy that eliminates the "drug problem" in the short run.

The model also allows for roles of variables such as extreme poverty, lack of opportunity for social mobility, and economic crises, which (as was shown above) have frequently been used to explain and justify the development of the illegal drug industry in the Andean countries. These can be latent and a given one moment in time they can contribute to the development of the industry.

Extreme poverty itself is only a latent cause. Most poor societies or social groups cannot be characterized as prone to high crime rates. Given a situation of stable extreme poverty—that is, where income is very low but does not decline—poverty becomes a "cause" of criminality only if the behavioral and repressive constraints discussed above weaken. Only when this happens does poverty contribute to the development of the illegal industry.

As was pointed out by Betancourt and García (1994), economic crises are only triggering factors. As these researchers explained, several Colombian regions experienced economic declines during the 1980s. As will be argued below, Colombia was the only Latin American country that avoided the external debt crisis of that decade and the only one whose gross national product did not decline in any year. During the 1980s, coca plantings grew in Bolivia, Colombia, and Peru, and Colombians developed and controlled the cocaine industry. The crises of many Latin American countries were very deep but did not result in the development of the illegal drug industry in those countries. Relatively mild crises acted as a trigger in Colombia during the 1980s because the institutional changes that the country had experienced made it very vulnerable to them. Without a social and institutional environment conducive to such development, the industry would have not grown.

Another important conclusion concerns policy effectiveness. If the growth of the illegal drug industry is caused by institutional and value changes in a society that weaken social and state controls, repressive policies might not be effective. As was discussed above (and is described in detail in chapter 10), the effectiveness of antidrug polices has been overestimated, leading to unrealistic expectations of policy success. It must be pointed out, however, that the failure of a policy to achieve an unrealistic goal does not necessarily mean that the policy should be discarded. It only means that expectations should be lowered to a reasonable level. It needs to be stressed that the long-term solution to the "drug problem" is an institutional one that requires significant changes in society, not just simple policies. Current policies could play important roles in mitigating some of the main negative effects of the problem, but if there is no real social change, very little will be accomplished in the long run. If surgery is needed, aspirin helps but does not do the job.

The model developed in this chapter differs fundamentally from the moralistic one on which many antidrug policies are based. The model does accept that some people could have a high propensity to become criminals, but it stresses the role of social institutions in allowing them to develop their tendencies.

The model described here also differs from the dependency-theory model. Institutional characteristics are used to explain the drug industry's development in both models. The dependency model emphasizes international relations, terms of trade, and the international division of labor. In our model, the important elements are internal and are determined by each society's institutions.

The moralistic and dependency models cannot and do not seek to explain the large differences in crime rates and crime types among countries. The model developed here will be used to explain at least some of these differences.

4

The Development and Structure of the Illegal Drug Industry in the Andes

As was noted in chapter 2, for a long time coca has been a product made, consumed in, and exported from the Andes. Domestic demand was the main factor determining a level of production that remained relatively stable.

Before the drug boom that started in the late 1960s, coca chewing was widespread among Indian peasants in Bolivia and Peru. This practice, though perceived as unhealthy by most governments, was nevertheless tolerated. In Colombia, coca chewing was practiced in only a few highland regions where Indian communities had survived. The consumption of other illegal drugs, such as cocaine and heroin, was limited to small groups of social outcasts, artists, and intellectuals (Camacho 1988).

Andean cocaine was produced in small quantities, mainly for export through connections with criminal organizations in Cuba and the United States (Thoumi 1995d, chap. 3). The Andean countries had signed the 1961 United Nations convention that committed them to prohibit coca chewing in 25 years, but traditional Bolivian and Peruvian production remained a domestic issue. As the international demand for illegal drugs grew during the 1960s, the Andean illegal industry experienced a boom that changed the role of coca and other psychoactive drug source plants and illegal drugs in the Andes.

This chapter surveys the development of the illegal drug industry in Colombia, Bolivia, and Peru. Its goal is to explain the evolution of the industry and to identify its main structural characteristics and actors.

The Industry in Colombia

The illegal drug industry in Colombia is more diversified and developed than in the other Andean countries, and Colombians' involvement in the industry is more complex. Indeed, Colombia is the only country where the three most important plants used to produce psychoactive drugs are grown in significant quantities.

In spite of its great social, political, and economic importance, it has been very difficult to draw an accurate picture of the organization of the illegal drug industry in Colombia. Drug organizations are continuously changing in their attempts to foil law enforcement efforts, and they are constantly searching for new raw material and intermediate good sources, export routes, and markets. The secrecy imposed by illegality precludes a highly structured and transparent organization in which workers know their bosses, what they do, and how they operate.

Existing industry networks are in constant flux to avoid detection. They continuously seek new routes, sources of chemical inputs; ways to disguise exports, and channels to influence politicians. High profits and low barriers to entry continuously attract independent operators that spring up at various stages of the business. In the past decade, guerrilla and paramilitary organizations became active participants in the illegal trade, and they developed links with international organized criminal organizations involved in illegal weapons trafficking. This has made it more difficult and dangerous to obtain current and reliable information about the industry and serve at the outset as a warning about possible inaccuracies in descriptions of it.

Marijuana

Marijuana began to be grown in the mid-1960s in response to increases in domestic demand, which echoed U.S. developments. Various researchers

(Arango and Child 1987; Camacho 1988) have argued that the Peace Corps made a substantial contribution to popularize the use of marijuana and several psychoactive mushroom varieties, although no evidence supports their actual involvement in marijuana exports.

Still, marijuana production and trafficking did not become important until the early 1970s. The 1960s growth in psychoactive drug consumption in the United States and Europe triggered the development of large marijuana plantings in Mexico and Jamaica. These countries became important marijuana suppliers to the U.S. market. Toward the end of the decade, the U.S. government promoted eradication programs in Mexico using paraquat, a herbicide known to have harmful health effects, which drove away American consumers. This measure created strong incentives to find other marijuana growing sites, and the marijuana crop was then displaced to Colombia (Tokatlian 1990, 300).

Marijuana originally grew mainly in the Sierra Nevada de Santa Marta on Colombia's Caribbean coast. At the beginning, American smugglers sought Colombian suppliers. Some local and American entrepreneurs provided seeds to poor peasants from whom they obtained the marijuana to be sold to Americans. After a short time, "Colombians seized the opportunity offered by the new market, and rapidly replaced the Americans organizing production to become marijuana exporters, but Americans retained marketing control" (Thoumi 1995d, 126). News about the good marijuana business spread rapidly, and by the late 1970s marijuana plantings had appeared in several other regions, particularly in distant, recently settled areas of the country (Ruiz-Hernández 1979).[1]

Marijuana exporting organizations were relatively simple. The peasants produced for a local exporter who controlled and/or owned one or a few landing strips or a port and negotiated with the American importer (Thoumi 1995d, chap. 3). Due to the lack of land titling and the very rudimentary and uncompetitive capital markets, the exporter frequently provided crop financing. Most peasants in the Sierra Nevada de Santa Marta had roots in that area, and many of them retired from the illegal business after a couple of successful crops provided them with enough capital to maintain a satisfactory living standard growing legal crops (Ruiz-Hernández 1979, 140).

---

[1]Gossaín's (1985) novel about the marijuana boom in the Sierra Nevada de Santa Marta provides good insights about the effects of the new crop on peasants, emphasizing the detrimental social dislocations it provoked.

In spite of its promising development, the illegal marijuana industry boom in the Sierra Nevada did not last. In 1978 it began to decline, the victim of several external forces. After Julio César Turbay became Colombian president in August 1978, the U.S. government questioned his antidrug credentials because of possible links between traffickers and some of his close political supporters. In response, the Colombian government engaged in an aggressive manual marijuana eradication campaign in the Sierra Nevada. It also confiscated boats and airplanes and destroyed some of the marijuana processing equipment (Thoumi 1995d, chap. 3). By that time, marijuana production in the United States had grown substantially after the development of the "sin semilla" variety, which is five times more potent and became highly popular.

These developments made the marijuana business somewhat less attractive, but they did not destroy it. Moreover, marijuana had infused Colombian entrepreneurs with an awareness of other potential illegal sources of wealth. Quaaludes began to be exported jointly with marijuana as a result of their diversification efforts. Some quaaludes were imported from Europe and reexported; others were produced by the domestic pharmaceutical industry using imported inputs (Ruiz-Hernández 1979, 180).

Marijuana did not disappear from the Sierra Nevada, but as the cocaine industry developed, the policy focus shifted away from it. This situation persisted until the end of April 1984, when Colombian minister of justice Rodrigo Lara-Bonilla was assassinated after a Senate confrontation with drug traffickers and the president, Belisario Betancur, took strong repressive measures against the industry. These included aerial fumigation of marijuana plantings in the Sierra Nevada. In fact, fumigation diminished the industry but did not make it vanish.

Traffickers' response to fumigation was to shift the location of marijuana plantings to Cauca Department, where yields turned out to be three times higher than in the Sierra Nevada (Tokatlian 1990, 324–26). Vargas (1994) showed that marijuana crop displacement also took it to other locations. In his work, he presented the detailed testimony of a peasant in the Serranía de Perijá who started to grow marijuana in 1978. He documented an absolute lack of state presence in the area, a very high level of violence generated by bullies who bought the crop and frequently stole the peasants' proceeds, and the arrival of a guerrilla organization that rooted out the bullies, established order, and gained peasant support.

Marijuana eradication campaigns continued during the 1980s with U.S. support, and by 1990 marijuana plantings had become relatively marginal in Colombia: "A major supplier of marijuana through most of the 1980s, Colombia has effectively eradicated most of that crop. Only about 2,000 [hectares] are now under cultivation" (U.S. Department of State, Bureau of International Narcotics Matters 1992, 104).

Because of the importance of cocaine, marijuana did not receive much attention during the 1990s. In the early part of the decade, marijuana seizures increased, suggesting a crop revival in the country. A few seizures of hashish and liquid marijuana offered clear indications of product diversification and significant technological changes. Official U.S. estimates show that marijuana hectareage increased from 2,000 in 1992 to 5,000 in 1993 and remained at that level through 1997.[2]

S. Uribe (1997) took field trips to marijuana-growing areas and concluded that in the mid-1990s there were about 6,000 hectares planted with marijuana concentrated in six regions of the country. Fieldwork in two marijuana-growing regions found that all plantings were small, of 1 hectare or less. Yields varied significantly between 300 and 1,500 kilograms per crop, depending on the techniques and inputs used. On average, peasants growing small quantities obtained family incomes equivalent to between three and four times the minimum wage.

Guerrilla groups provided protection to the crops, the peasants, and the buyers in the visited regions. They provided a regulatory framework for market operation and monitored transactions to make sure that the buyers did not take advantage of the peasants. In exchange for these functions, they charged fairly high "taxes" equivalent to one-third of the buyers' payments. One-half of these funds was returned to the community to finance communal projects, and the other half accrued to the guerrillas' general funds.

Marijuana buyers entered the region in trucks carrying presses to pack marijuana. They appeared to act with impunity, and when leaving the area they cleared police and army checkpoints with no problem. Interviews in rural producing areas indicated that peasants were not familiar with liquid marijuana, a relatively new product in world markets. Any liquid marijuana produced in Colombia is likely to be processed outside the growing areas, in urban environments where the pressed marijuana is processed.

---

[2]The data here are from U.S. Department of State, Bureau of International Narcotics and Law Enforcement Affairs (1998, 22). The stable levels of the estimate during the past few years could be an indication of the lack of importance that marijuana has relative to coca and poppies. It is possible that those charged with producing estimates simply devoted most of their efforts to other crops and reproduced the previous year's figures for marijuana.

S. Uribe's work (1997) also suggests that most marijuana production is likely to be aimed at the domestic market, although exports to the United States are likely to continue, albeit in smaller amounts than during the 1970s marijuana boom. Colombian marijuana is also exported to Europe, though in small quantities.[3]

Coca and Cocaine

The cocaine branch of the illegal drug industry in Colombia evolved differently. The success of marijuana was evidence of the lucrative appeal of illegal drugs. Marijuana was profitable but difficult to smuggle because of its volume and weight per unit of value. Cocaine, however, was a lot more appealing because it had much higher ratios of value to weight and to volume. Moreover, coca, its nonsubstitutable raw material, could not be produced in Europe or the United States, except in a few areas in Guam, Hawaii, and Puerto Rico, as was noted in chapter 3.

To grow coca does not require special skills; the plant is very hardy and fits very well in the tropical soils of the areas where it grows. It thrives in the humid, fragile low-altitude tropical forest environment.

Cocaine production is rather simple compared with other manufacturing processes. It requires coordinating several production steps, beginning with coca cultivation and harvesting, and moving on to the production of coca paste, cocaine base, and cocaine proper. These processes require locating and obtaining chemical inputs, such as sulfuric acid, sodium bicarbonate, potassium permanganate, ether, and acetone. It is also necessary to have access to electricity lines or generators, microwave ovens, and a few other materials. More important, it requires a good "cook," that is, someone with good practical experience and preferably some chemistry training. The processing of coca into cocaine is not very sophisticated as manufacturing processes go, but it does require a more complex organization than the one prevalent for marijuana production. It is likely that this was an important reason why the average marijuana trafficker did not make the jump into coca and cocaine.

In the mid-1970s, a few illegal entrepreneurs began to export small quantities of cocaine to the United States (Arango 1988). According to one

---

[3]Several visits to coffee shops in Amsterdam in 2001 and 2002 by the author found Colombian marijuana in all of them. However, its drug content was low and it had the cheapest price on all menus.

of the participants in the business at that time,[4] the Antioqueño cocaine business pioneers traveled by bus to Peru and Bolivia with very limited funds, and they established contacts with producers of coca paste in those countries. They began importing small quantities, which they refined into cocaine and then exported to the United States using "mules" (i.e., individuals who transport cocaine inside their bodies or concealed in their luggage) and small mail shipments.

Very high profits quickly allowed the business to become self-financing and expand. This included both developing stable links with coca paste suppliers following routes from Bolivia and Peru and with suppliers of chemical inputs to refine cocaine and also developing transportation systems for large shipments and distribution networks, especially in the United States. The large number of Colombian immigrants, many of whom were of Antioqueño origin, facilitated these developments. The growth of the illegal business promoted the development of increasingly sophisticated money-laundering systems, which were enabled in part by the large and complex contraband networks used to import many goods into Colombia.

The illegal cocaine traffic was a strong incentive for the development of coca plantings in Colombia, which appeared as a backward linkage of the cocaine trade during the mid-1970s (Thoumi 1995d, chap. 3). Their growth made them significant by the late 1970s. During the following decade, their growth rate accelerated, turning Colombia into a significant coca producer. On the basis of official U.S. government data, Sarmiento (1990, 69–70) estimates that in 1980 Colombia produced 3.7 percent of the world coca crop, a share that grew to 11 percent by 1987.

Coca production had an upward, albeit unstable, long-term trend. Coca prices have fallen in the long run and at times, when the government has intensified its antidrug fight against the "cartels," they have collapsed—causing deep depressions in coca growing regions. In 1983, for example, coca prices fell and generated a significant increase in violence in the Caguán growing area (Jaramillo, Mora, and Cubides 1989). In 1984, the government pressed its eradication campaign. These two factors led to a stop in coca planting expansion.

At the beginning of the twentieth century, Colombia was more an aggregate of regions than a nation. Its population was small, about 4 million

---

[4]This was reported in interviews by the author in Washington, D.C., in December 1997 and January 1998 with a former Colombian trafficker who participated in a U.S. government protection program.

in a country of about 522,000 square miles.[5] The country's geography is rough and awe inspiring, and throughout history it has been a great obstacle to travel and communications. The population was spread out in small concentrations, with scarce contacts among them. Most of the population was rural and maintained links only with the nearest city, which was generally the region's center. Only a small proportion of the country was settled, and the state's presence and actions were de facto limited to the cities and their areas of influence.

During the twentieth century, Colombia experienced a dramatic evolution. Rural–urban migration metamorphosed a rural country into a mostly urban one. Today, about 75 percent of the population is urban. Simultaneously, there has been a sizable rural–rural migration and smaller urban–rural flows toward the "empty quarters" (*terrenos baldíos*), where peasants and other migrants have squatted on unoccupied land.

Many of these migrations have been caused by the displacement of peasants in the wake of the frequent violent episodes that marked Colombia's twentieth-century history. Human flows have had varying degrees of notoriety: The swarming of people into cities has generated attention, whereas migrations to distant, unsettled, hard-to-reach regions have for the most part remained unnoticed. Almost all new settlements have been spontaneous, carried on by armed peasants prompted to resort to violence, and without state intervention (C. Leal 1995; Molano 1987, 1989, 1990). Settlements have had precarious infrastructure at best and have lacked government support; initially, the traditional power structure had no provisos to accommodate them.

Coca plantings in Colombia have developed almost exclusively in the areas recently settled by displaced peasants. These regions are isolated and distant from the main economic centers of the country, and the state has a weak presence if any. These are the cases of Caguán in the Caquetá Department, and the Guaviare and Putumayo Departments, the main centers of the coca economy.

The U.S. government estimated in 1991 that the area under coca cultivation had been 40,100 hectares the previous year. This was 18.8 percent of the total area under coca cultivation in the Andean countries. It was also estimated that Colombian coca productivity was lower than average, so that only 13.7 percent of the coca leaf volume was produced in Colombia

[5]The 1905 census reported 4,143,600 people.

(Thoumi 1995d, chap. 3). At that time, Colombia was the third largest coca producer in the world.

Official U.S. government data show few changes in coca hectareage during the early 1990s: 39,700 in 1993 and 45,000 in 1994 (U.S. Department of State, Bureau of International Narcotics and Law Enforcement Affairs 1998, 22). These figures contradicted frequent journalistic reports about the expansion of coca cultivation in the country. Field research done in 1995 and 1996 (S. Uribe 1997) studied illegal crops in detail and obtained data for the size of the areas under cultivation, production systems, yields, producers' associations, guerrilla participation, prices, and profitability. This study also obtained information about the refining processes near the coca fields and government policy implementation, including eradication efforts and communal perceptions about them.

S. Uribe (1997) had eight main findings. First, the area under cultivation with illegal crops in Colombia increased substantially during the early 1990s and reached much higher levels than had previously been estimated. In early 1995, approximately 100,000 hectares were cultivated with illegal crops, compared with 65,000 as officially estimated.

Second, the area under coca cultivation was estimated at about 80,000 hectares, placing Colombia in 1996 as the second largest coca-growing nation, substantially ahead of Bolivia and trailing only Peru. Before Uribe's work, official estimates of the area under coca cultivation were only about 45,000 hectares.

Third, cocaine yields increased significantly. Before this work was completed, it was commonly accepted that Colombian cocaine yields were significantly lower than those of Bolivia and Peru. Uribe found significant technological advances that increased Colombian yields to levels similar to those other two countries. These included adaptation of Bolivian and Peruvian coca varieties and the increased yield of Colombian coca due to the application of fertilizers, herbicides, and other techniques. (Indeed, peasants and chemists have continuously sought production improvements and frequently have achieved positive results.) Furthermore, improved refining techniques have become generalized among the population, and today most peasants are quite adept at producing at least coca paste. Some produce cocaine base and cocaine.

Fourth, Uribe found two main types of plantings: small, family-operated plantings of 1 hectare or less, which used hired labor only seasonally; and modern farming operations as large as 30 hectares, which both have their own laboratories to refine cocaine and also have export systems.

Fifth, this study also found important technological adaptations in cocaine refining. Peasants and chemists have found many ways to substitute inputs when some are not available; in extreme cases, they have innovated to the point that rudimentary artisanal methods can actually produce inputs, including small quantities of ether.[6]

Sixth, Uribe confirmed the participation of guerrilla organizations in the drug economy. No evidence was found that they had developed their own distribution networks abroad or exported directly, but it was clear that they profited substantially from the illegal industry. In coca-growing areas, the guerrilla front substituted for the state; it imposed a highly authoritarian regime, defined and applied its own laws and regulations, provided education and police services, and administered a primitive civil justice system to solve conflicts among the population. In exchange, the guerrilla fronts charged coca production and cocaine export taxes.[7]

Seventh, guerrilla involvement in drug-producing regions was a clear obstacle to past government policy success. Guerrillas opposed all government presence and set obstacles to state-sponsored programs like highway construction and communication systems that would integrate these regions to the power centers of the Colombian state. They were also an obstacle to alternative development and other programs that would strengthen the state presence in those regions.

Eighth, the large illicit crop increase in Colombia raised several questions related to changes in the structure of the illegal industry throughout the continent. One was the extent to which Colombian crops have substituted for imported coca by-products in the domestic industry. It appeared that at least paste and base imports had declined. Other crucial questions concerned the evolution of Bolivian and Peruvian production. (Where was it going? And who was controlling that trade?)

After Uribe's study, the U.S. government increased its estimates. The U.S. Department of State, Bureau of International Narcotics and Law Enforcement Affairs (1999, 22), gives a 1997 figure of 79,500 for total coca hectareage in Colombia.

By 1998, Colombia had become the world largest coca producer, ahead of Peru (U.S. Department of State, Bureau of International Narcotics and Law Enforcement Affairs 1998, 22). However, as will be discussed below,

---

[6]Interviews by the author with representatives of Colombian coca growers at a seminar in Cochabamba, Bolivia, in September 1997 confirmed these developments.

[7]Unfortunately, Uribe's study could not cover all guerrilla-controlled areas and did not eliminate the possibility that these organizations exported drugs from other regions.

Peru's output declined mostly because plantings were abandoned, not eradicated, and it may be possible for coca production to rebound quickly in that country if conditions are favorable.

The development of large coca plantings brought a complex set of new actors to the illegal industry. González-Arias (1998, 52–53) classified them as follows, distinguishing three types of peasants. Longtime settlers, who moved to the region to develop their farmer vocations, produce mainly foodstuffs and devote only a small part of their land (20 percent) to coca. Recent settlers devote most of their efforts to producing coca paste but also devote about 20 percent of their land to coca. Their main goal is to use their illegal activities to accumulate capital and establish a cattle ranch. Finally, recent migrants, who arrived in the region to grow coca, tend to have urban backgrounds, and they either rent small farms or cut down virgin forest to establish coca plantings.

There are also commercial farmers with large plantings of between 25 and 200 hectares and with direct links to traffickers; many have their own laboratories. These are the main rural employers in the region. Most workers in these farms are *raspachines*, who pick coca leaves and help in the manufacturing process. González-Arias (1998) argued that this is a heterogeneous group made up of three different types. The first includes peasants displaced by increased poverty and social decomposition and violence in their areas of origin.

The second type includes former rural hired workers and pickers who came from regions that produce coffee or modern crops and who expect to settle in coca-growing regions. And third are transient *raspachines* who expect to make some money before returning to their places of origin. Vargas (1999, 83) found that in Miraflores, Guaviare's capital, there were four hired farm hands for each farm owner. Policymakers and analysts were not concerned with *raspachines* until their 1996 marches protesting the aerial spraying of coca plantings showed their large numbers (González-Arias 1998).

Peasants, or *chichipatos*, also bought paste and processed coca into paste. The main function of *chichipatos* was to gather paste to sell in small quantities to *traquetos* or *propios*. These furnished the links to trafficking organizations, and some had been dispatched to the coca-growing regions by their organizations. The loyalties of this group belonged with those organizations, not with the coca-producing regions' residents (González-Arias 1998, 53). It was also common for *traquetos* to advance funds to *chichipatos*, who in turn financed peasants (Ramírez 1998).

There was also a group of "*parachuters.*" These were not people who actually parachuted into the area. They were called that because they did not live in the region, came in small planes, and left soon after. They brought large amounts of cash (pesos or dollars) and sizeable quantities of cocaine from the large factories and *traquetos.*

The illegal cocaine industry growth also generated strong incentives for illicit trade in chemical inputs. The Colombian government has tried to control ether and acetone, as well as other chemical imports, whose trade volumes have greatly exceeded the requirements of legitimate Colombian industries. But it is problematic that all these products, except ether, have myriad licit users and uses, making it very difficult to restrict their availability.

An additional problem arises from the drug industry's capacity to import contraband. Once the industry establishes export-smuggling capabilities, it also can import many products using many of the same smuggling systems. These are used to import chemical products required in manufacturing cocaine, fertilizers, herbicides, and more important, arms and other weapons. It should be pointed out, however, that on at least one memorable occasion, these imports were used to trace down the location of the refining center.[8]

In January 1999, Colombian president Andrés Pastrana gave the Colombian Revolutionary Armed Forces (FARC) guerrillas a demilitarized or "distension" zone in the Caquetá and Meta Departments with the purpose of starting peace negotiations. This zone included some of the main coca-producing areas and was used by FARC to expand its participation in the illicit drug trade. Unfortunately, scant research has been possible in that zone.

Coca hectareage has exploded during the past few years, particularly in the Putumayo Department's area bordering Ecuador. Here again, FARC has had a strong presence that has been challenged by paramilitary groups. Many peasants in this region are recent settlers displaced by several factors: declining prices of legal agricultural products, violence, and increased population in *minifundia* (very small rural family holdings that cannot

---

[8]In a well-known 1984 case, the U.S. Drug Enforcement Administration (DEA) installed a satellite-tracked radio transmitter in a couple of double-bottomed ether containers suspected of being purchased by drug traffickers. Their route was tracked down and led to the Tranquilandia laboratory in the middle of the Colombian jungle, which was destroyed. At the time, this was the largest cocaine seizure ever in the world (Gugliotta and Leen 1989, chap. 12).

yield enough to support a family). This region was the focus of a very aggressive aerial spraying campaign in 2000 and 2001. Still, the U.S. government estimates that in 2001 Colombia had 165,000 hectares of coca.

Poppy, Opium, and Heroin

Opiate production in Colombia has grown substantially, but relatively little is known about it. There existed strong incentives for Colombians to develop this branch of the illegal drug industry. During the 1980s, cocaine prices in the United States declined substantially, and by the 1990s this cocaine market appeared to be stagnant. During the past decade, the growth in cocaine demand has taken place mostly in Europe, where Colombians have not migrated in large enough numbers to facilitate the development of distribution networks.

Moreover, European and American prices of heroin have remained significantly higher than those of cocaine. And, as is discussed below, the large cartels were destroyed in the late 1980s and early 1990s, and the industry evolved into a large number of small trafficking groups more suited to lower-volume, higher-priced products. All these elements made it only a question of time before Colombians would get involved in opiates.

Poppy cultivation was first detected in Colombia in 1986 (Policía Nacional de Colombia, Dirección Antinarcóticos 1993). Colombian and U.S. fixation with cocaine allowed poppy, opium, and heroin production to grow unnoticed until the early 1990s, when official U.S. reports began to include Colombia as an important heroin supplier.

Available evidence indicates that traffickers who distributed seeds and guaranteed crop purchases to traditional peasants in *minifundia*, high-altitude regions promoted poppy plantings. Many of these peasants belong to Indian communities. Some poppy crops occupy plots used before to produce traditional crops. Others grow in newly cleared fragile, primary, high-altitude tropical forests that are very difficult to recover once destroyed.

Poppy plantings spread quickly over many areas of the Colombian Andes. By 1992, they were found in sixteen departments (Ramírez 1993). Vargas and Barragán's (1995) detailed study covering the social, economic, and political aspects of poppy, opium, and heroin production in the four largest production areas in the Cauca, Huila, Tolima, and César Departments found that almost all plantings were in small family plots. Poppy was the main cash crop for peasant families, but not their only crop. They had several other products, mainly foodstuffs for their own consumption.

In traditional Indian areas, poppy cultivation increased peasants' incomes, but not without creating social problems. The illegal business generated conflicts over payments and misunderstandings about business transactions, and it attracted undesirable outsiders to the growing areas, where violence has increased (Vargas and Barragán 1995). These researchers found that violence increased in most poppy-growing municipalities, where it was higher than in non-poppy-growing municipalities. They also found that traditional Indian communities had been disrupted and their ancestral authority structures had been challenged. This was a main reason for Indian community associations' attempts to negotiate possible eradication schemes with the Colombian government.

Migration toward poppy-growing areas and the advantages of growing illegal crops in government-owned "empty" lands (*baldíos*) to avoid legal responsibilities have been important causes of old primary forest destruction. Furthermore, the guerrilla presence in poppy-growing areas has increased. As was noted above, they enforced their own authoritarian order and imposed and collected production and trafficking taxes. Indeed, almost all poppy-growing areas have a strong guerrilla or paramilitary presence (Echandía-Castilla 1995, 61–65).

Vargas and Barragán (1995) also found that every region studied had experienced a significant economic shock before the development of poppy crops. In some regions, coffee prices had collapsed; in others, there had been peasant displacement due to land conflicts. Ramírez (1993) went farther and claims that the decline in coca prices in Caguán and Guaviare sent many coca-growing peasants back to their home regions, where they began to grow poppies!

As in the case of coca, poppy plantings are technologically diverse. S. Uribe (1997) found "commercial" and "peasant" crops. The commercial ones were generally in "empty" government lands, and growers used modern techniques, fertilizers, herbicides, and fungicides, many of which were sold by drug buyers.[9] These were larger than peasant plantings, but they generally did not exceed a total of 5 hectares, divided into several small plots to make detection difficult. Commercial plantings employed

---

[9]Some, like gramoxone (the commercial name of the infamous paraquat), are naively used by poppy farmers and peasants. These herbicides are banned in Europe and the United States, where they are considered strong carcinogenic agents. This practice can have disastrous long-term health effects. Indeed, gramoxone is the same defoliant used in the Mexican marijuana eradication of the late 1960s that led to the development of marijuana crops in Colombia.

hired labor, whereas peasant plantings employed only family labor, used less sophisticated production techniques, and were less profitable.[10]

S. Uribe (1997) also found that, in some places, traffickers had to refine morphine base at poppy production sites to avoid being tricked by peasants who found other types of latex that they could mix with opium. To ensure product quality, traffickers trucked small labs to poppy-growing regions and paid the peasants only for the morphine base refined from their opium.

Estimates of poppy, morphine, and heroin production are very uncertain. Official U.S. estimates show poppy crops of 1,600 hectares in 1991, 20,000 during the next 3 years, and 6,540, 6,300, and 6,600 hectares for 1995 through 1997 (U.S. Department of State, Bureau of International Narcotics and Law Enforcement Affairs 1998, 22).

S. Uribe (1997)—using several sources and fieldwork in 212 municipalities where illicit drugs were likely to grow—found that the poppy was the most widespread illegal crop. It was cultivated in small quantities in most municipalities in the highlands of the country. His total estimate came to 20,405 hectares for 1996, three times the official U.S. estimate. One reason for this discrepancy may be that because the poppy is a short-cycle crop (about 4 months), the estimates of the areas cultivated during a year can differ substantially from estimates based on one-time satellite pictures. The large differences between the two estimates also reflect the current lack of knowledge.

Cartels, Marketing Networks, Guerrillas, and Paramilitary Organizations

As was explained above, the Colombian illegal drug industry started with marijuana. This branch has survived, but its export dominance was rather short-lived, and it did not bring about the development of sophisticated international distribution networks. The growth of the cocaine industry that followed in the steps of marijuana produced more complex business enterprises.

Cocaine production takes several steps. First, it is necessary to grow coca. After the leaves are harvested, they have to be processed in three

---

[10]This was determined on the basis of a comparison with past export booms of short-cycle crops and the diverse quality of the Colombian opium and heroin found in the early 1990s, Echandía-Castilla (1995) asserts that the Colombian comparative advantage in heroin is likely to be transitory. By the late 1990s, this was clearly not the case.

stages. To begin with, coca paste is produced. This has to take place near coca plantings because of the difficulties involved in transporting large quantities of coca leaves. The next two stages produce cocaine base and cocaine proper. These operations can take place anywhere. The laboratories require little capital, and the machinery and equipment used are simple and easy to find in the market. In fact, laboratories are mobile, and in business jargon they are referred to as "kitchens." As was noted above, the chemicals needed are also commonly used in many industries and are easily found. Furthermore, all chemical inputs can be substituted, which weakens the effectiveness of market controls (Thoumi 1995d).

When the cocaine business started, coca did not grow in large quantities in Colombia, and the first contact between Colombian traffickers and coca paste producers in Bolivia and Peru resulted in small cocaine export volumes. These were made mainly to the United States using "mules." At this early stage, small Bolivian and Peruvian smugglers were doing the same.

The transition from small-scale artisanal operations to large businesses with sophisticated international criminal organizations was quite rapid in Colombia. The high profits generated by the business acted as seed capital for developing large organizations, and the potential profits provided strong incentives to do so.

By the early 1980s, Carlos Lehder had bought a small island in the Bahamas, where he supplied traffickers with an airport from which to send their larger shipments to the United States using small planes (Gugliotta and Leen 1990). This innovation changed the scale and structure of the business. It is also likely that other Caribbean bases were used.[11]

The development of large-scale smuggling methods increased potential gains dramatically and induced the creation of cartels or export syndicates. These organizations—which, again, are not cartels in the traditional economic sense because they do not control raw material production and most distribution systems in their main markets—could not prevent a large increase in coca cultivation and a long-term decline in cocaine prices.[12]

---

[11]In interviews in December 1997 and January 1998 in Washington, a former Colombian drug trafficker who helped Lehder in this endeavor explained that cocaine was also flown to the United States from other Caribbean bases in Haiti, the Dominican Republic, and Jamaica, among others.

[12]During the 1980s, wholesale cocaine prices declined by 75 percent in the United States. During the 1990s, the wholesale price fluctuated between $12,000 and $18,000 per kilogram.

Furthermore, they face competition from many small producers and smugglers and cannot block entry into the business (Thoumi, 1995d, chap. 3).[13]

True cartels are not functional for the illegal drug industry. First, "the risk minimizing strategies that must be followed to succeed as an illegal operation encourage a very loose structure, in which it is not possible to plan production levels and to give orders to be carried out through several layers of production and distribution. Further, the institutional organization of the industry is rather precarious, and precludes the development of anything resembling a bureaucracy, especially one that survives after the leaders are replaced" (Krauthausen and Sarmiento 1991, 36). A true cartel structure does not fully apply because

> relations between peasants who produce coca, those who gather the coca leaves, those who manufacture coca paste, those who transport it, those who refine it into cocaine base and cocaine, and those who distribute it in the main markets tend to be very fluid; the structure of the industry adapts itself to changes in the business environment brought about by the activities of law enforcement agencies and other factors. Hence, while there is no doubt that desires to preserve and increase industry profits encourage attempts to collude and create a suppliers' market agreement, or cartel, strong forces are also pushing in the opposite direction. (Thoumi 1995d, 143)

There is no doubt that at one time in the mid-1980s, drug traffickers tried to organize themselves, but "the most pressing reasons that the drug traffickers tried to organize themselves involved desires to counter the government's extradition policy and the threat of further kidnappings, two elements not directly related to cocaine pricing, market share fights, and other traditional goals of economic cartels." (Thoumi 1995d, 147).

These export syndicates were organized to minimize risk and guarantee profits. High risks and profits characterized contraband to the main cocaine markets and provided strong incentives for traffickers to search for ways

---

[13]Some analysts argue otherwise. Shelley (1995, 479) explains: "Colombian organized crime is quite different from the other organized crime groups because it operates as a cartel—its business is the monopolization of the illicit international narcotics trade. A cartel takes advantage of a monopoly position in the market to artificially control prices and access to particular commodities." The market price data cannot support this statement.

to lower risks. One of their simplest strategies consisted of combining exports from several producers and traffickers, making several shipments to scatter risk among those funding exports, with the awareness that some would be lost. This system guaranteed substantial profits for every partner (Thoumi 1995d, chap. 3).

Export syndicates coordinated the Colombian cocaine industry. They sent coca paste and cocaine base buyers to Bolivia and Peru, who organized shipments to Colombia, established laboratories to refine cocaine or subcontracted that process, and organized the illegal exports from Colombia and the wholesaling of the product in the United States and other markets. The extremely high profits of the cocaine business induced Colombians, but not Bolivians and Peruvians, to participate in all stages of the cocaine industry, including its distribution in the United States, where the large number of Colombian immigrants facilitated the establishment of distribution networks.

The development of distribution networks in the United States was also facilitated by the proclivity of Colombians to use violence against other smuggling organizations. Cuban criminal organizations controlled the illegal cocaine market before Colombians got involved in it, and they simply eliminated the Cuban mafias in Florida (Gugliotta and Leen 1990). Violence was also instrumental in deterring the development of export syndicates in Bolivia and Peru that would have competed with Colombians.

The large profits generated by the illegal industry also required the development of sophisticated money-laundering systems. Rapid wealth acquisition, furthermore, made it impossible for successful exporters not to be noticed. Their high notoriety increased their need for a social support network to protect their business, illegal profits, and accumulated capital. One of the early strategies for social support was to let wealthy Colombians buy shares in a cocaine shipment, under a system known as *la apuntada* (Krauthausen and Sarmiento 1991, 74; Arango and Child 1987, 130–31).

The illegal drug industry comprised a diverse group of participants: peasants, chemists, various types of suppliers, purchasers and intermediaries, pilots, lawyers, financial and tax advisers, enforcers, bodyguards, front men (*testaferros*), and smugglers that helped launder profits. They were tied to the central cartels in different ways. Some were directly part of the cartels, but many were loosely tied to them and acted more like independent contractors that sold their services for a fee. This arrangement was frequently preferred by the cartels, because when law enforcers captured subcontractors, they could provide only minimum information about the cartel's structure and membership.

Another social support network included politicians, police, guerrillas, paramilitaries, individual army members, public employees, bankers, loyal relatives, friends, and childhood friends. These benefited from the industry, condoned it, or provided protection to its members, but they were not directly part of it.[14] Such a social support network provides protection to the illegal industry, mostly at a price, and constitutes the main channel through which the illegal industry penetrates and corrupts social institutions. Through this network, illegal income is distributed to the rest of society, and strong loyalties are forged within the illegal industry.

During the 1980s, Colombians dominated cocaine production and exports to the United States and Europe. In Bolivia and Peru, the illegal industry was concentrated in rural activities, mainly in the Upper Huallaga Valley in Peru and the Chapare region of Bolivia. Trafficking organizations developed in those countries, but as is shown below, they exported relatively small amounts of cocaine and focused their activities on supplying coca paste and cocaine base to Colombian organizations.

In Colombia, there were several export syndicates. The Medellín cartel was the main one, followed by the Cali cartel. These two gained notoriety in international cocaine markets. Smaller syndicates remained in the shadow of the two main ones. These varied from relatively large organizations to "mom-and-pop" groups that exported small quantities. Most information about export organizations focuses on the Medellín and Cali cartels, and little is known about the rest. The frequent capture of "mules" carrying small amounts suggests that the number of small organizations may have exceeded 100.

The illegality of the industry motivates continuous change and adaptation to new government policies and a search for new operating modalities to keep ahead of law enforcement. Sometimes, the reaction of the illegal industry to government policy changes produces unexpected consequences. For example, the "war against narco-terrorism" declared by the Colombian government against the Medellín cartel after the assassination of Luis Carlos Galán in August 1989 opened up opportunities for the Cali cartel and other smaller export syndicates.

---

[14]Krauthausen and Sarmiento (1991) have provided an excellent analysis of this phenomenon in Colombia. Unfortunately, there are no comparable works in Bolivia and Peru. Gamarra's (1999) work on Bolivia begins to fill this void.

During the 1990s, the Colombian illegal drug industry experienced significant structural shifts in response to changes in demand or government policies. First, cocaine demand in the United States stagnated while cocaine production increased. The resulting lower prices encouraged traffickers to search for new markets. Second, the United States increased interdiction efforts in the Caribbean. Third, the Peruvian Alberto Fujimori administration took strong interdiction measures against illicit flights from coca-growing regions to Colombia.

Fourth, after Galán's assassination, the government of Virgilio Barco and its successor, that of César Gaviria, followed a war against narco-terrorism that destroyed the Medellín cartel. Pressured by the United States, the subsequent government of Ernesto Samper fought not only a war against narco-terrorism but also one against narco-traffic that led to the incarceration of all the leaders of the Cali cartel. This resulted in a breakdown of the industry and the proliferation of small *cartelitos*. Fifth, guerrillas and paramilitary groups became increasingly involved in the illegal trade, whose profits were used to fuel the Colombian conflict.

These changes have had important effects on the industry's structure. Lower international cocaine prices induced a search for new markets and products. Links were established between Colombian and European criminal organizations (Clawson and Lee 1996, 62–90; Krauthausen 1998). Bolivian producers searched other means to reach new markets, using links with Brazilian and Argentinean groups to export to Europe through Nigeria, Morocco, and other African countries that have easier access than Latin Americans to European markets.

It also needs to be noted that the expansion of old and the opening of new European markets has been greatly helped by the collapse of the Soviet Union and the strong growth in the underground economy in all countries previously under its influence. This has resulted in a substantial increase in European cocaine demand. Krauthausen (1998) compared the Colombian and Italian criminal organizations and presented detailed evidence about the links that they have recently developed. These provide openings for traffic in illicit drugs and other criminal activities like arms smuggling and money laundering. The links between Colombian and European criminal organizations also indicate that Colombian illegal drug issues and problems are evolving into organized crime issues that transcend drugs.

Bolivian and Peruvian traffickers have also tried to find marketing alternatives, and Bolivians have developed direct connections with Mexican criminal organizations, bypassing the Colombians. It appears that Peruvians have been much less successful than Bolivians in finding alternatives ways to market their coca products. There have been reports of attempts to grow poppies in Peru, but it seems that until 2000 they had not been successful and yields had been poor.

The interdiction efforts against illegal flights to Colombia from Bolivia and Peru by the Fujimori administration in the early 1990s contributed to a very large increase in coca cultivation in Colombia. This "import-substitution" phenomenon coincided with the falling in disarray of the Cali cartel that had strong links to Peruvian growers and with a fungus infestation dubbed as "El gringo." Purchasing coca paste and cocaine base abroad was more difficult for the new small *cartelitos* that took the place of the large export syndicates. These combined factors led to a dramatic fall of coca prices in Peru. Peruvian coca production was devastated, and the illegal Peruvian economy entered an unprecedented crisis.

The structure of illegal organizations also changed. In Colombia, the cartels became more and more sophisticated. The focus on the war against the Medellín cartel during the early 1990s allowed other syndicates to grow. The Cali cartel developed sophisticated intelligence systems and strengthened its social support networks. A prominent example of this was the Cali cartel's intelligence on its Medellín rivals, which was provided to the government and was instrumental in helping to locate the whereabouts of the drug lord Pablo Escobar, the leader of the Medellín cartel, who died trying to escape from police.

According to U.S. intelligence (Zabludoff 1997), in the early 1990s Colombia's drug exports were controlled by ten to fourteen large organizations. These coordinated the various stages of the business, from buying coca paste to selling wholesale in the United States and Europe, and in some cases, even established a few "cells" in the United States to sell to middle-level traffickers and obtain higher-than-wholesale prices. These sources also indicate that the Cali cartel controlled up to 80 percent of the cocaine marketed in the United States.

These large syndicates bought coca paste or cocaine base in Colombia and other Andean locations from independent producers. They subcontracted cocaine refining and also bought cocaine from independent manufacturers. They organized export shipments that frequently included joint ventures with other groups (Rocha 1997). Most export contraband was subcontracted with independent smugglers.

Structural sophistication and decentralization typically minimized risks of defection by turncoats after the capture of some member. In these syndicates, most individuals involved had contact with one or very few people and were ignorant of the actual structure of the organization and of who were its members. The most delicate operation to subcontract was money laundering, given the difficulty in keeping anonymity. To launder money, it is necessary to use totally reliable front people. In most cases, these must operate close to the traffickers, which increases identification risks.

Among the dozen or so organizations mentioned by Zabludoff, the Cali cartel was the largest, but it was undoubtedly not the only important one. The development of heroin production allowed some smaller syndicates to grow, because its potential profits per kilogram were larger and its distribution networks were not controlled by the established large export syndicates. In the early stages of the development of the heroin industry, new entrants did not have to compete head on with the large cocaine syndicates. Reports indicate that the North Valley cartel grew in importance, but there is little access to information about it.

Castillo's (1996) investigative journalism book argued that toward the mid-1990s there were several (and perhaps many) independent export syndicates. It appears that most were connected with the large cartels, leading to frequent cooperation and coordination. For example, Castillo attests that in the late 1980s Escobar required smaller organizations to contribute financially to his eventually successful efforts to have extradition declared unconstitutional by the 1991 Constitution. Castillo also points out that in 1994 the Cali cartel required contributions from the North Valley exporting syndicates to fund Samper's presidential campaign. He also notes that Escobar issued the equivalent of export "licenses" to the smaller groups and required the payment of an export "tariff."

In the early 1990s, vigorous U.S. interdiction efforts in the Caribbean induced Colombian traffickers to seek alternative routes. Links developed gradually between Colombian and Mexican trafficking organizations. At first, Colombians smuggled their cocaine to Mexico and consigned it to Mexicans, who in exchange for a fee smuggled it to the United States, where they returned it to the Colombians. Later, Mexicans began to be paid in kind with a share of the cocaine. For Mexicans, this change was welcome, because it was relatively easy for them to develop distribution networks on the West Coast among the large Mexican migrant population.

The reasons for the change in the payment system are not clear. From the Colombian point of view, in-kind payments eliminated the need to smuggle large amounts of cash into Mexico to pay for the Mexicans' services. Nevertheless, this change introduced stiff competition in the U.S. wholesale cocaine market, which reduced Colombians' profits substantially. It is likely that the pressure by the U.S. and Colombian governments on Colombian trafficking organizations played an important role in encouraging this change that lowered the profile of Colombian traffickers while raising that of Mexican ones.

Another factor likely to have played a role was the link of Mexican trafficking organizations with the Mexican police. Indeed, it may be argued that the negotiations between Colombian and Mexican traffickers were not between two trafficking organizations but rather between Colombian traffickers and franchisees of the Mexican police. One consequence of this development has been the Colombians' loss of market share on the West Coast and in the Western mountain regions of the United States, where Mexicans now dominate the market. This change has also had an important indirect effect: It broadened the U.S. antidrug foreign policy focus to include Mexico rather than only Colombia.

It was reported that the Mexicans gradually increased the percentage of the shipments they charge the Colombians. A rate of up to 50 percent was frequently mentioned. This induced Colombian exporters to seek other routes, particularly in the Caribbean.

As has been noted, guerrillas and paramilitary organizations have also participated in the Colombian illicit industry. In the early 1980s, there were reports of a developing relationship between guerrilla groups and drug-trafficking organizations. In 1984, after the capture and destruction of the Tranquilandia cocaine laboratory in the Amazon jungle, "there was evidence that the guerrillas had provided such protection, a fact that led United States Ambassador Lewis Tambs to formulate a theory about a 'Narco-Guerrilla' drug conspiracy" (Thoumi 1995d, 159).

There is no question that guerrilla groups provided protection for processing labs and coca plantings, but their relations with trafficking organizations have been complex and at times conflictive:

The illegal psychoactive drug (PSAD) industry and the guerrillas have been odd bedfellows. At times the government has been their common enemy, but they have fundamentally opposite goals. The illegal PSAD industry represents a crude, unrestrained form of capitalism, while the guerrilla organizations have their origins in their fight against the unfair, crude capitalism that has prevailed in the country. The conflict between the long-run goals of these two social groups is irreconcilable. (Thoumi 1995d, 159)

Gugliotta and Leen (1990, chap. 16) presented evidence of links between the Medellín cartel and both the Sandinistas and the M-19 guerrillas, whose takeover of the Supreme Court building on November 6, 1985, benefited traffickers by destroying criminal files of cases against them. These findings supported the guerrilla–drug link hypothesis.

It needs to be noted that the Medellín cartel also developed connections with other Central American and Caribbean governments and subversive groups. Scott and Marshall (1991) assert the cartel's links with the Nicaraguan Contras, General Manuel Noriega in Panama, and Cuban government officials. They also argue that the U.S. Central Intelligence Agency was involved in some of these activities.

"The 'Narco–Guerrilla connection' provided the United States with the possibility to kill two birds with one stone, since it could link its antidrug policies with anticommunist policies in the region" (Thoumi 1995d, 159). However, the alliances between the illegal drug industry and the guerrillas proved to be temporary and fraught with conflict. In some guerrilla-controlled areas, coca growing started being promoted by the illegal industry. This weakened the guerrilla organizations because the loyalty of the peasants was considerably affected.

"As illegal drug businessmen invested in other guerrilla-controlled areas, such as in the Middle Magdalena Valley, the guerrillas tried to apply the same 'taxation' methods used on traditional landowners, and in cases, they went as far as kidnapping the industry's entrepreneurs and their relatives to extract ransom payments. These tactics led to a strong reaction by the drug traffickers and to the formation of paramilitary groups that made use of the legal framework provided for the establishment of self-defense community groups" (Thoumi 1995d, 159–60).[15] Not only did those protect the industry's investments; they also resorted to violence against anyone who sympathized with social reform. The illegal drug industry in essence, substituted their own protection organization for the guerrillas.

The drug industry also established links with gangs of young assassins-for-hire (*sicarios*), who have been used to dispose of a gamut of enemies or rivals, to settle accounts with business partners, and to eliminate

---

[15]The first ones appeared around 1980 in the Middle Magdalena Valley, where drug traffickers had invested in large ranches. See also Clawson and Lee (1996, 186–90).

competitors. Salazar's (1990) work, based on in-depth interviews with *sicarios*, showed that some of them were first trained by the M-19 guerrilla organization. Allegedly, these youngsters found the Marxist rhetoric rather irrelevant to their life experiences, but their newly acquired skills proved quite instrumental in the capitalist marketplace.

To sum up, connections were established during the 1980s between the guerrillas and the illegal drug industry, but these proved fundamentally unstable, because the main long-term goals of the two groups were diametrically opposite. The nature of these relationships followed the logic of expediency that characterized the illegal drug industry. When it was convenient, the illegal industry sought to form alliances or bought military personnel, judges, politicians, bankers, and other professionals.

During the 1990s, the Colombian illegal drug industry experienced significant changes that compounded its complexity, increased the number and types of active actors, and most crucially, intertwined the illegal industry and other key Colombian problems, particularly subversive and antisubversive movements, thus affecting the possibilities of peace in the country. These changes have made the "drug problem" more intractable.

The large increase in coca plantings and the development of the poppy industry introduced new actors to the illegal drug drama in Colombia. In several regions, significant numbers of peasant families depend on illegal crop income, linking illicit drugs and employment issues. Guerrilla organizations capitalized on this development and tried to organize peasant political movements against the state. Guerrilla and paramilitary organizations and peasant groups became influential political actors in issues related to illegal drugs. In late 1996, for example, the guerrilla-organized peasant marches protesting aerial spraying of coca plantings forced the government to negotiate policy changes.[16]

However, the lack of a similar reaction in response to widespread aerial fumigation in 2000 and 2001 suggests that the guerrillas' support has not run deep in most peasant communities.[17] And in a more crucial change, illegal crops and drug trafficking have become one of the main sources of guerrilla and paramilitary revenues and now fuel the country's conflict.

---

[16]The marches mobilized up to 120,000 peasants and their families. It is likely that at least a proportion of them did not participate voluntarily because the fear of guerrilla retaliation was always present.

[17]Guerrilla and paramilitary support in these communities depend on the way in which those violent organizations treat peasants. In many instances, peasants have been ordered around and put in peril, and their support is likely to be superficial.

Beginning in the 1970s, guerrilla groups started to kidnap and extort Colombian landlords and a few prominent businesspeople. As was noted above, they also charged to protect illegal drug crops, laboratories, and smuggling activities. After the collapse of the Soviet Union, and the consequent termination of foreign assistance funding, the guerrillas had to rely almost exclusively on domestic sources.[18] The explosion in coca and poppy plantings offered a golden opportunity for guerrillas. Once guerrillas became involved at that level, drug trafficking also became a main source of their funding during the 1990s. Their other significant fountains of income are extortion and kidnappings.

During the 1990s, Colombian guerrillas secured financing from several sources, mainly taxes on the illegal drug industry, kidnappings, and extortion, including "protection" for foreign oil companies. During this period, guerrilla organizations became significantly larger, sophisticated, and better armed. They developed intelligence systems, urban networks, and established foreign representations in Costa Rica, Mexico, Venezuela, and Europe. These changes prove that current guerrilla financing is much higher than what they had available in 1990.

The guerrilla–drug nexus is not questioned, but its specifics are difficult to determine. Villamarín (1996) argued that FARC, the oldest guerrilla group, constitutes a "drug cartel."[19] His work provided insights into FARC control of some of the main coca- and-poppy growing regions, their various "taxes," FARC links to trafficking organizations, and some estimates of drug related revenues. Villamarín argued that the type of rule imposed by guerrilla organizations on the areas they controlled is authoritarian and antidemocratic and that the guerrillas applied force liberally to impose their will. Using data from the president's staff, Villamarín estimated that in 1994 FARC received $260 million from illegal drugs.[20]

---

[18]It is impossible to determine the value of the assistance provided by communist countries to Colombian guerrillas before 1990, and some would argue that it was not significant.

[19]Villamarín was an army major at the time of his writing. His book has a prologue by Harold Bedoya, the right-wing retired general who ran unsuccessfully for the presidency in 1998 and 2002. The work is based on former guerrillas' testimonies, published material, and presumably confidential intelligence information. It lacks rigor, but does shed some light on the FARC finances and the army's perspective on the guerrilla organization.

[20]Villamarín does not provide any methodological explanation to allow for an evaluation of the accuracy and biases of these estimates.

La Rotta (1996) argued that Colombian guerrillas have exploited the Colombian nation and provided many estimates of different guerrilla funding sources. His estimates are based on testimonies of former guerrillas, police and army personnel, government officials, journalistic reports, and other sources. Most of his estimates are based on testimonies, but his methodology is not clear. Some of the oral evidence he gathered indicates that not only were the guerrillas taxing the drug industry, but that they were also growing coca and poppies and manufacturing cocaine and heroin.[21] His main point is simply that the guerrilla organizations have enriched themselves at the expense of the nation. His estimate of guerrilla drug income is three to four times larger than that of official sources or Villamarín.[22]

Lee (1998) used Colombian government data and journalistic reports to estimate the illicit drug income of the main guerrilla organizations: FARC, the National Liberation Army (ELN), and the Popular Liberation Army (EPL). His 1997 estimates were $381 million for FARC, $35 million for ELN, and zero for EPL. According to his estimates, 70 percent of FARC revenues were related to illegal drugs, whereas only 8 percent of ELN's came from this source. Indeed, 92 percent of this guerrilla group's sources came from kidnappings and extortion, particularly of foreign oil companies.

According to Lee's research, the differences in the guerrilla groups' funding sources were due to the ELN's policy of attacking foreign investment in primary-product extractive industries, which according to its economic development theories represent the root cause of Colombia's poverty and the reason for the nation's underdevelopment. Another reason for the differences is the lack of EPL presence in coca- and poppy-growing regions and the rejection of the drug trade by some ELN guerrilla fronts whose members have devout Catholic backgrounds and take a strong moralistic position against drugs (see chapter 9).

Vargas (1999, 48) used journalistic reports to arrive at a figure for the income of all guerrilla groups from 1991 through 1996. These figures are difficult to interpret because they are given in then-current pesos and annual inflation during the period remained about 20 percent. The breakdown of funding sources is likely to be more valuable than the total:

---

[21]It must be pointed out that academic research pieces like those of Vargas and Barragán (1995) and S. Uribe (1997) did not arrive at similar findings.

[22]Unfortunately, this book lacks rigor, and it is impossible to evaluate the validity of its estimate.

44.4 percent drug trafficking, 27.4 percent extortion and various types of robberies, 21.9 percent kidnapping bounties, and 6.3 investment returns and government funds obtained from guerrilla-controlled municipal governments.

Independent of the possible inaccuracies, the available estimates indicate that during the 1990s illegal drugs became the main source of guerrilla funding in the country. This increased the complexity of drug issues in Colombia as the internal conflict and the illegal drugs industry became intertwined. Illegal drugs became a main funding source for every actor in Colombia's ambiguous war, and they turned into a key issue and a main obstacle to the country's peace agenda. There is no question today that peace and drugs are closely intertwined and that the solution of one problem hinges on the other. This will be explored in chapter 7. One consequence of these changes has been to make illegal drug research more difficult and dangerous, and it has been very difficult to follow up the industry's evolution.

As has been noted, soon after President Pastrana took office in 1998, he granted the FARC guerrilla group a "distension zone" in an area of heavy FARC presence to facilitate peace talks. This region was a center of coca production in which FARC had controlled the countryside for a long time. The government withdrew the army and police, and FARC took over the urban areas and established a de facto government. It created a conflict resolution and justice system, oversaw education, and developed infrastructure. This safe haven was used by FARC to organize its guerrillas, keep military personnel it had captured and kidnapped civilians held for ransom, and control the illegal drug trade. Paramilitary organizations were created with support from the drug syndicates, and they have extensively relied on illegal drug funding.

Interviews with U.S. and Colombian government officials and Colombian researchers suggest that at least some guerrilla groups have tried to develop drug export trafficking networks using the remnants of the Latin American leftist movements as conduits. Moreover, it is also believed that guerrillas were only able to export limited amounts this way and that the prices they obtained were significantly below international wholesale levels, which are, however, substantially higher than Colombian wholesale prices.

After the departure of government forces from five coca-growing municipalities of the "distension zone" in early 1999, the guerrillas began to rid the region of coca paste, cocaine base, and cocaine intermediaries (*chichipatos*). Guerrilla organizations took over coca paste and cocaine base manufacturing and drug market intermediation, and they established marketing systems to sell to wholesale refiners and exporters. In 1999, they also established support prices that raised peasants' income and export drug prices in an apparent move to increase their peasant support.

It needs to be underscored that guerrillas and drug traffickers are strange bedfellows. They use illegal drug money for essentially divergent ends. The former's expenditures support mainly subversive activities and their political agenda, and the latter's lead to individual profits. There is no evidence that many individual guerrilla members are becoming rich in the drug industry, although there are reports that some have pocketed guerrilla funds. In short, guerrillas benefit institutionally while drug traffickers profit personally from drug trafficking. Many years ago, "Tirofijo"[23] himself was aware of the deleterious effect of individual enrichment on guerrilla morals and attributed the weakening of the liberal guerrilla groups of the 1950s partly to cattle rustling, extortion, and armed robberies (Alape 1998, 246).

The divergent goals of traffickers and guerrillas and the attempts by FARC to control the coca and coca paste markets are likely a reason that, since 1999, coca planting expansion in Colombia has taken place mainly in Putumayo, outside the distension zone.

In summary, the main Colombian guerrilla organizations unquestionably depend on the illicit drug trade financially. There is, however, no evidence that they have developed significant international marketing networks. In that sense, therefore, there is no guerrilla "cartel." The guerrilla involvement in the drug trade has intensified in the past few years, and they have appeared intent on increasing their share of the illegal business. Moreover, estimates of the extent of their involvement cannot be established accurately and is still much a matter of conjecture.

Paramilitaries are also important actors in the illegal trade. Such organizations originated in the late 1970s and flourished during the 1990s, partly as a response to the strengthening and consolidation of the guerrillas. These are right-wing guerrillas with questionable origins and membership. Some of the main leaders of these groups originated in the emerald underground market trade and have developed links with smuggling organizations. They are supported by various sources: individuals

---

[23]In English, "Sure-Shot"; this is Pedro Antonio Marín, a.k.a. "Manuel Marulanda-Vélez," the indisputable head of the FARC guerrilla organization.

who have been threatened, extorted, or kidnapped by guerrilla organizations (landlords, businesspeople, their relatives, and others);[24] former military personnel frustrated with the armed forces' inability to subdue guerrillas; and illegal drug organizations that seek its alliance for the protection of land investments, to expel peasants from coveted lands, or to protect laboratories and trafficking operations.

The links of these organizations to the illegal drug trade are also complex and difficult to determine. That the paramilitary groups and guerrillas struggle to control such areas as the Urabá and Putumayo regions indicates competing efforts to control illegal production regions and routes that are crucial for drugs and other illegal trade such as arms and chemical precursors for illicit drugs.

Peasant testimonies in coca- and poppy-growing regions also implicate the armed forces in the illegal trade. The seizure of more than 600 kilograms of cocaine on board a Colombian Air Force C-130 transport plane in Fort Lauderdale in late 1998 confirmed these testimonies. At the time, the press devoted a lot of space to the existence of a "Blue Cartel," (the color of the Air Force uniform) but again, there is no solid evidence about the extent of the drug industry's infiltration of the country's armed forces. Ramírez (1998) argued that military personnel have enriched themselves personally through their involvement in the illegal industry, and that such money does not contribute to the armed forces' coffers. The armed forces as an institution are not tainted by drug money, despite the incriminating behavior of some of their members.

It is ironic, in this regard, that the corrupting force of drug funds undermines the armed forces. But those same funds strengthen guerrilla and paramilitary forces by enabling them to afford soldiers and weapons. Illegal drugs contribute to the armed forces' budget indirectly through the foreign aid they receive as part of the antidrug efforts of the U.S government.

In February 2002, the peace dialogue between the Pastrana administration and FARC broke down, and the government rescinded the distension zone. This is seen as a move toward a more open war. The effects on the illegal drug industry are unpredictable. At this time, the future of the drug industry in Colombia and its role in the country's conflict are more difficult to predict than at any time in the past 30 years.

---

[24]E.g., guerrillas killed the father of the Castaño brothers, the principal paramilitary leaders, after they had paid an agreed-to ransom.

The Industry in Bolivia

To study the Bolivian and Peruvian psychoactive drug industry, it is necessary to separate traditional coca plantings that provide leaves for coca chewing, a few industrial processes (coca tea, toothpaste), medical uses and legal exports,[25] from other plantings that produce inputs to the illegal industry. In Bolivia, Law 1008 of 1988 recognizes legal coca plantings in two traditional coca-growing regions: Yungas of La Paz Department and Yungas of Vandiola in Cochabamba Department. The legal coca-growing areas in Yungas of Vandiola are very small so that Yungas of La Paz accounts for most of the legal plantings.[26]

Traditional Coca

Coca has been consumed continuously in Bolivia, like in Peru, for as long as one can remember. Until the 1950s, most coca grew in the Yungas region of La Paz Department. Coca in that area can be traced back to the seventeenth century when free Indians, independent from the haciendas, began to grow coca in the region. Land tenancy in Yungas became concentrated over time, and by the 1720s the development of haciendas had already been consolidated. This evolution continued, and by the late nineteenth century there were only a few landowners. By 1900, José María Gamarra, the "coca king," dominated the coca market.[27] At some point in time, he owned 32 percent of all haciendas in the main coca-growing area of the Yungas (Quiroga 1990).[28]

The Yungas landlords, under the leadership of Gamarra, developed a tightly knit association—the Society of Landowners of Yungas and Inquisivi, or SPY[29]—which became a strong pro-coca lobby against international pressure in the League of Nations to restrict coca cultivation

---

[25]These are mainly made to multinational pharmaceutical and soft drink companies.

[26]In most coca literature, the use of the word Yungas refers to that region in La Paz Department.

[27]The characteristics of the coca market and the structure of property in Yungas of La Paz in the late nineteenth and early twentieth centuries were studied in detail by Soux (1993).

[28]See also Bascopé (1993).

[29]Gamarra never actually presided over SPY, but he was always the power behind the throne (Bascopé 1993, 21).

and consumption,[30] and against domestic opposition to coca chewing (Lema 1997).

During the first half of the twentieth century, coca consumption became generalized to the point of becoming a staple in Bolivian diet. SPY sought to develop several coca uses and funded studies that showed "that coca's vitamin content was indeed high" (Lema 1997, 109), but traditional uses prevailed. The importance of coca to the Bolivian economy and its widespread use for both work and other social activities are reflected in the inclusion of coca in the 1940 government's list of "indispensable articles" required to be available in all mining and railroad business locations (Quiroga 1990, 12).[31]

Bolivia experienced a significant revolution in 1952. A land reform program was initiated in 1953, and many haciendas were split up and distributed among a large number of peasants. These changes produced a decline in coca demand, which most analysts attribute to an increase in the peasants' real standard of living that improved their diets and thus released them from the compulsion to chew coca to placate hunger. Quiroga (1990, 14–15) argued that this fall was simply due to a supply decline caused by the hacienda breakup, which according to Bascopé (1993, 30) destroyed the coca marketing systems previously controlled by the landowners.

This situation resulted in notably higher urban coca prices. Independent of the reasons for the decline, it is significant that coca chewing fell in the 1950s and 1960s. Blanes and Mansilla (1994, 15) argued that social change and economic development (albeit slow) in Bolivia resulted in a degree of Westernization that produced a secular decline in coca demand for traditional uses. They also pointed out that during the 1980s traditional coca uses were discouraged simply because higher prices could be charged for the deviation of legal coca to illicit drug production (p. 22).

Traditional coca growers in Yungas also planted other crops, particularly coffee. They used environmentally friendly systems and cultivated their coca in terraces that prevented soil erosion.[32] Coca cultivation has expanded in the Yungas since the 1970s, but the terracing system has not been used in the new plantings (Quiroga 1990; Joel 1999). Some of these

[30]As early as 1923, the League of Nations had labeled coca leaves as a narcotic (Musto 1999).

[31]These lists were common in most Latin American countries and included goods whose price and availability was considered politically sensitive by the government. In many cases, these goods' markets were regulated and their prices controlled.

[32]Spedding (1997a) has provided a detailed description of these methods.

are geared toward the legal coca market, but many are not (Joel 1999), and as noted above, some of the old coca has also been supplying illegal markets.[33] This shows a changed peasant attitude toward land management and an increase in the importance of short-term profits in their decision-making process—a development that foretells grave ecological problems in a not-too-distant future.

New Coca

New coca plantings developed in the 1970s in response to increased world cocaine demand. Most of those new plantings are in Chapare, but there are other regions as well where new coca has also been planted in smaller quantities.

Chapare, or "Tropic of Cochabamba," is a low-altitude, extremely rainy and humid region that until recently was covered almost completely by primary humid tropical forests. The colonization of Chapare has been a goal of successive governments since colonial times. From 1940 on, their promotion of settlements in Chapare formed part of attempts to solve the land tenancy problem, and to offer non–urban migration alternatives to peasants. The settlement of Chapare, however, was accompanied by increases in coca production. In 1937, 97 percent of Bolivian coca hectareage was in the Yungas. The 1950 census showed that this proportion had fallen to 67 percent, with Chapare gaining most of the balance. By 1967, more than 50 percent of Bolivian coca hectareage was in this area (J. Painter 1994, 3).

Coca production in Chapare differed from that in Yungas. Farms here were more modern and employed salaried workers, in contrast to Yungas, which relied exclusively on family labor. This evolution broke with the tradition of subsistence farming of producing mostly for self-consumption and reserving only small quantities for the market (Quiroga 1990, 14).

---

[33]An April 1999 interview with a Yungas coca growers' leader by the author implicitly confirmed this. The coca grower explained that in Yungas there were only about 9,000 hectares planted with coca, whereas the limit authorized under Law 1008 was 12,000. He acknowledged that traditional coca demand was satisfied, but he complained bitterly about the government efforts to eradicate new coca plantings that would have supplied only the illegal industry. He simply appeared to believe that coca growers had the right to increase their plantings to the maximum allowed by law, independent of legal coca demand and coca uses.

The government sponsored many Chapare settlements, whereas others developed spontaneously. The state was always present in this. Large infrastructure projects were partially financed by multilateral and bilateral lending agencies, mainly the World Bank, the Inter-American Development Bank, and the U.S. Agency for International Development (J. Painter 1994). Both multilateral banks helped finance the road between Cochabamba and Santa Cruz, one of the main thoroughfares of the country, which crosses the Chapare. Government investment in Chapare has been significant, with the result that today it has by far the best infrastructure (electricity, education, health services, communications, transportation, etc.) of any rural Bolivian region.

In addition to the government, civil organizations also participated actively in this process, with peasant *sindicatos* playing a key role. These are fairly democratic institutions peculiar to Bolivia.[34] *Sindicatos'* membership is determined by residence. Each *sindicato* covers a particular area, and each family that settles on a parcel of land within its jurisdiction becomes a *sindicato* member. *Sindicatos* require their members' presence at periodic meetings, where many of the community's problems are vented.

Sindicatos have developed communal conflict resolution systems, the decisions of which are enforced by the community. They "possess the authority, legitimacy, and power to establish private land boundaries for new colonists, to influence transport fares, and to manage and tax coca-leaf markets in the towns of the Chapare, with the funds so raised to be used for local, small-scale public works programs" (Healy 1991, 89).

The *sindicatos* are grouped in federations that form confederations. These organizations provide coca growers with political representation, acting as mediators among peasants, the state, and foreign donors like the United Nations Drug Control Program and the U.S. Agency for International Development. Evo Morales, the most prominent *sindicato* leader, has been a member of the Bolivian Congress, as have been a couple of other *sindicato* members.[35]

---

[34]I use the word "fairly" for the reason that they are not totally democratic because they implicitly discriminate against women and their modus operandi is a traditional blend of paternalism and authoritarianism.

[35]In February 2002, Evo Morales was expelled from Congress in a remarkably fast reaction by that institution to what the establishment perceived was Morales's encouragement of violent Chapare peasant protests. This reaction dramatically increased Morales's popularity. To the surprise of most analysts, in late 2002 he was the runner-up in the presidential election and became a key power broker in the country.

The *sindicatos* were originally organized after the 1952 revolution in the peasant Sierra communities, the home of most migrants to Chapare. Their cohesion reflects the strong community infrastructure among Bolivian peasants. Although the peasants' decision to move was made individually, migration to Chapare was communal. Sierra peasants from a particular village migrated to the same Chapare area, so Sierra *sindicato* members are also members of a parallel *sindicato* in Chapare.[36]

It may be argued that the peasants migrated with their institutions on their backs, and indeed, most Chapare migrants did not sever their links with their original Sierra communities. Indeed, many migrants have been seasonal. Traditional Indian communities in Bolivia cultivated plots at several altitudes, in which they grew different crops that provided a diversified diet. Following this tradition, many migrants maintained their small plots in the Sierra and established new ones in Chapare where they worked only part of the year.

Chapare's weather is extremely hot and humid. Many migrants used to more benign Sierra conditions do not feel comfortable in Chapare. In spite of Chapare's relatively high income levels, very few peasants invest in good housing in the region. Indeed, Chapare's housing is remarkably primitive. A typical peasant house consists of a mere roof supported by a few pillars to protect the family from rain, a hearth floor, and no side walls. Sanabria (1993) found that Chapare settlers invested most of their savings in their original Sierra villages and that their accommodations there were significantly better than those of nonmigrants. Indeed, one remarkable aspect of Chapare migration has been the survival of community organizations.

The settlement of Chapare accelerated during the 1970s and continued at a fast rhythm in the 1980s. The collapse of the Bolivian economy and the closings of the tin mines in the mid-1980s provided other incentives to migrate. Quiroga's (1990, 19) estimations indicate that 70 percent of Chapare residents in 1989 had moved to the region in the past two decades. This was accompanied by a large increase in coca acreage, which remained stable from 1988 to 1997 (Joel 1999).

As a result of these migrations, Chapare's population is made up of three main groups. The first consists of former highland peasants who are landowners in Chapare. They migrated to a large extent because of a land shortage in their regions of origin, where population increases led to the

---

[36]Sanabria (1993) has provided an excellent anthropological analysis of this process and the nexus that has developed between the Sierra and Chapare communities.

subdivision of family plots and land overuse reduced productivity. These factors encouraged many peasants to search for other land sources. Economic crises in the same regions also provided migration incentives.

The second group consists of former miners displaced by the economic crisis of the mid-1980s who are also Chapare landowners. The third group consists of former highland peasants and miners who do not own land in Chapare but who work either as farmhands or in the illegal drug industry.

Among all groups in Chapare, the large majority was former highland peasants. J. Painter (1994, 17), on the basis of a very large sample, estimated that in the early 1990s, 65 percent of Chapare's population came from Cochabamba Department, of which only about a quarter came from Chapare itself. Migrants from Potosí and Oruro, the main mining regions, accounted for about 16 percent. Mansilla (1994, 50, 65) found that in a sample of 100 Chapare peasants there were only 15 former miners, but only 5 of them attributed their own migration to mine closings. Seventy-seven explained that they had migrated because of a lack of land and declining land productivity in their region of origin.

It is not surprising, given the illegality of coca-related activities, that violence in Chapare is higher than in other rural areas of Bolivia but much lower than in Colombia. Coca traffickers introduced arms to Chapare; in contrast to Colombia, social organizations in Chapare neutralized this problem, thus preventing general increases in violence (Irusta 1992, 34–35). Anthropologists have explained in this respect that in Bolivian Indian culture a crucial value is placed on avoiding violence, using peaceful conflict resolution systems and enforcing respect for human life (Spedding 1997a).

Bolivia is the Andean country with the most extensive crop-substitution and alternative development experience. Since the mid-1970s, Bolivian governments and foreign donors have attempted to find alternatives to coca cultivation, particularly in Chapare. These attempts have brought significant foreign aid to the country, and Bolivians in general and peasants in particular have become accustomed to being compensated for eradicating coca (see chapter 11). Peasant *sindicatos* have played a key role in mediating between foreign donors and the government on one side and coca growers on the other.

Since the late 1990s, there have been reports of new coca plantings outside Yungas and Chapare, particularly in Beni Department. Unfortunately, no analytical work or information is available about these possible new coca fields.

In July 1988, "the Bolivian government, bowing to pressures emanating primarily from the United States, passed the Ley del Regimen de la Coca y Substancias Controladas, popularly known as Ley [Law] 1008" (Léons and Sanabria 1997, 22).[37] The new law decreed stiff penalties for drug-trafficking activities and regulated coca cultivation. It established three coca-planting categories. The first includes legal coca, grown in traditional Yungas of Cochabamba and Yungas of Vandiola areas. The second includes "surplus" coca grown in Chapare, to be eradicated gradually after compensating peasants. And the third includes illegal coca plantings in other regions, which are subject to rapid eradication without any compensation for peasants. The debate on this law was most acrimonious. Opponents of the law advanced extensive nationalistic arguments against imperialism and in defense of cultural values.

U.S. influence unquestionably played a central role in the law's formulation and eventual approval. Nevertheless, its final form shows a substantial accommodation reached by the various interests involved, as is attested by the three planting categories, the banning of aerial spraying and the use of defoliants and herbicides in coca eradication efforts (Malamud-Goti 1994, 81), and the requirements for international funding of alternative development and peasant compensation programs in Chapare.[38]

Law 1008 has remained a subject of debate in Bolivia. Some of its provisions have been attacked as unconstitutional and as eroding civil liberties. It has been alleged that its implementation has been biased against the poor, who are the great majority of those detained and jailed in its application (Farthing 1997, 254–55). The law's interpretation has also been questioned, particularly among peasants.

According to peasants, the formal definition of most coca plantings as illegal is only a quid pro quo for the international funding of alternative development programs. Furthermore, they interpret the law as requiring the government to develop Chapare, not just to implement alternative

---

[37] All students of Bolivian illegal drugs acknowledge the role of the United States in formulating and passing Law 1008. See, e.g., Gamarra (1994) and J. Painter (1994).

[38] Among significant political American sectors, peasant compensation has been very difficult to accept because it is held tantamount to paying someone not to commit a crime. Quiroga (1990, 68) also raised this point and commented ironically that if paying criminals not to commit a crime were a generalized anticrime policy, all the governments' budgets would have to be assigned only to that purpose and that amount still would not be sufficient.

development projects. From their point of view, "lack of compliance with the requirement for provision of viable alternatives invalidates the other requirements of the law" (Léons and Sanabria 1997, 27), including eradication, dismissing the relevance of coca as part of the illegal cocaine trade.[39]

The Industry's Organization

Bolivians tend to divide their illegal drug industry into two different branches. The first branch comprises the peasants and their hired laborers in Chapare, a group closely tied to traditional Indian values originating in the highlands and used to the seigniorial productive system that prevailed in Bolivia before the 1952 revolution (Rodas 1996, 40–47). They are referred to as Collas.

The second branch is made up mostly of mestizos and whites from Santa Cruz and other lowland prairie departments that have adopted Western attitudes. According to Rodas (1996, 36), the "bourgeois" authoritarian capitalist values of this second branch resulted from the failure of the 1952 revolution to produce a real democracy.[40] Hence, it is not surprising that they devote themselves to the more profitable aspects of the industry: making cocaine base and refining cocaine, marketing illegal coca derivatives, smuggling precursor chemicals, and exporting cocaine base and cocaine. They are called Cambas. The differences in culture, ethnicity, and social class between the two groups has fostered traditional confrontation and mistrust among Collas and Cambas.

Quiroga (1990, 29) described the industry toward the late 1980s as follows. Peasants grew "surplus" coca. Coca leaf purchasers ("rescuers") gathered larger amounts of coca and sold them to be processed into paste at a laboratory owned by an independent processor. "Coca stompers" (*pisacocas*) were employed at the lab to extract coca paste. Couriers then transported the paste to laboratories, where it was processed into cocaine base or cocaine. Most of these couriers were "ants" who carried small

---

[39]This author's interview with a coca growers' leader in April 1999 in La Paz who requested anonymity confirms this perception. The coca leader simply insisted that economic development had not taken place in the coca growing regions. Moreover, his conception of development was unclear except that it appeared to entail a much higher standard of living than the currently prevailing standard in coca growing communities.

[40]See also Malamud-Goti (1994, chap. 1).

amounts by foot or mule. Others were more sophisticated and used small riverboats (*lanchas*). Quiroga explained that people did not specialize in one of these tasks and that many exchanged roles frequently.

According to Quiroga, the "rescuer" had the riskiest task and was the key to the business's success. Besides having to be continuously on the move to avoid detection and to carry large amounts of cash, "on the one hand he has to dodge police operators in the highest risk areas. On the other, he frequently faces competitors from other 'lines' or trafficker groups" (1990, 29).

Other participating actors include airplane pilots and boaters, chemists, laboratory managers, packers, dryers, and guards. Coca base and cocaine laboratories or factories were located mainly in the Beni and Santa Cruz Departments and were apt to employ up to 100 people. "Conditions in a large factory are similar to those in a rigorously controlled camp" (Quiroga 1990, 30). In some cases, the factory manager may be a "family head," that is to say, the boss of the Bolivian organization, but most frequently he is someone very close to the boss.

Peasants, *pisacocas*, "ants," and other low-level industry members were Collas, while most rescuers and higher-level players were Cambas (Rodas 1996; Malamud-Goti 1994). This cultural and ethnic division concentrated drug profits in the hands of Cambas, preventing Collas' advancement possibilities in the industry. Because most captured illegal industry actors are low-level participants, the jail population accused of drug related crimes is heavily Collas (Malamud-Goti 1994).

Coca-growing peasants were increasingly involved in the production of cocaine paste, cocaine base, and even of cocaine. Malamud-Goti (1994, 45) asserted that as early as 1992 peasant cooperatives of Shinaota and Ivirgarzama, two important Chapare coca-growing towns, were producing coca paste. Hargreaves (1992, 28) reported that in 1984, paste-making do-it-yourself kits were for sale in Sinahota. Other studies confirm these reports.[41] Most researchers have attributed this phenomenon to the decline in coca prices generated by repressive government policies that lowered coca prices and drove peasants to produce at least coca paste in an effort to preserve their scant incomes.

Malamud-Goti (1994, 48) provided a different explanation based on the Colla–Camba clash. He argued that, an indirect effect of those repressive policies, Colla peasants were forced to produce coca paste by Camba

[41]See, e.g., J. Painter (1994) and Rodas (1996).

traffickers in an attempt to avoid the risks involved in transporting large quantities of coca leaves by truck or plane to Beni laboratories to manufacture coca paste or cocaine base. From an economic perspective, these analyses are surprising because the large volume of coca leaves and their potential deterioration during long trips provide strong incentives for them to be processed into paste very near their source. Furthermore, the incentives for peasants to produce paste are very high, independent of the level of coca prices. Their main obstacles had been a lack of knowledge and access to the appropriate chemical precursors, and these should have been overcome in a short time.

During the 1970s, the emergence of Bolivian trafficking organizations paralleled the expansion of illegal crops. These did not evolve into complex export syndicates, as was the case in Colombia. They coordinated coca paste purchases, cocaine base and cocaine refining, and sales in Bolivia of most of their cocaine base and cocaine to foreigners, mainly Colombians linked to the Medellín and Cali cartels.

There has been a general belief that these groups acted independently of each other. Rodas (1996, 217–18) asserted that trafficking organizations incorporate mainly members of a particular family, that they try not to interfere with organizations of other families (that are their friends), and that they shun violence. Levine (1991) was the exception.[42] He argued that in the mid-1980s drug traffickers in Bolivia organized themselves under the leadership of William "Pato" Pizarro in one very large group, La Corporación, which controlled most Bolivian exports. Levine also asserted that this syndicate had many large laboratories throughout Santa Cruz and Beni Departments that produced most of the cocaine consumed in the United States at the time, but that their members were not high risk takers, shunned violence, and sold their cocaine only in Bolivia.

---

[42]Levine was a star DEA agent for more than 25 years. His exploits were the subject of a couple of best-selling books written by professional writers. He was a main actor in the drug war in Bolivia in the late 1970s and through the 1980s. After he retired from DEA, he wrote a book in which he vented his frustrations over the U.S. bureaucracy's inept handling of the drug war and in which he described the actions of "La Corporación." His assertion about this group exporting mostly cocaine is based on testimony of a DEA pilot and David Wheeler, a well-known former drug trafficker who became an informer. In his book, Levine frequently raised doubts about Wheeler's veracity, which contributed to making it impossible to evaluate to what extent La Corporación actually functioned as a centralized organization focused on cocaine manufacturing and selling.

Hargreaves (1992, 58) and Rodas (1996, 219) argued that in about 1990 there were thirty-five Bolivian drug-trafficking organizations, based mainly in Beni and Santa Cruz Departments. These Camba organizations comprised mainly cattle ranchers and agricultural entrepreneurs. Rodas (1996, 58) traced the involvement of these ranchers and large farm owners in the illegal drug industry to the collapse of the international cotton market. He argued that after Hugo Banzer took power in 1971, the Inter-American Development Bank informed him confidentially of a forthcoming cotton price boom, whereupon Banzer's government obtained international credits and financed a large cotton expansion. In 1975, however, the international cotton price collapsed and many borrowers got caught in a bind. To resolve their financial crisis, they had to resort to the illegal industry.[43]

The largest Beni trafficker was Roberto Suárez (dubbed "the King"), who became the main Bolivian supplier to the Colombian cartels. "During the dictatorship of General Banzer, a friend of his, Suárez knew the authorities would not trouble him on his remote Beni ranches" (Hargreaves, 1992, 71). "Through Banzer, Suárez had made the acquaintance of another man of German descent [*sic*] called Klaus Barber, once the head of the Gestapo in Lyon, who had been living in Bolivia since 1951 under the name of Klaus Almann" (p. 72).

Suárez used this contact to organize a group of thugs who terrorized his critics (journalists, analysts, law enforcers) and competitors. It was also used for protection against Colombian traffickers. All analysts agreed that the illegal drug industry not only boomed during the Banzer dictatorship (1971–78) but also that he either protected it, or at least condoned it (See, e.g., Aguiló 1992, 52; Rodas 1996, 53; Hargreaves 1992, 58; Gamarra 1994, 20; Lee 1990). As is shown in chapter 8, Banzer's name has frequently been linked to people who have been active in the illegal industry.

---

[43]I cannot give any credibility to this story. For 12 years (1977–89), I was a section chief in the Economic and Social Development Department of the Inter-American Development Bank. For several years, I headed the International Economics Section, which had to follow international commodity prices. Nobody at the Inter-American Development Bank had the ability to make credible price forecasts. It is more likely that after the commodity price boom that was accompanied by the 1973 "oil crisis" many people expected commodity shortages and increasing commodity prices for the foreseeable future. None of these predictions materialized, although the multilateral lending agencies based their projects on them.

Bolivian governments have been known as the most unstable in Latin America since independence. Indeed, Luis García-Meza's July 1980 takeover was the "189th coup in Bolivia's 154 years of independence" (Hargreaves 1992, 102). Throughout the country's history, the military has unarguably played a key political role. Of the 20 presidents and dictators that Bolivia had from the 1952 revolution until the establishment of a new electoral regime in 1982, 16 were military and 6 civilian (Lavaud 1998, 15). From November 1964 to October 1982, constitutional governments were in power for 476 days and de facto military regimes for 3,488. Within this context, the 7-year Banzer dictatorship (August 21, 1971–July 21, 1978) was a remarkable exception.

Several factors—the authoritarian tradition emanating from a seigniorial society, the grip that the military had on power, and the small size of the country—made it unfeasible for the illicit drug industry to operate in the country without strong links to the military. Compounding this problem, the land reform program allowed the government to distribute unsettled lands, and during the 1960s and 1970s many military officers received such grants in Beni and Santa Cruz Departments. Some of them became prominent traffickers whose labs and airstrips were located on those distant ranches and farms.

Links between military personnel and the illegal drug industry were tolerated by the governments of the 1970s and by the U.S. bureaucracies whose main goal at the time was to prevent a possible expansion of communism in Latin America (Gamarra 1999). By the late 1970s, a number of Bolivian military personnel were profiting from the illegal business. Roberto Suárez's organization developed strong links to a group of military personnel, particularly General García-Meza. The military and politicians involved in illegal drugs were aware that several groups, particularly those related to organized labor, were willing to denounce their involvement. On July 18, 1980, García-Meza orchestrated a military coup "to prevent the rise to power of the left-leaning coalition of the Popular Democratic Unity (UDP) that won the June 1980 election" (Gamarra 1994, 25).

García-Meza's regime used the group of thugs previously employed by Suárez to concentrate under his authority and that of his inner group, including Suárez, the illegal industry's sales to foreign buyers. This period was characterized by particularly tense United States–Bolivia relations, which led Washington to put an end to U.S. aid (Gamarra 1994). Fortunately, the narco-government led by García-Meza was short-lived. "General García-Meza was overthrown in August 1981 by a Military Junta made up of three officers that were primarily interested in preserving some semblance of institutional honor" (Gamarra 1994, 26). The García-Meza episode can be referred to as the only case of a true narco-government in the Andean countries.

Members of García-Meza's government who were implicated in drug trafficking managed to flee, but two of the main characters, interior and culture minister Luis Arce-Gómez (a cousin of Suárez), and his partner Erlan Echavarría, were captured several years later, in 1989, and extradited to the United States. Suárez, the main trafficker and supporter of García-Meza, was caught on July 21, 1988, on one of his Beni ranches. He was sentenced to serve 15 years in prison.

This sketch of the Bolivian illegal industry indicates that foreigners, mainly Colombians, have marketed most Bolivian production internationally. Smaller independent cocaine-exporting operations run by Bolivians have indeed existed. The best-known case is that of Roberto Suárez' nephew, Jorge Roca-Suárez (a.k.a. "Techo de Paja" or "Thatched Roof" on account of his blond hair). According to Hargreaves (1992, 78–79), in 1984 the Colombian traffickers lowered the price of coca paste from $14,000 to $8,000. Suárez appears to have perceived the drop in price as a simple attempt of the Colombians to manipulate the market, hence refusing to sell. In reality, it was the murder of justice minister Rodrigo Lara-Bonilla on April 30, 1984, ordered by Escobar, which unleashed a very harsh Colombian government response, in turn lowering coca prices throughout the Andes.

Roca-Suárez had lived a substantial part of his life in the United States; he perceived an opportunity for him to by-pass his uncle's organization and to develop a network to produce cocaine and to export it to the United States. Techo de Paja succeeded for several years and developed what could be considered a medium-size cocaine-smuggling network in the United States. "By the time of his arrest in December 1990 in Los Angeles ... Techo de Paja had built-up an impressive array of properties in Bolivia and the United States. He was arrested in a luxury nineteen-bedroom mansion in San Marino (valued at $11 million), and later discovered to have properties worth $9 million in the United States and $30 million in the Santa Cruz and Beni departments" (J. Painter 1994, 59).

The Industry during the 1990s

The Bolivian illegal drug industry experienced important changes during the 1990s, some of which began in the late 1980s. The stagnation of cocaine demand in the United States encouraged Bolivians and other traffickers to export to Europe (Irusta 1992, 34–35; Malamud-Goti 1994, 33). The decline of the Medellín cartel, which had provided their main export networks to the United States, also contributed to this development.

In Bolivia itself, many of the export organizations from Beni and Santa Cruz Departments were disrupted. Bedregal and Viscarra (1989, 162–70) asserted that the capture of Suárez led to a dismantling of trafficking organizations, which implies that the illegal industry was centralized and controlled by one main trafficker. Perhaps more important, in 1991, the Jaime Paz-Zamora administration, following César Gaviria's example in Colombia, offered not to extradite and to administer relatively short sentences to traffickers who turned themselves in and confessed to one crime. This offer produced seven "repented ones," ranchers and pilots from Santa Ana de Yacuma in Beni.[44]

This episode was both peculiar and illuminating. Most repented traffickers argued that they surrendered to cleanse their family name, to avoid stigmatizing their children and relatives, and to vindicate themselves. Irusta (1992, 83) argued that "behind their surrender was an attitude akin to valor, dignity and honor," and believes that although some of the repented ones met together before their surrender, they did not coordinate their confessions but did so to contemplate their common vindication. Repented traffickers received sentences averaging 5 years.

The vertical integration of production detected in Colombia also occurred in Bolivia. As was noted above, peasants had been producing coca paste since at least the mid-1980s. Mansilla (1994) found that peasants in all coca-producing regions had learned to process coca leaves. Most produced coca paste, a good number cocaine base, and some produced cocaine. As was noted, some have argued to explain this evolution that peasants have been "forced" to enter the manufacturing process because of their need to maintain a minimum standard of living in the face of government repression on cocaine trafficking that resulted in falling coca prices.

These changes in the peasants' role in the illegal business are important because they strain the credibility of the traditional argument that peasants do not participate in criminal activities and are only poor people who cultivate a traditional crop with strong cultural roots. In this case, the

---

[44]Irusta (1992) commented on this process and summarized the confessions and life histories of the "repented ones."

popular argument—"If coca prices were fair, no peasant would be 'forced' to produce paste or get involved in other illegal activities"—is simply an attempt to "export" the responsibility for criminal actions. To sustain this argument it would be necessary to explain how coca prices could be "fair" without the illicit demand for leaves to be used in the production of cocaine.

It is probable, indeed, that the fall in coca price triggered the peasants' involvement in coca paste production. It is also very likely that they would have undertaken those tasks sooner or later because coca paste and cocaine base production are very simple processes whose profits are very high compared with coca growing.

There is no question that the best-known traffickers of the 1980s were apprehended. However, this did not lead to the disappearance of the Bolivian illegal industry. Indeed, until 1997 total coca hectareage had not declined, and coca by-products had to have been made somewhere. Trafficking organizations have also evolved in Bolivia, although available information is weak and sketchy.[45] The production of cocaine base and cocaine has increased, and a few export networks to the main markets have been developed. It is likely that these organizations are multinational and include traffickers of Bolivian, Colombian, Brazilian, and other nationalities (Clawson and Lee 1996).[46]

Some of these networks have established direct links to Mexican traffickers, bypassing Colombian intermediaries, and have searched for markets outside the United States. The publicized 1994 seizure of a large plane loaded with 8 to 10 tons of cocaine at Lima airport, where it stopped for refueling on the way to Mexico, provides clear evidence of the development of Bolivian cocaine exporting capabilities and organizations. One of the big mysteries behind these developments is just what happened to the 35 drug exporting organizations reported about in 1990.

The decline in coca prices from their 1980s heights, coupled with a much more efficiently managed economy, has made the illegal drug industry substantially smaller relative to Bolivia's gross national product in the 1990s than in the 1980s (see chapter 5). One indirect result of this

---

[45]The Bolivian literature on this issue is virtually nonexistent, and in the United Nations Development Program–funded research project I coordinated in 1994 and 1995, it was not possible to find a Bolivian researcher willing to study this issue.

[46]Mendoza (1993) asserted that new Bolivian organizations have developed export networks through the Amazon jungle into Brazil using rivers and jungle trails, avoiding the traditional use of airplanes in Bolivia.

change is a loss in the relative economic importance of drug traffickers, who now may be less conspicuous and harder to detect. Chances are that current Bolivian traffickers have learned the value of following a low profile and limiting ostentatious consumption and signs of wealth and that they are successfully camouflaged.

Laserna, Vargas, and Torrico's (1999) very detailed study of the illicit industry in Cochabamba in 1995 found that the industry had successfully adapted to government policy and international market changes. They reached eight main conclusions:

1. Cochabamba's illegal industry was made up of small, family-based productive units in which trust plays a key role.
2. These productive units were independent of each other, which endowed the coca and cocaine industry with flexibility and the corresponding capacity to adapt in response to changes in the environment in which it operated.
3. The simplicity of cocaine production technologies had given peasants access to the chemistry needed for the production of coca paste and cocaine base. A very high number of peasants was involved in these activities.
4. Coca paste "factories" were very primitive, and their operations were organized to minimize the risk of detection and seizure.
5. The illegal industry employed mainly young men in numbers that accounted for approximately 12 to 16 percent of Chapare's workforce.
6. The number of participants in the illegal industry decreased substantially as elaboration advanced from coca paste to base and cocaine. The same occurred in marketing.
7. Most chemical inputs were smuggled from abroad.
8. Repressive polices had favored small-scale production in "factories" that were difficult to locate. The criminalization of coca growing implicitly turned every peasant into a criminal, which debased social stigmas and moral qualms attached to illegal activities. These two factors contributed to involving peasants in illegal coca processing. It is not surprising that as peasants' involvement in the industry expanded, the average size of laboratory seizures declined over time.

According to Laserna, Vargas, and Torrico, the characteristics of Chapare's illicit industry are responsible for the many battles won by law enforcement even while they lost the war: They captured many small laboratories and traffickers but could not control the overall illegal activity.

The second Banzer administration inaugurated in August 1997 developed Plan Dignidad—"For the Country's Dignity!"—to rid the country of the "scourge" of drugs (República de Bolivia 1998).[47] This plan emphasized eradication, some actions against money laundering, and drug consumption treatment and prevention. Curiously, attacking trafficking organizations was not one of its main concerns. The plan's implementation was very aggressive and concentrated on a very active eradication campaign with strong support from the U.S. government. According to U.S. embassy sources,[48] the emphasis brought to bear on the eradication campaign was justified because Bolivia did not have significant trafficking organizations and illegal exports were handled by only small mom-and-pop operations.

In any case, all the other evidence suggests that Bolivia is very vulnerable to the influence of international trafficking organizations and that it is very likely that the participation of Bolivian entrepreneurs in the illegal business has increased. First, coca prices rose substantially in Peru from 1998 on, suggesting that Bolivian traffickers were substituting Peruvian coca for eradicated Bolivian production. Second, in mid-1999, Marino Diodato, an Italian married to a niece of General Banzer and an officer of the Bolivian armed forces,[49] was indicted on drug-trafficking charges. The indictment alleges that Diodato was part of a trafficking network with links to the Italian Mafia and Camorra.

The success of Plan Dignidad has been remarkable. By late 2001, there were only about 6,000 "surplus" coca hectares in Chapare and a few more new plantings in Yungas. However, forced eradication has produced a large decline in the real living standard of Chapare peasants and led to much social unrest and many protests in that region. Some of these have been violent and led to the deaths of several peasants and police personnel. And though Plan Dignidad has been remarkably successful within Chapare, international cocaine prices have not increased, suggesting that source displacement to Colombia and Peru has taken place. The success of the plan requires a sustained repressive force in Chapare. Important current issues (as of early 2002) are whether the eradication is sustainable

---

[47]Plan Dignidad was the brainchild of former vice president and president Jorge Quiroga, a member of a small party that joined the coalition formed by Banzer.

[48]This is based on the author's interview with U.S. ambassador Donna Hrinak in La Paz in April 1999.

[49]His appointment to the Bolivian armed forces has been questioned as unconstitutional.

in the long run, whether peasants' organizations will succeed in pressuring the incoming government to change policies, and whether alternative development programs will receive sufficient international funding.

The Industry in Peru

As in Bolivia, coca has a long tradition in Peru, a country that for a long time has been the world's main producer. Yet despite Peru's predominance in the world coca market, coca and cocaine receive much less attention in the Lima media, and the illegal cocaine industry has been much less studied there than in Bolivia and Colombia. Most studies of the illegal drug industry in Peru have been commissioned by official national or foreign organizations; their circulation is quite limited, and they have focused on estimate of the industry's size and its macroeconomic effects.[50]

These reports are informative but they skirt many important issues. There is a lack of debate and a scarcity of studies of the industry's structure and its nexus with the rest of society. It is almost as if Lima did not want to find out what happens in that distant, wild "deepest Peru" beyond the Sierra. For these reasons, it is more difficult to draw a good picture of the Peruvian industry than that of the other two coca-producing countries.

Traditional Coca, Settlements, and the Illegal Industry in the 1970s and 1980s

Before the cocaine boom, coca was produced in Peru for coca chewing, coca tea, and legal exports to soft drink companies.[51] Traditional coca chewing was tolerated but looked down upon by "white" society, and the government did not have any qualms about signing and ratifying the 1961 Vienna convention committing it to eliminate all coca cultivation and use in 25 years (Cotler and Zárate 1993). When coca plantings grew during the 1970s in response to increased international demand, the government took measures to control the market.

---

[50]See, e.g.: Alvarez (1993), CUÁNTO S.A. (1993), Astete and Tejada (1988), MACROCONSULT S.A. (1990), Figueroa and Matuk (1989), and Cotler and Zárate (1993). As far as I am aware, none of these works has been published as a book or in a journal.

[51]It is well known that the original Coca-Cola formula contained cocaine. Early in the twentieth century, cocaine was eliminated from it, but coca continued being used. Coca-Cola is the largest legal coca importer.

In 1978, the military government of General Francisco Morales-Bermúdez issued Legal Decree 22,095, aimed at repressing "traffic of dependency producing drugs, prevent their inappropriate use, to psychosocially rehabilitate addicts, and reduce coca cultivation" (Cotler 1996, 61). To achieve these goals, it established the Multisectoral Drug Control Committee, made up of the ministers of interior, presidency, foreign relations, agriculture, health, education, industry, and justice, and the attorney general.

The military government took these measures partly believing that traditional coca consumption caused degeneration of the Indian race (Cotler 1996).[52] A few months later, the government established the National Coca Enterprise (ENACO), which substituted the Coca Estanco (government monopsony to buy coca from peasants and monopoly for wholesale transactions). ENACO's functions included the "establishment of a register of all legal coca producers, to act as the monopolist in coca leaf commercialization and industrialization and to control the traffic in industrial inputs required in the production of illicit drugs" (Cotler 1996, 62). From that moment on, the unregistered producers were clearly illegal. Registered farmers cultivate approximately 18,000 hectares of coca (MACROCONSULT S.A. 1990). As is shown below, these have accounted for a small percentage of total coca hectareage.

Illegal coca has grown primarily in "Selva's Eyebrow" (Ceja de Selva), the recently settled mountainous jungle on the east side of the Andes that remained almost totally unpopulated for centuries. Settling and colonizing this region was an old goal of Peruvian governments and the elite:

Since the nineteenth century, the Peruvian elite had conceived the jungle as a inexhaustible source of richness. The rubber boom that stimulated several failed colonization projects reinforced this idea. Later on, peasants' pressures for land, the migrations to the cities during the 1950s, and the geopolitical worries of the military added up,

---

[52]In the literature on Andean coca of the 1940s and 1950s, there were frequent references to the "degeneration of the Indians" but remarkably, no evidence was presented. It is true that Indians tend to be short and undernourished, and that many are illiterate and are likely to have low intelligence quotient levels measured by standards of industrial countries. But it is not clear that these conditions could not be changed with a couple of well cared for generations. In other words, if there was a "degenerative" process, its more likely causes are poverty, segregation, and discrimination rather than coca chewing.

so that the governments implemented colonization projects sponsored by international organizations. All were convinced that the Amazon region was to become not only Peru's, but also the world's food basket. The certainty that the Amazon sub-soil contained large mineral resources also contributed to this decision. (Cotler 1996, 35)[53]

Fernando Belaúnde-Terry expressed this vision of the jungle's role in Peruvian society and economy with particular vehemence during his two governments in the 1960s and 1980s and made the development of that region a very high government priority. Indeed, the "Marginal Jungle Highway" was always his pet project.[54] In his first campaign, he ran on the slogan "Let's conquer Peru for the Peruvians."

Government policy during the first Belaúnde administration contributed to the jungle's colonization, integrating that region with Peru's coastal markets, particularly Lima's. In 1966, the Inter-American Development Bank financed a settlement project in the Upper Huallaga Valley (Tarazona-Sevillano and Reuter 1990, 101). Policies changed substantially after the 1968 coup by General Juan Velasco that implemented a land reform in the Coast and High Sierra, promoted cooperatives in the Huallaga, and increased the pro-urban bias of its overall policies.

According to Cotler (1996), the persistence of these policies led to a gradual decline in rural incomes and an increase in rural poverty that made illegal coca-related activities increasingly attractive. In this process, coca substituted for legal traditional crops in places like the Upper Huallaga Valley. Tarazona-Sevillano and Reuter (1990, 104–7) added other elements to this explanation. Velasco's forced cooperative organization in the valley resulted in lower outputs because that form of organization was alien to peasants. They also argued that the low fertility of the jungle soil resulted in quickly declining crop yields. Contrary to other crops, coca is perhaps the most environmentally friendly crop for this type of soil and grows for a long time.

[53]See also Tarazona-Sevillano and Reuter (1990,100–4).

[54]I was fortunate to share membership with Belaúnde in the Latin American Studies Council of George Washington University in 1975–77, where we were faculty members before his second presidential period of the early 1980s. In my conversations with Belaúnde, he always dismissed the arguments about the low quality of the jungle soils and the danger of environmental destruction associated with the jungle's settlement. His passion and single mind focus on the "Marginal Jungle Highway" as the most important nation-building project in Peru were remarkable, even though puzzling to my economist mind.

Gonzales-Manrique (1990, 208) traced coca cultivation in the Upper Huallaga back to the 1940s, when a Huanuco pharmacist bought the coca crop and produced cocaine that he sold openly. This activity disappeared a decade later when cocaine was declared illegal. His work documents that Peruvians had the know-how and ability to produce cocaine before the 1970s coca boom, which is not surprising in light of the simplicity of the manufacturing processes involved.

Available studies indicate that during the 1970s and 1980s Peru produced mainly coca paste that was exported mostly, but not exclusively, by Colombians. CUÁNTO S.A. (1993, 21) estimated total coca paste, cocaine base, and cocaine production in Peru from 1980 to 1992. This study argued that through time Peruvians increased their production of cocaine relative to the other two products and that by 1992 they were producing 165 tons of cocaine. MACROCONSULT S.A. (1990) presented a similar argument and went one step further, claiming that by 1989 Peru was not exporting any coca paste, but only cocaine base and cocaine.

These studies assert that because of widespread impoverishment, some rural areas of Peru were ready to respond when demand for cocaine grew and potential buyers appeared searching for coca paste supply. Since the beginning of the coca boom in the 1970s, two parallel illegal industrial branches have developed. One Peruvian-controlled branch, which can be characterized as artisan, produces and exports in small quantities. The other, commercial branch, dominated by Colombians, makes large-scale exports.

The commercial networks can be schematically described as including the coca growing peasants or *cocaleros*; the *traqueteros*, or coca collectors; the storers, who process coca and store coca paste or cocaine base; and the *boss chargé*, who organizes shipments and works directly under the boss (who generally is a Colombian residing outside Peru). The network also includes those who supply chemical inputs, chemists and lab assistants, guards, bodyguards and other security personnel, pilots that transport the product out of the country, and others.

Morales (1989) asserted that in Peru there is an ethnic division of labor similar to the one discussed above in the Bolivian context. Indian peasants cultivate coca and process it into paste, and mestizos do the more profitable downstream processes: base and cocaine manufacturing, marketing, and exporting. This reproduces the traditional economic divide among those who have kept Indian traditions and values on one hand, and foreigners and those who have adopted foreign values on the other.

Each of these networks is called a "firm" in Peruvian jargon. They are commonly associated with a *boss chargé*, almost always a Peruvian or Colombian who runs the business in Peru. Available studies indicate that the industry is made up of forty to fifty "firms" (Alvarez and Associates 1996).[55]

Morales's (1989, 78, 82) subsequent work reported that natives of the traditional coca-growing regions, many of them authorized to produce legal coca, have learned to process coca leaves even to the point of producing cocaine, which then was marketed in Lima. Coca paste produced in small quantities in other regions was also sent to Lima, where it was processed into cocaine. This trade was independent of the large firms linked with the Colombian bosses and, most likely, produced the cocaine smuggled in small quantities by "mules," frequently caught at Lima airport.

As was noted above, illegal drug crops were recognized as a problem by the Morales-Bermúdez government in the late 1970s. After the election system was reinstalled and Belaúnde was elected for a second time, the Peruvian government under U.S. pressure from and with U.S. support started the Special Coca Control and Eradication Project in the Upper Huallaga (CORAH). This was complemented a year later by a crop-substitution Special Upper Huallaga Project (PEAH).

CORAH employed 480 peasants to eradicate coca manually. This is a very labor-intensive and slow process. According to Obando (1993, 82), 30 workers eradicated 1 hectare per day, resulting in 8,666 hectares eradicated in the 1983–85 period, during which total coca hectareage increased several-fold. The small eradication advances obtained manually led to proposals to aerially spray coca plantings using Tebuthiuron, also known as "Spike," which generated great public reaction because of environmental damage fears. The debate over this issue was diffused when Ely Lilly, the producers of Tebuthiuron, announced their refusal to supply it to coca eradication programs in Latin America (Obando 1993, 82). According to Obando, after 10 years of CORAH activity, a total of only 18,000 hectares had been eradicated.

PEAH began searching for suitable alternative crops for the Upper Huallaga. As usual, this was a slow process. Furthermore, not enough

---

[55]Cabieses (1998) has contended that the organization of these groups is so weak that they should not be called "firms" but just "bands," and that Peru should consider itself fortunate not to have firms or cartels but simple bands.

attention was given to marketing, and peasants who had agreed to eradication and those forced to do it found that their expectations of government help were frustrated. It was not surprising that the peasants considered the police and government officials involved in eradication to be their enemies. This provided an opportunity for the Shining Path guerrilla organization, which entered the Upper Huallaga Valley in 1984 (Obando 1993, 84). Labrousse (1995, 110) explains that the arrival of Shining Path was facilitated by the existence in the region of Puka Llacta ("Red City"), another Maoist group.

Moreover, peasant organizations were rather weak, in contrast to the Bolivian *sindicatos* (Lee 1990). At the end of 1984, after the military offensive in the Ayacucho and Huancavelica Departments, Shining Path moved into the Huallaga with the support of Puka Llacta and systematically attacked government officials working in eradication and crop-substitution programs and the leaders of the weak peasant organizations (Dreyfus 1999). Shining Path then mediated between peasants and traffickers, setting minimum prices and becoming "the only intermediary between the traffickers and the peasants. They became the only source of protection for both groups against the police" Dreyfus (1999, 382). They also required peasants to diversify their production, insisting that they devote a proportion of their land to food crops.

The army was called to action in the Huallaga Valley to confront the guerrillas. They realized that it was necessary to avoid confronting the peasantry and opted not to fight drug trafficking and to focus strictly on the guerrillas (Obando 1993; Labrousse 1995). Furthermore, the army simply refused to provide protection to CORAH's eradication teams, some of which were massacred by Shining Path and drug traffickers. "This move quickly turned the support of the peasants (and, paradoxically, of the traffickers) in favor of the army" (Dreyfus 1999, 383). This provided the key to the army's success against Shining Path, which was expelled from the valley.

The following Alan García administration had the view that "the guerrilla movement stemmed from socioeconomic problems, therefore programs of social assistance and economic development in poor rural areas should take precedence over repression. Moreover, he sought to reduce the high degree of autonomy that the armed forces had in managing the repression of Shining Path in areas that were declared under a state of emergency" (Dreyfus 1999, 283), and the army was moved out of the Upper Huallaga Valley. Furthermore, García's policies were more aggressive against the illegal crops and traffickers, a fact that weakened the peasants' support for the government.

The overall economic deterioration of Peru offered new opportunities for Shining Path and the Tupac Amaru Revolutionary Movement (MRTA) to establish themselves in the Huallaga. This led to a confrontation between these two groups, which Shining Path won (McClintock 1988; Obando 1993, 84). By then, García's policies had the police change tactics and had them focus on capturing *traqueteros*, storers, and traffickers and leave peasants alone. This worked in the short run and produced a substantial decline in coca leaf prices (McClintock 1988). In the medium run, peasants realized that the police were still responsible for their income decline, that the government did not provide any reasonable alternative, and that once again they were opposed by the police and the government (Obando 1993, 85).

Shining Path took the opportunity to establish strict control of the Huallaga. It "reorganized all narcotrafficking relations: it fixed coca leaf prices, got rid of all intermediaries, determined how leaves were to be weighed,[56] fixed the dollar exchange rate and established a system of delegations" (Obando 1993, 85). A delegation was a group of guerrillas charged with negotiating with traffickers.[57] "To be able to buy, traffickers had to register themselves with the delegation. The registration cost $15,000 of which 50 percent went to the central Shining Path accounts, 40 percent was used to purchase communication equipment and 10 percent was left with the delegation" (p. 85). Shining Path also benefited from drugs in other ways. It killed the traffickers' security guards and replaced them with Shining Path members and established a tax of 15,000 pesos on each trafficking airplane that landed to pick up coca paste (p. 86).

Shining Path's control of the Huallaga rang Washington's alarm bells. Several U.S. government reports pointed out the Peruvian military's incompetence and accused the army of corruption and human rights abuses. In some cases, the threat of decertification was clear.[58] García

---

[56]Peasants had always complained that traffickers used altered weights.

[57]Dreyfus (1999, 383) dated the first delegations to 1984 during the first Shining Path penetration of the valley. He also asserted that they were made up of peasants led by a guerrilla.

[58]Many in Washington's intelligence community were concerned. The Center for Strategic and International Studies published Tarazona-Sevillano and Reuter's (1990) book warning the establishment of an imminent narcoterrorist threat by the Shining Path.

reacted, decreeing an emergency zone, which again gave control to the army. It appears that Shining Path overplayed its hand and "captured the Uchiza police post in the center of the Upper Huallaga after a bloody night-long battle. The interior minister resigned in disgrace and a new commander was appointed for the Huallaga emergency zone" (Clawson and Lee 1996, 218).[59]

These events turned the government policy focus from fighting drugs to fighting guerrillas. The new commander, brigadier general Alberto Arciniegas-Huby, realized that he could not destroy the peasants' livelihood and win the war against Shining Path. He threatened to destroy Uchiza if the citizenry did not support government institutions, restricted eradication activities, and "carried out aggressive military actions against Shining Path without particular regard for human rights" (Dreyfus 1999, 385). Arciniegas mediated between peasants and police and managed to restore peasants' support for the government, which used the army backed by the air force to defeat the guerrillas.

The Industry in the 1990s

The relations between the United States and the García administration had been rough. Besides, at the end of it, the Peruvian economy was in shambles (see chapter 8), which limited the government's ability to implement a strong antidrug campaign. The 1990 arrival of Alberto Fujimori in the presidency improved bilateral relations, but its first priority was to eliminate Shining Path, not illicit drugs. Still, after the economic collapse during García's presidency, the United States was eager to cooperate with the new Peruvian government. Fujimori's policy was based on the recommendations of his close adviser Hernando de Soto, who a few years earlier had written an international bestseller about the informal economy in Peru (De Soto 1996).

De Soto defined the coca problem as one of poverty and not of criminal behavior and emphasized alternative development programs that would provide secure titles to the peasants' lands and markets for their products. This "Fujimori Doctrine" defined coca growers as individuals outside the criminal drug organizations and who required large infrastruc-

---

[59]These researchers believed that Shining Path's action was triggered by a field test in preparation of CORAH's eradication with Tebuthiuron (Spike).

ture development in transportation, storage, and other facilities and aid from the international community, including private-sector companies that would guarantee the purchase price for alternative development products (Obando 1993, 90). Fujimori's policy was to postpone attacking drug trafficking directly until the guerrillas were eradicated.

It should be noted that most migrants to Selva's Eyebrow came from the Sierra, and as in Bolivia, they belonged to structured communities. Even though their community organizations did not reproduce themselves in settled areas (see chapter 9), the colonization of the Huallaga Valley was relatively peaceful. The level of violence in the coca-growing region is higher than in other parts of the country, but it does not compare at all with that in Colombian coca-growing areas.

Huallaga coca growers organized themselves first against eradication and later against Shining Path. The guerrilla group at first protected the peasants against traffickers and government polices, but its strong Maoist ideology made it indoctrinate peasants and force them to undertake many actions that the communities rejected. "Shining Path appeared as a dogmatic force that tried to keep the peasants under control" (Obando 1993, 92). The lack of army actions against drug trafficking also contributed to the peasants' disenchantment with the guerrillas, as did the elimination of the eradication program when Fujimori came to power.[60] Besides, in 1991 "Fujimori eliminated coca cultivation from the penal code" (Jones 1999, 45). This move left coca plantings in a legal limbo, but it was equivalent to a de facto decriminalization of coca growers, who no longer needed the protection of Shining Path.

The peasants developed 175 committees organized in the Defense Front Against Coca Eradication in the Upper Huallaga (FEDECAH) and a smaller Agrarian Federation of the Selva Maestra (FASMA) that had the support of the National Agrarian Confederation (CAN). Many of these groups were armed and organized peasant self-defense groups (rondas campesinas) to fight Shining Path (Jones 1999, 45). This was a broadly based development that transcended the Huallaga Valley. Indeed, the most important rondas developed in areas where Shining Path had a strong presence and had several times massacred peasants, particularly in Ayacucho Department. The government took advantage of these conditions and en-

---

[60]Labrousse (1996) argued that the MRTA had greater appeal to the peasantry because it promoted traditional populism compared to the more ascetic Shining Path.

couraged the creation of the rondas that played an important role in weakening Shining Path.[61]

The regained military control over the Huallaga had an undesirable by-product: It put the army and some politicians with decision-making power at risk of corruption by traffickers (see chapter 8).[62] This risk became particularly great after April 1992, when Fujimori closed down Congress, weakened or eliminated democratic controls on the executive power, and started a process to build a "new Peru" independent of the old, ineffective, and corrupt political parties. This was an authoritarian coup d'état against the president's own government (*auto-golpe*), which succeeded because of the support of the armed forces. This act aimed to eliminate the political opposition, distanced Fujimori from the political establishment, and led to a de facto civil dictatorship dependent on the armed forces.

As it has happened across the Andes, during the 1990s the structure of the Peruvian illegal industry experienced substantial changes. The most obvious one was a coca crisis caused by a price collapse. Cabieses (1998, 202) reports that according to his best price data source, in 1992 in the Upper Huallaga Valley a kilogram of coca leaves sold for $2.50, one of coca paste for $295, one of cocaine base for $708, and one of cocaine for $1,172 at the laboratories' door. In June 1997, these prices respectively were $0.70, $121, $265, and $829. Roncken and Associates (1999) report that "between January and September of 1995, coca prices in the Huallaga fell from $3.00 to $0.40 per kilo, and [cocaine base] prices from $850 to $100 per kilo."

This deepest and longest coca industry crisis in Peru since the 1970s boom was caused by a combination of supply and demand factors. The supply was hurt by the infestation by a fungus (*Fusarium oxysporum*), which peasants call "El gringo" or "Clinton." The coca price decline can be traced to four elements. First, the Peruvian and U.S. governments' active anti-illegal flight policy led to the shooting down of a few trafficking airplanes and substantially increased transportation costs to Colombia. Second, a decline in the Colombian cartels' demand was caused by the

---

[61]See, e.g., Degregori (1996a, 1996b), Coronel (1996), Del Pino (1996), and Starn (1996). Gorriti (1990) is the classic Shining Path history.

[62]Academic research on these events is almost impossible to carry out in Peru. Very brave journalists have collected most of the available evidence, particularly Gustavo Gorriti, who has been in exile in Panama. Peruvian academics have shied away from this issue. A foreigner, Labrousse (1995), provided a summary of the military–drug nexus.

dismembering of the Cali cartel by the Colombian government that eliminated many export networks. Third, a preference for the domestic supply of the smaller *cartelitos* replaced that of the large Cali and Medellín cartels.[63] Fourth, the Colombian guerrillas and paramilitary groups encouraged Colombian peasants to grow coca as a means of developing a financial and political base.

The coca industry has also changed geographically in response to the fungus. "Farmers moved into areas where land was readily available, primarily to the east. Some went directly east into the Aguaytia Valley; others went northeast into the Central Huallaga; still others went southeast into the Apurimac Valley. Those regions generally lack economical access to the legal market, making coca the most attractive crop" (Clawson and Lee 1996, 136).

Eight other changes were identified by the 1995 fieldwork of Alvarez and Associates (1996).

- First, all peasants learned to produce coca paste. Indeed, in many locations it was difficult to determine the coca price because there was no coca market. As in Bolivia, most analysts attribute this change to the peasants' need to maintain a minimum income level.[64]

- Second, *traqueteros* and storers, who used to buy and process coca leaves, now bought mainly coca paste or cocaine base from peasants. *Traqueteros* acted in the name of wholesalers, whose organization or "family" processed the leaves and readied the final product to be sold to exporters who arranged for international shipment. These were linked directly to international criminal organizations, mainly Colombian cartels.

- Third, "firms" exported almost exclusively high-quality cocaine base, which in Peruvian jargon is called "queen base" because it converts one-to-one by weight into cocaine.

- Fourth, "firms" developed their own facilities to reprocess low-quality cocaine base to make it exportable.

---

[63]As was noted above, they have few members and try to keep a low profile. They did not have the capacity or the desire to buy abroad.

[64]This has shrunk the coca leaf market, which casts some doubts on the accuracy of coca price estimates that are based on fewer and fewer observations.

• Fifth, transportation costs increased substantially because it became necessary to transport coca paste, cocaine base, and cocaine by surface transport to distant landing strips, many of which are near the Colombian and Brazilian borders. This time-consuming process uses several slow and expensive transportation means: mules, humans, and small riverboats. Besides, the constant tracking by law enforcement forces required frequent changes in storage facilities (*caletas*) and landing strips (*medias*).

• Sixth, even though Peruvian participation in the export market gained ground, it was not possible to establish the magnitude of this change. It is safe to say that it has been slow and that the Peruvian industry was not able to satisfactorily substitute for the Colombian "bosses." Only two Peruvian "families" were found that could export their products on their own. The remaining ones encountered substantial difficulties to market their products. The persistence of low coca prices reported until 2000 indicates that most Peruvian "firms" were able to develop satisfactory export alternatives.

• Seventh, many producers decided to save the coca paste, hoping for price increases. When buried, coca paste lasts up to a year without losing its value.

• Eighth, in spite of the crisis, the number of "firms" appears to have remained constant, at about forty.

Cabieses (1998) and Ronken and Associates (1999) reported large coca production declines in the late 1990s in response to the price fall. Even though there was a lack of rigorous research,[65] the coca production reduction could not be attributed to a successful manual eradication program. U.S. government officials reported, off the record, that about a third of the decline was attributable to eradication and two-thirds to the abandonment of many fields in response to very low prices. In these fields, coca was not cut down, in the hope of a future price increase.

It appears that Peruvians have not been successful in developing extensive international drug distribution networks. However, increased

---

[65]The authoritarian tendencies of the Fujimori administration and the apparent involvement of Vladimiro Montesinos, his closest ally, in drug trafficking made it very dangerous to do research in Peru during the late 1990s. The available data were provided by reports of a mainly journalistic nature and U.S. official sources.

cocaine seizures in Peru indicate increases in cocaine processing capacity and point in the direction of efforts to develop new export channels. The Observatoire Geopolitique des Drogues (1999, 4–5) indicates that from late 1997 on, coca prices in Peru recuperated substantially. Indeed, they state that the price of 1 arroba (12.5 kilograms) of dried coca had fallen from an earlier average of $50 to $5 by 1996 but that in late 1998 they had reached $37 in the Upper Huallaga Valley.

If these estimates prove correct, they furnish the evidence that Peruvians have succeeded in developing new drug export networks and that whatever success antidrug polices have had could be reversed. It is also likely that this rebound in coca prices in Peru was the result of the strong eradication campaign of the Banzer government in Bolivia. Most likely, Bolivian cocaine producers and traffickers have substituted Peruvian coca and cocaine for domestic products.

The positive trend of the Peruvian industry appears to be reinforced in early 2002. Journalist Roger Rumrrill (personal communication) has reported that the deepening of the Colombian conflict, coupled with the troubles of the Peruvian government, has resulted in the return of Colombian buyers. He has asserted that in March 2002 the coca leaf arroba price in the Huallaga Valley was $40. High coca prices and the collapse of the price of other agricultural products were causing a large coca hectareage increase.[66] According to Rumrril, Peru had 60,000 to 70,000 hectares of coca, instead of the officially estimated 34,000. In the ever-changing picture of Andean illegal crops and drugs, it will not be surprising if these reports turn out to be accurate.

---

[66]He reported that 10 papayas were selling for 2 cents, 1,000 bananas for $25, and 50 kilograms of clean rice for $10. Coffee and cacao did not have buyers.

Part II

The Effects of the Andean Illegal Drug Industry

5

The Size of the Illegal Drug Industry

The size of the illegal drug industry is a key determinant of the industry's effects on a society. But estimates of illegal drugs' total revenues, inputs, value added, employment, exports, the amount of narco-dollars that enter a country's economy, and other related economic indicators are highly uncertain and difficult to ascertain. Data on the size and ownership structure of the industry are inaccurate, difficult to obtain, and frequently derived from secondary and indirect sources that provide, at best, a fuzzy approximation to reality. This inaccuracy is mainly due to the industry's illegality, which challenges scholars in their research. Obviously, researchers cannot go to the industry's association or government statistics office and ask for balance sheets and other relevant data. Indeed, they are reduced to largely indirect and highly speculative estimates.

The difficulties inherent in the data and the estimates based on them are well known (e.g.: Thoumi 1993, 1995d; Clawson and Lee 1996; Reuter 1996; and Steiner 1997). Still, the pressures on some entities to produce data and the publicity benefits that can be obtained by doing so lead sometimes to arbitrary estimates. Three cases illustrate this point. Freemantle (1986, 211) claimed that "drugs provide Colombia's biggest source of foreign income, nearly 36 percent of its total gross national product." Giorgio Giacomelli, the United Nations Drug Control Program (UNDCP) executive director in 1996, gave $500 billion a year as the size of the world illegal drug economy. UNDCP's (1997) *World Drug Report* provided a lower figure ($400 billion). More recently, in a late 1999 speech, Michel Camdessus, the International Monetary Fund executive director, claimed that the money-laundering volume was between 2 and 5 percent of the world's gross product. These figures are credible because they came from apparently authoritative sources. Still, none of these statements were backed by serious research, but they have been widely used and abused.[1] Steiner (1997) provided an excellent review of such estimates and charitably referred to them as "folkloric estimates."

A listing of the steps required to estimate the size of the illegal coca and cocaine industry will highlight the uncertainties found at each stage of the business. To estimate coca and cocaine value added in each of the three Andean countries studied, it is necessary to first figure out the size of the coca crop in Bolivia, Colombia, and Peru. One must then estimate conversion factors from coca leaves to coca paste, coca paste to cocaine base, and cocaine base to cocaine. These vary depending at least on the following factors: the type of coca plants and their age; weather conditions; coca plant density per hectare; the amount and types of fertilizers and herbicides used; the frequency of pruning; the skills of chemists and the type and quality of the chemicals used; and the time between the moment leaves are harvested and the actual refining process begins. Furthermore, because improved varieties have been developed and yields have increased, it is also necessary to continuously update the conversion factors to take technological improvements into account.

Other data requirements to estimate the industry's value added are the actual inputs used in the chemical and agro-industrial processes and their

[1]E.g., this occurred at an international conference in September 1998 organized by the U.N. International Scientific and Professional Advisory Council in Courmayeur Mont Blanc, Italy. Some participants contested the United Nations Drug Control Program's (UNDCP's) $500 billion a year figure frequently reported by the media. A high-level U.N. official at the conference had to humbly explain that such a figure was just a back-of-the-envelope estimate that he had made under pressure a few years earlier when he had to provide a figure for a U.N. speech. In early December 1999, I interviewed several International Monetary Fund officials in Washington and could find no source for Camdessus's estimate or anyone working on money laundering.

prices;[2] price data on coca paste, cocaine base, and cocaine;[3] the share of the Bolivian and Peruvian paste and base that is controlled and internationally marketed by Bolivians, Colombians, and Peruvians; and the share of each country's traffickers in the value added generated by smuggling drugs within the Andean countries and outside the region. These figures hinge on the availability of data on the amounts paid to foreign pilots and smugglers, in bribes, and for other transportation costs. The shares of each foreign market where wholesale prices are different (European countries, Japan, the United States, and other countries) that are controlled by traffickers of each Andean nationality need to be known. And data on losses in the production process, and through law enforcement seizures, are also needed. Every estimate adds uncertainty to the final figure.[4]

Other drugs present different estimation problems. For example, the estimation of poppy hectareage must be made quite rapidly and frequently over all the area of a country because it takes only 4 months from planting to harvesting.

A simple example illustrates the problems encountered in these estimations. Cultivated hectareage can be estimated in two ways. The first is by using reports made by government officials, journalists, or researchers who either reside in or have visited the growing areas. These secondhand reports do not and cannot use accepted sampling techniques but must rely on interviews with informers, law enforcers, and other area residents.

The second approach uses satellite photography. This method is more sophisticated, but it is not necessarily more accurate, because it depends on the observers' often diverging perceptions. Air photography does not reveal plants grown under tree cover; moreover, it is quite inaccurate in the many spots where illicit crops are mixed with other legal plants or when they are grown in the shade of other plants. Similar examples can be given for each of the estimation steps needed to obtain final figures. In spite of these limitations, there have been numerous estimates of the size of the illegal industry in the Andean countries. In fairness to the estimators, it must be acknowledged that most of them are aware of

[2]All inputs used to produce cocaine can be substituted. When one input market is controlled, producers use others or develop new ways to obtain the same input.

[3]It is recognized that price data, collected in undercover transactions, are more accurate than volume data.

[4]Similar estimation problems arise in poppy-opium-morphine-heroin, marijuana, and synthetic drugs.

the limitations of their own estimates and that in spite of the obstacles confronted, these estimates are probably more sophisticated than those made in other regions of the world.

The industry's size may also be estimated from the consumption side. Such a calculation would have to be based on consumption estimates, from which one would then derive the market share that corresponds to each of the Andean countries. This approach also presents myriad weaknesses. Little is known about consumption in any market, and prevalence data based on surveys do not provide detailed consumption information.[5] It is well known that consumption-based estimates are substantially lower than production based ones, which suggests a permanent oversupply condition and raises further doubts about the estimates' accuracy (De Rementería 1995; Steiner 1997; Reuter 1996). Consumption estimates first establish a figure for drug addicts and drug users in the main markets. The various doses demanded by addicts and the frequency of use of addicts and nonaddicts are then estimated. Total consumption is figured out from these figures. Yet, a comparison of this figure with some production and smuggling estimates may lead to absurd conclusions. Some estimates of marijuana produced in Mexico and smuggled to the United States require for example, that about one-third of Americans 15–50 years of age be marijuana addicts (Reuter 1996)!

The impact of the industry on a country depends not only on the industry's value added within that country, but also on the amount of illicit revenues that its nationals generate abroad and repatriate—and, conversely, on the amount generated domestically that is transferred out of the country. Further methodological problems arise if one takes into consideration the involvement of Andean expatriates, mainly Colombian, in drug-marketing activities outside the country. Their profits are not Andean value added, but they can be invested in the Andean region, and as evidence indicates, at least a share of them are (Thoumi 1995d).

A very large share of the industry's value added captured by Andean residents is generated by the roughly tenfold increase in the cocaine price

---

[5]Some typical questions asked in these surveys: Have you ever consumed a particular drug? Within the last year? Within the last month? These questions do not provide good data about frequency, patterns, amounts, and environments in which drugs are consumed. Indeed, they are not conceived to determine drug consumption volume and causality but rather to identify lawbreakers and are reminiscent of those asked by Catholic priests at confession who aim to find out what sins were committed but not much more than that.

between Andean and U.S. wholesale prices, and an even larger difference between Andean and European wholesale prices. To illustrate this point, it is useful to take a look at the Colombian cocaine industry's price structure circa 1995.[6] The coca leaves required to produce a kilogram of cocaine cost from $400 to $600. A kilogram of coca paste cost about $800, and a kilo of cocaine base $1,000. Cocaine wholesale prices were in the range of $1,500 to $1,800 per kilogram. Wholesale cocaine sales of 200 or more kilograms, at the U.S. port of entry sold for about $18,000. This price increases rapidly with each subsequent transaction.[7] At the retail level, a kilogram of cocaine sold by the gram cut to 60 to 70 percent purity can fetch $120,000.[8] European prices have been significantly higher. Cocaine wholesale prices in many European cities can be about $25,000 per kilogram, though recent reports indicate that they have been falling to levels similar to those in the United States, and that in such cities as Amsterdam, cocaine prices are already comparable to those in the United States (Thoumi 1999).

This price structure has three important implications. First, drug profits in mainly producing countries strongly depend on who does the smuggling to external markets. If it is country nationals, country profits are dramatically larger than otherwise. In spite of high transportation costs between Latin America and the United States—which reach from $2,500 per kilogram (Zabludoff 1997) to even 50 percent of the drug weight—the profits that traffickers make at this stage of the business are extremely large compared with those made at earlier stages.

Second, Andean cocaine and heroin exporters do not need to bring back to their countries most of their profits to pay for the drugs they export. Most of their profits can be laundered and invested anywhere. It is not surprising that studies show difficult-to-explain capital flows in the Colombian balance of payments, a significant share of which are likely to be funded by illegal drug money (Correa 1984; Urrutia and Pontón 1993; Rocha 1997), showed that they are statistically explained by interest-rate differentials in the United States and Colombia, and by devaluation expectations in Colombia. Drug traffickers are good capitalists, and illicit

---

[6]These figures are based on Rocha (1997) and (S. Uribe (1997) and are comparable to those used by UNDCP (1997, 126).

[7]U.S. intelligence services indicate that there are four to five transactions before cocaine reaches its final consumer.

[8]This figure exaggerates the traffickers' income because many dealers are also users or addicts who sell to support their habit.

drug capital flows behave in a way similar to any other international capital flow: They are influenced by macroeconomic conditions in the Andean countries, the United States, and other countries, as well as by fiscal and monetary policies in the Andean and other countries.

Third, it is necessary to point out a "political" source of estimate bias. The estimates of the size of the drug industry are not only of analytical interest, but they also have policy and political implications. During the past 25 years, for instance, coca-growing countries have received foreign aid to help eradicate coca plantings. Hence, many local politicians believe a successful foreign aid request is directly related to the size of the illegal industry. In Bolivia, this is particularly noticeable, and it is not surprising that past Bolivian estimates by researchers close to the government tended to be substantially higher than estimates made by the United States.[9]

All the methodological issues and difficulties discussed raise warning flags about the figures frequently used, particularly when there is no detailed description of the successive steps used to ascertain them. There is no question that any analysis of the illegal drug industry should use extreme caution when using any data.

The Colombian Estimates

During the last 25 years, there have been several attempts to establish the size of some parts of the illegal drug industry (e.g.: Junguito and Caballero 1979; Ruiz-Hernández 1979; Gómez 1985, 1988, 1990; Gómez and Santa María 1994; C. Caballero 1988; Kalmanovitz 1990; Sarmiento 1990; Urrutia 1990; Kalmanovitz and Bernal 1994; Vargas and Barragán 1995; Steiner 1997; Rocha 1997; and S. Uribe 1997). These are the more serious studies in this field, and they were surveyed by Thoumi (1993, 1995d), Steiner (1997), and Rocha (1997, 1999). There have been other estimates and journalistic reports that give much higher figures, which sometimes are drastically out of the realm of possibility (e.g., Freemantle 1986 mentioned above).

---

[9]E.g., Machicado (1992, 93) estimated that the coca produced in Bolivia in 1988 was sufficient to produce 546.9 tons of cocaine. The U.S. Department of State, Bureau of International Narcotics Matters (1990) estimated worldwide cocaine production in 1988 at about 750 tons, and maximum coca production in Bolivia at 34 percent of the world total, a much lower figure.

Table 5.1. *Illegal Drug Income in Colombia (billions of U.S. dollars)*

	Steiner					Rocha				
Year	Cocaine	Heroin	Marijuana	Total	Cocaine Minimum	Cocaine Maximum	Heroin	Marijuana	Total Minimum	Total Maximum
1980	1,386			1,386						
1981	1,933		137	2,070	1,358				1,358	
1982	1,819		65	1,884	2,484			133	2,617	
1983	1,868		79	1,947	1,294			133	1,427	
1984	4,093		79	4,172	671			83	754	
1985	2,933		20	2,953	947	3,817		26	973	3,843
1986	939		34	973	845	3,340		21	866	3,361
1987	1,311		152	1,463	493	2,386		57	550	2,443
1988	1,395		290	1,685	533	3,658		49	582	3,707
1989	2,485		94	2,579	677	6,677		22	699	6,699
1990	2,341		48	2,389	503	6,435		20	523	6,455
1991	1,400	756	83	2,239	161	3,965	27	45	233	4,037
1992	1,822	756	89	2,667	331	3,323	163	53	547	3,539
1993	1,363	756	368	2,487	357	2,999	270	140	767	3,409
1994	1,176	756	329	2,261	194	2,625	424	182	800	3,231
1995	1,446	756	333	2,535						

Sources: Steiner (1997) and Rocha (1997).

Most serious estimates are based on U.S. government figures of coca hectareage in the Andes. However, the assumptions about each required variable mentioned above vary widely, so the estimates fall within a very wide range. Table 5.1 presents the results of the most recent studies (Steiner 1997; Rocha 1997). Steiner's estimate of total illicit drug income for the early 1980s was about $2 billion a year; it rose dramatically to more than $4 billion in 1984 and fluctuated widely between $1 billion and $3 billion for the rest of the decade. From 1989 to 1995, it tended to be stable at about $2.5 billion.

Rocha estimated total income from 1981 to 1994. For the 1985–94 period, he also produced minimum and maximum estimates, depending on what assumptions were made about cocaine. The minimum figures were quite low; after 1983, they never exceeded $1 billion. Rocha's maximum estimate was in the range of $2.5 to $4 billion for the 1984–88 period, then rose to $6.5 billion during the next 2 years, and then fell to $3 to $4 billion for the last 4 years. Rocha's estimate also showed the importance of possible alternative assumptions because for several years his maximum estimate was ten or more times larger than his minimum one.

Steiner's (1997) and Rocha's (1997) figures highlight the importance of the sharp drop in cocaine prices from the early 1980s on, which reduced total cocaine income. The figures also coincide in showing a decline in the importance of marijuana during the 1980s, then a rebounding of that illegal industry branch in the 1990s. Both caution the reader about the greater uncertainty about heroin revenues. Indeed, none had estimates for the years before 1991, in spite of police reports about the existence of poppy plantings (see chapter 4), and Steiner considered that it was not feasible to develop a good estimate and opted for a constant figure for all years.

As was noted above, drug income estimates are very uncertain and frequently contradictory. For example, S. Uribe's (1997) study—based on the usual hectareage estimates plus fieldwork in illegal crop regions—estimated cocaine and heroin domestic value added generated in the processing of locally grown coca and poppies at $1.2 billion (excluding coca paste and cocaine base imports from Peru and Bolivia). This estimate only covered value added generated in the production process up to the point at which laboratories sell their drugs in Colombia. It provided an order of magnitude of the value added generated in the illicit crop regions by peasants, collectors, chemists, refiners, and so on. Uribe's estimate was higher than the minimum cocaine estimates of Rocha and similar to total cocaine income as estimated by Steiner. Because Uribe's estimate did not include the most profitable smuggling part of the business, it clearly implied substantially higher total cocaine revenues.[10]

As was noted in chapter 4, the illicit industry's structure has changed substantially in the past few years as illegal hectareage has exploded, the Colombian Revolutionary Armed Forces (FARC) guerrillas were granted control of the "distension zone," and paramilitary forces increased their role in drug production and trafficking. These changes led to significant changes in illicit revenues and their distribution, but they have not been researched.

All estimates have important biases, among which five come easily to mind: First, reliable data on actual transportation costs throughout the Caribbean and Central America to the United States are not available. As was discussed in chapter 4, Mexicans can be charging Colombians up to 50 percent of the cocaine to smuggle it from Mexico to the United States. Traditionally, the U.S. Drug Enforcement Administration has estimated

---

[10]Rocha's and Uribe's studies were part of the same United Nations Development Program–sponsored project that I coordinated. Each author had very strong convictions, and because I simply did not succeed in having both authors agree to a common set of assumptions about the variables discussed above, I opted to publish both studies in the same book in spite of these obvious inconsistencies.

transportation costs in the range of 10 to 15 percent of the wholesale price at American ports of entry. These estimates, however, crucially hinge on what proportion of the exports is assumed to go through Mexico. In any case, this means that those who transport cocaine make as much as all producers and traffickers up to the point at which the drug is exported from the Andean countries.

Second, the large number of Colombians jailed around the world on narcotics charges evidences involvement in trafficking within the United States, Europe, and other markets, but there are no studies that estimate these Colombians' income or the proportion that they send back to Colombia. Third, Colombians are also involved in Bolivia and Peruvian exports. Moreover, Steiner's and Rocha's estimates focused on Colombian value added and did not include either Colombians' profits from trafficking within the United States, Bolivia, or Peru.

Fourth, the estimates did not include illegal industry revenues from domestic sales in Colombia. Fifth, both sets of estimates deducted money-laundering costs from gross revenues. This implicitly assumes that the costs of money and asset laundering are foreign value added and/or that money laundering is not part of the illegal drug industry. Either way, this assumption creates a downward bias in the estimates, particularly because there is no doubt that many Colombians participate in and profit from asset laundering activities (as will be shown in chapter 7).

If one is interested in studying the impact of the illegal drug industry on a country, one should not look only at domestic illegal value added but also at the amount of resources that the industry can command at one particular moment in time. The point is simply that estimates of illegal revenues relevant to the Colombian economy should include the industry's value added that ends in Colombians' hands in and out of the country. It may be argued that domestic value added is likely to have a greater impact on Colombia than value added accruing to Colombians outside the country. In this case, it would be necessary to determine a proportion of the foreign value added that could be transferred to the country and its impact on the Colombian economy.

A further point should be made about the income generated by drug industry funds already laundered. Some estimates show higher illicit income in the early 1980s than in the 1990s due to the approximate 75 percent decline in international cocaine prices. However, by the 1990s the illegal drug industry had accumulated large investments that were producing income. These revenues are also part of the industry's economic base and influence its ability to affect the Colombian economy. Unfortunately, it is very difficult (if not impossible) to assess this share of the illicit industry's income, and no estimates are available.

To evaluate the estimates of the size of the illegal industry's revenues, it is necessary to compare the undervaluation arising from not considering the income generated by heroin, cocaine, and other drugs marketed outside Colombia that can be transferred to the country, which is likely to be "large," against the possibly underestimated costs paid by Colombian traffickers in the smuggling stage. On balance, it is likely that the studies of the size of the illicit drug industry underestimated the relevant Colombian drug income, which could have been be somewhere around $4 billion a year, without including income from laundered assets.

It is interesting to point out that the size estimates indicate a declining weight of the illegal drug industry on both exports and gross national product (GNP). In the early and mid-1980s, GNP was about $36 billion, measured in current dollars. During the 1990s, it grew substantially, to $68.6 billion in 1994 and $96.3 billion in 1997.[11] According to these estimates, the value added generated by the illegal drug industry in the early 1980s was in the range of 7 to 10 percent of GNP, but by the late 1990s it dropped to 3 to 4 percent.

A similar conclusion is obtained when illicit drug revenues are compared with total exports of goods and services. In the early 1980s, they fluctuated between $4 and $5 billion. Beginning in 1987, total exports increased and reached $12.1 billion in 1994 and $15.9 billion in 1997. There is no question that in the early 1980s illegal drug exports were a much higher proportion of total exports than in the late 1990s.

Employment is another important drug industry size variable. As would be expected, employment estimations are also subject to large error margins. In spite of measurement difficulties arising from the natural reluctance of both employers and employees to give information, the seasonality of many drug jobs, and the multiproduct nature of many small family farms where family members work on several crops, S. Uribe (1997) estimated that in 1995 coca and poppy production generated the equivalent of 40,000 full time jobs.

[11]All data on GNP, total exports of goods and services, population, and economically active population for Bolivia, Colombia, and Peru used in this chapter are from the Inter-American Development Bank online database. All data are in current dollars. The bank's export data come originally from the International Monetary Fund.

Zabludoff (1997), using U.S. intelligence data, estimated that the managerial core of the 10 largest Colombian "cartels" was made up of about 500 people. These also employed 5,000 people, counting laboratory employees, transport personnel, money launderers, and order and contract enforcers. One should add to these 1,000 specialized free-lancers: pilots, chemists, lawyers, assassins for hire (*sicarios*), financial advisers, and the like. Some of these are permanently employed, but many work only part time for the illegal industry. The drug industry also used the services of about 10,000 technical and nonqualified personnel.[12] These were also employed on a permanent and part-time basis, and included guards and bodyguards, "mules," radio operators, messengers, heavy equipment operators, surveillance teams, and "smurfs." (Smurfs are individuals used to break down a large quantity of cash to be deposited into several smaller deposits that can be made in various financial institutions, thereby avoiding the requirement that the financial institution report large deposits to the authorities. For example, the United States requires banks to file reports on every cash deposit in excess of $10,000. Smurfs take a large amount and make several deposits of less than $10,000 in accounts in several institutions, avoiding the reporting requirement.) Moreover, an indeterminate number of people serve in airlines, airplane and communications equipment maintenance, banks and other financial institutions, chemical input suppliers, and the like.

There is no question that there is a complex job structure related to the illegal drug industry. The industry, however, was not a large employer in the country until the mid-1990s. The total population in 1995 was 35.8 million, and the economically active population was more than 23.7 million. These figures show that the illegal drug industry's employment in Colombia was not important at a global level, although it was extremely important in coca- and poppy-growing regions. The changes that have taken place since 1999 might have changed this. The explosion in coca plantings increased the importance of the illegal industry for rural employment but, as noted in chapter 4, the increased involvement of guerrilla and paramilitary organizations in the illegal trade and the intertwining of illegal drugs and armed conflict have prevented rigorous research on these topics. However, it is safe to state that illegal crop employment in Putumayo, Caguán, Guaviare, and a few other regions could

---

[12]The roundness of these figures, all thousands that are multiples of 5 and 10, makes me question whether they are anything more than educated guesses.

have accounted for 200,000 jobs by 2001. These figures are consistent with reports that total coca cultivation exceeds 130,000 hectares.

The Bolivian Estimates

It is not surprising that the estimates of the size of the illegal drug industry in Bolivia also fluctuate over a wide range.[13] Most these estimates are based on assumptions that, according to the estimators, reflect the country's peculiar involvement in the illegal trade. The estimates assume that all illicit coca is converted into coca paste in Bolivia and that the value added generated in this process is Bolivian. They also assume that non-Bolivians buy and export part of the paste output and that the rest is processed into cocaine base in Bolivia. Part of the value added of this process is Bolivian, and part is attributed to foreigners. Part of the cocaine base is exported, and part is processed into cocaine, and again the value added is divided among Bolivians and foreigners.[14] Most estimates assume that the foreigners involved are Colombian.

These studies also make another peculiar assumption: that a significant proportion of the Bolivian value added and profits obtained in cocaine base and cocaine manufacturing are invested abroad and never get back into the national economy. This assumption is based on the beliefs that part of this value added ends up in foreign hands and that the absorptive capacity of the Bolivian economy is very small—that is to say that there are not enough domestic investment opportunities for all the capital accumulated by Bolivian traffickers.

Bolivia is a small, poor economy that historically had been subject to large international price fluctuations of its main exports. Its governments did not manage these external shocks well and during the 1970s borrowed heavily in international markets. During the early 1980s, a combination of very high international interest rates, a collapse of international tin prices, and a free-spending populist government produced hyperinflation and a deep recession.

---

[13]J. Painter (1994, chap. 3) summarized the available estimates a few years back. See also Doria-Medina (1986). More recent estimates are found in Ayala (1999), Joel (1999), and Steiner (1997).

[14]All these estimates have a key weakness because there is no solid basis to figure out the proportions of Bolivian and foreign controlled processes. These amount to "educated guesses."

The country's GNP in the early 1980s fluctuated between $4 and $7 billion, depending on international prices for its exports and the availability of borrowed funds. In 1985, a new government introduced drastic adjustment reforms. The 1986 GNP was $4.5 billion. The late 1980s was a period of slow growth, with GNP reaching $4.8 billion by 1990. Afterward, the economy grew steadily, with GNP reaching $7.8 billion in 1997, a level only slightly higher than the $7.2 billion of 1984!

Official exports of goods and services were $1.030 million in 1980 and declined steadily to $650 million in 1987. From then on, they recovered slowly, reaching $1.181 million in 1994, the first year that they exceeded the 1980 level! In 1997, they reached $1.362 million.

The longest series of Bolivian drug exports covers the 1980–93 period and was produced by Steiner (1997, 43). Shorter series, none exceeding 8 years, are found in J. Painter (1994), Alvarez (1993), De Franco and Godoy (1992), and Antezana (1995). All series showed a sharp decline in value added and exports during the mid-1980s.

Steiner's (1997) figures were total export estimates independent of the amount actually repatriated to Bolivia, although they included a 20 percent laundering deduction, which implied that there were no Bolivians involved in money laundering. These also assume that exporters get only the free-on-board price, that is, that they did not benefit from the highly profitable international smuggling and marketing operations. These figures during the early 1980s oscillated between $700 and $800 million, a level of the same order of magnitude as official exports. From 1985 to 1993, they were at the level of $300 to $400 million.

The declining trend was due to lower coca and cocaine prices and not to a decline in the coca cultivated area,[15] and it has been maintained even as productivity in the coca farms has increased (Ayala 1999). All coca hectareage estimates showed a substantial increase from 1985 to 1993, from about 15,000 to 50,000 hectares. Coca acreage remained stable through 1997 and declined sharply after 1998, when the newly elected Hugo Banzer government implemented its forced eradication plan.

Joel (1999) presented relatively low figures. He estimated direct Bolivian value added in the illegal industry in the range between $152 and $204 million. His estimates of the value added that actually remained in

---

[15]E.g., see Antezana's (1995) study. This author is the economist who followed the illicit industry at the U.S. Agency for International Development office in La Paz.

the country were only between $115 and $133 million. All these estimates assumed that all Bolivian exports were made free on board. Ayala's (1999) estimates were in the range of $200 to $300 million, as were Antezana's (1995).

Joel also estimated direct plus indirect value added, which included the industry's multiplier effects on the rest of the economy. These were in a range between $227 and $263 million, or between 3.8 and 4.4 percent of GNP. Joel also considered a few scenarios in which Bolivians controlled a proportion of their exports and sold them on American and European markets. Assuming that a quarter of Bolivian drug exports are handled by Bolivians, and that one half of the profits from international marketing are repatriated, Joel found that the direct contribution of the industry increased to somewhere between 4 and 7 percent of GNP.

The same study estimated gross coca paste, cocaine base, and cocaine exports at $156 to $242 million. Of these, between $73 and $109 million actually entered the country. These figures were only between 8.8 and 13.2 percent of official export figures.

Summarizing the evidence, there is no doubt that in the early 1980s the illegal drug industry generated an important share of GNP, somewhere in the range of 10 to 15 percent, and higher if Bolivians themselves did any drug exporting. At that time, the illegal industry's importance as a foreign exchange generator was much greater because illegal exports were similar in magnitude to official ones.

The sharp coca price fall of the mid- and late 1980s combined with the renewed growth of the Bolivian economy during the 1990s resulted in a notable decline in the magnitude of the illegal industry relative to the rest of the economy. The illegal industry was more important as a foreign exchange source than as an income generator, and in the 1990s it accounted for export revenue levels of 15 to 25 percent of total official exports. The issue of export revenue repatriation has been important in Bolivia, and there is a consensus among researchers that a significant proportion of exports' revenues remained abroad. Unfortunately, there is no solid evidence to determine the correct proportion, and all researchers use rules of thumb.

Employment in illegal coca and cocaine in Bolivia has been more important than in other Andean countries. According to Joel (1999), the illicit industry generated 71,300 direct jobs in Chapare and estimated total direct and indirect employment of between 107,000 and 135,000, or the equivalent of between 5 and 6.4 percent of the licit employment in the country.

Earlier employment estimates placed direct coca-cocaine employment at between 120,000 and 300,000. Most of these jobs were agricultural. These figures imply that the coca-cocaine industry employed between 6.7 and 13.5 percent of the economically active population. Ayala's (1999) figures were somewhat higher than Joel's. Independent of the accuracy of these estimates, there is no question that Bolivian employment depended heavily on the illicit industry and that its reduction through the implementation of Plan Dignidad has had grave social and economic implications.

It is quite clear that assumptions about the proportion of illicit value added and profits that remain in the country are key determinants of the effects of the illegal industry in Bolivia. If the large majority of the illicit income that remained in the country was generated by coca growing and was distributed among poor peasants, the industry had very positive effects on the country and did not cause significant changes in its power structure. If this was the case, most illegal income was spent on consumer goods, rural home improvements, and education, and it did not alter the property structure of manufacturing, real estate, and other urban sectors. If Bolivians are involved in international cocaine trafficking, a few individuals will make large fortunes that will allow them to gain great clout on the formal economy and the country's government. In this case, the effects of the illicit activity will prove substantially more complex.

The successful eradication program of the Banzer administration has dramatically changed the structure of the illegal drug industry in Bolivia. Peasant income and employment in coca declined sharply. However, because there is no solid evidence about the extent of the Bolivians' participation in drug manufacturing and trafficking, it is not possible to determine the current impact of the illegal industry on the country's economy, although it is possible to assert that it is certainly significantly lower than in the past.

The Peruvian Estimates

As was noted above, until recently Peru has been the main world coca producer and a main exporter of coca paste and cocaine base to Colombia. Traditional coca plantings were concentrated in a few Sierra locations. During the 1970s and 1980s, coca plantings expanded significantly and spread to about ten departments. The main concentration of illegal coca was found in the Upper Huallaga River Valley. Morales (1989), after doing extensive fieldwork in five peasant communities, estimated that in 1985 there were 100,000 hectares of coca. CUÁNTO S.A. (1993, 20) surveyed all available data and produced a series from 1980 to 1992.

This series showed coca hectareage of about 128,000 for 1980 to 1983, about 150,000 hectares for the following 6 years, a sharp increase to 207,000 hectares in 1990, and further increases to 257,000 hectares in 1992. It also estimated increases in coca productivity from 1985 on due to increased use of fertilizer, herbicides, and better agriculture techniques. CUÁNTO S.A.'s methodology probably overestimated the area cultivated. It first estimated the total population of the coca-growing regions, then estimated the population needed to produce the legal crops reported in those regions, assuming that everyone who is not employed in legal crops is engaged in coca production. In other words, it assumed that land supply is infinitely elastic and that the only constraint on production is a labor shortage.

Alvarez and Associates[16] (1996), on the basis of a detailed revision and evaluation of available estimates, and particularly on fieldwork, produced what are likely to be more reliable estimates. For 1993, they figured coca cultivation in the range of 145,000 to 175,000 hectares.

Since the early 1990s, there had been several police and journalistic reports about the presence of poppy fields in Peru. Some of these reports also suggested that poppy plantings were not very successful. Alvarez and Associates simply could not find data, nor could they safely visit suspected poppy regions. Whatever poppy fields existed at the time, therefore, could not be studied.

As was the case in the other coca-growing countries, coca hectareage grew substantially from 1980 on. However, the relative weight of the coca and coca products industries in the Peruvian economy has declined drastically, due to a combination of factors. On the one hand, coca and coca products' prices declined sharply. On the other hand, during the late 1980s during the Alan García presidency, Peru suffered a depression cum hyperinflation. During the 1990s, the Peruvian economy recuperated and grew at relatively high rates. MACROCONSULT S.A. (1990) estimated that the GNP contribution of the coca-cocaine industry in the early 1980s could have been as high as 11 percent. Alvarez and Associates (1996) estimated, due to the changes mentioned, that coca and its products

---

[16]That included the authors of CUÁNTO S.A. study.

accounted for approximately 8 percent of the country's GNP in 1988, and fell to less than 2 percent in 1995.[17]

As was mentioned above, a combination of factors contributed to a sharp coca price decline during the mid- and late 1990s. As it happened, in the other coca growing countries, coca growers have evolved into producers of coca paste and cocaine base, and on occasion even into cocaine refiners. Another important change occurred in the geographical distribution of coca plantings, which are present in an increasing number of departments, a development that makes any eradication strategy more and more difficult.

The contribution of the illegal drug industry to the balance of payments was, at least during some periods, a lot more important than its contribution to GNP. Steiner (1997, 43) produced a series of total gross drug revenues for Peru from 1980 to 1995. In the early 1980s, these revenues increased while official total exports of goods and services declined. In 1980, illegal revenues were 16 percent of total exports registered in the balance of payments. Their share increased steadily, and in 1985 and 1986 they exceeded 26 percent. From then on, total official exports recuperated and illegal revenues declined, so that in 1995 illegal revenues were only 6 percent of legal exports.

It was not surprising that coca-growing families enjoyed higher incomes than other peasants did. Alvarez and Associates (1996) placed coca peasants' family per capita income at about $1,500, a level close to the national average.

CUÁNTO S.A. (1993, 22) estimated direct rural employment for 1980 to 1992. Its series started at 123,300 in 1980 and increased continuously to a hefty 293,800 in 1990. It assumed that every family has 1.9 members employed in coca-cocaine, resulting in a series from 64,900 families in 1980 to 154,600 in 1992. Alvarez and Associates (1996) estimated 1993 direct rural employment in the illicit industry at between 150,000 and 174,000 jobs, or about 7 percent of the rural economically active population or 2 percent of the countries' economically active population.

Backward linkages of the illegal industry with the rest of the Peruvian economy are not very large but are significant. Alvarez and Associates

---

[17]These figures are consistent with those used by Steiner (1997, 43). Alvarez and Cervantes (1996) and Alvarez (1998) summarized the results of Alvarez and Associates (1996). However, Alvarez (1998) gave a figure of less than 1 percent for the 1995 share of Peruvian GNP generated by the illegal industry.

(1996) estimated them at between 13 and 18 percent of the illicit industry's intermediate goods' demand.

To conclude, in the early and mid-1980s, the illicit industry in Peru was an important source of foreign exchange and income, and there is no doubt that it helped the country maintain some of its populist policies of the time. However, the weight of the illegal industry on the Peruvian economy dropped substantially, and similar to Colombia's, Peru's economy on the whole could do well without drugs. In the mid-1990s, the illegal industry still represented an important source of rural employment in all coca-growing regions that attracted migrants.

As in Bolivia, coca hectareage declined sharply in the late 1990s. There is no doubt that the weight of the illegal industry on the Peruvian economy also fell sharply, but as in Bolivia, little is known today about the magnitude of the decline.

6

Economic, Environmental, Social, and Political Effects of the Illegal Drug Industry

During the past 30 years, the illegal drug industry has had pervasive effects in Bolivia, Colombia, and Peru. Because the consequences of the industry's development have been complex, the structure of the relations between causes and effects has frequently been unclear and difficult to identify or measure. It is not surprising that many opinions are voiced regarding how good or bad illegal drugs have been to the Andean region. On the positive side are those who argue that the illegal industry has provided significant employment and foreign exchange, facilitated the structural adjustment of Bolivia in the late 1980s and of Peru during the early 1990s, has prevented their economic collapse, and more recently, has promoted economic growth.

On the negative side are those who argue that the industry has had typical boom-and-bust effects in many regions and that it has not set the basis for sustainable economic growth. More important, they point to the increased violence, organized criminality, and the corruption that have caused the business climate to deteriorate, increased costs to the formal economy, and lowered the countries' rate of economic growth (particularly Colombia's). Others focus on the industry's effects on behavior, income expectations, moral values, and political corruption. Before discussing the effects in each country, it is useful to dwell separately on those effects that are mainly economic and environmental and those that are primarily political and social.

Economic Effects

The illegal drug industry has many possible economic effects on the Andean countries, among which the most important and likely to have occurred are that

1. The industry can cause regional booms and busts in coca-, poppy-, and marijuana-growing regions and in the cities where drug traffickers are concentrated.
2. Illegal drugs can generate a significant number of jobs, particularly in coca- and poppy-growing regions.
3. The illegal industry promotes money laundering.
4. It can distort consumption, investment, and import patterns as traffickers and their associates invest in real estate, machinery, equipment, and goods that are not the most profitable or socially productive ones but which facilitate laundering. A similar situation occurs with consumer goods.
5. The abundance of foreign exchange it generates can be a cause of currency overvaluation and a loss of competitiveness for other exports and the domestic production that competes with imports.
6. The illegal industry can also increase expectations of quick wealth and encourage high-risk, speculative investments.

Many complex and difficult-to-answer questions can be posed about the possible economic effects of illegal drugs: What is the actual industry's weight in a country's economy? Would the destruction of the industry cause an economic crisis? What are its effects on the balance of payments and fiscal and macroeconomic policies and management, on employment and economic growth, on regional economic development, or on the environment? This section attempts to provide some answers, recognizing that the complexity of most of these issues may preclude obtaining many definite ones.

The effects of the illegal industry on a particular country depend minimally on the following: the structure of the industry, that is, the number of participants and firms at each stage of the production and marketing process; the role that the country plays in the overall world drug industry, whether it is a producer of agricultural raw materials, a drug manufacturer, a transshipment or money laundering center, and so on; the way in which drug income is generated, distributed, and laundered; the industry's size relative to the rest of the economy; the ways in which illegal foreign exchange is brought into the country; and the channels and ways used to launder the industry's illegal income and accumulated assets. It is necessary to focus on these factors to explain the industry's effects.

Effects of the Industry's Structure on Income Distribution

The price, revenue, and profit structure of the illegal drug industry implies that the industry's impact on a country crucially depends on the stage of the business in which the country participates, for three reasons. First, as was shown in chapter 5, drug prices increase sharply as drug processing advances and as drugs move from mainly producing countries to mainly consuming ones. Income is much greater at the smuggling and marketing stages than at the agricultural and manufacturing ones.

Second, peasant employment is very large. As the refining of coca into cocaine and of opium poppies into morphine and heroin advances, rural employment declines at each stage. Cocaine and heroin refining can be rural or urban and employ few people. There are relatively few smugglers. When drugs reach the mainly consuming countries, employment increases as the marketing chain advances from wholesaler to retailer. At the retail level, there are again a large number of participants.[1]

---

[1]The industry's employment structure is like an hourglass: At the bottom, there are many peasants who participate in the industry, the number of actors declines, and there are few at the smuggling stage. In the drug-importing countries, the number of participants expands at each stage and there are many retailers. This fact is used as an argument to justify the focus of repressive policies on large international drug traffickers, of which there are few and which may be easier to target.

Third, income is distributed very widely at the agricultural stage. It is larger and becomes more and more concentrated as the manufacturing stages advance, it is large and highly concentrated in the smuggling phase,[2] and from then on the level is high but it becomes deconcentrated to the point at which retailers' income distribution is also very dispersed.[3]

Money-Laundering Constraints

The economic effects of the illegal drug industry depend on how easy it is to launder illegal income and capital.[4] Asset and foreign exchange laundering are complex phenomena. They have received the attention of academics and policymakers for only a few years, and there is no consensus about their definitions. The United Nations Convention Against Illicit Traffic in Narcotics and Psychotropic Substances defines money laundering as a process through which the illegal source and the ownership of cash or other assets is concealed to project a perception of legitimacy. A United Nations–sponsored study defines money laundering as a "dynamic three-stage process that requires: firstly, moving the funds from direct association with the crime; secondly, disguising the trail to foil pursuit; and, thirdly, making the money available again to the criminal once again with its occupational and geographic origins hidden from view (United Nations Office of Drug Control and Crime Prevention 1998, 4).[5] The U.S. Department of State does not formally define money laundering but describes it thus: "Money laundering generally involves a series of multiple transactions used to disguise the source of financial assets so that those assets maybe used without compromising the criminals who are seeking to use the funds. Through money laundering, the criminal tries to transform the monetary proceeds derived from illicit activities into funds with an apparent legal source" (U.S. Department of State, Bureau for International Narcotics and Law Enforcement Affairs 1999, 565).

---

[2]This is one important reason that the economic effects in Colombia are different from those in Bolivia and Peru (Thoumi 1995b).

[3]Falco et al. (1997) and Reuter (1996, 1997) showed that this is a characteristic of the illegal drug market.

[4]This section is based on Thoumi (1996).

[5]This publication was written by Jack A. Blum, Michael Levi, R. Thomas Naylor, and Phil Williams.

Some of these definitions and descriptions imply a coincidence between legitimacy and legality, but in the Andean countries, where there is a great gap between de jure and de facto behaviors, it is important to separate them (Thoumi 1995d). Indeed, in the Andean ethnically mixed societies, where a dominant culture has been forcibly imposed on large segments of the population, many actions are deemed illegal but legitimate. These actions are approved by the mores and values of the society or of some of its subgroups but reproved by formal laws.[6]

In these cases, at least some asset and income laundering can be considered legitimate. This factor is frequently related to the degree of legitimacy of the state's laws and property rights, as well as to the former's ability to mediate and solve private conflicts and enforce contracts.

Until recently, asset and income laundering was not a subject of academic studies and research. Although the emerging literature on this topic relies on the definition mentioned above, for the purposes of this work, it is useful to use a different one that allows for more nuances that reflect the Andean social realities. Asset and income laundering are here defined as the processes through which illegally obtained assets and income are disguised and become identified as legal, separating the concepts of legality and legitimacy. According to this definition, assets and income can be legal and legitimate, legal and illegitimate, illegal and legitimate, or illegal and illegitimate.

The transformation from illegality to legality launders assets and income. It requires hiding the origin of the assets and income and minimizing the risk of the origin's being identified after the process is completed. The risks inherent in the laundering process depend on whether laundered income and capital are legitimate; when they are illegal but legitimate, laundering risks and costs are substantially lower than when they are illegal and illegitimate.

Asset and income laundering imply the existence of converse processes that dirty assets and income (Thoumi 1995d, 1996). In the Andean countries, where many laws and regulations related to economic activity are evaded, legality and illegality convey costs and benefits (De Soto 1986). Any profit-maximizing firm will try to capture the benefits of legal

---

[6]Importing contraband of cigarettes, small appliances, and other consumer goods falls in this category in the Andean countries.

and informal operations, while avoiding the costs of both. This is why there is a long tradition for people and businesses to continually dirty and clean assets, that is, to hide legal capital and turn it illegal and vice versa.

From an entrepreneur's viewpoint, the decision to keep a proportion of operations above board and maintain the rest under board is similar to any portfolio management decision that involves a choice between assets that provide different risks and returns. In the Andean countries, most dirty capital has traditionally been legitimate; that is, its accumulation obeys the mores of society and no one questions its origin. In these cases, the most common reason to hide dirty capital has been to evade taxes.

In any country, every individual has the capacity to dirty and launder an amount of income and capital. Specifically, there is an amount of illegal income that an individual may spend and of capital that can accumulate without risks of confiscation or penal sanctions. These risks increase with income and asset size, but also depend on the individual's behavior, on the ability to develop a social support network, on the type of assets invested, and on the degree of legal compliance in the society. The keys to successful laundering are to conduct it through socially legitimate ways and not to attract the law-enforcing authorities' attention.

Conspicuous personal behavior lowers laundering capacity, whereas a modest and low profile increases it as it heightens the probability that the laundering operation will not be identified. Any criminal organization lowers its risks if it develops a support network in the society. Success in these operations is higher when the launderer can count on a loyal and large group of relatives, childhood friends, classmates, and other close ones who collaborate in the process. The need to develop these networks is directly related to the size of the income or assets to be laundered. Assets that are difficult to price and those widely used by other businesses to hide capital are good means of laundering. Real estate and art objects are good laundering assets in the Andes. Last, in societies where breaking commercial and economic laws and regulations is a widely accepted and legitimate practice, laundering is easier than in the opposite case.

It needs to be noted that what is sometimes called asset laundering does not increase the amount of laundered capital in the society. For example, if a real estate transaction is recorded for a lower sum than the actual price, the purchaser who paid illegal cash obtains a legal asset while the seller has to hide the excess price. This amount of illegal capital is just transferred from one individual to another. The seller may have a higher capacity to hide such assets or engage in other activities that can be used to shelter them, but they are still illegal.

Conversely, some activities enter the classification of money laundering even when they are not considered as such. For example, if a U.S. ghetto crack cocaine dealer goes on a cash-spending shopping spree at a luxurious shopping center, he or she is laundering income according to the definition used in this study. However, U.S. legislation (and all other legal systems) and government officials do not consider this action as part of money laundering on the grounds that spending on nondurable consumer goods does not lead to wealth accumulation and seizable assets. This might be a practical rule that does not mean that the activity in question is not analytically, in effect, money laundering. According to this perspective, a person would launder money only if he or she ends up with an asset to show for it. Merely buying nondurable consumer goods does not represent money laundering. This might be a practical rule that does not mean that the activity in question is not analytically in effect money laundering.

The prevalence of dirtying and laundering activities in a society implies that formally or informally, a lot of money dirtying and laundering will go unpunished. Attempts otherwise create an open conflict between the laws and regulations of the state and social mores and common social practices. For this reason, laws that define laundering to cover all illicit income and capital face strong social opposition and are either not enacted or enforced. Thus, most legislation criminalizes laundering only when the income or assets are related to illegal drug trafficking. Laundering other illegally obtained income and wealth can be an infraction of the law but not a criminal act. These laws implicitly differentiate between dirty but cleanable and dirty but noncleanable assets. In the Andes, Colombia was a pioneer in expanding its legislation to cover income and assets obtained from the illegal drug industry, kidnappings and extortion, and public-sector corruption (Garzón 1997). Peru sanctions drug money laundering and can impose up to life in prison without parole if the drug trafficker has collaborated with subversive guerrilla organizations (Lamas 1995).[7]

---

[7]There has been a recent international trend to expand the coverage of money laundering to include funds used by terrorist groups and those generated by public-sector corruption, kidnapping, and extortion.

Money laundering of funds that originated in tax evasion present particular problems. Current legislation does not consider these funds to be part of money laundering. Indeed, offshore and international banks strongly oppose expanding current money-laundering legal definitions to cover these funds. The legal argument is simply that legislation to attack tax evasion already exists and that no new laws are necessary. In reality, many financial institutions and offshore jurisdictions benefit greatly from handling these funds and insist on separating "hot money" coming from tax evasion from "dirty money" generated by criminal acts and international organized crime.

As was argued above, individuals have a limited capacity to dirty and launder capital without risk of confiscation. Countries also have limits on the amounts that they can launder. These depend on the size and structural characteristics of the economy.

Because of the international nature of the drug market, laundering the proceeds of the drug industry in the Andean countries requires two different and related steps. First, dollar-denominated assets have to be brought into the country and converted into local-currency-denominated assets. Second, those assets have to be disposed of (consumed or invested) in the local economies, minimizing the confiscation risks.

There are a limited number of ways to bring illegal assets into the Andean countries, and each has limits. Besides, as was noted above, bringing money into the country per se does not launder it. The most common ways to bring illegal assets from abroad are contraband of goods; "technical contraband" (import underinvoicing; export overinvoicing; and other trade-related tricks, e.g., misclassifying imports); foreign exchange cash imports sold to central banks as labor remittances and other transfers, or on the underground or parallel market; purchases of assets in the Andes paid abroad; and establishing fictitious transnational corporations that invest in the Andean countries. There are also other less known financial systems, particularly the purchase of a type of Colombian foreign debt bond issue that is sold in foreign currencies but may be redeemed in pesos.

All these channels to bring illegal foreign exchange into a country are limited. Contraband is limited by local demand; by the need to bring goods that are easy to hide and sell and whose origin does not have to be justified by the purchaser;[8] by export controls in foreign countries; and by the need to have a collaborating exporter.[9]

"Technical contraband" is limited by the demand for imported goods and price information available to customs officials. It frequently requires the complicity of customs officials and the trade partner (exporter or importer).

Central bank foreign exchange purchases as labor and other remittances depend on the bank's willingness to accept those funds without asking too many questions about their origin.

Asset purchases paid abroad are also limited and require finding an Andean resident who wants to invest abroad and who is willing to become a laundering accomplice.

The creation of fake transnational corporations to bring in capital is limited by the need to justify their expertise in a particular field where they claim to be operating. Furthermore, if these are used to purchase existing enterprises, they are likely to require the sellers' complicity.

As was mentioned above, certain means that are used to bring the foreign exchange generated by the drug industry into a country do not launder it. For instance, contraband sales in a country do not launder those assets because they remain illegal. There is no question that the sale proceeds of contraband imports are more protected from government seizing actions than actual drug revenues and that they might actually become legitimate

[8]E.g., an importer frequently uses legal imports to shield similar goods imported illegally.

[9]One of the most notable examples of complicity has been the U.S. and British tobacco industries, which have exported large quantities of cigarettes to Panama, Aruba, Curaçao, Margarita, and other Caribbean islands knowing that many of those products are smuggled into Colombia. The case of Aruba is remarkable in this respect, because its cigarette imports were 25 percent of the island's national income (Steiner 1997)! Curiously, for many years Philip Morris's advertising budget in Colombia exceeded the value of its official cigarette exports to Colombia! The official Philip Morris response to Colombian officials who questioned these expenditures was simply that it was trying to increase its market share, even though it has more than 70 percent of the market already! (Interview with Miguel Fadul, Jr., director of the Colombian Commercial Office in Washington, D.C., August 1998). These facts became known and generated a public opinion outcry against tobacco companies. Besides, the Andrés Pastrana administration appointed a new national tax and customs director, the remarkable Fanny Kertzman, who was bent on attacking contraband. As a result, the main tobacco companies have taken measures to control their sales to money launderers and have made a deal with the Colombian government to prevent cigarette contraband.

if society condones such transactions. In Bolivian, Colombian, and Peruvian cities, contraband has been sold openly for years in some clearly limited zones or neighborhoods. In these cases, the need to hide these assets decreases because the government will find it very difficult to expropriate a large number of small traders. In spite of this, these assets are illegal, and their owners cannot justify them as generated by legal economic activities.

The structure of the Andean economies also imposes important restrictions on the use of the illegal capital once it is in the country. Indeed, one of the problems faced by Andean traffickers is that the "Laundromat" is small. In these countries, people who launder significant amounts of capital become clearly conspicuous and easy to identify. This makes it difficult and costly to launder large amounts of capital. Rocha (1997) has shown that the Colombian economy is very vulnerable to illegal capital precisely because it is difficult to launder large amounts. As was noted in chapter 5, all Bolivian analysts who estimate the size of the country's illegal industry assume that significant proportions of traffickers' illegal profits are not brought back into the country because of "lack of investment opportunities." Perhaps another reason is that if they do it, everybody will identify them and then they will have to face very high capital protection costs.

Environmental Effects

Illicit drugs crops and antidrug policies have important environmental effects. Unfortunately, studies on these environmental issues are few and far between and leave many important questions unanswered.

A substantial proportion of the coca and poppy crop expansion in the Andean countries has been done at the expense of primary tropical forests. Low-altitude humid forests have been destroyed to plant coca, and high-altitude forests have been cut to plant opium poppies. The environmental loss exceeds the area planted with illegal crops because for each hectare of coca or poppy peasants cut down 3 or 4 hectares of forest.

Illegal crops have other negative effects on the environment. Peasants use smuggled herbicides and fertilizers that are banned in the United States and Europe because of their damaging effects on the environment or the peasants' health. Chemicals used to refine drugs are frequently stored without concern for safety and can leak into the environment. One of the worst practices observed was hiding chemical containers in rivers to avoid detection

(S. Uribe 1997). After chemicals are used or when law-enforcement forces approach, peasants are known to throw them on the ground in an attempt to destroy criminal evidence, contaminating underground water supply, or to dump them into rivers and streams, causing much damage.

The destruction of high-altitude forests has extremely negative effects on the water supply. Indeed, parts of the Andes that have been singled out for their great abundance of water are at risk of losing this most valuable resource. A high-altitude tropical forest is extremely difficult to recuperate once it is lost. This problem is particularly important in Colombia where opium poppy crops grow.

Some antidrug policies also cause environmental damage. This has been a strong argument against eradication and aerial spraying in all illegal-crop-producing countries. The herbicides used in eradication campaigns, such as glisofate (sold in the United States under the Roundup brand), have many agricultural uses and are considered rather mild. However, when they are used to spray coca, they are applied in a way for which they were not designed or mixed with other ingredients that make them more damaging. Furthermore, it is probable that the main negative ecological effect of eradication does not take place in the eradicated areas themselves but in others. As was shown in chapter 4, the history of illegal plantings in Latin America shows that eradication causes crop displacements. If this happens, one by-product of eradication is further deforestation!

Unfortunately, there are many unanswered questions about the environmental effects of illegal drugs and the policies to fight them. Three of the main unresolved issues are as follows. First, there is no doubt that without illegal crops peasants would still migrate to unsettled rural areas because of population increases and economic difficulties. It is not known what proportions of the migration and environmental damage are due to drugs. Second, the lands where coca grows are ecologically very fragile, and coca is an excellent plant for them. Most other crops exhaust those lands at a very fast rate. It actually may be argued that planting coca is a way to minimize ecological damage, but the magnitudes of the differences in ecological impact of various crops are not known. Third, land reform in nonillicit crop regions is frequently mentioned as a policy to prevent migration to virgin areas, but there is no knowledge about how effective this policy could be.

To conclude, the environmental effects of illegal crops and antidrug policies are grave, but there has been little research and there are many "black boxes" and unknowns about them. As will be shown below, many difficulties in the study of this topic stem from the highly political implications of any conclusion. The lack of sensible debate on the environmental effects of illicit drugs and antidrug policies forebodes bad effects on the environment, which is likely to be one of the main victims of both the drug industry and the "war on drugs." Indeed, both are important contributors to the deforestation of the Amazon basin and the high Andean forests.

Social and Political Effects

The illegal drug industry has had a profound and complex influence in the Andean countries and many important social and political effects. The list of possible social and political effects is long and includes, among others, (1) changes in values that include increased materialism and consumerism, the search for quick profits, increased display of wealth as status symbols, and disregard for the effects of individual actions on the rest of humanity; (2) other behavioral changes, including the increased use of violence to solve conflicts and to obtain individual goals; (3) more government and private-sector corruption; and (4), as is argued elsewhere (Thoumi 1995d), the growth of the illegal industry as a catalyst that accelerated the weakening of the Colombian state and traditional social controls.

Unfortunately, it is easy to agree about the importance of these effects but it is very difficult to establish and to measure their exact causality. The rest of this section explores the relationship between illegal drugs and corruption.

Illegal Drugs and Corruption

It is frequently argued that the development of the illegal drug industry in a country leads to a substantial increase in corruption. But the relationship between illegal drugs and corruption is difficult to determine clearly, for at least four reasons. First, there is no consensus on a definition of corruption.

Second, the concept of corruption is difficult to measure, and its size, scope, importance, causes, and consequences are difficult to establish. As was shown in previous chapters, the same can be said about the illegal drug industry.

Third, the relationship between illegal drugs and corruption is circular: Corruption may encourage the development of illegal drug activities, and vice versa. Fourth, corruption and drug trafficking are generally symptomatic of deeper social problems and are frequently the result of processes that delegitimize the political system and weaken civil institutions, and of the lack of bridging social capital and trust within a society.

The Nature of Corruption

Corruption can be and is defined in many ways, partly because it is a concept shrouded with cultural elements and because political science does not have a unifying paradigm that allows for a consensus. Perhaps for these reasons, many authors just discuss corruption without defining it. Indeed, in many cases corruption is treated as something that does not need to be defined but rather as a phenomenon that "you recognize when you see it."

Corruption was not a frequent research topic among academics before the late 1960s. In recent years, the academic literature on corruption has grown significantly. Most studies limit corruption to the public sector and define it either as a "public service misused for private gain, the abuse of government as a 'bounty' to be distributed among a privileged group, or as public sector behaviors that benefit private individuals, harming social welfare" (Restrepo 1994, 1997). Bardhan (1997) and the World Bank (1997) used a simpler approach and defined corruption as "the use of public office for private gain."

Following these definitions, corrupt actions often break laws, as in the case of public servants who receive "commissions" or "fees" for performing their services. In other cases, corruption can exist without being accompanied by any law's violation. For example, a public-sector employee can assign a contract to a relative, friend, or fellow party member without charging a commission and complying with all legal requirements, but harming social welfare. In the first case, corruption implies breaking a law and an ethical norm; in the second, it could be argued that only an ethical norm is infringed on. Bardhan (1997) considered that it is possible for some individuals to participate in corrupt acts without breaking ethical norms—for example, when an official is bribed not to torture a prisoner. In this case, the briber may act in defense of an ethical norm. However, the potential torturer is breaking one. Unquestionably, corruption is always related to ethics.

Corruption is a generalized phenomenon encouraged by bureaucratic discretionary powers. Any decision made by a person or group within a governmental decision-making process that is not totally transparent is vulnerable to corruption. "Corruption occurs at the interface of the public and private sectors. Whenever a public official has discretionary power over distribution to the private sector of a benefit or cost, incentives for bribery are created" (Rose-Ackerman 1997, 31).

Most of the literature on corruption excludes many behaviors within the private sector that are similar to corrupt public ones. For example, a public employee who charges a commission is corrupt. A person who does the same in a private-sector transaction is not corrupt. This literature implicitly assumes that private-sector entrepreneurs and capitalists have strong incentives to protect their interests and establish control systems lacking in the public sector, and that for this reason the public justice and law enforcement systems may disregard private-sector corruption.

From an analytical point of view, it may be convenient to limit corruption to the public sector. But there is no doubt that public-sector corruption is related to fraud and other crimes in the private sector. When a society encourages or condones rapid private enrichment without caring for the origin of the capital, public-sector corruption and private-sector economic crime feed on each other. The acceptance of a bribe in the private sector by a person is a good indicator of his or her willingness to do so in the public one.

Some economists studying corruption depart from this tradition and look at corruption as something that can occur in any sector. Weinschelbaum (1998) used a game-theory model to study corruption in only private-sector transactions, partly because of difficulties modeling government behavior.[10]

It is possible to study corruption without making value judgments about it. But in many cases, ethics, morals, and culture condition studies and debates on the subject. The literature offers many examples in which corrupt behaviors are justified or condoned; the "weak" and "poor" who bribe a corrupt public official are described as "poor victims" and "good," but the "strong" and "rich" who do likewise are shown as "bad."

Others perceive corrupt public officials as mere followers of informal social norms in view of "very low" and "unjust" salaries that "force" public employees to charge "commissions" or a *mordida* (bite) for their services. For example, the Andean illegal drug industry literature is full of references to poor peasants who are "forced" by circumstances to produce coca and coca paste, and who "must" bribe local authorities (government officials, paramilitary groups, or guerrillas) so as to continue producing illegal goods in order to survive.[11] The gist of these approaches to the study of corruption make it very difficult to have constructive policy debates

---

[10]Profit maximization as a private-sector goal is easy to model, but the objective function of the government sector is difficult to define and to formulate mathematically.

[11]For examples on Bolivia, see Quiroga (1990); on Peru, see Morales (1989); and on Colombia, see Cano-Isaza (1997), Santos-Calderón (1989), Tovar (1994), and Vargas and Barragán (1995).

between those who have different opinions because the discussion easily drifts into a question of morals and values.

As was noted, corruption studies in the Andean countries are scarce. Cepeda's (1994b, 1997) study of Colombia was a comprehensive attempt to deal with this issue.[12] It included theoretical discussions of corruption, case studies surveying five important government agencies, as well as public education, evaluation of red tape procedures (*tramitología*), citizens' perceptions of corruption, and discussions of several policy strategies. As part of this study, Restrepo (1994, 1997) surveyed corruption literature.

---

[12]This study's publication has been a saga that illustrates the importance of ethics, morals, and institutions in defining corruption and the politics involved in dealing with it. The study was sponsored by the Colombian Controller's Office. Manuel F. Becerra, the controller, who served a sentence for illicit enrichment, introduced the 1994 volume at the time. Furthermore, the coordinator of that volume thanks "Doctor Fernando Botero-Zea, one of the pioneers of the study of corruption in Colombia, who several years ago taught a course on the subject at the Universidad de Los Andes" (Cepeda 1994a, xiv). Botero-Zea, Ernesto Samper's 1994 campaign director, was accused of receiving $6 million from the Cali "cartel." The Comptroller's Office withdrew this volume from circulation soon after its publication.

An expanded volume was reissued in 1997 with a somewhat different title. This volume does not have Becerra's introduction or the references to Botero. In the new introduction, dated June 1995, Fernando Cepeda praises Samper's government for implementing at least six important anticorruption strategies and defends it aggressively against well-known drug-money campaign funding accusations: "Samper's administration, starting before its inauguration on August 7, 1994, established ethical controls in his electoral campaign that included a campaign code of ethics, an ethics investigator ('fiscal') and during the campaign he publicly expelled several political leaders. He presented to Congress an anti-corruption bill that he defended during the campaign. His election opponent (Andrés Pastrana) paradoxically questioned the efficacy and sincerity of these measures five days before and immediately after the victory. In his concession speech to Ernesto Samper he made some insinuations, made more explicit two days later in a press conference, casting a shadow of doubt that gravely hurt relations of Colombia with the United States and other countries. The Samper administration's political commitment to fight drugs and corruption yielded overwhelming facts that in less than a year after the victory cleared those suspicions that never should have been raised. They were the result of the perverse environment product of the deals and misbehaviors linked to the drug world. This environment promotes rumors, mistrust, insinuations, falsehoods, and distortions that stress human relations and open a space for anyone that feels with a right to say or hint anything to harm or destroy the image or career of a person as part of a game or a playful and wicked exercise" (Cepeda 1997, xvi–xvii).

It is difficult to understand why Cepeda, who wrote this introduction in 1995, did not change it before the book was printed on February 1997 after the blatant failure of Samper's anticorruption campaign measures and the confirmation of widespread drug trafficker funding of his campaign.

She defined corruption as "a consensual exchange involving at least two capable parties—one of which holds a powerful position that is used in that person's self-interest—who are aware of the fact that they are breaking the rules or values that support the general interest of a system or society" (Restrepo 1994, 3).

This definition illustrates some problems posed by the concept of corruption. To begin with, it assumes that society is sufficiently cohesive so that in it exists a consensus about the common good. Colombia is a stratified, fragmented, and deeply individualist society with little social cohesion or trust. What groups or individuals consider to be to their personal benefit can conflict directly with that of other groups, whether individuals or the majority of the population. In this case, how and who defines the "general interest of a system or society"? Because of a lack of a social consensus, the definition of corruption for one part of society may differ substantially from that accepted by other groups. For instance, contraband in Colombia has been widespread for at least four decades, and bribes of custom officials have been institutionalized. Those involved in contraband consider their behaviors to be accepted by social norms, and most Colombians buy contraband without thinking of themselves as being corrupt. But for other segments of the population (perhaps a minority), these are viewed as corrupt behaviors.

Furthermore, some have argued that corruption is benign and even necessary under some circumstances. Studies of the informal Latin American sector (De Soto 1986; Tokman 1992) argued that some forms of corruption result from the informal sector's overregulation. In this case, many socially productive economic activities could not take place without corruption. In this instance, what represents corruption for some is an economic survival strategy for others. Following this line of thought, laws and regulations can be classified as "good" and "bad," and breaking "bad" laws is "good." Yet the fact that there is no way to get entrepreneurs to break only "bad" laws and comply with "good" ones is problematic. Once it is perceived as justified to break one economic regulation or law, the probability that economic actors will accept the violation of other laws becomes very high.

Bardhan (1997) surveyed the literature on the costs and benefits of corruption and concluded that under some circumstances, in the short run, corruption can "grease the machine" and facilitate economic transactions and activities, whereas in the medium and long runs its negative effects are very likely to outweigh positive ones. This means that in the long run corruption will strain economic growth.

Restrepo's (1994) definition also highlights other important aspects of corruption. What a particular society considers corruption varies over time and depends on prevailing values and political institutions, as well as on social ethics and morals. The concepts of corruption that appear in the current literature tend to reflect the values and political systems of advanced industrial societies (Restrepo 1994, 5–12). Today, the importance of institutions and culture in determining corruption is widely accepted. In reference to bureaucratic bribes, Rose-Ackerman (1997, 31) stated: "Every state must decide when to legalize such payments and when to label them illegal corruption. The proper link between money and politics is a deep one and will be resolved differently by different countries."

The adoption by a poor society of anticorruption policies developed in rich ones can cause great difficulties. According to conventional wisdom, for example, low public-sector salaries are a cause of corruption, and therefore they should be raised to "decent" levels. It might be true that low salaries encourage corruption, but in most countries it is impossible to pay decent public-sector salaries without increasing overall poverty.

For example, in the Andean countries, a minimum decent salary may be defined as the equivalent, in real terms, of $20,000 to $30,000 a year. Because per capita income in Bolivia, Colombia, Ecuador, and Peru is at or below $2,000, one is talking about salaries at least ten times larger (and in most cases much higher) than per capita incomes.[13] On the one hand, these would be impossible to fund with the regular budget so that the public-sector employees' expectations would be unmet. On the other hand, even if it were politically viable for the government to raise the required funds, the limited size of the country's gross national product would force significant sectors of the population to receive much lower real salaries. In this particular situation, corruption is a structural result of the gap between real income expectations and low average productivity in a particular country.

Institutional, historical, and cultural differences across countries also make it difficult, if not impossible, to apply a unique definition of corruption across countries. Latin America has had an authoritarian tradition accompanied by an ethics of inequality (Kalmanovitz 1989). These have led to extensive power abuse by national and local leaders. Applying

---

[13]In the United States, a similar salary ten times the country per capita income would be more than $250,000 a year!

Restrepo's (1994, 3) definition of corruption, one must conclude that leaders and elites who do not seek to improve social welfare are corrupt. The same can be said of many actions and measures that have led to their enrichment.

The case of past Latin American dictators provides a good illustration of the difficulty of applying a single definition of corruption in all political contexts. Dictators of small Central American and Caribbean countries of the 1950s and 1960s managed their countries' economies as if they were their own haciendas and factories to be exploited for their private benefit. For example, in the Dominican Republic "General Rafael Leonidas Trujillo Molina amassed a large fortune by coaxing entrepreneurs into making him a business partner on favorable terms, receiving portions of their assets as gifts, and so on" (Thoumi 1991, 101). The difference between the private and public sectors in this and other countries was impossible to establish, so the dictator and his close allies had many "private" firms that benefited directly from government policies, which he formulated and implemented. When Trujillo fell, all his properties were confiscated and put together under a large official financial conglomerate that became "the people's inheritance."

Moreover, predatory capitalism and authoritarian traditions prevailed in the Dominican Republic, and the conglomerate's firms were exploited and decapitalized mercilessly by the political parties and politicians that controlled government. In the end, they became white elephants that generated large government deficits (Thoumi 1991, 103). Ironically, dictatorial corruption required a minimum of economic efficiency and reasonable management because the dictator sought large profits but "democratic" corruption bankrupted those firms because most managers transferred funds to their parties or their own pockets. Something very similar happened during the 1990s in Colombia, where fiscal decentralization led large sums to be transferred to many municipalities with weak institutions, and powerful local groups ended up distributing the official largesse.[14]

Authoritarianism has deep roots in the Andes, where governments have not had a tradition of accountability. At best, they have to account for their actions to powerful economic groups but are not accountable to the

---

[14]Investigative journalistic reports and daily news during 1998, 1999, and 2000 highlight the fleecing of public funds that is currently going on in Colombia in spite of gallant efforts of the Prosecutor General's (Fiscalía) Office.

general public, and individuals lack mediating institutions that could exact government accountability.[15]

It can be argued that in traditional predemocratic systems the leaders' actions are not corrupt because prevailing social values allow them to profit from their positions. The point is just that in patrimonial and clientelistic political systems the enrichment of those in power by the use of power is a normal way of life. Corruption makes sense only when private benefit is gained through the abuse of power within a democratic context.

All Latin American countries are evolving from traditional authoritarian systems and developing new institutions and political and economic systems. In these countries, the roles of the state, political parties, and the various forms of private property (capitalist, communal, cooperative) are not clearly established. Many governments have clear ideas about policies and reforms to be implemented, but in many cases the social consensus on them is weak. In many of these countries, corruption can become a big obstacle for democratic development, for it is a great obstacle to accountability.

Corruption and Countries' Propensity toward Corruption

Some societies are more prone to corruption than others. Restrepo (1994, 26–27) argued three factors promote corruption in a society. The first is when in a command economy corruption becomes necessary for it to function "like in the old Soviet Union and today's Cuba." The second is when corruption is functional for a market economy and economic efficiency requires corruption. The third is "when a society has had very rapid economic, political and social changes that have not benefited large sections of the population and thus, have not been legitimized by the society."

The first two factors are clear. The third one is not. There is no question that the greater the regime's legitimacy, the weaker the society's propensity toward corruption. The point is, however, that greater legitimacy can be achieved even if income inequality and concentration increase. For example, Chile's experience under Augusto Pinochet suggests that economic stability and drastic inflation decline after economic crises

---

[15]Significantly, Spanish does not have a word for "accountability." The Inter-American Accounting Association and the U.S. Agency for International Development have proposed using *respondabilidad*, a term that has not caught on in spite of the agency's publication of a newsletter with the name *Respondabilidad: Anti-Corrupción*.

and hyperinflation can be legitimating even if they are accompanied by in-come-concentrating economic growth.

It is also possible to list other characteristics that increase a society's propensity toward corruption. The first is the size of the "bounty" relative to total gross national product and income per capita. Second, corruption is dynamic. Changes in corruption are associated with past corruption levels and changes. The greater and more widespread the corruption in a society, the more costly it is for individuals not to become corrupt. High levels of corruption tend to generate even greater corruption.[16] Third, the greater the social segmentation and group differences, the stronger the loyalties to family, clan, and other minor social groups as opposed to the country or nation, the greater the corruption propensity. Fourth, the higher the level of trust and social solidarity, the lower the propensity toward corruption. Fifth, the stronger the authoritarian tradition of a society, the more difficult it is to generate accountability systems to control corrup-tion. This list is not exhaustive, but it highlights some factors that make societies vulnerable to corruption.

Corruption is multidimensional and complex, which makes it necessary to study various types. Nadelmann (1993, 266–86) developed a useful ty-pology to classify various forms of corruption and distinguished three kinds: individual, organizational, and moral:

> The typology of individual corruption distinguishes corrupt officials by the degree of complicity in criminal activity. The least corrupt is best described as a passive cooperator, the moderately corrupt is typically a facilitator, and the most corrupt is the initiator. At one end of this con-tinuum is the honest police officer who cooperates only because his or her family has been threatened. At the other end is the drug dealing po-lice chief, general or dictator. … [At the organizational level, one can distinguish] the organizational networks of corrupt officials by size, so-phistication and hierarchical structure. At one end of this continuum is corruption that may be deemed sporadic. In the middle are two forms of what may be termed systemic corruption. And at the other end is what may be called institutionalized corruption. (Nadelmann 1993, 267–69)

---

[16]Bardhan (1997) explained in detail Andvig and Moene's (1990) model, which showed that when there are many dishonest people in a society, the cost of honesty in-creases for everyone, and those who acted honestly in the past will tend to act dishon-estly. Thoumi (1987) argued that Colombia had fallen into a "dishonesty trap" from which it is very difficult to escape.

Sporadic corruption is not part of a generalized pattern and involves public employees who receive bribes individually or as part of small groups. Systemic corruption is pervasive and may be unorganized or organized. The difference between these two is that in organized corruption there is a hierarchical payoff system and low-level workers give most of the bribes collected to their superiors. In a particular country, there may be several of these "payoff cones." In the case of disorganized systemic corruption, these cones do not appear. "When all 'payoff cones' fall within the umbrella of a centralized national 'payoff cone,' or when only one 'payoff cone' exists for the entire country, the nation may be said to have institutionalized corruption" (Nadelmann 1993, 270).

Bardhan (1997) classifies corruption according to its degree of centralization. When corruption is centralized, one single government agent negotiates bribes, and the quid pro quo is highly certain to occur. When government decision making is decentralized and many agencies can collect bribes, the bribing procedure is more complex and the bribing results are more uncertain. These factors lead to significantly higher economic welfare losses under decentralized than centralized corruption.

Corruption and Politics in the Andes

Two aspects of the Andean narcotics industry have contributed most significantly to political corruption in the region. One is the industry's sheer size. Independent of the estimates used, the industry's revenues are simply very large relative to the incomes and salaries of all public officials. A related problem is that traffickers need to buy political support to operate the industry and launder their vast earnings in relatively small economies, but the corrupting effects of the industry are related to the industry's structure in each country.

Large-scale transfers of funds and investments are necessarily conspicuous in such a setting, and the dominant elites must acquiesce. As has been observed elsewhere,

> for the most part the drug cartels require only local support networks to allow them to grow coca and poppies and to manufacture and export drugs. However, when it comes to laundering money these cartels often need to win favor with ranking officials of the central government. Such favor affords protection from the law. The reason that drug cartels have turned to corrupting high-level government officials involves

the Colombian economy's modest capacity for absorbing and hiding illegal funds. (Thoumi 1997a, 95)

A third factor that conditions the illegal industry's corrupting effect is
the ability of traffickers to collaborate in influencing government policy,
the law enforcement environment, and the political system in general. The
stronger and more sophisticated their organizations and the more willing
to resort to force and violence, the easier for them to corrupt the political
establishment.

There is no doubt that the polities of the Andean countries are vulnerable to the illegal drug industry's power. However, differences in the industry's size and structure and in each country's institutional strengths and
weaknesses determine how vulnerable each country's polity is to the industry. Because of these differences, no direct correlation exists between
corruption indexes and drugs. It is well recognized that these indexes are
subjective and are based on the perceived corruption by a group of (mainly
foreign) entrepreneurs (Bardhan 1997). Still, as was noted in chapter 3,
Transparency International's corruption index is totally unrelated to the
degree of development of the illegal drug industry in the Andes.[17] The next
chapters will attempt to throw some light on the differences between corruption and illegal drug development.

---

[17]Bardhan (1997) presented other corruption indexes for earlier years that confirm
this point.

7

The Illegal Drug Industry's Effects in Colombia

The illegal drug industry's effects in Colombia have been deeper and wider than in any other Andean country. The list of the effects of the industry's growth is long. It includes the accumulation of very quick and large individual fortunes that changed the power structure and the nature of the elite in many regions,[1] regional economic booms and busts, an overvalued currency, substantial increases in contraband incentives, rural land tenancy concentration and government corruption, conflicts with the United States, a strengthened guerrilla movement, the establishment of paramilitary organizations, a substantial increase in violence, and the funding of the main actors in the violent conflict experienced by the country. This is only a partial list because the industry undoubtedly has had additional effects.

---

[1]The folk culture recognized this from the early 1970s, when drug traffickers were referred to as "magicians."

Besides the large number of possible effects, they can be very complex and difficult to identify and measure. This chapter surveys the available evidence, and it discusses and evaluates some of the main effects of the industry.

Economic Effects

As was discussed in chapter 6, the economic effects of the illegal drug industry are complex. These effects depend, at least, on which social groups profit from the illegal activity, on the structure of the economy, on the difficulty or easiness of laundering money, on the way in which illegal assets are laundered, and on government policies and the government's ability to implement them.

Money-Laundering Constraints and Effects

Asset and income laundering in Colombia has some peculiar characteristics. As was noted above, money laundering itself is a relatively new policy issue, and it was not considered a crime in many countries. Following an old Spanish legal tradition, Colombia had long-standing legislation against "illicit enrichment," but it was not "typified,"[2] and thus it was unenforceable. Only in the mid-1990s did Colombia develop legislation that typified asset laundering as a crime (Garzón 1997).[3]

As was argued in chapter 5, breaking multiple economic laws and regulations has long been common and considered legitimate in Colombia. Indeed, the government has accepted this reality and has periodically taken measures to adapt to it. Since 1974, there have been more than fifteen tax reforms, many of which have included ample amnesties implicitly acknowledging the existence of dirty capital and encouraging capital dirtying because they have created the expectation of further amnesties that would allow capital laundering if needed.

---

[2]I.e., the specifics of what constituted a crime, what proofs are needed, and other technical legal aspects required to apply the law were not established.

[3]The late development of the anti-laundering legislation is not unique to Colombia. Indeed, during the past decade, the promotion of this type of legislation has been one of the main activities of the Organization of American States's Inter-American Commission for Drug Abuse Control (CICAD) and the Global Program Against Money Laundering of the United Nations Office of Drug Control and Crime Prevention.

As was noted in chapter 6, drug money laundering requires several steps. First, foreign currency has to be brought to the country, converted into local currency, and then invested. In spite of a legal and institutional environment conducive to money and asset laundering, the Colombian economy has many structural constraints on those activities. As was noted above, all channels to bring in illegal foreign exchange are limited.

Until exchange controls were eliminated in 1991, the Colombian parallel foreign exchange market was small and highly volatile; at any time, a few million dollars had significant effects on the exchange rate. That the size of this market is a money-laundering restriction is reflected in the fact that for long periods of time the parallel exchange rate has remained below the official one, a unique case in the world.

Detailed work by Rocha (1997) on illegal flows hidden in the current account of the balance of payments indicated that the value of "technical contraband" (underinvoicing imports and overinvoicing exports) plus Central Bank foreign exchange purchases of fake labor and other remittances—to be modest—averaged about $1 billion a year until the mid-1990s.[4]

Similar work by Steiner (1997, 87–88) argued that technical contraband and the tourism account in the balance of payments do not appear to have been used to launder money because their trends are stable through time and their levels are not out of line with those of other countries. Conversely, he also concluded that expatriates' remittances and contraband do appear to have been widely used to bring in illegal drug money into the country. His estimates indicated that contraband could have accounted for about $1.5 billion a year and that there were other difficult-to-explain flows of about $1.2 billion during the period 1990–92 and of $800 million a year from then until 1996. Steiner was cautious in attributing all these sums to the illegal drug industry because that is not the only source of funding for contraband and difficult-to-explain flows. However, he concluded that most of the income generated by Colombian traffickers abroad during the 1990s likely was repatriated.

---

[4]Since the mid-1970s, the Central Bank has frequently changed its foreign exchange purchase policies. When the bank eased its purchase requirements, it was said that it "opened its sinister window"—and vice versa when it increased them. These changes were particularly important before 1991, when the country had strict foreign exchange controls. Since then, under a system in which there is a legal parallel market, the sinister window has lost its importance.

The Colombian government has intermittently issued foreign debt bonds sold in foreign currency, but redeemable in pesos or foreign currency at the owners' will, a practice that began in about 1975. These bonds are issued to the bearer, and the interest and possible capital gains are exempted from Colombian taxes.[5] Bonds issues approved by Law 55 of 1992, Decree 700 of 1994, and Decree 4308 of 1995 fell into this category. These issues were not large. The one in 1995 was for only $80 million. Whoever bought these bonds abroad can use them to convert foreign exchange into pesos, making the state a possible accomplice in a money-laundering operation (Thoumi 1996).

Until the late 1990s, drug inflows used to finance capital flight were also likely to have been small. Because in Colombia the return on capital was high and the risk of expropriation by the state very low, capital flight was not significant. Indeed, capital flight was a vehicle to obtain "revolution and kidnapping" insurance, because in Colombia the risk of expropriation by insurgent forces and common criminal organizations has been much greater than by the state. The deterioration of the armed conflict from 1999 on has induced much capital flight.

Once illegal capital was brought to the country and converted into pesos, it had to be used domestically. It was reported that there were three main investment channels for illegal funds brought into Colombia: the purchase of existing firms, and both urban and rural real estate purchases. These and their limits are discussed below.

The Colombian private sector developed in the midst of a lack of trust among market participants, high transaction costs, and uncertain and weak property rights. Moreover, there is no impartial judge or referee to enforce contracts and solve conflicts. The structure of the private sector reflects these characteristics. The public sector's failure to provide effective contract enforcement mechanisms is a strong incentive to integrate vertically and to form economic conglomerates that include financial, manufacturing, advertising, marketing, and retailing firms. These conglomerates allow for many transactions within the group that are in keeping with its internal contract enforcement systems.

Some of these groups have become monopolists in some markets. But contrary to what took place in the United States in the nineteenth century, their rents are not just monopolistic; they also result from the

---

[5]It seems that these bonds were implicitly designed to be sold to Colombians who had taken capital out of the country, legitimating exchange control evasion.

entrepreneurs' ability to transact within the conglomerates at lower costs than their competitors (Thoumi 1996).[6]

The development of economic conglomerates is a private-sector reaction to the market environment in which it operates. The existence of these conglomerates has been a major obstacle to the development of a meaningful stock market because almost all companies whose shares are traded on the stock exchange are controlled by conglomerates, but they also have protected large parts of the formal sector from being penetrated by drug capital. Stock purchases are not attractive to drug entrepreneurs, foreign mutual funds, or many domestic investors because the firms are closed companies managed following the strategy of the conglomerate that controls them.[7] Large investments have to be made only in agreement with the conglomerate owners and are very difficult to accomplish through the stock exchange. To launder large quantities using any stock traded on the stock exchange, it is necessary to have the complicity of the financial conglomerates that would have a lot to lose by doing so.

Urban real estate has been used to launder drug capital, but the process is not as simple as most people suspect.[8] In Colombia, it is very common to record real estate transactions at values substantially below the real prices.[9] This practice allows buyers to transfer hidden capital to sellers. If illegal drug funds are used to finance a building project that is sold when finished and deeds are recorded at lower than real values, the buyers launder capital through the purchase. In this case, the drug industry that finances the project launders somebody else's dirty capital!

Thus, to launder using real estate, the traffickers have strong incentives to keep the properties in their possession or in the hands of front men (*testaferros*). Urban real estate has been used to launder drug money, but

---

[6]In spite of some monopolistic positions, they confronted price restraints either from actual or possible imports or from price controls. E.g., for a long time the core of the main financial conglomerate was a beer monopoly, but price controls kept beer prices in Colombia among the lowest in the world.

[7]This is an important reason why very few Colombian households invest in the stock market and why 90 percent or more of the transactions on the Colombian stock exchange are of bonds.

[8]Giraldo (1990) detected a substantial decline in capital market financing of new construction projects during the 1980s, a phenomenon related to the growth of the illegal drug industry.

[9]To prevent this, the Colombian legislation does not permit real estate transactions to be recorded below the assessed value of the property. However, in most cases, the assessed values have substantially lagged behind the real ones.

it has limitations because the cost of social support networks and front men increases with size and limits the number of properties that can remain in the hands of drug traffickers.[10] It should be acknowledged, however, that it is possible to launder in real estate if the capital is used to fund real estate construction and recycled into new projects. After this "layering" has been repeated several times, the drug entrepreneurs can argue that their capital comes from real estate ventures and not from drug trafficking. This is a feasible but complex laundering method, and it depends on high, continuous demand for new buildings.[11] These characteristics of urban real estate money laundering imply that real estate is a good laundering venue for small traffickers who buy residences and a few investment properties for themselves and their extended families, but that it is a less efficient venue for laundering very large amounts.

Drug money has also flown into rural land. Illegal entrepreneurs or their *testaferros* have bought large tracks of land, mainly in areas of recent settlement where property rights and state presence are weak.[12] These purchases frequently took place in areas of strong guerrilla activity where drug entrepreneurs contributed to the creation of self-defense paramilitary groups that fought the guerrillas raising land values. Rough estimates (Reyes 1997) indicate that illegal drug money has been used to purchase about 4 to 5 million hectares of grazing land. These include a large proportion of the best grazing land available in the country. Further investments are likely to be smaller than in the past because available lands are of lower quality. Legislation that facilitates land expropriation has added a disincentive to further land purchases by drug entrepreneurs.

Money laundering in Colombia was done rather openly during the 1970s and 1980s. In a sense, it was not laundering, because traffickers did not necessarily try to hide the origin on the funds. They simply invested excess profits from their illegal business. The government began to pass anti-money-laundering legislation in response to the narcoterrorism of 1989 and early 1990s. Throughout the 1990s, the government perfected

---

[10]There are many reports about the several hundred apartments that the Cali cartel had in that city. Most of them were vacant. One has to wonder how many more would have been purchased if they had not been captured; chances are, very few, because they simply were an economic waste.

[11]The real estate boom in urban real estate during the 1990s could have been partially attributed to this process.

[12]Reyes (1997) has given a detailed picture of this process.

this legislation and developed a corresponding jurisprudence. By the end of the 1990s, money laundering was a constant political issue, and a large number of properties had been confiscated—although final expropriation has been unsuccessful (see chapter 10).

Macroeconomic Effects

The macroeconomic effects of the illegal drug industry are also complex. There is no doubt that the industry increased the supply of foreign exchange and that it had similar effects to other export booms. In contrast with Latin American countries of similar and larger size, Colombia has distinguished itself by avoiding populist governments, runaway fiscal deficits, and hyperinflation periods characteristic of those countries until the 1990s (Urrutia 1991). Indeed, until the late 1990s, Colombian macroeconomic management was remarkably stable, the country was able to cope with export booms and busts relatively well, and it was the only one in the region that had avoided the Latin American debt crisis of the 1980s.

The increased supply of foreign exchange generated by the illegal drug industry had different effects in Colombia than in the rest of the region because they were less direct. As was noted above, because most profits are made in the smuggling stage, the amount needed to pay for illegal exports is only a small proportion of total export revenues. This makes drug capital inflows similar to other capital inflows that are responsive to interest-rate differentials between Colombia and the international markets, mainly the U.S. one, and to the devaluation expectations in Colombia (Urrutia and Pontón 1993).

Colombian macroeconomic policies changed significantly in 1990 when the country engaged itself in an economic liberalization process similar to that followed by other Latin American countries. There were seven main economic policy changes:[13]

- The first was the elimination of exchange controls that had originally been put in place as far back as in 1931 and tightened in 1967. These changes allowed Colombians to have financial accounts and borrow abroad and legalized the parallel foreign exchange market.
- Second was a decline in import tariffs and the elimination of import quotas and of most import licenses.

[13]See Thoumi (1997a) for a detailed discussion of these events.

- Third, the labor market was liberalized, making it easier to lay off and fire workers.
- Fourth was the establishment of a program to privatize publicly owned companies, including banks that had been purchased by the government during a financial crisis in the early 1980s.
- Fifth was the promotion of direct foreign investment.
- Sixth was the promotion of private retirement funds as an alternative to public social security.
- Seventh was a decentralization program that transferred a large proportion of central government revenues to local governments that were supposed to assume new responsibilities.

Complementary measures included a modernization program for the judicial system, development of simpler ways to enforce contracts, support of alternative development programs in coca-growing areas (and later in poppy-growing regions), reform of the state bidding systems, and other measures to eliminate privileges and corruption. All these changes were designed to create a modern capitalist society and had the support of the Inter-American Development Bank, the International Monetary Fund, the World Bank, and several U.S. government agencies.

After these policy changes, Colombia experienced large foreign capital inflows. At issue is what caused the inflows. The opening of the economy in other Latin American countries had also led to similar capital inflows. Colombia's opening and privatization was milder than in the rest of Latin America—because state ownership was limited and contraband had already de facto opened the economy—and the capital inflow was due mainly to other policy changes. The 1991 Constitution led to a dramatic increase in government spending due mainly to the transfers of central government funds to local governments that were not accompanied by similar reductions in central government expenditures. These changes generated large government deficits, which were funded with new taxes, the sale of state enterprises, and large increases in domestic and external debt (Kalmanovitz 2001).

In late 1994, the U.S. Drug Enforcement Administration (DEA), wary of the growing international influence of Colombia's illegal drug industry, argued in a study that Colombia's new economic policies had provided the illegal industry with inroads into the international marketplace that would make it much more difficult to monitor and control (DEA 1994). DEA officials insisted on four points:

- First, the elimination of exchange controls made it easier to bring large sums of drug money into the country disguised as foreign investment capital.
- Second, the privatization of publicly owned banks allowed drug lords to purchase these banks and develop an ostensibly legitimate infrastructure through which to hide and launder capital.
- Third, officials warned that Colombia lacked restrictive money-laundering laws, which made it easy for drug money to enter the country and penetrate the national economy.
- Fourth, U.S. officials maintained that the recent construction boom experienced in the country "has been financed primarily by large investments using drug proceeds."

The Colombian government's response to the DEA study was quite forceful (Banco de la República 1994). It argued that the DEA's paper "was without any empirical and theoretical basis,"[14] was biased against the government, contradicted many "statements from other U.S. agencies and the Federal government," and "expresses implicitly its preference for a heavily nationalized economy with very little space for the private sector." But six important points were raised by the government: (1) The large capital inflows received by Colombia had occurred in all Latin American countries that had followed similar policies. (2) Earlier controls had not prevented drug money from coming into the country. (3) Liberalization did not eliminate the requirement to register capital brought into the country. (4) The construction boom was being financed by a significant increase in credits from savings and loan associations. (5) The financial system liberalization required "financial institutions to get to know their customers and carry out direct surveillance of transactions." (6) The privatization of financial institutions had been under the surveillance of the banking superintendent and no drug money had been detected in bank purchases.

This debate illustrates the difficulty of determining strong macroeconomic causality relations.[15] On the one hand, it is likely that economic

---

[14]Indeed, the DEA does not have a strong economics department, and its paper lacked the rigor of World Bank or International Monetary Fund reports. Apparently, the author of the DEA paper was Donald Im, a young DEA economist. What is essentially the same DEA paper was presented under Im's (1994) name at a conference in November 1994.

[15]Urrutia and Pontón (1993) and O'Byrne and Reina (1993) are good examples of solid opposite views about the importance of illegal drug capital flows. The former researchers argued that these flows have not been very important. The latter argued the opposite.

liberalization programs facilitate money laundering. On the other hand, it is also true that illegal drug capital flows follow the same pattern as other capital movement and that the government has instituted systems to control illegal flows. However, within the Colombian environment of widespread acceptance of illegal economic activities, corruption, contraband, and a large underground economy, one has to question whether many of the Central Bank policies are likely to be effective.

The DEA's paper also illustrates the effects of placing illegal drug policies in a paramount position to which all other policies have to be sacrificed. Indeed, one of the main problems raised by antidrug policies anywhere is the sacrifice in other policies and human rights that they require.[16] The DEA's implicit request that Colombian macroeconomic policies should be shaped by the U.S. antidrug effort is a good example of the high costs that society must pay to achieve success following mostly repressive drug policies. In this case, following DEA's reasoning, Colombian's efforts to liberalize its economy should be sacrificed to other antidrug goals.

Structural Effects

Independent of the actual amount of foreign exchange brought into the country by drug entrepreneurs, and of its macroeconomic effects, there is no doubt that the impact of the industry on Colombia has been quite large. According to national accounts figures, the private-sector capital formation during the 1980s averaged $2.8 billion a year (Thoumi 1995d). Furthermore, any criminal organization exporting 50 or more tons of cocaine a year would have profits that until the late 1990s competed with those of the country's largest financial conglomerates.[17] After the 1999 economic crises, drug profits remained positive while those of several conglomerates fell into the red. Any estimate of the size and profits of the illegal drug industry, no matter how conservative, highlights the industry's

---

[16]The literature on these issues is substantial and growing. See, e.g., Balakar and Grinspoon (1984), McWilliams (1996), Husak (1992), and Peele (1989).

[17]A back-of-the-envelope estimate can place export profits net of transportation costs at about $10,000 per kilogram or $500 million per 50 tons. According to one estimate, in 1995 the four largest financial groups had profits of $530, $140, $480, and $190 million respectively. In 1999, several of these conglomerates have had losses while illegal drug profits continued ("Los Cuatro Grandes," *Semana*, April 30–May 7, 1996).

capacity to change the country's economic power structure (Thoumi 1995d).

Although it can be argued that the drug industry penetrated many economic activities, it cannot be argued that the performance of the Colombian economy improved because of drug income. Indeed, the rate of growth of Colombia's gross national product during the post-cocaine era (1980 on) through 1997 was about 3.2 percent, whereas it had averaged 5.5 percent during the 30 previous years. This decline cannot be explained by the 1980s' Latin American foreign debt crisis, which Colombia avoided, or by worse international terms of trade or other external conditions during the 1980s than during the three earlier decades (Thoumi 1995d). During the late 1990s, the performance of the Colombian economy declined sharply, and in 1999 it registered a decline of about 5 percent of gross domestic product (GDP). This was the first year since the end of World War II in which income fell.

It is commonly accepted, particularly outside Colombia, that the country's economy benefited from the large illegal drug revenues. This could be possible in the short run, but in the long run it is a mirage. Most Colombian economists who have studied this issue concur that on balance, the illegal drug industry had a negative effect on the performance of the Colombian economy. In particular, the industry acted as a catalyst that accelerated a process of "delegitimation of the regime" that has contributed to the country's stagnation (Thoumi 1995d).

This delegitimation process produced a sharp decline in trust, which increased transaction costs;[18] contributed to increased violence and impunity that induced "clean" capital flight as well as larger security costs; and promoted expectations of very rapid wealth accumulation that produced highly speculative investments, along with increases in bankruptcies, embezzlements, and so on. The increased level of criminality had a significant declining effect on the country's income growth rate. Indeed, Rubio (1996a, 32) found that "the cost of crime in terms of lost growth exceeded 2 percent per year, without including its longer term effects on factor productivity and capital formation."

Most economists agree that Colombia could have done quite well without the illegal drug economy. The country had a diversified economy, and before the growth of the illegal drug industry it generated a significant

---

[18]Earlier works (Thoumi 1995a, 1995d) identified the high level of transaction costs in Colombia. Recent work by Rubio (1996b) has confirmed this point.

amount of manufacturing and other exports. Its macroeconomic management has been very prudent and stable and, as was noted, it was the only
country in Latin America that avoided the 1980s' external debt crisis.
Earlier studies concluded that if drugs were to disappear, the worst-case
scenario would be a mild recession for a couple of years (Sarmiento 1990).
Furthermore, after the 1999 recession and the accentuation of the armed
conflict funded substantially with drug funds, there is no question that the
impact of the illegal drug industry on the Colombian economy has been
very negative and that it is necessary to eliminate it if sustained economic
growth is to be renewed.

During the 1990s, the final use of illicit revenues changed dramatically.
Those funds were used mainly to purchase real estate and some productive enterprises. Beginning in the early 1990s, the participation of guerrilla
and paramilitary organizations in the illegal trade increased substantially,
and drug revenues were used more and more to purchase weapons and pay
guerrilla and paramilitary personnel. This drug money has been used to destroy productive assets and has had a very negative effect on the economy.
Unfortunately, the effects of the illegal economy evolved from causing
regional and national booms in the 1970s and 1980s to becoming a main
cause of a social, political, and economic crisis from the late 1990s on
(Thoumi 2002).

Regional and Sectoral Effects

The impact of the illegal drug industry at the local level has been large
at times in cities like Barranquilla, where many marijuana exporters
were located, and Medellín, where a large proportion of the 1980s' cocaine
entrepreneurs lived. These cities experienced "Dutch disease" symptoms
when marijuana and cocaine were booming. Similar effects are evident in
coca-producing regions, where income boom-and-bust cycles follow coca
prices (Thoumi 1995d).

During the 1980s, the Medellín export syndicate invested heavily in
rural land in the Middle Magdalena Valley. This was a recently settled
region, where property rights were not well established, and where there
was a strong guerrilla presence. The drug investors promoted the establishment of "self-defense" paramilitary groups that fought the guerrillas
and attacked many who sympathized with the goal of a more egalitarian
society. During the 1990s, rural land investment continued to be made by
the drug industry.

Reyes (1997) showed that drug-funded rural land purchases have been large, though obviously accurate figures are impossible to obtain. In spite of measurement difficulties, he suggests that drug money had purchased about 4 to 5 million hectares, that is, about 10 percent of the country's grazing lands. Reyes's findings indicated that most purchases had been of large ranches, and that drug money had not penetrated *minifundia* or modern agricultural areas. Small purchases took place only in areas near cities or in tourist places, where land value increases were expected. However, these were minor. Reyes also found that those grazing lands are among the best ones of the country and are easy to administer. Thus, further purchases would be less attractive than those already made.

Other export syndicates followed a low-key profile and invested in manufacture, urban real estate, services, and other economic activities. Although there is some evidence on investments of this type, little or nothing is known about the money earned by others—those who have sold chemical precursors; those who have helped drug traffickers launder their capital; police, armed forces, guerrillas, and paramilitary personnel who "sell security" services to the industry; chemists who help refine cocaine and heroin; smugglers who help launder drug capital; small drug dealers who have returned from the United States; and so on. It must be stressed that a significant proportion of drug related income might not be evident, and thus, may be laundered easily, particularly in a country were money laundering and dirtying is an old art.

For most of the past 25 years, the employment effects of the illegal drug industry have been significant in a few isolated regions of Colombia but not at the national level. However, the rapid growth of coca and poppy plantings during the 1990s and the guerrillas' support led to the political organization of coca and poppy growers, which by 1996 had become a force the government had to reckon with. In late 1996, peasant protests against aerial coca fumigation, instigated by guerrilla organizations, mobilized about 120,000 peasants and turned coca spraying into a social issue of national magnitude.[19]

The Costs to the Government of the "War on Drugs"

The "war on drugs" forced the government to use resources that otherwise would have been allocated to other purposes. In spite of the importance of

[19]"Aquí estamos y aquí nos quedamos," *Semana*, August 13–20, 1996, 32–35.

this issue, and perhaps due to the difficulties in obtaining reliable data and to the possible political implications of this type of research, until 2000 there had been only one attempt to analyze and estimate these government expenditures, by López (1997). He looked at government antidrug costs before the large increase in military expenditures generated by the fight against the subversive drug-funded forces and Plan Colombia, which was implemented after 1999. He could not obtain estimates of the total government expenditures on the war on drugs, but he made significan advances in that direction. Specifically, he identified important characteristics and patterns of antidrug expenditures.

The first problem López faced in this endeavor was to identify all government agencies involved in the antidrug effort and their links to each other. Unfortunately, not only do they form a complex policy network, but many of them are engaged only marginally in fighting drugs, which makes it very difficult to identify what resources are devoted to those tasks.

As expected, there were at least five problems that made it difficult, and at times impossible, to obtain reliable expenditure information. First, an important share of total antidrug expenditures is complementary to military foreign assistance programs that are secret for national security reasons. Second, large military expenditures had been devoted to fight simultaneously armed subversion and illegal drugs, and it was not possible to separate each purpose's share.

Third, other large social sector expenditures like those of the Presidential Advisory Board on Medellín (Consejería de la Presidencia sobre Medellín) were related to fighting drugs, but only an indeterminate share could be attributed to this end because Medellín had many other problems. Fourth, the accounting practices of many government agencies did not permit determining the end uses of their expenditures. Fifth, the accounting systems of many government agencies were frequently confusing and disorganized, and government bureaucracies were reluctant to provide information.[20]

In spite of these limitations, López (1997) reached important conclusions. Feasible expenditure estimates showed that until 1989 the antidrug effort was concentrated on control and repression. Eradication and police and military expenses accounted for almost all antidrug expenditures. From 1989 on, the expenditure composition was substantially altered.

---

[20]Indeed, in some cases López had to formally appeal to freedom of information legislation to obtain access to some of the data.

The Ministry of Justice's share increased from 0.2 percent in 1989 to 25.4 percent in 1990 and 29.6 percent in 1991. These changes were required mainly by the elimination of the extradition of Colombian citizens in the 1991 Constitution (formulated in 1990) and the César Gaviria's administration *sometimiento* policy, which encouraged several of the main traffickers to turn themselves in.

Antidrug expenditures were made in reaction to specific events. For example, Pablo Escobar's escape from his infamous "Cathedral" prison in 1992 led to a large increase in repressive expenditures that increased 8 percentage points that year to 78.4 percent and to 80.4 percent in 1993. After Escobar's death in late 1993, the Ministry of Justice's expenditure share increased again to 34 percent in 1994, while repressive expenditures' share fell to 61.2 percent.

Government expenditures in demand control (prevention, treatment, and rehabilitation) had been marginal, and before 1993 they did not exceed 1 percent of the total. In 1994, they increased to 4 percent in response to an apparent increase in social concern.

Some changes in the expenditures' composition cannot be explained easily, perhaps because of the secret nature of many decisions related to national security. For example, available data show that in 1992 and 1993 the armed forces' repressive expenditures increased substantially. These increases were concentrated in the navy, something that the available information could not explain. A similar difficulty is found trying to explain the expenditure shares of the Departamento Administrativo de Seguridad (DAS),[21] the armed forces, and the antinarcotics police. Their shares vary from year to year in a way that the outside analyst cannot decipher.

Quantifiable antidrug expenditures have been augmented in response to the assassination of important politicians and to narcoterrorist actions, but they have not been high. In 1978, total measurable antidrug expenditures were only 0.15 percent of GDP. In the following years, this figure declined and reached 0.09 percent in 1982. This share remained stable until 1990, the year after the assassination of presidential candidate Luis Carlos Galán, when it rose to 0.17 percent. From then on, it continued rising, reaching 0.24 percent in 1994.

Measurable antidrug expenditures as a proportion of total public expenditures were also low. During the 1980s, they were about 0.6 percent, and they had increased to 1.5 percent in 1993. Remarkably, antidrug

[21]This is the Colombian equivalent of the U.S. Federal Bureau of Investigation.

expenditures did not exceed 2.8 percent of social-sector expenditures in any of the years studied. López (1997) was very cautious in his conclusions, but his careful study of antidrug patterns led him to conclude that antidrug expenditures have been reactive to narcoterrorism and foreign pressures and have not been proactive.

Illegal Drugs and the Environment

It is undeniable that the illegal drug industry has many negative environmental effects. Unfortunately, there is a lack of in-depth studies on the impact of illegal drug production and antidrug policies on the environment, and attempts to advance in this field have been thwarted by political considerations.[22]

In spite of these deficiencies, the evidence available indicates that the environmental effects are not only highly negative, but they can become devastating in the medium and long terms. The nine main nefarious points listed by many analysts are similar to those discussed in chapter 6. First, coca and poppy plantings in previously unsettled areas have caused the destruction of large amounts of primary tropical forest. This destruction is much larger than the hectareage devoted to illegal crops. Ramírez (1998, 20) estimated that 2 hectares of forest are destroyed for each hectare of new coca plantings that is destroyed; in the case of opium poppies, $2^{1}/_{2}$ hectares are destroyed.

Second, after the original forest is cut, the vegetal material is simply burned. This process kills almost all of the soil microorganisms that facilitate the soil nutrient absorption, lowering soil fertility (Vargas 1999, 72).

Third, the illegal industry's impact on the country's freshwater supply is highly negative. The destruction of high-altitude primary tropical forests

---

[22]E.g., in 1996 the Inter-American Development Bank, which had funded an alternative development program in Colombia, was interested in determining these environmental effects. I headed a research group that made a proposal for such a very detailed study that included soil tests in illicit crop regions, health effects studies, an evaluation of eradication programs, etc. In a letter to Asunción Aguilá, the head of the environment division of the Inter-American Development Bank, Héctor Moreno, the head of Colombia's alternative development program (PLANTE), vetoed Alejandro Reyes and Francisco Thoumi from participating in this research effort, which was canceled. I was shown the letter, but unfortunately, I was not allowed to copy it.

has a direct effect on the water volume carried by the country's main rivers, and significant declines have already been detected. Colombia has been endowed with one of the most abundant freshwater supplies in the world. There are now well-founded fears that in a few decades Colombia might face a water shortage.

Fourth, some of the drug production practices are also very damaging to water supplies. Peasants use strong herbicides, fertilizers, and chemical products, which are spilled or whose residues are dumped into the rivers or seep into the ground, contaminating underground water supplies (S. Uribe 1997). Sometimes, peasants keep their supply of chemicals submerged in rivers and creeks to prevent their detection. Any leaks in the chemicals' containers cause grave damage.

Fifth, peasants' practices also generate large potential health hazards. Most chemicals are handled without appropriate equipment and some are known to be carcinogenic and are banned in the United States and Europe. These are quite cheap on international underground markets and are smuggled to illicit-crop regions. S. Uribe (1997) and Vargas (1999) found that coca growers use gramoxone, the infamous paraquat, a strong carcinogenic agent that is outlawed in the United States, European countries, and other countries. Paraquat is particularly bad for the environment because it blends into the clay soils of the Amazon basin, where it has a mean lifetime of 20 to 25 years (Vargas 1999, 75).

Sixth, most peasants use chemicals without appropriate protective equipment, causing blisters and other skin problems and even grave poisoning (Vargas 1999). Seventh, Colombia's rich biodiversity is also threatened by the growth of the illegal drug industry. The decline and contamination of the water supply, as well as widespread and indiscriminate chemical use, are likely to hurt the country's flora and fauna. Furthermore, as was noted by Vargas (1999, 76), many chemicals aimed at particular pathogens also kill many other microorganisms, destroying the natural equilibrium among the species in the region.

Eighth, antidrug policies are also very damaging to the environment. Aerial spraying and other eradication policies have severely negative environmental effects and generate strong social and political opposition. Indeed, Colombia is the only Andean country where aerial spraying is used. Aerial spraying destroys illegal crops—and frequently also other crops. It is difficult for airplane pilots to spray only coca and poppy fields, especially when they fly high to lower the risk of being shot down by guerrillas. In many cases, they also spray nearby crops.

Another defying element arises from the peasants' practices to plant coca and poppies mixed with other crops to avoid detection. All this means that to eradicate 1 hectare of illegal crops using aerial spraying, it is required to spray a larger area. Eradication by ground-based methods is less damaging to the environment, but it requires the presence of crews in the actual plantings, which can be very dangerous given the large guerrilla presence in those regions.

Ninth, eradication induces peasants to penetrate further into the jungle, destroy more forest, and establish new plantings. The displacement of coca and poppy fields is perhaps the greatest source of environmental damage caused by eradication, even if done from the ground and by hand (Ramírez 1998; Vargas 1999).

There is no doubt that the environmental damage caused by illegal crops and drug manufacturing is extensive and that in the long run it can increase exponentially. Indeed, the Colombian Amazon jungle is becoming one of the main victims of illegal drugs and antidrug activities. Regrettably, the debate on these issues has been highly political and ideological.

Those siding with coca growers argue that peasants' pressure for land is very strong and their migration into the empty forests (*terrenos baldíos*) cannot be stopped, so deforestation would have taken place with or without coca. Furthermore, because this crop represents what can be sustained on these fragile lands for the longest period, it is the one that minimizes environmental damage.[23]

Those who oppose illicit crops argue that illegal profits are a strong incentive for migration and forest destruction. Furthermore, for each hectare of coca or poppy, peasants destroy several more of primary forest. Finally, it is argued that most peasants are opportunistic—are devoid of local roots or of long-term plans to settle in those regions where their sole goal is to grow illegal crops.[24]

In a debate of this type, many important questions are not raised. For instance, how much actual migration would there be without illegal crops? How much migration has been caused by violence and peasant displacement in other rural areas? How has the failure of land reform promoted peasant migration?

---

[23]Of course, a similar argument cannot be made for the opium poppy in high-altitude lands whose bush forest are crucial determinants of the water supply.

[24]This is more likely to be the case for coca than poppy growers.

The debate about the effects of aerial spraying is also confusing and value laden. On the one hand, peasants and guerrilla organizations have opposed aerial spraying of glisofate and other herbicides on the grounds that it causes permanent desertification and presents a health hazard for pregnant mothers and young children. They avoid explaining why those negative effects do not appear to be associated with 80 percent of the glisofate used in modern Colombian agriculture or with its widespread use in the United States, where it is sold under the Roundup brand name (and where it is the most commonly used household herbicide). Conversely, those who advocate eradication tend to minimize the negative effects of the chemicals used.[25]

It must be noted that in spite of these policy debates, several branches of the Colombian government and important segments of the public have been concerned with the environmental effects of the illegal industry and of antidrug policies. The Colombian government has formulated and implemented policies aimed at protecting the environment on its own, without foreign pressure. The Gaviria administration identified the threat to the environment represented by the expansion of poppy plantings and attempted to thwart it in the early 1990s. The decision to spray the early poppy fields was made in part to prevent further destruction of high-altitude forests (Tokatlian 1997). This attempt to nip the poppy industry in the bud did not succeed, and today Colombia is an important heroin producer on the South American continent.

To conclude, there is a consensus that the environmental damage caused by the illegal drug industry is very large, but the politicization of the debate about the actual effects of various policies and industry practices has led each side to blame the other, without providing viable solutions. Under these conditions, there is a very high probability that in the long run Colombia's tropical forests will be one of the main victims of the illegal drug industry and the war on drugs.

Social and Political Effects

The social and political effects of the illegal drug industry have been pervasive in Colombia. The industry has unquestionably permeated Colombian society. But its main role has been that of a catalytic factor that

[25]E.g., in late 1998 another herbicide, tebuthiuron ("spike"), was used over the objections of many environmentalists.

has sped up and aggravated a process of social decomposition already under way. It must be stressed that the concentration of the industry in Colombia is hardly accidental, but rather a consequence of the country's historical development and institutional weakness.[26]

General Considerations

The illegal drug industry has, nevertheless, been a main driving force behind the country's horrifying increase in violence and criminality.[27] It has also been instrumental in increasing political corruption and putting many democratic institutions at risk. It has contributed to a growing social tolerance for criminal and deviant behavior and a get-rich-quick mentality. It has funded all actors of the country's ambiguous war, and has strengthened guerrilla and paramilitary groups. Illegal drug policies in general and illicit crop eradication in particular have become key issues and obstacles in peace negotiations with guerrilla groups. This is not meant as an exhaustive list of relevant effects, but as an illustration of the complexity and diversity of the industry's social and political effects. As a whole, they are more important than the economic ones because they destroy the social fabric and institutions and the state's ability to govern the country.

Camacho and López (1999, 47) have summarized the consensus found in an opinion survey of Colombian experts:

Drug traffickers have absolutely reactionary and violent values. At the same time, and without attempting to do so, they contributed to the de-

---

[26]The reasons that the illegal industry became concentrated in Colombia are elaborated on in chapter 9.

[27]The homicide rate in Colombia has been high for a long time. During La Violencia in the 1940s and 1950s, it was obviously high. In 1958, at the beginning of the National Front, it "peaked at 51.5 per 100,000 inhabitants. It fell continuously during the 1960s and early 1970s, bottoming out between 1973 and 1975 at about 16.8 per 100,000 inhabitants" (Thoumi 1995d, 72). However, in the late 1970s and 1980s, it increased rapidly. By 1990 it was about 90 per 100,000, an unprecedented level except in societies waging an open war (Rubio 1999, 36–38). Since then, it has fallen to about 60 per 100,000 inhabitants. Data on kidnappings are weaker than those for violent deaths because many of them are not reported to the authorities. Pax Christi Netherlands (2001) estimated that in 2000 there were more than 3,700 reported kidnappings in Colombia; it reviewed the various kidnapping systems and kidnappers' strategies, and it estimated kidnapping and extortion revenues at about $450 million in 1999; i.e., about 0.6 percent of GDP! Although kidnapping data are weak, it can be said that during the past decade Colombia has experienced 40 to 50 percent of all the kidnappings in the world!

struction of traditional Colombian society. The relationship between certain last names and social position was lost. It can be asserted in a general way that within large segments of the middle and lower classes drug trafficking is seen as a legitimate upward mobility channel and a way to accumulate wealth. At the same time, it also confirms the conviction that it is impossible—or at least very difficult—to achieve a comfortable economic position through persistent work.

It must be stressed that the Colombian political structure made the country's polity very vulnerable to the illegal drug industry and facilitated the industry's growth (Thoumi 1995d). Political parties in Colombia have not had a strong ideology or centralized organizations. They have been associations of local political leaders (*caudillos*) whose main function has been to deliver votes (F. Leal 1989a, 1989b; Leal and Dávila 1990). This structure facilitated the development of local support networks for the drug industry and eliminated the need for national-level support.

As was noted above, geographic segmentation and the isolation of many regions with virtually no state presence implied that only local and cheap support networks were required to produce and smuggle drugs. In many of these areas, guerrilla organizations substituted for the state and provided the needed support and protection to coca and poppy plantings and laboratories (S. Uribe 1997). However, the "Laundromat" is quite small in Colombia relative to the income and capital generated by the illegal drug industry. This is why the main social and political effects are the result of the need to launder large sums. Small farmers, manufacturers, and exporters can use their own families and friends to launder sums considered large relative to Colombians' incomes but rather small compared with drug traffickers' total revenues.[28]

However, laundering large sums requires support and protection at high social and political levels. In Colombia, it is impossible to launder $10 million inconspicuously, and this requires high-level political support. The concentration of the industry's smuggling activities in a few large "cartels" has compelled them to seek political support at the highest political level. Extradition has also contributed to this need and has encouraged extraditable traffickers' attempts to influence legislators, presidents, and other high-level officials, and to threaten members of the judiciary.

---

[28]E.g., a drug-trafficking family is likely to be able to launder about $100,000 to $200,000 a year without raising suspicions.

The amounts spent by drug-trafficking organizations in their attempts to buy political protection may be very large compared with the budgets of all political campaigns in Colombia, but they are very small relative to the estimates of their earnings. A simple fact of Colombian life is that politicians are "very inexpensive" relative to the wealth and income of drug traffickers (Lee and Thoumi 1999).

As Colombian authorities (with some prodding from Americans) sought ways to crack down on the drug trade and drug-trafficking groups acquired more power and visibility, noneconomic forms of collaboration became central to the cartels' activities. Trafficking organizations pooled information on law enforcement activities (e.g., planned raids on major leaders), developed joint counterintelligence and counterenforcement strategies, funneled cash to political parties, and sought collaboration to improve their bargaining position vis-à-vis the state. To date, such patterns of cooperation have developed largely within specific regions, but narcotraffickers also exercised political influence at the national level (Lee and Thoumi 1999).[29]

Colombian society has been ambivalent toward the illegal drug industry. An environment that is characterized by extreme individuality, lack of human solidarity, and an ethics of inequality that encourages individuals to improve themselves economically at any cost and in which virtually everybody breaks economic laws is also one that is very tolerant of illegal economic activities. Indeed, in this environment it is very difficult, if not impossible, to single out one illegal economic activity as evil while others are socially tolerated. The development of important collusive relations between politics and the illegal drug industry is therefore no surprise.

The threat of organized crime to the political order has proven greater than to the country's economic structure. It has been subtle and insidious rather than direct and overt, but it has been pervasive. Unlike terrorists or guerrillas—who operate more or less outside the system and who may

[29]E.g., Cali cartel leaders and a number of smaller Valle traffickers reportedly established a common $8 million fund (in a special account in the Banco de Colombia in Cali) to influence the outcomes of the 1994 presidential and congressional election campaigns (Castillo 1996, 204). In addition, in the late 1980s and early 1990s, leaders of the Medellín and Cali cartels negotiated as a group with the Colombian government in an effort to obtain collective judicial benefits, e.g., short jail sentences, favorable conditions of incarceration, an end to extradition, and even amnesty for their crimes.

seek to overthrow the government—these criminals usually seek to manipulate the system from within. Indeed, well-organized groups conduct their business with the protection and sometimes the active support of governments.

Collusive ties between government and criminals are manifested in a number of ways. The most basic, of course, is the nexus of criminal money and functions of government. The aim in this case is to protect the integrity of the organization and its leaders, to promote legislation favorable to criminal interests, and in general to ensure a crime-friendly environment.

On an operational level, corrupted law enforcement officials allow individual illegal transactions (e.g., drug processing or shipments) to proceed unhindered. Officials provide their criminal clients advance warning of government raids and dragnets.[30] Similarly, judges and police officials on traffickers' payrolls make a mockery of the criminal justice system.[31] Corruption has become almost inseparable from the activities and purposes of statecraft in Colombia. Here the issue now is no longer the delivery of specific services or favors in return for bribes but rather the management of relations with a powerful (if illegal) interest group to achieve specific political objectives.

Drugs and Politics in the 1980s and Early 1990s

As was argued above, criminal economic activities require strong social support networks to operate and grow. As the illegal cartels accumulated wealth, their need for these networks became apparent and they began to establish links to the political system. In the early 1980s, members of the Medellín cartel tried to obtain power directly. Pablo Escobar ran as a

---

[30]A case in point was the conspicuous failure of the government to arrest Pablo Escobar in 1992 and 1993, despite a series of encirclement campaigns conducted by thousands of soldiers and elite police (*bloque de búsqueda*) troops. The degree of social support that Escobar received in Medellín was also remarkable (though partly attributable to slum-rebuilding and other civil-sector projects sponsored by the trafficker in the early 1980s), and this was perhaps the main reason that it was so difficult to capture him (García-Márquez 1998).

[31]It was reported that henchmen for the Medellín cartel offered judges trying drug cases *plata o plomo* (silver or lead)—money if they let the trafficker go free, a bullet if they convict him. It was not surprising that most judges chose the former option. The Cali cartel's technique was somewhat more refined: "We don't kill ministers or judges; we buy them," remarked Cali kingpin Gilberto Rodríguez Orejuela on one occasion.

backup for Congress and got elected.[32] He also developed a strong support base, mainly in some of Medellín's suburbs and his nearby hometown of Envigado, where he financed public works, housing, and a welfare system.[33] Carlos Lehder established a political movement with strong nationalistic overtones, but it did not flourish.

The Medellín cartel invested heavily in rural land, mainly in the Middle Magdalena Valley and areas of Antioquia and Córdoba Departments. In these regions, the cartel promoted the formation of self-protection paramilitary groups that fought the guerrillas. These groups have been funded by traditional landowners and the drug industry, and they have responded to the need to protect property and life in those regions where guerrillas used kidnapping and extortion to finance their subversive activities. In these regions, entrepreneurs in the illegal drug industry have used a simple investment strategy: buying distressed properties that their owners could not exploit because of guerrilla threats and bringing in their paramilitary groups to raise land values.

A leadership structure of sorts existed within Colombia's cocaine establishments exercised by the heads of the dominant trafficking organizations that facilitated negotiations. In Medellín, Escobar's pioneering role in establishing export routes, his access to the means of violence, and his ruthless domination of smaller exporters held the coalition together and established its identity. In Cali, Gilberto Rodríguez-Orejuela retained what he called his *poder de convocatoria* (power of assembly) with other Valle drug dealers, and together with his brother Miguel defined the common position of this Valle group in surrender negotiations with the Colombian government in 1993–94 (Clawson and Lee 1996, 47, 55).

The Medellín cartel did not hesitate to use violence against the public who opposed it or who simply tried to enforce laws as their duties required. Its early victims were judges and law enforcement authorities. In late April 1984, it killed Rodrigo Lara Bonilla, the justice minister who had challenged Escobar in Congress. This event escalated the conflict. President Belisario Betancur, who had been a staunch opponent of extradition on principle, began to extradite traffickers to the United States.

[32]Before the 1991 Constitution was approved, every senator and representative had a backup or substitute who would take his or her place in case of absence. This system allowed Escobar in effect to buy himself a politician who got elected and got him into Congress.

[33]Indeed, the town of Envigado was the only municipality in Colombia that provided unemployment compensation to its citizens, a program funded by Escobar.

The illegal industry responded with a vicious narcoterrorism campaign that included frequent bomb explosions in public places and the assassination of politicians, cabinet ministers, judges, journalists, policemen, military personnel, presidential candidates, and others who opposed the drug trade.[34]

Extradition has been a great source of conflict between the government and drug traffickers, who have used all available resources to fight it.[35] When the extradition treaty with the United States was signed and ratified during the Julio César Turbay (1978–82) administration, some legal technicalities were not complied with. The traffickers' lawyers appealed to these to argue in the Supreme Court against the treaty, which was invalidated on June 25, 1987 (Thoumi 1995d, 218; Tokatlian 1990, 349). In response to this setback, the government, led by justice minister Enrique Low, "began to search for other ways to extradite, appealing to and reviving old treaties dating back to the 1880s" (Thoumi 1995d, 218). These efforts failed but made Low a target for traffickers' retaliation.[36]

The traffickers' responded to the government efforts with a new wave of narcoterrorism. The victims of the violence generated by the Medellín cartel transcended the establishment, for they also used terrorism as a weapon. During the late 1980s and early 1990s, large bombs were frequently detonated against targets such as police headquarters, the secret police, and random public places. These simply aimed at creating chaos.

The 1989 presidential campaign was a bloody one, particularly for left-wing candidates of the "Patriotic Union" (UP) with links to the former M-19 guerrilla organization that had negotiated with the government its reinsertion to civil life:

> UP leader Jaime Pardo Leal was killed late in 1987. Another UP possible presidential candidate, José Antequera, was gunned down in Bogotá's airport on 4 March 1989 while waiting to take a plane. Also shot in this incident was Ernesto Samper Pizano, a young Liberal

---

[34]Thoumi (1995d, 217) provided a partial list of the targeted victims.

[35]Their claim of their preference of a tomb in Colombia over a jail in the United States is well known.

[36]Enrique Low, a remarkable, brilliant, honest, and kind man, was assassinated on April 30, 1991, the seventh anniversary of Rodrigo Lara-Bonilla's (another justice minister) assassination.

politician with an excellent chance at a future presidency, who just happened to run into Antequera and was greeting him. ... The increased level of violence associated with drug trafficking and the apparent lack of success that the government campaign was having despite impressive data about drug seizures and destroyed laboratories, inclined President Barco to search for other ways to extradite. On the morning of 18 August 1989, the Council of Ministers decided to establish an extradition system as an administrative measure, not a judicial one. (Thoumi 1995d, 220, 221)[37]

It appears that for President Virgilio Barco, extradition was still the main weapon against drug trafficking, perhaps because he could not see any other alternatives. "Lacking other imaginative options, and imprisoned by a repressive logic, President Virgilio Barco worked until the end of his period with an instrument that did not provide any realistic solution to the Colombian drug trafficking problem" (Tokatlian 1990, 353). Coincidentally that evening, Luis Carlos Galán, the leading presidential candidate and odds-on favorite, was assassinated (Thoumi 1995d, 221).

   "The reaction of the Barco administration was swift and strong, declaring an all out war against the 'narco-terrorists' that led to an unprecedented increase in militarization of the anti-drug effort. The day after Galán's death President Barco made public the extradition decree signed the day before, and issued a series of new ones that allowed the arbitrary confiscation of cartel properties, and for the first time made shadow ownership of these properties a crime" (Gugliotta and Leen 1990, 559–60). With the new decrees in place, the government concentrated all its efforts in capturing the drug traffickers, confiscating their assets and destroying their producing capabilities and their networks. Large numbers of properties were immediately seized, hundreds of individuals were arrested, and extradition resumed within days when some "extraditables" were captured (Thoumi 1995d, 222).

   The new crackdown was different from the previous ones because it appeared to have actually harmed the Medellín cartel, and for the first time the Colombian government actions began to resemble a frontal war (Gugliotta 1992). However, the government's attack on the illegal drug industry was only partial, because its primarily target was the Medellín cartel that was associated with anti-state violence (Thoumi 1995d, 223).

---

[37]See also Tokatlian (1990, 351).

On August 24, this group issued a communiqué declaring "total and absolute war" against anyone that had opposed them, including government officials, the industrial establishment, judges, and union leaders. "In the month after Galán's murder, the drug traffickers had set 36 fires and detonated 37 bombs, including a large one that on 2 September caused extensive damage to the *El Espectador* building in Bogotá in an obvious attempt to silence the most outspoken anti-drug newspaper" (Thoumi 1995d, 223). The terror campaign continued in spite of government pressure, and the drug organizations demonstrated they could freely attack individual targets, particularly in Medellín, where a former mayor and several *El Espectador* employees were assassinated (Castillo 1991, 269).

"On 3 October President Barco appeared to have had another success when the Supreme Court ruled the new extradition procedures constitutional" (Thoumi 1995d, 224). However, it "ruled unconstitutional the decree by which Colombian security forces had arbitrarily confiscated more than a thousand drug trafficker properties" (Gugliotta and Leen 1990, 574). And the situation became even worse:

> While the frequent bomb explosions injured and killed relatively few people, they had a damaging psychological effect on Colombia and generated widespread fear and a feeling of insecurity among the citizenry. Media surveys showed that public opinion supported strong government actions; however, as the war environment expanded and no key "cartel" figure was caught, public support for the war on "narco-terrorism" began to diminish. A particularly serious blow to the government was the explosion that destroyed an Avianca plane that had just taken off from Bogotá for Cali on 27 November. This terrorist act killed 111 people. A week later, on 6 December, a massive truck bomb virtually destroyed the twelve-story headquarters of the National Security Forces (DAS) in Bogotá, killing 72 people and injuring hundreds. (Thoumi 1995d, 224)

What could be done? The government

> needed some victories. On 14 December the government achieved one of these objectives when Gonzalo Rodríguez-Gacha died in a shoot-out with the army. This important event is likely to have been perceived by other top traffickers as a sign they were not invincible after all. [The violence continued and in early 1990, Bernardo Jaramillo, UP's

presidential candidate, was killed, as was his successor, Carlos Pizarro, a couple of months later.] ... From then on, one of the primary concerns for the Barco administration was to guarantee the life of whoever was going to represent the UP in the presidential election. This was the first presidential campaign in Colombia in which problems associated with the illegal drug industry became the main political issue and the industry's negative effect on the imperfect Colombian democracy became clear. ... The heightened violence and insecurity generated strong public pressure on the government to "do something." President Barco seized this opportunity and initiated procedures to change the constitution in an effort to make the government more responsible to the people and to break the grip of the clientelistic system on the state. Simultaneously, the government began a process to open the economy to international competition in an attempt to revive economic growth. (Thoumi 1995d, 220, 225)

In contrast with the Medellín cartel, the Cali cartel has followed a low-profile political strategy. None of its members has attempted to become a political figure. Instead, it has chosen to "buy" political support. The Cali syndicate certainly succeeded in developing a support network in Cali that included public employees, politicians, and a large cadre of taxi drivers and other common folk. They did not use violence openly against the political establishment and did not appeal to terrorism. Indeed, some of their violence was applied to gain public support. Their "social cleansing" of petty thieves, prostitutes, homosexuals, and other "throwaways" (*desechables*) in Cali was designed with this purpose.

By 1990, when César Gaviria was elected president, the Colombian regime was in a war against narcoterrorism and a deep delegitimation crisis that expressed itself in:[38]

- An elitist and exclusionary political system that appealed to widespread clientelism to co-opt the opposition but that was unable to cope with the fast rate of change in Colombian society that demanded democratic political option (F. Leal 1989a; Leal and Dávila 1990).
- A very inefficient state, including a congested and dysfunctional judicial system that nobody trusted. The state had lost not only

[38]These points were developed in Thoumi (1997b).

its monopoly on violence but also its capacity to enforce contracts and protect property rights.

- A very rapid growth of criminal and noncriminal underground activities, particularly marijuana and coca growing, and cocaine manufacturing and exporting.
- Extremely high levels of violence, comparable to those of countries at war.
- Guerrilla organizations that had operated for more than 45 years and that controlled large rural areas.
- Paramilitary groups that grew as self-protection landowner organizations against guerrilla extortion and kidnapping. They also controlled parts of the country and had links to the armed forces.
- A very high level of nonpolitical and nonmilitary associated violence, which has prompted many analysts to claim that Colombians have few internalized behavioral constraints and that they show a total disregard for the effect of their actions on other people (Kalmanovitz 1989; Herrán 1987).

The deep social crisis and the need for significant reforms were first recognized by the Betancur administration (1982–86), which promoted a dialogue and negotiations with guerrilla movements. The Barco administration (1986–90) continued seeking reforms, which led to a National Assembly to reform the constitution. The Gaviria administration (1990–94) approved the new constitution in 1991 and implemented drastic institutional changes.

Political reforms were of paramount importance in tackling the crisis, and in 1990 the government convened a Constitutional Assembly, which produced a new Constitution in 1991. This very long and complex document aimed to introduce many changes in Colombian society. Its main goals were to "modernize" the country and promote democracy. Therefore, it established systems to encourage political participation and the development of grassroots organizations. It also established large financial transfers from the central government to local governments, which historically had been deprived of funds. The Constitution also aimed to improve the justice system; it created mechanisms to protect human rights and to speed up the resolution of legal conflicts.

Many of these changes were designed to promote the government's accountability. Another important feature, one that has played a key role in government, has been the creation of a strong and independent prosecutor general (attorney general) office. The Constitution thus has been a very ambitious project, which has tried to legislate many social changes, including the protection of many individual rights, but has been found wanting in practice because the state does not have either the resources or the organizational capability to guarantee those rights. The large transfers to local governments have been particularly troublesome because they have not been accompanied by parallel declines in central government expenditures and most municipalities did not have the capability to handle large budgets. This has been a main cause of the dramatic increase in government deficits and corruption since the mid-1990s (Kalmanovitz 2001).

Since the early 1970s—when the drug trade began to grow in Colombia until the end of the Gaviria administration in August 1994—Colombian governments had argued that drug trafficking was a global problem that Colombia could not solve and that its fight was against "narcoterrorism." This position minimized the importance of the industry's links to politics. As part of its fight against narcoterrorism, in 1991 the Gaviria administration established a policy of negotiated surrendering (*sometimiento*) of drug traffickers, which allowed most of the Medellín cartel members to turn themselves in, in exchange for light sentences. Escobar negotiated the terms of his surrender, which included the construction of a special jail in the countryside near his hometown of Envigado (a Medellín suburb) in a farm in La Catedral's municipal district (*Vereda*).[39]

Escobar selected his own guards, furnished his jail with comfortable appliances and furniture, developed an active social life, including cocktail parties, and continued his trafficking operations from jail. When the government tried to control these activities and transfer him to a regular prison, he escaped in July 21, 1992. From then on, the government's main antidrug goal was to capture Escobar, who declared an open war against the government—resorting to many terrorist attacks, mainly large bombs against government targets or randomly placed in shopping centers and other public places where explosions would generate great public fear. This challenge forced the Colombian government to focus all its efforts on catching Escobar. He died of bullet wounds in Medellín on a house roof

---

[39]Méndez-Bernal (1996) described in some detail the process by which the municipality of Envigado bought the land and built the jail, presumably funded by Escobar himself.

trying to escape from the police search brigade (*bloque de búsqueda*) on December 2, 1993.

According to the DEA,[40] the two main cartels had fought for control of some U.S. markets, mainly New York City, and had other conflicts in Colombia. The two cartels formed alliances with different segments of Colombian society, with disastrous effects. The Medellín cartel promoted the development of paramilitary groups to protect their rural investments, and in doing so, developed links with army personnel. The Cali cartel established alliances with the police and politicians. Members of the police helped in Cali's "social cleansing," and army personnel helped "cleanse" the Middle Magdalena Valley of guerrillas. Furthermore, the Medellín syndicate led by Escobar offered a bounty for each policeman killed, and many, mainly in Medellín, suffered that fate. These alliances resulted in a rift within the government and widespread distrust among officials fighting the war on drugs.

The war against narcoterrorism had other important effects: It eliminated some of the main illegal industry bullies, and it promoted an increase in sophistication among the remaining traffickers. The Cali organization took advantage of Colombia's clientelistic system to build an extensive base of political support. This was accomplished mainly funding politicians and their campaigns. Campaign financing by drug traffickers had been a long-accepted practice since the mid-1970s (Lee and Thoumi 1999), but the Cali cartel's financing of the 1994 elections led to an unprecedented political crisis.

Drugs and Politics in the Samper Administration

A succession of scandals besieged the Ernesto Samper administration after it took over in August 1994 and brought the country to the brink of political and economic collapse. Telephone conversation tapes made public right after Samper's election revealed that drug money had heavily funded his campaign. After a lengthy and traumatic legal process that indicted and found guilty several important politicians, the president himself was exonerated on the grounds that he did not know about such funding, which in his own words: "took place behind his

---

[40]This is based on an interview with DEA Washington personnel in December 1992. Castillo's (1996) journalistic research and Clawson and Lee (1996) have confirmed the DEA version.

back."[41] The highlight of the crisis was the presidential trial in Congress, forced by the attorney general. The trial had to deal with two main issues: first, whether President Samper knew that illegal drug money had entered his campaign, as Fernando Botero, the campaign director claimed; and whether campaign expenditure limits had been broken and the campaign accounting falsified to collect state matching funds.

Whether Samper was aware or not was very difficult to prove in a legally satisfactory way. On the one hand, he alleged that he had been too busy with the political aspects of the campaign to bother with its finances. On the other hand, Botero claimed that he had discussed campaign finances with the former candidate but could not present definitive proof.[42] Two related points strengthened the president's position. One was simply that at the time of the campaign, Colombia did not have enforceable anti-money-laundering legislation. Another, perhaps more important, was that drug traffickers had funded the campaigns of many elected politicians, including many in Congress who were trying the president.

The second issue concerned violation of campaign expenditure limits. One of the provisions of the 1991 Constitution established that the government would provide matching campaign funds as long as total campaign expenditures did not exceed a certain limit. This was a stronger accusation, and one that Samper could not dodge because compliance was legally his responsibility, independent of whether he was aware of any violations. The accusation was simply that Samper's campaign had exceeded the expenditure limits and had altered its accounting to claim

----

[41]By the end of 1996, Fernando Botero, the former director of Samper's campaign and former minister of defense, Santiago Medina, the former campaign treasurer, and former senators Gustavo Espinosa and Alberto Santofimio were serving sentences. Former *procurador general* (a function similar to a societal ombudsman) Orlando Vásquez-Velásquez, former comptroller Manuel Francisco Becerra, former senators Eduardo Mestre, Armando Holguín-Sarria, and José Guerra-de-la-Espriella, former representatives Tiberio Villarreal, Alvaro Benedetti, Ana García de Petchalt, and Rodrigo Garavito, former presidential military assistant colonel Germán Osorio, and General Farouk Yanine were detained and being tried. In spite of having a large number of his close associates indicted and jailed, Samper remained in power and was able to finish his presidential period.

[42]Although it cannot be proven that Samper knew, chances are very slim that he did not. During the campaign, he and Botero spent many hours together every day, and campaign finances were a key issue that they should have discussed. This was particularly the case after the first round, when the campaign found itself very short of funds and received large inflows from the Cali cartel.

government funds. This implied that the campaign had defrauded the state of more than $2 million, a crime clearly defined and easy to prosecute.

However, Samper got off on a technicality. Because of the continuous inflation experienced in Colombia, expenditure limits have to be established before each campaign. To ensure that people could not claim ignorance of the laws, any Colombian law has to be published in the *Official Daily* before it can be enforced, and campaign limits were not published on time. The limits applied to only two campaigns, there was clear evidence that both presidential candidates had expressed knowledge of the limits, and both campaigns had sought ways around them,[43] but these facts were not sufficient to convict, and Samper was exonerated by the Lower House of Congress in an overwhelming vote (111 to 43) in June 1996.

Independent of the president's verdict, the trial forced Colombians to acknowledge the existence of a very close nexus between politics and the illegal drug industry that polarized the country and weakened the government.[44] Vice President Humberto de la Calle resigned in protest against Samper, corruption charges were raised against several key government figures, and ministerial changes became common. Furthermore, the relations between Colombia and the United States deteriorated to a point unknown since the independence of Panama in 1903.[45] The Colombian economy, traditionally resilient, began to show signs of cracking down during the Samper administration as investment and growth declined. At the end of the Samper administration, urban unemployment had increased 5 percentage points to more than 15 percent, a trend that carried over into the new Andrés Pastrana administration and reached 19 percent by 1999.

---

[43]The campaign of Andrés Pastrana, the other main candidate, and subsequent president, got off the hook when it received a favorable ruling that established that the actual campaign limit was equal to the limit set plus the matching funds received. This interpretation presents another problem because the amount of matching funds is not determined by the amount spent itself but by the number of votes received, which implies that the limits are determined after the election returns are known.

[44]Investigative journalists Vargas, Lesmes, and Téllez (1996) presented a detailed chronicle of the events from 1994 to early 1996, when President Samper was close to resigning. López-Caballero (1997) studied Samper's trial in Congress. He argued (correctly) that what should have been a political trial became a weak legal trial in which the president was accused of non–legally defined crimes like receiving checks from legal banks' accounts of legal companies, which led to his exoneration. F. Leal (1996) provided a more academic study of the crisis.

[45]Indeed, Colombia has been the first "friendly" country decertified by the United States for its lack of cooperation in the drug war.

President Samper survived politically and finished his term, but at a high cost. The country was polarized, and government expenditures and policies were used to anchor the weak administration. Indeed, labor unions, financial conglomerates, guerrillas, paramilitary groups, some private-sector associations, some political groups, and nongovernmental organizations sensed the weakness of the government and tried to extract from it as many favors as possible in exchange for their support or nonagression.

The Samper administration had arrived in power with the goals of lowering inflation, increasing social-sector expenditures, and deepening democracy. These fell victim to an administration whose main goal was to survive. Thus, the "social pact" established to control price increases caused mainly by inertial inflation was not respected because any group that felt it was needed by the government demanded favorable increases. Other groups simply forced the government to increase expenditures for their benefit, and it is not surprising that the budget deficit ballooned.

During the 1990s, but mainly during the Samper administration, guerrilla and paramilitary organizations gained strength relative to the forces of the state and became the recognized de facto power in many regions.[46] As was noted in chapter 4, the growth and strengthening of insurgent groups have been funded to a significant extent by the "taxes" they levy on the illegal drug industry.

Colombia–United States relations deteriorated to historically low levels. In 1996, the United States government "decertified" Colombia for the first time since the certification process was established in 1986. Decertification prohibits export–import bank credits (which are not relevant for Colombia) and requires the U.S. executive directors at the Inter-American Development Bank and the World Bank to oppose any project for Colombia except for those dealing directly with the antidrug effort.

However, the United States does not have veto power in any of these institutions, and it has not lobbied other countries to block any loans. Perhaps the most important effect was the elimination of U.S. government foreign investment insurance for American firms wanting to invest in Colombia. Decertification also allows the U.S. government to impose

---

[46]E.g., in August 1996, a Colombian Revolutionary Armed Forces (FARC) guerrilla commando killed 30 soldiers and captured 60 more in an attack on a military post in Caquetá. Eight months later, after protracted negotiations with the government, they returned the captured soldiers after the government ordered its army to vacate for about a month a large area of the country where the guerrillas had been operating. During 1998, FARC scored similar victories against army bases in isolated regions.

discretionary economic sanctions, which potentially could be very important to Colombia. These, however, were not applied, and the only discretionary measures taken were rather symbolic, like the cancellation of President Samper's and other politicians' visas.

The indirect decertification effects can be important. It is possible for the threat of economic sanctions to be a significant element affecting Colombian and direct foreign investment.[47]

Partly in response to U.S. pressure, the Colombian government responded to the decertification with a strong antidrug effort. Eradication was intensified, and most leaders of the Cali cartel were captured. The official U.S. version discounted Colombia's efforts on the ground that they were the result of its pressure and not of the Colombian government's antidrug position. On March 31, 1997, the U.S. government again decertified Colombia, a very controversial decision in view of the simultaneous full certification of Mexico, a country whose government has also been infiltrated by the illegal drug industry.[48]

The large growth in coca and poppy plantings continued during the Samper administration. As was noted in chapter 4, it had to contend with organized peasant marches as well as increased guerrilla influence over illegal crop peasants. The government continued its eradication campaigns, complemented with an alternative development program (PLANTE). At the same time, the U.S. government developed strong links to the Colombian police under the leadership of General Rosso José Serrano. The U.S. government helped Serrano clean up the national police, which, as noted above, had been linked to the Cali cartel, and supported its anti-narcotics branch.

By the time the 1998 certification decision had to be made (March 1), the U.S. government had a trusting relationship with the Colombian police. Colombia was not certified but was granted a "waiver" on national security grounds.[49] It was clear then that although the United States had

---

[47]E.g., Colombian flower producers have moved some of their operations to such countries as Costa Rica and Ecuador.

[48]The U.S. Department of State's official version was that Colombian president Ernesto Samper actively sought campaign funds from the drug industry while Mexican president Ernesto Zedillo actively opposed the industry. It was not important being Ernest, but it was important being Zedillo.

[49]Mexico was fully certified again in 1998, an event that made it more and more difficult for the U.S. administration to decertify Colombia. By then, the difference between the U.S. treatment of Colombia and of Mexico had become too glaring, and an important segment of the U.S. public opinion had questioned the fairness and efficacy of the decertification exercise.

censured President Samper, it realized its need to work with other elements of the Colombian government.

The political crisis during the Samper administration highlighted the depth and complexity of the criminal–political nexus in Colombia. Many actors with various interests play a role in the Colombian narco-drama: illegal drugs and other criminal organizations, guerrillas, paramilitary groups, the army and the police, the government and its bureaucracy, political parties, the U.S. government, civil society organizations (including the main legal economic interests of the country), and others. The nexus between these players is intertwined and difficult to ascertain with a high degree of certainty. The following section, based on Lee and Thoumi (1999), explores this issue in more detail.[50]

Specific Aspects of the Criminal–Political Nexus

Examples of two types of the criminal–political nexus can be cited: criminal–political collusion, and drug money and electoral politics. Let us briefly examine each type.

---

[50]This section draws liberally from that study. I thank Rensselaer W. Lee III, the coauthor of that article, for the use of this material. During the last week of July and first week of August 1997, the authors interviewed the following actors in Bogotá: (1) Horacio Serpa, perhaps the closest Samper associate, his former minister of the interior, and 1998 and 2002 presidential candidate for the Samper faction of the Liberal Party; (2) Alfonso Valdivieso, former prosecutor general and 1998 presidential candidate, who is heir to the legacy of his cousin, assassinated presidential candidate Luis Carlos Galán; (3) Humberto de la Calle, former Samper administration vice president who resigned in protest for the links of Samper's campaign with illegal drug organizations; (4) Felipe López, president of *Semana*, the country's most influential weekly magazine and son of former president Alfonso López-Michelsen; (5) Manuel Francisco Becerra, former secretary of the departmental government of Valle del Cauca (whose capital is Cali), former representative and former governor of that department, former comptroller and former minister of education, detained and waiting to be sentenced on illicit enrichment charges; (6) Rodrigo Garavito, Oxford-educated former representative from the Middle Magdalena region, waiting to be sentenced on similar charges; (7) Santiago Medina, former treasurer of Samper's campaign, serving a house arrest sentence, who died in late 1998; and (8) Juan Manuel Avella, former administrative manager of Samper's campaign, who was serving time at La Modelo jail in Bogotá. The interviews followed an open format designed to let the interviewees talk about a few issues. Each interview lasted from $1^1/_2$ to 2 hours. In one case, the authors were requested to come back for an extra hour. The authors agreed to use the interview findings with discretion, giving direct attribution to those interviewed only selectively.

Criminal–Political Collusion

Three specific examples of the collusive pattern can be mentioned: The first is the bizarre history of negotiations between the Colombian government and leaders of the Medellín and Cali cartels. In no other country has a government negotiated with criminals so openly and for such a long period. In those negotiations (which have occurred sporadically since 1984), the government has sought various outcomes: to diminish the size of the drug trade, to reduce societal violence and narco-terrorism, to achieve the release of kidnapping victims, and to bring traffickers to justice. Traffickers have sought mostly guarantees of judicial leniency— nonextradition, amnesty or minimal jail time, and the chance for "reintegration" into Colombian society.

In the negotiations, traffickers have made several grandiose (and probably dubious) offers to retire from the narcotics business, to dismantle trafficking routes, and to surrender assets such as laboratories, aircraft, and weapons. The Colombian government, though viewing some offers with skepticism, nevertheless has found it expedient to maintain a dialogue with the criminals.

Usually, the criminals have initiated government–trafficker negotiations, although the government at times has been an active and interested participant in such talks. The extreme violence of 1989–90, the period of most intense hostilities with the Medellín cartel, prompted prominent members of society to become intermediaries in the conflict. In 1990, a Committee of Notables—consisting of three ex-presidents of Colombia, a former minister of government, a widely revered Catholic priest, and a leader of the leftist Unión Patriótica Party—attempted to negotiate peace and surrender terms on behalf of the Medellín Extraditables.

Moreover, the Notables—in effect representing the government— sought and achieved the release of a number of hostages held by the traffickers, among them, members of prominent Colombian families. The activities of the notables and general popular pressure for peace prompted the government to issue a succession of *sometimiento* decrees in late 1990 and 1991 that allowed traffickers to submit to justice under extremely favorable terms. Leading Medellín traffickers, including Escobar, took advantage of these concessions and turned themselves in.

In at least two recorded cases, in Panama City in May 1984 and in Bogotá in January 1994, cocaine kingpins held direct fact-to-face meetings with government representatives. In Panama, leaders of the Medellín cartel—Escobar, Rodríguez-Gacha, and Jorge Ochoa—presented a surrender proposal directly to Colombian attorney general Carlos Jiménez-Gómez following an earlier meeting with ex-president Alfonso López-Michelsen. (At the time, traffickers were in hiding in the aftermath of a massive government crackdown mounted after the April 1984 assassination of justice minister Rodrigo Lara-Bonilla.)

During the early 1990s, Colombian prosecutor general Gustavo de Greiff held successive private meetings with three important Cali bosses: Helmer Herrera-Buitrago, José Olmedo Ocampo, and Juan Carlos Ramírez. The traffickers were seeking to clarify their legal status and to explore surrender options. Another source, former Cali cartel accountant Guillermo Palomari, claimed in a 1997 testimony in the United States that de Greiff held seven meetings with Miguel Rodríguez-Orejuela in the presence of the latter's lawyer, Bernardo González, in a Rodríguez-owned apartment in Bogotá. De Greiff denies this version.[51]

A second politically noteworthy area of collusion has occurred in Colombia's ongoing conflict with antigovernment insurgent groups. The focal point of cooperation among these groups has been paramilitary forces—in effect rural vigilante groups—which over the years have developed a broad anti-leftist agenda. Traffickers who are landlords also have had their channels of communication with the army. For example, in the 1980s, it was reported that drug lord Gonzalo Rodríguez-Gacha maintained direct radio contact with the military command center of the army's Bárbula battalion in the Middle Magdalena Valley—a major counterinsurgency battleground in Colombia (Clawson and Lee 1996, 187).[52]

A third significant link in the criminal–political nexus in Colombia, and the one that has received the most public attention, is the pervasive

---

[51]"La Película en Inglés," *Semana*, July 28–August 4, 1997, 35. De Greiff was an unfortunate choice as a government negotiator. At one point, he proposed legalizing drugs, a position that undermined his credibility outside Colombia. More important, before his appointment as prosecutor general, he had been a shareholder and the president of a company, Aerolíneas El Dorado, in which Gilberto Rodríguez had owned 42 per cent of the shares. Certainly this was a potential case of guilt by association (see Castillo 1996, 52–53).

[52]To be sure, the Colombian pattern is not unique in the annals of statecraft. U.S. history offers several examples of government collusion with criminals to accomplish specific political or foreign policy objectives. U.S. naval intelligence's understandings with Lucky Luciano to help undermine the Fascist regime of Southern Italy, the Central Intelligence Agency's dealings with Sam Giancana's organization in two assassination attempts against Fidel Castro, and U.S. collaboration with Laotian warlords to fight the Pathet Lao Communists are obvious cases in point.

influence of drug money in national presidential and congressional campaigns. As former vice president Humberto de la Calle noted, "Campaign finance is the principal point of entry into the political system."[53] Given the economic clout of the cocaine industry, traffickers' contribution can make the difference between success and failure for aspiring politicians in Colombia. In some parts of the country (Antioquia, Valle, and the North Coast), drug income is probably the leading source of private political funds.

The Samper administration corruption scandal in Colombia intimates the dimension of the problem. By 1997, at least 12 Colombian legislators as well as an attorney general and a defense minister had been jailed for accepting money and favors from Cali traffickers in the 1994 elections. Santiago Medina, Samper's campaign treasurer, believed that at least 70 members of Congress were elected with funds provided by the cartel and that Samper himself solicited donations from traffickers.

Drug Money and Electoral Politics

As was noted above, Colombia's party structure and the clientelistic system have proven extremely vulnerable to the illegal industry. During the past 50 years, political parties have become depoliticized, largely forfeiting ideological considerations, and turned into electoral machines designed to distribute the state bounty. The widespread practice of buying votes allowed the system to be controlled by those with the most money to spare.

Electoral reform was one of the main concerns of those who wrote the new 1991 Constitution. Four types of changes were designed to make the system more democratic and to make it more difficult to purchase votes on election day. The first change was the establishment of two rounds of presidential elections, requiring a runoff if a candidate did not win a majority of votes in the first round (this encourages coalitions and power sharing with smaller parties). The second change was that senators were elected by all voters instead of by departments, to allow smaller parties to be represented in Congress.

The third change was in the voting system. Under the old system, a voter had a small envelope with his candidate's name written on a piece of pa-

---

[53]This is based on Lee and Thoumi's interview with Humberto de la Calle, Bogotá, August 1997.

per inside. This system made it easy to purchase votes because the buyer would give the voter the envelope with a candidate's name and could see when it was placed inside the ballot box. In the new system, the election witnesses give the voter a *tarjetón*, a large piece of paper with the names of all candidates, among which the voter has to choose in private. The fourth change was allowing for paid political advertising in the main media (television, radio, and newspapers).

All interviewees concurred that Colombia, a country of low-cost elections before these changes had been turned into one of high-cost elections. There is no doubt that those with greater capacity to finance elections have become more politically influential. These include the large financial conglomerates and the illegal drug industry. Democracy is expensive!

The interviews highlight two types of drug-trafficking pressure on the system, reflecting different goals of both relatively prominent and obscure drug entrepreneurs. In the past, the traffickers could be separated into extraditables (those singled out for eventual prosecution by U.S. authorities) and nonextraditables (those whose activities were sufficiently circumscribed to merit little attention in the United States).

In small nonmetropolitan areas, low-level and perhaps middle-level participants in the drug industry, who do not feel threatened by extradition, feel safe enough and do not seek any political favors from the political establishment. Their goal when they establish a link to politicians is social acceptance. According to Rodrigo Garavito,[54] "A typical narco has low education. His activity calls for strength and courage. He comes from the middle or lower middle class. He first acquires a house for himself, then one for his mother, a car and later on he buys a *finca*. Finally, he purchases other urban properties. They want social acceptance. At banquets they want to be placed at a table near the politician." Their behavior is akin to that of any other rich individual who wants an active role in the community. They first approach the politician with support offers and do not establish a direct quid pro quo. It is not known how many low-level provincial narcos there are, but Zabludoff's (1997) work suggests that there can be several thousands, a number large enough to influence local politics in most municipalities.

[54]This is based on Lee and Thoumi's interview with Rodrigo Garavito, Bogotá, August 1997.

Politicians realize that some of their supporters have questionable associations, but they prefer not to probe too deeply into the origins of campaign funds. They are willing to accept illicit monies but not to assume responsibility for the crime. At the same time, many campaign contributors prefer formal anonymity, that is, they want the politician to know who they are but they shun public disclosure. This is the case for the large financial conglomerates that finance competing campaigns.[55]

At local and provincial levels, several systems have been used to maintain donor anonymity. Raffles are one. For example, a car is raffled and a contributor, who does not claim the prize if he or she wins, buys most or all tickets.[56] Another more overt system is the issuance by the politician of a set of "bonds" consisting of bearer-denominated receipts that are given in exchange for the contributions. These are "don't tell, don't ask" funding systems, enabling politicians to receive questionable funds without having to acknowledge their source.

The availability of illegal drug funding for political activities has increased its own demand. Drug funds have increased the level of campaign expenditures and tempted other politicians to seek or at least to be willing to receive them.

The need for formal anonymity and the danger of direct politician–narco contacts have spawned the development of an intermediation industry. The system is quite simple. The intermediary approaches a politician with an offer of funds from rich unknown contributors who want to remain anonymous and lets the politician or his campaign manager decide whether to accept the funds. Many times, after a deal is made and the money flows to the campaign, the intermediary takes a cut.

Larger and more powerful narcos worry about the passage of strong drug laws through Congress. They have been particularly, but not exclusively, concerned with extradition legislation. Their behavior toward Congress is similar to that of other powerful economic groups in the country. They contribute funds to their political campaigns without any specific request. But when relevant legislation is being discussed, they try

---

[55]Because parties are depoliticized and devoid of ideologies, it really does not matter who wins; what counts is to have supported the winner.

[56]E.g., Manuel Francisco Becerra explained in the interview that in Cali it became known among politicians that the drug store La Rebaja, which belonged to the Rodríguez-Orejuela brothers, bought more raffle tickets than any other company in town from virtually any candidate, and that they did not claim their prizes when they won.

to leverage past contributions to request favorable votes in the issue at hand. Their contributions can be compared with a joker or a wild card that they can use at appropriate times. Here there is an implied threat of scandal or political ruin if the congressman does not comply. On several occasions, narcos have funded lawyers who write memoranda in support of their desired legislation and distribute them throughout Congress. In this sense, the narco lawyers function as staffers of members of Congress.

Interviews indicate that drug money has financed presidential political campaigns in Colombia during most of the past 25 years. Betancur's unsuccessful 1978 campaign received substantial funds from the illegal industry. Drug funds played an important role in Betancur's and López-Michelsen's campaigns in 1982. Samper, in his capacity as director of López-Michelsen's 1982 presidential campaign, met with Escobar, Gonzalo Rodríguez-Gacha, Ocampo, and other Medellín kingpins in the "Medellín Suite" of that city's Intercontinental Hotel. The outcome was that Samper obtained contributions totaling 19 million pesos ($317,000) from the businessmen.[57]

Betancur, the winner in that election, is reported by his campaign treasurer in Antioquia to have received significantly larger sums. It must be pointed out that the 1982 presidential campaign probably did not cost more that $1 million. This means that the drug money funding López-Michelsen's 1982 campaign was proportionally comparable to what Samper received in 1994. In the next two presidential elections, in 1986 and 1990, it is likely that drug money played a smaller role because in both cases there was an ongoing war between the then dominant Medellín cartel and the government.

The 1991 Constitutional Assembly, which made extradition of nationals unconstitutional, is widely believed to have been highly influenced by drug money. However, the interviews hint at a more complex situation. Escobar opted to pressure the establishment and society at large but not the Assembly itself. As was noted, his strategy was based on exploding

---

[57]Carlos Lehder reported a contribution of 24 million pesos ($400,000). In his recently published memoirs, López-Michelsen (2001, 142) has acknowledged that they received about $400,000, but he claims that this money did not enter the campaign coffers but was used by Antioquia's Liberal Party. This version contradicts our informant's assertion that "it is possible that an intermediary pocketed the difference between the $400,000 contributed by the traffickers and the $317,000 received by the campaign."

bombs in heavily populated places and kidnapping important members of the establishment.[58]

The Medellín cartel's fearful terrorist activities—as well as Colombia's nationalistic resentment against U.S. pressure—had swayed most of the Colombian public against extradition. The Assembly also included a heavy leftist representation that opposed extradition on ideological grounds. The point is simply that most Assembly members opposed extradition, without any pressure from bribes by the drug industry.[59] This is not meant to imply that no Assembly members had strong contacts and links to the illegal drug organizations, or for that matter to the guerrilla movement.

After the new Constitution was approved, a special Congress, known as El Congresito, met to decide whether to approve the decrees passed during the interim period while the new Constitution was being approved. The interviews indicate that drug industry pressure on El Congresito was significant because some of the decrees had to do with the *sometimiento* policy of the Gaviria administration.

During the 1994 presidential campaign, both main candidates were approached with contribution offers from the Cali cartel. Pastrana refused them outright. However, his campaign was broken down into "his" central campaign in Bogotá and seven other Conservative Party campaigns in other regions of the country. This probably was done to circumvent the campaign spending limits, because it could be argued that the regional ones were not part of his campaign. The central campaign rejected all drug contributions, but it is not known what happened in the others—though the interviews indicate the very high probability that drug money did enter those campaigns.

The flow of Cali cartel funds into Samper's campaign was the main political issue in Colombia during the 1994–98 Samper administration and has been the immediate cause of the political, social, and economic crises that the country is experiencing. Cali's contributions, which totaled at least 5 billion pesos ($6 million), played a very important part in the campaign and possibly affected the outcome of the election. The decision-making process by which the money entered the campaign and the impact of the

---

[58]García-Márquez's (1998) best-selling book is a story of these kidnappings.

[59]It must be stressed that when it became known that extradition was declared unconstitutional, there was no public or press outcry against a measure that at the time was quite popular.

funds are not entirely clear. Accounts of various participants, however, seem to agree on seven points.[60]

First, the Cali leaders initiated the relationship. An offer of funding was made to Samper's campaign treasurer, Medina, in April 1994, roughly a month before the start of the campaign. A Colombian journalist with close ties to the cartel, Alberto Giraldo, communicated the offer to Medina in the latter's office in Bogotá.

Second, Samper's campaign manager, Fernando Botero (subsequently the defense minister in Samper's cabinet) accepted the offer. To formalize arrangements for the donations, Medina traveled to Cali in early May and met with Miguel and Gilberto Rodriguez as well as two other Cali leaders, Helmer Herrera and José Santacruz. At the time, he asked for 2 billion pesos, half of which he received.

Third, the campaign also solicited funds from the Cali traffickers. Samper and his campaign members expected to win in the first round, but they came in a very close second to Pastrana, trailing by 14,000 votes. After this failure, and confronted with the need to spend large sums of money that they did not have, it appears that many in the campaign decided to actually ask the Cali cartel for support during a 3-week period before the second round. Medina traveled to Cali in June to deliver the request and at the time received 4 billion pesos in additional funds from the traffickers.

Fourth, some quid pro quo was involved in the campaign nexus. In contrast to the general pattern of drug-funded campaigns, Cali traffickers wanted specific understandings and assurances from the candidate in return for their donations.

Fifth, to orchestrate the illegal fund operation, the campaign treasurer created what amounted to a double bookkeeping system. A foundation was set up, the Asociación para una Colombia Moderna, to run the campaign's legal finances. The foundation took checks and cash from legitimate donors up to the prescribed campaign expenditure limits (established by

---

[60]Principal sources include Samper campaign officials Juan Manuel Avella and Santiago Medina, interviewed in Bogotá in July and August 2002, and Guillermo Palomari, formerly Miguel Rodríguez's accountant, who has recently testified in the United States under a witness-protection program. Useful published material includes "La Indagatoria de Samper," *El Tiempo*, August 3, 1995, 8A, 9A; "Por Qué No Se Cayó," *Semana*, December 10–17, 1996, 45–48; "La Película en Inglés," *Semana*, July 28–August 4, 1997, 35; Castillo (1996, 204–6); Vargas, Lesmes, and Téllez (1996, 112–50); and López-Caballero (1997).

the National Electoral Council) of 4 billion pesos. A parallel system appears to have been established by Medina and Botero to receive and distribute dirty money, including the donations from Cali. There is agreement that campaign expenditures exceeded the legal limits by significant amounts and that drug money entered the campaign. The most likely version indicates that the excess expenditure was 7.3 billion pesos (approximately $8 million); 5 billion of this could be attributed to the Cali cartel.[61]

Sixth, the deal was a cash transaction. According to different sources, Cali funds originated in the account of Miguel Rodríguez-Orejuela's front company—Exportcafé—in the Banco de Colombia in Cali. As was noted above, that account had been set up by a coalition of Cali and Valle traffickers specially to support presidential and congressional campaigns.[62] It was reported that the money was packed in boxes and gift wrapped (each box held 500 million pesos) in the presence of Rodríguez-Orejuela himself and then flown by private plane to Bogotá. Their cartel intermediary picked up the money and delivered it directly to Medina and Botero, who then arranged the distribution of the funds to cover campaign expenses in different regions of the country.

Seventh, the cartel's donation possibly made the difference between victory and defeat for Samper. Some of the money was used to cover media advertising costs (mainly television), which according to Medina's calculations reached 8 billion pesos ($9 million) during the campaign. Some was used for outright vote buying. One clear case was in the Córdoba Department; Samper received 31,000 votes in the first round of the campaign, but 3 weeks later he obtained 87,000 votes!

In sum, campaign corruption, like other kinds of collusive behavior, represents an exchange of values. The motives of the campaigns obviously are to raise money and to win elections. Traffickers' requirements (like those of, say, American corporate donors in U.S. elections) tend to

---

[61]It must be pointed out that most evidence about these expenditures is based on individual testimonies only. Because most expenditures were in cash, it has been impossible to follow up on most of them. López-Caballero (1997) argued that in Samper's trial in Congress, it was proven that only a fraction of those funds entered the campaign and that it is likely that Medina keep a large sum for himself.

[62]Funds from the same Exportcafé account, about $250,000, also supported the congressional campaign of Orlando Vásquez-Velásquez, who was later named procurador general. At the time of the interviews, Vásquez-Velásquez was awaiting sentencing at a DAS facility outside Bogotá.

be diffuse and generalized. A bribe delivered to a judge, a police officer, or a government official implies an expectation that a specific service or favor will result from it.

More generally, during the campaigns, traffickers seek to create a relationship of goodwill that will pay off in allowing subsequent access to the new incumbent. An apparent exception was the Samper presidential campaign; before giving money to the campaign, traffickers asked for and received general assurances relating to their legal status. In any event, the entry of drug money into election contests itself establishes a nexus to the political elite. Traffickers, like large legal contributors, give money with the expectation that when a legislation or policy issue will be at stake, they will be able to request particular favors from such and such politician.

The criminal–political nexus has conferred some benefits to both sides in Colombia. For the narcotics establishment generally, the benefits have included the opportunity to legalize drug earnings; to invest relatively openly in companies, real estate, and rural land; to cultivate personal ties with political leaders and other establishment figures; and, in general, to acquire a modicum of social acceptance and respectability. For traffickers under pressure from authorities, ties to the political system have paid off in relatively short prison sentences, favorable "plea bargaining" legislation (which allowed sentences to be cut by two-thirds or more under various pretexts), a constitutional ban on extradition and in individual cases, and the opportunity to be integrated back into society after serving time.

For the Colombian government, the benefits have been less obvious. Surrender negotiations with traffickers have brought about a reduction in anti-state violence and also have brought those traffickers whom the authorities were unable to apprehend behind bars. Yet such deals also have highlighted the weaknesses of the criminal justice system. The short sentences meted out to top Medellín and Cali kingpins, the farce of Escobar's designer prison in his hometown of Envigado (from which facility he could exit at will to attend soccer matches and carouse in local discotheques), and the apparent ability of Cali's Rodríguez-Orejuela brothers to run their trafficking empires from jail are testimonies to this unfortunate situation.

In Colombia's troubled hinterland, traffickers' contributions to local security forces may have played a role in expelling guerrillas from some important rural zones in Colombia (e.g., the Middle Magdalena Valley). Yet the narco-backed paramilitaries accentuate the problem of govern-ability in Colombia even while performing positive security functions. Paramilitaries are in effect right-wing guerrillas who contribute to rural strife and instability. Furthermore, traffickers' ability to purchase the services of legislators and top government officials—as well as the infiltration of drug money into political campaigns—degrades the political environment in Colombia. The result is to underscore the government's weakness and to accelerate the delegitimation of the Colombian regime.

Finally, the 1994 campaign scandals and evidence of widespread corruption at the topmost echelons of Colombia's political system have complicated Colombia's international relationship, especially with the United States. In two successive years Washington "decertified" Colombia as an unfit partner in the drug war—a decision that carries the potential of economic and diplomatic sanctions.

Drugs and the Pastrana Administration

Andrés Pastrana, the president elected in 1998, had narrowly lost to Ernesto Samper in 1994, and many believed that his loss had been due to the large contributions of drug money during the final days of Samper's campaign. In contrast to his predecessor, Pastrana had the trust of the U.S. government, and his election was accompanied with high hopes of better relations with the United States. He had run on a peace campaign and owed his election to a substantial degree to his visit to guerrilla-controlled areas, where he had taken a widely circulated picture with Pedro Antonio Marín (a.k.a. Manuel Marulanda-Vélez and Tirofijo), the undisputable Colombian Revolutionary Armed Forces (FARC) leader, and other members of FARC's secretariat.[63]

Since day one, Pastrana's main priority had been to start, and it was hoped conclude, a peace process with FARC. To start the process, he agreed to remove all government armed and law enforcement forces from a five-municipality area in the eastern jungle, one of the main coca-growing and -processing regions. There is no question that the state's presence in that region was limited almost exclusively to the urban areas and that FARC had been the main de facto authority in most of it.[64] This

---

[63]FARC played a key role in Pastrana's 1998 election because that picture increased his support among Colombians hungry for peace. Ironically, 4 years later Alvaro Uribe was elected on a war platform in response to FARC actions.

[64]The international press repeated in almost every relevant article that Pastrana had granted a "Switzerland-size" area to FARC. In fact, the Colombian state never had real control of it.

"distension zone" was to provide a good environment in which peace negotiations could proceed.

It appears that the granting of the distension zone to FARC was decided as a result of Pastrana's campaign visit and that the new administration did not really have a plan about how to proceed. Before vacating the area, the administration did not set clear rules about the FARC and the state's roles in the region. FARC insisted, and obtained, a total military and police withdrawal from the region, including all nonarmed personnel. This allowed the FARC to impose its own law on the municipal and other government officials. Furthermore, the distension zone provided a safe haven in which FARC could concentrate its secretariat, organize and coordinate its military operations, keep its kidnap victims, and control the drug trade.

When FARC took over control of the distension zone, it proceeded to impose its own law and order and began to restrict and regulate the illegal drug industry. To start, in order to strengthen peasant support, it decreed a minimum coca price and eliminated some of the intermediaries between the peasants and the traffickers. First, it took over the activities of the coca gatherers and then established control over the refining process. Independently of who owned the labs, they were controlled by the FARC. Second, it took control of sales to cocaine wholesales and exporters. Third, it built several airplane runways to facilitate the drug trade and illegal weapon imports. These developments increased FARC's involvement in the illegal drug trade. It is not surprising that there have been many journalistic and political references to FARC as a drug "cartel," even though there is no evidence that it has been able to develop international distribution networks. It cannot be denied, however, that FARC has developed strong links with international criminal organizations that purchase drugs and sell weapons and other war supplies.

It is also true that it is very difficult for Colombian guerrilla organizations to develop their own international drug distribution networks. First, they do not have many members that speak foreign languages or that can safely reside abroad. FARC certainly finds it more difficult to set up distribution cells in the United States and Europe than other Colombian trafficking organizations Second, any guerrilla member abroad directly involved in the illegal drug business would face substantially longer sentences than a common trafficker. Similarly, drug traffickers would also risk higher sentences if caught purchasing from guerrillas abroad because they could also be accused of being guerrilla members. These facts suggest that the FARC would have a strong preference to sell drugs to international traffickers in Colombia and not become too involved in international trafficking. Colombian guerrilla difficulties in the drug trade were likely to increase after they were declared terrorists by the United States and the European Union.

During the Pastrana administration, paramilitary organizations also gained strength and contested with the National Liberation Army (ELN) and FARC for control over coca- and poppy-growing areas and export corridors. The Middle Magdalena Valley and Putumayo are examples of such regions in which paramilitary forces gained power. The paramilitary–guerrilla fight put many peasants at risk of being accused by either group of helping the enemy and generated a massive peasant displacement, most of it to urban areas, creating a grave social problem.

The peace negotiations with FARC did not advance during the Pastrana administration. The government did not take a proactive position and did not propose an agenda responding to FARC grievances. Three years were spent discussing how to start negotiating. Indeed, the "peace process" could be described as dialogue without negotiations. In the meantime, both sides made preparations for an open war. During this time, FARC continued kidnapping civilians and attacking targets, many of them civilian. Finally, in February 2002, the government gave up its peace attempts and cancelled the distension zone. Throughout the peace talks, FARC presented a very intransigent position. It is as if it believed that the Colombian state was growing weaker and weaker while FARC's financial resources had increased and allowed it to wait for the state's collapse.

The internationalization of the Colombian armed conflict has been an important by-product of the growth of the illegal drug industry. As soon as Pastrana took over, the Colombian government made a plea to the international community to fund a "Marshall Plan" for that country. The plea was based on the Colombian government's belief that the illegal drug industry was the main cause of the country's problems and that the international community was partly responsible. The European countries did not respond quickly, but several countries expressed interest in collaborating a year or so later. This left the United States as the main contributor. Plan Colombia spells out the U.S. contribution.

There is a debate about the authorship of Plan Colombia. Many in Colombia argue that it was written in Washington with very little, if any, input from the Colombian government, whose officials adamantly respond that it was their plan. The head of Colombia's National Planning Department argues that the plan was formulated quickly but that it dovetailed with the development philosophy of the government and was conceived as a complement to its national development plan, which had been carefully formulated by a team working on it for a long time. However, critics argue that there is no single Plan Colombia, that the English version presented to the U.S. Congress differs from the Spanish version circulated in Colombia, and that the plan has varied through time.

Plan Colombia originally called for $7.5 billion, most of which was to be funded by the Colombian government. The European contribution was to be more than a billion dollars, but it was never forthcoming. The United States contributed $1.3 billion during a 2-year period. These funds were assigned to fight illicit drugs. Most of the U.S. contribution was military; $450 million were used to fund the U.S. military bases in Manta (Ecuador) and Aruba. The rest was used to provide the Colombian government with mostly military hardware (Blackhawk helicopters), military training and assistance, and the illicit-crop aerial spraying program. A residual amount was assigned to alternative development and social problems.

The Colombian government argues that most of the social component of Plan Colombia was domestically funded and included several social programs already in the government's pipeline. Critics equate the plan with the U.S. contribution and argue that it is simply a military campaign against coca- and poppy-growing peasants and fails to deal with the drug industry in a realistic way. Some argue that it is just an excuse to increase the U.S. military presence in the Amazon, a region where the U.S. has a long-term strategic interest because of its natural resources.

The use of military hardware has been a source of contention. The U.S. Congress required that the U.S. funds had to be used only to fight drugs. They could not be used to fight subversive forces. Given the guerrilla involvement in the drug industry, it is difficult to draw a line between fighting drugs and fighting guerrillas. The Colombian government requested unsuccessfully that this restriction be eliminated. However, after September 11, 2001, the Colombian guerrilla and paramilitary organizations were declared terrorists by the United States, opening the way for the use of U.S. contributed hardware against subversive forces, which was authorized in April 2002.

Independent of its components, the U.S. contribution is remarkably small relative to the size of the Colombian economy. Excluding the expenditures in Manta and Aruba, the balance amounts to 0.5 percent of the country's gross national product. One certainly can argue that if the drug "problem" in Colombia could be solved with that amount, why should foreign assistance be required?

Plan Colombia has had two different effects. First, it has helped strengthen the Colombian military. There is no question that if Colombia is to survive as a nation, its military must become more professional—it should control the country's territory, respect human rights, and gain social respect. The plan contributes effectively to all these goals. And indeed, there are signs that the Colombian armed forces are moving in that direction with U.S. assistance.

Second, Plan Colombia has promoted ineffective repressive antidrug policies that tend to aggravate the Colombian conflict. Alternative development is not effective, but it appeases the peasantry (see chapters 11 and 12). Plan Colombia has promoted aerial spraying. Manual eradication in Colombia is more difficult than in Bolivia and Peru (and probably impossible in most places) because of the lack of state presence in producing regions and the lack of organized stable communities in most illegal crop zones. In many areas, fumigation represents the main state presence. "State presence by fumigation" increases resentment against the state and undermines any other of its activities in those communities. The success of aerial fumigation requires the use of pesticides against which peasants cannot devise protective methods. This is likely to increase environmental damage. Besides, in the case of opium poppy, a short-cycle, 3- to 4-month crop requires a credible threat of continuous fumigation to avoid replanting.

During the Pastrana administration, illegal drugs have had important effects on the Colombian conflict. First, the main violent actors (guerrillas and paramilitary) have increased their warring capabilities, using the drug industry as the main funding source. Second, illegal drugs have contributed to the internationalization of the Colombian conflict. Indeed, Plan Colombia would not have been developed if Colombia had not been a main illegal drug producer. Unfortunately, the antidrug policy component of Plan Colombia has had conflicting effects on the government's capacity to cope with the guerrilla and paramilitary problem, and the plan's emphasis on repressive policies—particularly aerial spraying—has not contributed to a long-term resolution of the Colombian conflict.

8

The Illegal Drug Industry's Effects in Bolivia and Peru

The illegal drug industry's effects in Bolivia and Peru have been significantly different from those in Colombia. These have been determined by the industry's structure in both countries, their governments' economic policies, and the countries' institutions and social capital. On the whole, the industry's effects in these two countries have been milder and more benign than in Colombia.

Economic Effects

Illegal Drugs and Structural Adjustment

During the postwar period, until the 1980s, macroeconomic management in Bolivia and Peru was very unstable. Economic policies changed frequently, and populist governments led to episodes of grave macroeconomic disequilibria and very high inflation. In the early 1980s, both countries experienced the Latin American external debt crisis, deep declines in national income, and sharp increases in the proportions of their population living below the poverty level. Both countries also had to undertake profound macroeconomic adjustment processes, even though their timing and specifics did not coincide.

In 1984 and 1985, Bolivia suffered a hyperinflationary period and a deep crisis that led to structural economic adjustment. This included the closing of important tin mines and the privatization of public enterprises designed to encourage social participation (Alvarez 1995, 128). Inflation declined dramatically, and the Bolivian economy has remained quite stable since then, even though the reforms have not led to sustained growth.

Noneconomists frequently criticize the structural adjustments that most Latin American countries undertook in the mid- and late 1980s on the grounds that they hurt the weakest members of society. To understand structural economic adjustment, it is useful to review some elementary national accounting identities.

Total aggregate demand confronted by producers (Y) in a country is equal to the consumption expenditures of the household sector (C) plus the investment expenditures of private business (I) plus government expenditures (G) plus external demand for exports (X) minus the demand satisfied by imported goods and services (M). Thus $Y = C + I + G + X - M$.

The same income Y received by all households is used to purchase consumer goods and services (C), to pay taxes (T), and to save (S). Thus $Y = C + T + S$.

From these to identities, one gets $C + I + G + X - M = C + T + S$, which can be rewritten as $(S - I) + (T - G) = (X - M)$. In a very simplified way, this shows that the financial balance of the private sector (its savings minus what it invests) plus the balance of the public sector should (taxes minus government expenditures) equal the surplus or deficit in the current account of the balance of payments (exports minus imports).

If the total of the balances of the private and public sectors is negative— that is, private-sector savings plus taxes are less than private investment plus government expenditures—then imports must be greater than exports by the same amount.

Focusing now on another balance of payments identity, the balance in the current account must be equal to the balance in the capital account plus changes in reserves. That is, if a country runs a current account deficit (i.e., it imports more goods and services than it exports), this has to be financed by borrowing abroad or selling international reserves. In most cases, such a deficit is financed through external borrowing. Therefore, total domestic deficits must be financed by borrowing abroad (or selling international reserves).

These accounting identities can be used to illustrate in a nutshell what happened to Bolivia and Peru during the late 1970s and early 1980s. For several years, the private sector in those countries invested more than it saved, and the public sector ran deficits. These had to be financed abroad, and the countries had large deficits in their current accounts ($M > X$). When this happens, the countries' total "absorption" ($C + I + G$) is larger than their total production.

Because the capacity of any country to borrow abroad is limited, an economic system that is functioning on the premise of ever-larger external debt sooner or later has a crisis. Very frequently, an unexpected event such as a decline in the price of the country's exports triggers and receives attribution as "the" cause of the crisis, even though the crisis would have occurred anyway at a later time. The large increase in international interest rates in the early 1980s triggered crises in all of Latin America and the Caribbean, except Colombia. This dried up the sources of external funds and actually forced Bolivia and Peru to pay their debts, which required these countries to run a surplus in their current account ($M < X$), which in turn forced an adjustment in the private and public sectors, which were forced to generate a surplus ($S + T > I + G$). To resolve the crisis, the countries had to increase X, S, and T and lower M, I, and G.

It must be stressed that this analysis is based on accounting identities and is independent of any economic theory. Because these are identities, they cannot be circumvented and act as a straitjacket on any economy. The structural adjustment programs forced countries that had been accustomed to large external capital inflows to generate capital outflows, which required sharp cuts in investment and government expenditures and increases in taxes and domestic savings. In this situation, every government is forced to distribute a fall in total "absorption" ($C + I + G$). In other words, the total of consumption plus investment plus government expenditure must decline.

The attempts by the Bolivian and Peruvian governments to circumvent the macroeconomic-balances straitjacket led to very large government deficits, which accelerated inflation,[1] which in turn aggravated the deficits and led to hyperinflation. In these conditions, the government cannot avoid raising taxes and cutting government expenditures. The nature of the country's political economy will determine how this adjustment is borne by the citizenry, that is, which expenditures and subsidies are cut and which taxes are increased. It is not surprising that those who are politically the weakest tend to pay a high price in this process!

It must also be stressed that structural adjustment is the other side of the coin of a process of overspending and heavy external borrowing. In other words, when countries overspend and do so with financing from abroad, eventually they will have to adjust. In this sense, structural adjustment was unavoidable in the Latin America of the 1980s. Many critics of structural adjustment point to the many injustices it generates, but they generally fail to provide viable alternatives. Furthermore, they do not explain what would happen if a government refuses to adjust, in which case the country's economy would simply collapse, generating social costs that could easily be larger than those of the adjustment. At the end of the day, the dismal science confirms that life is unfair!

Alvarez (1995, 129) characterized Peruvian postwar policies as a pendulum that goes from periods of strict government controls to periods of market liberalization and vice versa. These swings accounted for a substantial degree of economic instability and were instrumental in a lackluster growth record from the mid-1960s to 1990. During the external debt crisis of the 1980s, the Alan García administration tried to postpone structural adjustment on account of its large foreign exchange reserves. To do so, it announced a limit on payments of the country's external debt to 10 percent of exports and increased salaries to promote domestic demand. This program could be maintained as long as the country could draw on foreign exchange reserves to fund the current account deficit ($X > M$) it generated. The program appeared to succeed for a couple of years, but when reserves ran out it resulted in hyperinflation and a sharp economic depression.

During the 1990 presidential campaign, the right-of-center candidate, Mario Vargas-Llosa, advocated a structural adjustment program. When President Alberto Fujimori took over in 1990, he surprised most observers

---

[1]The increases in inflation result in lower tax collection in real terms (deflated by inflation) because of the lag between tax accruals and tax collections. In simpler words, by the time taxes are collected, they already have lost a proportion of their purchasing power.

when he proceeded to implement the policies advocated by the election's main loser. In reality, the straightjacket was on, for Fujimori did not have alternatives. During the 1990s, the Peruvian economy was stable and regained most of the lost income, although there are questions about its sustained growth possibilities.

Adjustment took place in Bolivia and Peru after both countries experienced significant declines in gross national product, increases in absolute poverty, very sluggish private-sector investment, and runaway inflation. The illegal drug industry played important roles in Bolivia and Peru's economic adjustment.

In Bolivia, the crisis of the early 1980s and the 1985 adjustment coincided with a substantial expansion in coca cultivation. As was seen above, the main coca-producing region (Chapare) received large numbers of new immigrants, many of whom were impoverished peasants and a few unemployed miners. Besides, the illegal industry also created significant indirect employment in the urban informal sector involved in money-laundering activities and contraband (Alvarez 1995, 135). In this case, it may be argued that the combination of low international tin prices and macroeconomic mismanagement contributed to illegal crop growth. At the same time, the employment and foreign exchange generated by the expansion of the illegal industry allowed macroeconomic mismanagement to last longer and made the economic adjustment somewhat easier.

Bolivia and Peru dollarized their economies to a much greater extent than Colombia, in part as a result of the hyperinflation that they experienced. Contracts, bank accounts, and transactions in dollars are common in both countries. The widespread use of the dollar for domestic transactions makes it easier to launder illegal drug revenues than in Colombia because at least part of the drug revenues do not have to be changed into local currencies to be laundered.

Other Economic Effects in Peru

Peruvian economists have had a lively debate about the economic effects of the illegal drug industry. This has centered on the impact of the illegal industry on the exchange rate and the possible negative effects of exchange rate overvaluation. Given the great macroeconomic and policy instability experienced by Peru from 1968 to 1991, it is very difficult to determine in a clear-cut fashion the macroeconomic consequences of the illegal industry's growth. This period included episodes of strict foreign exchange controls and liberalization, attempts to centrally control the economy, populist policies, and hyperinflation. Thus it was not surprising that economists' opinions about the illegal drug industry effects varied.

Vega and Cebrecos (1991) argued that the recession of the late 1980s and the very high interest rates experienced by Peru were more important causes of currency overvaluation than the foreign exchange generated by the drug industry and concluded that the latter did not have an important effect on the exchange rate. Cruz-Saco, Revilla, and Seminario (1994) found that from 1985 to 1990 the Peruvian currency appreciated continuously while illegal industry revenues varied around a declining trend. On the basis of these findings, they also argued that illegal-industry revenues were not important determinants of the exchange rate.

Alvarez and Associates (1996) and Alvarez and Cervantes (1996) used more elaborate and sophisticated econometric techniques. They used monthly data from 1979 through 1994 for the real exchange rate, total international reserves minus gold, and coca export estimates. This series showed growing illegal industry exports until 1983 and almost continuous declines after then until 1992. International reserves increased in 1979 and remained relatively stable until 1986 (the beginning of the García administration), when they experienced a sharp drop and remained quite low from 1988 through 1990.

After 1990, when Fujimori took over, international reserves had a dramatic increase. This series varied mainly with presidential and policy changes, that is, with the Peruvian pendulum, and it was not related at all to illegal drug exports. Indeed, during the 1990–92 sharp increase in international reserves, illegal drug exports were much lower than during the early and mid-1980s. The series of real exchange with the country's seven largest commercial partners was flat from 1979 through 1981, and then increased exponentially from 1982 to 1986. During the next 3 years, it was flat after the currency was replaced (the sol was replaced by the inti). During the next 3 years, it was flat again and increased from 1990 on.

The statistical analysis by Alvarez and her colleagues found that, in the long run, the exchange rate was "cointegrated" with their estimates of illegal drug exports, which implies that illegal revenues, although declining, have had an effect on the exchange rate. Their analysis also showed that an important part of this effect takes place through the process of "securitization" and money laundering. Securitization occurs when traditional funding through bank loans to corporate customers, including traffickers, is replaced by the issuance of securities, mainly bonds and short-term money market paper, placed directly with investors (Alvarez and Associates 1996, 71). In simpler words, the development of an active bond market allowed traffickers to launder their profits and revalue the exchange rate.

Alvarez and Associates (1996) and Alvarez (1998, 111) also argued "that the coca boom can ultimately increase poverty in the areas concerned" because of two perverse effects on the food-growing sector, which competes with imported foods and on producers of tradeable goods. Alvarez and her colleagues based this argument on two facts: The illicit industry generates inflationary food pressures, and it increases the supply of foreign exchange. These two effects result in a currency overvaluation that "serves to make the overall economic adjustment more difficult" (Alvarez 1995, 136).

These arguments are somewhat confusing. It is one thing to have increased food prices in a region that is experiencing a boom, and it is something else to argue that the development of the illegal industry will eventually make peasants poorer and will make macroeconomic structural adjustment more difficult. If structural adjustment is understood as explained above, there is no question that the illegal drug industry facilitated adjustment in Bolivia and Peru. One of the key characteristics of the crises was a foreign exchange deficit, and any exports contributed to improving the macroeconomic imbalances of those economies. Any increase in exports meant that consumption, investment, and government expenditures had to have smaller cuts or that taxes and savings had to increase less.

There are, however, other possibly important effects. To explain the food inflation effect discussed by Alvarez, it is necessary to clarify three points. First, the development of any large new export industry generates foreign exchange, income, and increased demand. These developments change some relative prices within the country and generate winners and losers. Winners are involved in the production of goods whose relative prices increase, and losers are involved in the production of goods whose relative prices decline. Among consumers, winners spend large amounts on the goods whose prices fall, and vice versa. In this sense, the illegal drug industry is not different from any export industry.

Second, the illegal industry has regional effects, one of which is the increase in prices of nontradeable goods and services in the coca-growing regions. This is a change in relative prices within a particular region that is different from inflationary pressure. It may or may not contribute to inflation in the rest of the country.

Third, if coca plantings substituted for food crops, then food prices would go up in the country and imports would also go up. Because the illegal industry's value added is mostly exported, the industry itself generates large amounts of foreign exchange and, as Alvarez and Associates pointed out, revalues the currency. Thus, food imports will be cheap and food prices will tend to fall.

It is possible for some to see any change in relative prices as a cost,[2] and indeed, politically these changes can be costly. However, changes in relative prices are not costs in an economic sense, and indeed, the ones caused by the illegal drug industry are similar to those generated by any expanding export industry. These are independent of the structural adjustment process experienced by Bolivia in the mid- and late 1980s and Peru in the early 1990s.

Backward-Linkage Effects in Peru

As was noted in chapter 5, on the one hand, in Bolivia and Peru the illegal industry's value added as a percentage of the countries' gross national product reached a maximum in the early 1980s and has declined significantly since. On the other hand, rural employment in the illegal industry has been and remains important in both countries.

The backward-linkage effects of the industry on the countries' economies have been thought to be small because almost all intermediate products used by the illegal industry are believed to be imported. This is certainly the case of Bolivia. In the case of Peru, Alvarez and Cervantes (1996, 153) referred to Alvarez's (1993) estimates of "the value of the coca sector's purchases from other sectors [which] ranged from 1 to 5 percent of the sector's total intermediate demand. The major implication of findings is that the coca industry has limited importance from an interindustrial perspective."

Alvarez (1998, 109) used the estimates of Alvarez and Associates (1996) to provide a different view: "Coca's backward linkages show that they may be higher than previous estimates suggest. For instance, 15–17% of the sector's intermediate demand is for chemical products and 16–17% for transportation and storage." As the illegal industry becomes more vertically integrated in Bolivia and Peru, one would expect larger indirect effects because of the industry's greater need for chemical products, hideouts, and transportation.

---

[2]This appears to be the case in Alvarez (1998, 119–20).

Peculiarities of the Estimated Effects on Bolivia

As was explained in chapter 5, the estimates of the illegal drug industry's revenues in Bolivia are based on some peculiar assumptions about the share that remains in the country. It has become a "fact" of conventional wisdom that a significant proportion of the value added of Bolivian illegal drugs does not remain in Bolivia and is invested abroad (Doria-Medina 1986, 70; Malamud-Goti 1994, 33; Mendoza 1993, 17; Aguiló 1992, 45; Cortez 1992, 119). Of these researchers, only Doria-Medina spelled out the proportions of income generated by coca paste, cocaine base, and cocaine that are assumed to stay in Bolivia. The rest simply state as a fact that income generated in Bolivia leaves the country. Joel (1999) followed the same tradition and assumed

1. That 100 percent of the value added generated in coca growing is retained.
2. That there is no real market for coca paste and that coca is processed straight into base.
3. That 50 percent of the base is exported and 50 percent processed into cocaine, and that 70 percent of the base generated value added is retained.
4. That 35 percent of the value added generated in cocaine manufacturing is retained.
5. That Bolivians do not participate in international smuggling and do not receive any revenues generated in smuggling or foreign markets. In other words, all their exports are F.O.B. ("free on board").

These percentages were not derived from any serious research and are only widely used "guesstimates."[3] The estimators used several underlining arguments to justify these figures. The first is that a proportion of the Bolivian value added accrues to Colombians and other foreigners who take it out of the country. The second is that a proportion of the amount made by Bolivian drug traffickers is also invested abroad because there are no investment opportunities in Bolivia.

As was noted in chapter 5, this argument implies that the "absorptive capacity" of Bolivia is so limited that the country somehow

[3]Joel is a former economist at the U.S. Agency for International Development who worked in Bolivia. His study was part of a United Nations Development Program (UNDP) project that I coordinated. I discussed these figures with Joel on several occasions and came to the conclusion that they were simple educated guesses based on conventional wisdom and journalistic reports.

has excessive funds available for investment. Because Bolivia borrows large amounts abroad and real interest rates are high, this argument is quite questionable. A more likely reason for Bolivians' propensity to invest drug revenues abroad is simply that the "Laundromat" in the country is just too small. That is, any trafficker with a few million dollars in a country as poor as Bolivia becomes very conspicuous if he tries to invest his fortune in Bolivia. In this case, the incentives to invest abroad could be very strong.

Even if it is true that a proportion of Bolivian illicit drug revenues is invested abroad, there are at least three interesting questions that researchers have not addressed. First, if it is accepted that international traffickers pay in dollar bills, then what happens to the funds that are taken out of Bolivia? Are they deposited in Bolivian banks, from where they are transferred to financial havens? Are they smuggled out of Bolivia? As far as I have been able to ascertain, there has never been a seizure of funds of this type leaving Bolivia.

Second, another interesting issue is how long investments remain abroad. As was shown in chapter 7, the volume of illicit drug funds that flows into Colombia varies in response to domestic and international investment environments. If Bolivian traffickers invest part of their profits abroad, do they never bring them back? Is the proportion of expatriated profits constant, independent of international and domestic market conditions?

Third, the structure of the Bolivian industry has changed over time. As was shown in chapter 4, there is evidence that in the 1990s the industry became more integrated and the proportion of coca processed into cocaine in Bolivia increased. Simultaneously, Bolivians became more involved in international drug trafficking. Have these changes affected the proportion of revenues expatriated?

The lack of serious studies about the actual proportion of illicit value added that is retained in Bolivia is very unfortunate because these estimates are crucial to determining the impact of the coca-cocaine industry on the country. As long as most of the income generated by the industry that remains in the country is a remuneration to rural labor and coca growing, poor peasants and the economy benefit, without generating wealth concentration and drastic changes in the power structure of the country. If this is the case, most coca-cocaine income is spent on consumer goods and improvements to peasant housing, education, and health, but very little drug money is invested in urban real estate and in the industrial and service sectors.

This perception of the Bolivian industry is widely held (at least as part of official discourse) and leads to the conclusion that the industry's effects on Bolivian society are very benign. This corresponds to what one might call the "evil Colombian" or "evil foreigner" model of Bolivian drugs. According to this model, most benefits of the industry in Bolivia accrue to "good guys" and the "bad foreign guys" make most of the money (Thoumi 1995b). The real impact of the illegal drug industry on Bolivia is, however, extremely dependent on the validity of the assumptions of the "evil foreigner" model, particularly on the lack of Bolivian participation in the export and marketing businesses in Europe and the United States, and on the reluctance of Bolivian traffickers to invest in the country.

Bolivia is a small country with a very concentrated income distribution, and its economic elite likely consists of fewer than 50,000 people. In these circumstances, any industry that grows to the point of generating between 10 and 15 percent of gross domestic product for a few years has to involve the country's elite and must be a very important (perhaps the main) upward mobility channel. In reality, Bolivian society is very vulnerable to the illegal industry and, as will be shown below, it has been deeply affected by drug trafficking. However, the "evil Colombian or foreigner" model provides a smokescreen behind which many of the social, political, and economic effects of the illegal industry can be hidden and denied. For example, this model allows researchers to avoid serious analysis of such key issues for Bolivia as money laundering, land concentration in traffickers' hands, and the relationship between politics and drug money.

The opening during the 1990s of new cocaine markets in Argentina, Brazil, and Europe and other places where Colombian drug traffickers do not have the same capacity as in the United States to develop distribution networks increases the incentives for Bolivians to involve themselves in the cocaine export business. This clearly raises the country's vulnerability to the illegal industry.

Following the "evil Colombian" model, many Bolivians see coca as an economic godsend. When the mineral-based economy of Bolivia collapsed in the late 1970s and early 1980s, coca growing provided the only reasonably good employment alternative for many unemployed people. Furthermore, coca is perceived as a very good crop: It uses a fair amount of labor, it does not require great skills, it grows in areas where it is difficult to cultivate other crops, it generates badly needed foreign exchange, and the growers do not have marketing difficulties.

As was shown in chapter 2, a significant part of the Bolivian literature sees coca as a regular primary product whose terms of trade deteriorate in favor of industrial consumer countries, portrays U.S. policies simply as protectionist, and argues the unfairness of the small share of the cocaine street value that goes to pay the poor Bolivian grower. Furthermore, though violence in coca-growing regions is higher than in other parts of Bolivia, in reality it is not very high. Therefore, Bolivians do not perceive the industry as generating many negative effects.

Besides, as was noted above, there is growing evidence that peasants are increasingly processing coca leaves into paste, base, and occasionally cocaine. The popular Bolivian explanation is that they were "forced" to do so to maintain their levels of income when coca leaf prices fell. These changes are important because they destroy the argument that growing coca is qualitatively and morally different from producing cocaine and that peasants are not engaged in criminal activities. In this case, again, the Bolivian popular position blames exports: If coca prices were "fair," peasants would not process coca leaves. Of course, Bolivians do not explain that the only way for coca prices to be "fair" is if coca is used to produce cocaine.

Employment Effects

Recapitulating from chapter 5, estimates for the Bolivian illegal drug industry indicate that it employed anywhere between 5 and 13.5 percent of the labor force, mostly in coca growing. In Peru, these figures are about 7 percent of the rural labor force and 2 percent of the country's labor force.

It is clear that the employment effects of the illegal industry are extremely important for Bolivia and are also important in rural Peru. This suggests that any policy aimed at cutting illegal production would have to contemplate employment alternatives; otherwise it would likely generate other undesirable effects, such as increased rural–urban migration to already congested cities and possible peasant uprisings.

Regional Effects

The illegal drug industry has had significant regional effects in Bolivia and Peru. In Bolivia, the illegal industry has accelerated the migration and settlement of Chapare and Beni. Among the country's cities, the greatest impact has likely been on Santa Cruz, where it is commonly acknowledged that its fast growth and real estate boom have been supported, at least partially, by illegal funds. Santa Cruz is the heart of Camba culture and is where most of the known Bolivian traffickers have resided. A real estate boom was also experienced in La Paz, where many skyscrapers have been built. The conventional wisdom also relates this development to illegal funds. Unfortunately, there are no rigorous studies that test these hypotheses.

Laserna, Vargas, and Torrico (1999) studied some of the effects of the illegal industry growth on Cochabamba. They found that the industry has changed the nature of the city and its surrounding region. Before coca, Cochabamba Department was a source of migrants to other regions and the city's growth was controlled and planned. Coca made the department a magnet for migrants, and fast city growth has made it very difficult to have orderly city development. These effects are the result of Colla participation in the industry. Because Collas are underrepresented in the high-income-generating activities of the industry, the impact of the industry on Cochabamba is likely to be weaker than on Santa Cruz.

Other Bolivian cities and regions have also felt the effects of the illegal industry. SEAMOS (1993) studied the effects of drug trafficking in Tarija Department. This is a border region with Argentina that is used to export cocaine base and cocaine and to import chemical precursors for the illegal industry. The study was done in 1992 and 1993 and found that the border city of Yacuiba, where contraband was centered, had clear "Dutch disease" symptoms: higher real estate and service prices than in Tarija, the department's capital. These effects changed the nature of Yacuiba, as many bars, nightclubs, and other adult entertainment establishments popped up in the small city.

According to Peruvian conventional wisdom, illegal drug money has funded some of the real estate developments in Lima and other cities. The country's formal agriculture sector has suffered several crises, and coca has provided an alternative that prevented greater migration to the cities. The Upper Huallaga Valley was originally settled by peasants who grew several crops. When agricultural prices collapsed, coca provided a viable alternative (De Rementería 1995). The same can be said of other regions where coca plantings have grown in the 1990s. Unfortunately, the regional effects of the drug industry in Peru have not been studied in detail.

Alvarez and Associates (1996, 91–104) surveyed four rural regions to look for the effects of illegal coca. Their surveys were done in 1993 and

1995 in four rural districts: (1) Shamboyacu, a heavily coca-dependent district, where two out of three peasants acknowledged producing coca; (2) Tocache, an old coca-producing region, where it appears that there had been a coca decline and several peasants acknowledged being coca growers; (3) Pedro Abad District, which had been heavily into coca but that at the time of the survey was diversified, producing mainly bananas, corn, cassava, and coca; and (4) Nueva Cajamarca, a non-coca-growing district.

The surveys found, as expected, higher prices for nontradeables and services in Shamboyacu and Tocache. Perhaps the main difference found was in average peasant income. Peasants reported monthly incomes of $549 in Shamboyacu, $345 in Padre Abad, $294 in Nueva Cajamarca, and $281 in Tocache. These data are not strictly comparable because each survey was done at a different time. Nevertheless, they support the conclusion that coca-growing peasants have significantly higher incomes than non-coca-growing ones or that a peasant in "a predominantly coca area would (have) double the income of a non-coca area" (Alvarez and Associates 1996, 103).

It is interesting that income concentration does not seem to be affected by coca. In all districts, the top 20 percent of the population receives between 43 and 48 percent of the income (Alvarez and Associates 1996, 103). Furthermore, "the income of the coca growers is transformed in savings and in highest [*sic*] consumption and also increase the income of the retailers who have the opportunity to sell goods at higher prices. In Shamboyacu, residents save 28 percent of their incomes in contrast with 10 percent in Nueva Cajamarca" (p. 103). As was noted above, Alvarez and Associates (1996) posited a possible impoverishing effect of the illegal coca industry via increased food prices. It is interesting to point out that their own figures show that this is simply not the case!

Environmental Effects

The growth of the illegal drug industry in Bolivia and Peru has had similar but weaker negative environmental effects than in Colombia. First, a significant share of coca grows in areas that have been cultivated for a long time (e.g., Yungas and Cuzco). Second, the settlement of Chapare and the Upper Huallaga Valley, the main coca-producing regions of Bolivia and Peru, had been encouraged by various governments before the development of the illegal coca industry. Thus, significant primary forest destruction had occurred before this took place. Third, there has not been significant development of opium poppies, which destroy high-altitude forest and water sources. Fourth, the governments of Bolivia and Peru do not use aerial spraying to eradicate illegal crops.

The debate about the environmental effects of the illegal industry in Bolivia is interesting. As in Colombia, most authors have acknowledged their ignorance and the need for detailed research to clarify some of the main effects (Mansilla 1994, 39; J. Painter 1994, 65–66; Salm and Liberman 1997, 226). The lack of knowledge is not limited to the physical and chemical effects of the illegal crops but also includes many social aspects of the phenomenon.

It is clear that any exploitation of the Bolivian Oriente using traditional means will cause environmental degradation. At issue is whether the development of the illegal drug industry accelerates and compounds that phenomenon. There is no question that coca is one of the most suitable crops for areas such as Chapare (Salm and Liberman 1997). At the same time, "farmers in the Chapare are estimated to clear between 2 and 6 hectares of land for every one in (coca) production" (J. Painter 1994, 66). Are these figures the result of peasants' desire to diversify their crops or just the effect of coca illegality? We do not know for sure, although one could venture to say that coca illegality plays a role. If coca and cocaine were legal, their prices would be much lower and the incentives to migrate to Chapare to grow them would be much weaker. However, we do not know the magnitude of such an effect.

The lack of solid knowledge results in authors frequently taking positions that are educated guesses and/or are influenced by their own ideological and political perspectives. J. Painter (1994, 67) accepted that coca is the least damaging crop in Chapare and stated that "perhaps, the most damaging effect resulted from the processing, rather than the growing of coca."[4] This view implies that there is no substantial abuse of fertilizers and herbicides, and that the main culprit is the disposal of chemical leftovers from the refining process on the ground and in rivers. To this one should also add the burning and/or dumping of chemicals by law enforcement units during laboratory seizure-and-destruction operations.

Several researchers have argued that traditional coca growing is very environmentally friendly and have cited as an example the millenary terraces used in the Yungas to grow coca (Spedding 1997a, 1997b; Salm and Liberman 1997). There is no question that traditional coca-growing

---

[4]Salm and Liberman (1997) concurred with these points.

methods in Yungas have been environment friendly, although it appears that new plantings, perhaps because they are liable to be eradicated, have not been placed on terraces.[5] However, as Mansilla (1994, 40) pointed out, the Aymara *Andean logic* cannot be applied in Chapare, where an *Amazonic logic* is needed. From a purely environmental point of view, such logic would require the exploitation of the diverse primary forest without destroying it. This is technologically feasible, would employ fewer peasants, and is very unlikely to take place on a large scale.

Mansilla (1994, 31) argued that the ecological effects of the illegal industry in the coca-growing areas are alarming. It is true that the Chapare settlement would have eventually taken place without the development of the coca-cocaine industry. However, the speed of the settlements would have been much slower. Unfortunately, there is no way to estimate how much less forest destruction would have occurred without coca-induced migrations. Mansilla's (1994, 31–45) work, which was based on extensive field interviews, concluded that many Chapare migrants consider their own migration as temporary and look at their highland region of origin as the home to which they would eventually return.

Although traditional institutions, mainly the *sindicatos*, were transplanted in the migration process; the migration itself weakened some of the migrants' traditional community links. This prompted Mansilla (1994) to consider three main ecological effects of the Chapare coca industry: the destruction of primary forest; the effects of the misuse and disposal of chemicals used in paste, base, and cocaine production; and the illegal industry's effects on social ecology. It was interesting that Mansilla devoted most of his work to the last.

Laserna (1996, chap. 8) concurred with Mansilla on the negative environmental effects of the illegal drug industry but attributed most of them to the illegal nature of the industry. His point is that illegality is a very strong disincentive to long-term investments in terraces and laboratories, encourages chemical dumping, and shortens the time horizon of all actors.[6] Mansilla (1994) gave more weight to the weakening of the social fabric and the decline in social controls. He also argued that most Bolivians do not see the ecological effects of the illegal industry as significant. They consider that the area planted with coca is very small in relation to the "immense"

[5]This is based on interviews with United Nations Drug Control Program (UNDCP) personnel in La Paz in April 1999.

[6]As will be seen below, these arguments are akin to those used by Hernando de Soto in Peru to design the antidrug strategy of the Fujimori government.

Amazon basin and that ecological arguments are only another smoke screen thrown in by the Americans who want to impose their imperialistic policies. Mansilla (1994) also argued that there is a great difference between the Yungas and Chapare peasants. The latter need an exculpatory ideology to justify their involvement in the illegal industry, and the imperialist explanation of ecological concerns is justified by their ideology.

To these differences, one could add that many Chapare peasants did not come from coca-growing regions and did not have firsthand experience in coca cultivation and environmentally friendly agricultural practices. Furthermore, Mansilla asserted that the interviews that he has carried on in Chapare indicate that the arguments about the peasants' traditional concern with environment preservation are exaggerated and that many traditional practices are not necessarily environmentally friendly.

The short time horizon of Chapare peasants is also due to the lack of long-term settlements and their links with their original high-altitude communities. If you move from a dry high altitude village where you are part of a closely knit farm community to an awfully hot and humid region, planning to return to your original one, why would you have a long-term horizon in your newly settled place? There is no denying that there is a little of the predator in most Chapare settlers. Summarizing, the environmental damage caused by the coca-cocaine industry can be attributed to the illegal nature of the industry, the weakened community structure and sense of belonging caused by migration, and the possible predatory attitude of most migrants. Unfortunately, there is no possible way to determine the relative importance of each of these factors.

It should also be mentioned that a peculiarly Bolivian antidrug policy has generated some important negative environmental effects. As will be discussed in detail below, Law 1008 provides for compensated coca eradication in Chapare, and peasants received up to $2,500 per eradicated hectare.[7] This policy created a very peculiar situation not only because it paid peasants not to break a law, but also because it created a benefit accessible only to those who had planted coca. Many peasants eradicated old coca fields and used the money they received to move further into the forest and plant new coca.

In the 1980s, several studies looked at the environmental effects of the illegal drug industry in Peru (Bedoya 1990; Dourojeanni 1989; Marceló

---

[7]This figure could have been lower in many cases because of corruption and bureaucratic delays (Léons 1997).

1987). These were surveyed by Alvarez (1992). The main conclusions of these works were:

1. Most coca in the Upper Huallaga was planted in lands not fit for agriculture of any kind (Dourojeanni 1989). The only long-run sustainable activity in those regions should be based on the exploitation of the primary forest itself.
2. The illegality of coca encouraged extensive agriculture in titled and untitled lands (Bedoya 1990).
3. Shining Path required peasants to plant food crops alongside coca. This practice aggravated the deforestation associated with coca cultivation (Bedoya 1990).
4. The river contamination caused by dumping chemicals has devastated the environment, and the contamination of the rivers in the Upper Huallaga exceeds the standards of the World Health Organization (Marceló 1987).
5. The total deforestation attributed to illegal crop development is about 700,000 hectares, or about 10 percent of the Peruvian Amazon Basin deforestation of the twentieth century (Dourojeanni 1989).

The surveys by Alvarez and Associates (1996) mentioned above showed that the illegal drug industry had significant negative health effects on the population involved. The two coca-producing regions covered showed significantly higher morbidity rates than the non-coca-producing regions. During the two weeks before the surveys, the proportions of people reporting to have had an illness in the two coca-producing regions were 37 percent in Shamboyacu and 35 percent in Tocache, compared with 24 percent in Nueva Cajamarca and 20 percent in Padre Abad.

The main illnesses reported were the common cold in Tocache, stomach problems in Nueva Cajamarca, vomiting and diarrhea in Shamboyacu, and a mix of all these in Padre Abad. It is clear that the coca-growing areas have more health problems than the non-coca-growing regions, and that they are likely to be more complex. It is likely that these are related to the widespread use and misuse of fertilizers, pesticides, and chemical products used in paste and base production.

Social and Political Effects

The social and political effects of the illegal drug industry on Bolivia and Peru have also been quite different from those in Colombia, for at least five reasons. First, as shown above, in both countries drug revenues have been higher relative to the countries' economies than in Colombia, but the accumulation of wealth based on illegal drugs has not been as concentrated. The lack of large Bolivian and Peruvian benefits from smuggling into American and European markets produced fortunes that were large relative to the standards of both Bolivia and Peru, but substantially smaller than those of large Colombian traffickers.

Second, in Bolivia and Peru the illegal industry has employed large numbers of peasants and a high proportion of the countries' rural labor force, resulting in a large share of drug profits being distributed in small amounts to large numbers of people. Third, government power in Bolivia and Peru has been more centralized in those nations' capitals, and the central government has been better able to exert control over the country's territory than its Colombian counterpart.

Fourth, the military has played a very active role in government. Both countries' histories include large periods of military rule and frequent cases of former military leaders being elected to the presidency. This contrasts with the long sequence of civilian governments in Colombia, where military rule has been exceptional by Latin American standards. Military power in Bolivia and Peru has translated into the military's active participation in economic activities and has made it vulnerable to the attractions of the illegal drug industry.

Fifth, Bolivia and Peru have very strong Indian societies that value peaceful conflict resolution and appeal to violence only in extreme cases. These behaviors have transcended native groups, are widespread across the social spectrum, and have been an obstacle to the development of drug "cartels," hampering Bolivian and Peruvian competition with Colombian groups. There is no doubt that illegal drugs have had a deep effect on Bolivia and Peru, but the factors listed have made the social and political effects of the illegal industry more benign than in Colombia.

Effects in Bolivia

The illegal drug industry has had a widespread impact on the main institutions and social groups of Bolivia. These effects have been felt mainly on the state, peasant communities, the armed forces, some of the regional elites, especially that of Santa Cruz, and on Bolivia–United States relations.

Perhaps the main difference from Colombia has been the strength of the Bolivian illegal industry's challenge to the state. In contrast to Colombia,

Bolivian drug traffickers have not confronted the state and illegal drug funds have not funded subversive organizations. Rather, in a country with a small elite, a very strong authoritarian political tradition, and a powerful army that was deeply involved in politics, the illegal drug industry had to involve people close to the top of the power structure to operate successfully.

The Narco–Politics–Military Nexus

In particular, the vulnerability of the Bolivian army to the attractions of the illegal industry has unquestionably been greater than in Colombia and Peru. Throughout Bolivian history, the army has been a major political player. Besides, the very strong authoritarian tradition of the culture has shielded its leaders from any accountability needs. Power obtained through the control of the armed forces has been frequently abused. In this environment, the illegal drug industry could have not grown without some links to those forces.

During the dictatorship of Hugo Banzer in the 1970s, the illegal industry grew and developed a tight nexus with Santa Cruz's elite and the military.[8] One factor contributing to the armed forces' vulnerability to the penetration of the drug industry was the result of the land reform enacted after the 1952 revolution, which broke up large haciendas among peasants but also allowed the distribution of large ranches in unsettled areas.

Many military officers benefited from this policy. Indeed, some of the lands in which General Luis García-Meza operated illegal laboratories were granted to him that way. During the Banzer administration, the distribution of land in the Beni and Santa Cruz Departments to powerful capitalists and military officers accelerated (Rodas 1996, 55). One of the military leaders who benefited from land grants during Banzer's administration included Colonel Ariel Coca, a reputed trafficker who later became a minister of education during the García-Meza regime (Rodas 1996, 108). Both members of the capitalist elite and of the armed forces, which often overlapped, were frequently involved in the illegal industry.

It has frequently been reported that Banzer has had strong links to the illegal drug industry. For example, Federico Aguiló (1992, 52), a well-respected Spanish priest and researcher, referred to Roberto Suarez

---

[8]See, among others, Hargreaves (1992, 166), Aguiló (1992, 52), and Gamarra (1994, 20).

as Bolivia's drug-trafficking godfather and reserved the title of "under-cover father" for Banzer. Although there has not been an incontestable proof of Banzer's direct involvement in illegal drug activities, he was surrounded by those for whom there was. Indeed, "it is clear that if the General was not personally involved in the cocaine trade, at least he looked the other way when his relatives and friends were" (Malamud-Goti 1994, 121).[9]

Some of the elite Santa Cruz families that helped finance Banzer's 1971 coup d'état later were proved to have participated in the illegal industry (Gamarra 1994, 20). José Gasser, a member of one of the most powerful Santa Cruz families, sold a ranch in San Javier to Banzer at a greatly undervalued price and later was indicted for drug trafficking (Rodas 1996, 55).[10]

In 1980, during Lidia Gueler's administration, the Narcotics Division of the Santa Cruz police searched two ranches in San Javier: El Potrero, which belonged to Banzer, and another one belonging to Wilder Razuk, a suspected trafficker. Air Force personnel in the area that opened fire on the police opposed the search. The police officer in charge of the operation persisted and seized a Colombian airplane containing some coca paste (Aguiló 1992, 52; Rodas 1996, 68). Banzer explained, as later also did several of the "repented" traffickers, that his ranch had been used without his permission (Rodas 1996, 68).[11]

Luis F. Valle, Banzer's son-in-law, who was Bolivia's consul in Ottawa in the 1970s, was declared persona non grata and expelled from Canada after being found in possession of several kilograms of cocaine

[9]In April 1999, Carlos Felipe Martínez, the UNDP representative in Bolivia, and I visited U.S. ambassador Donna Hrinak to ask for her support in the publication of a book summarizing the research results of a UNDP program that I coordinated and that had been objected to by a UNDCP representative in Bolivia on the grounds that it was not very kind to Banzer. Ambassador Hrinak indicated that the U.S. government had suspected Banzer, but no smoking gun had ever been found. Furthermore, his eradication program was advancing successfully, and thus it was important not to stir the beehive with old stories. Therefore, my politically incorrect book, coedited with Eduardo Gamarra (1999), included in this book's reference list, could not be published.

[10]The fact that the ranch was sold for a very low price might not be indicative of the real price because in Latin America it is very frequent to underreport prices of real estate transactions to avoid taxes.

[11]Sandro Calvani, a former UNDCP representative in Bolivia, told the author on May 1999 in Vienna that in a personal interview with Banzer, the retired general also argued that the finding was not relevant because at the time cocaine base manufacturing was not an act sanctioned in the criminal code.

(Malamud-Goti 1994, 121–22; Rodas 1996, 55). The Canadian government did not want to create an international incident over the event, but Alberto Sánchez-Bello, one of the couriers who delivered the cocaine to Valle, had to serve 5 years in a Canadian prison (Aguiló 1992, 52).[12] After Banzer took over as elected president in 1998, he appointed Valle to the prefecture of La Paz. Guillermo (Willy) Banzer-Ojopi, Banzer's cousin[13] and Bolivia's consul in Miami, was arrested and accused of drug trafficking after depositing $10 million in a Miami bank (Rodas 1996, 55). Even Banzer's wife, Yolanda Prada de Banzer, "had drug trafficking difficulties with Canada's Mounted Police and at Barajas airport in Madrid" (Aguiló 1992, 52).[14]

The latest episode of this saga, as was noted in chapter 4, was the mid-1999 arrest of Marino Diodato, an Italian married to a niece of Banzer, and an officer in the Bolivian army, who was indicted on money-laundering charges and is suspected of having links to Italian organized crime. Apparently, in a way similar to what President Ernesto Samper claimed in Colombia in 1996 (see chapter 7), all these incidents "happened behind Banzer's back," without his knowledge. It should be noted that during his term as elected head of state in the late 1990s, Banzer became a "born-again eradicator," which helped silence some possible critics.[15]

Independent of whether Banzer has had direct links to traffickers, it is clear that during his 1971–78 dictatorship the illegal industry developed and that many members of the military actively participated in it. This could not have been otherwise in a country were the military were part and parcel of the small economic power elite. The García-Meza coup in July 1980 was the culmination of the symbiotic relationship between Bolivia's power structure and the illegal drug industry. This administration was known as the only real drug government that has existed in Latin America. During the short 13-month narco-regime, García-Meza, with the support of other military officers, particularly his interior minister Luis Arce-Gómez (Roberto Suárez's cousin,[16] and also known as "minister of

---

[12]Sánchez-Bello was the personal secretary of Edwin Tapia-Frontanilla, a Banzer minister (Rodas 1996, 55).

[13]Aguiló (1992, 52) referred to Banzer-Ojopi as Banzer's half-brother.

[14]In an October 1999 interview, Alain Labrousse, the director of the Observatoire Geopolitic des Drogues in Paris, asserted that many testimonies confirmed all these ncidents.

[15]This was particularly true for those in the U.S. embassy.

[16]See Aguiló (1992, 53).

cocaine" (Léons and Sanabria 1997, 13), tried to control and tax all production and export trafficking of coca paste, cocaine base, and cocaine. Individual producers and traffickers were required to pay a "tax" to García-Meza's group in a "formalized system of corruption" (Hargreaves 1992, 169). Then, through threats, detentions, and killings, they eliminated many small competitors (Mendoza 1993, 61).

Indeed, capturing competitors was a strategy to make the government look good internationally, particularly in the eyes of the United States. Government terror was applied through a paramilitary group, the Fiancés of Death, "a band of young neo-Fascists and Neo-Nazis" (Hargreaves 1992, 107), which had originally been organized by Nazi refugee Klaus Barbie under the auspices of Roberto Suárez.[17]

Unquestionably, drug trafficking has had a great influence on the Bolivian state; however, this does not mean that the state and politics are dominated by drug-trafficking interests (Rodas 1996, 83). This point was highlighted by the political response—albeit made under pressure by the United States—to the García-Meza regime. Bolivian institutions including the armed forces reacted, and the regime was overthrown after a little over a year in August 1981. It was replaced by a military junta that transferred power to an elected president, Hernán Siles-Zuazu, in 1982.

Scandals related to drug-trafficking activities in Bolivia continued throughout the 1980s and early 1990s. On September 5, 1986, a botanic and ecological expedition headed by Professor Noel Kempff-Mercado stumbled into a very large cocaine laboratory in the Huanchaca region of Beni. Kempff-Mercado and two of his companions were killed in cold blood, but Vicente Castelló, a Spanish researcher, managed to escape.[18]

The debate about what happened in Huanchaca and why left many questions unanswered. Retired Colonel Ariel Coca reported to several government and U.S. Drug Enforcement Administration (DEA) officials his suspicions about a landing strip and frequent airplane activity in the

---

[17]As was noted in chapter 4, during World War II, Barbie was head of the Gestapo in Lyon, where he was known as the "Butcher of Lyon." During the Siles-Zuazu administration, Barbie was captured and extradited to France, where he was convicted of war crimes and sentenced to life in prison.

[18]The Huanchaca case was analyzed in detail by Rodas (1996) in a book of that name, and also by Malamud-Goti (1994), Gamarra (1994, 48–52), and Cortez (1992, first part), among others.

Huanchaca area.[19] U.S. officials have conflicting versions. Apparently, a DEA pilot who flew over in a mission reported a large laboratory and a landing strip. Official correspondence from the U.S. embassy to the Department of State indicated that no suspicious buildings or activities were sighted (Gamarra 1994, 50).

The Bolivian Congress opened an investigation on this matter headed by Edmundo Salazar, a young house deputy (representative), that found evidence that suggested that "Interior Minister Fernando Barthelemy and a large network of hundreds of prominent members of important Santa Cruz families" (Gamarra 1994, 51) were involved in the Huanchaca trafficking operation. Salazar's public stature provided no immunity and he was gunned down by a couple of *sicarios*. Barthelemy ordered the capture of dozens of suspects but was forced to resign under pressure from the U.S. embassy. "Two years later, despite overwhelming evidence against those accused, the Santa Cruz Court absolved and freed most suspects" (Gamarra 1994, 52).

The contradictory versions of the DEA pilot and the U.S. embassy—and an apparently procrastinating attitude on the part of the embassy and the Bolivian government, which delayed sending search planes after Kempff-Mercado's plane went missing—have led to much speculation about the actual control and purpose of the Huanchaca laboratory. One such version, accepted by Scott and Marshall (1991), was that Huanchaca was a Central Intelligence Agency laboratory established by Oliver North of Iran-Contra fame to produce and sell cocaine to fund the Nicaraguan Contras.

New narco-political scandals developed in 1988. In late March 1988, a videotape that became known as a "narco-video," delivered by an army captain and shown by a television station, showed a meeting of two former Banzer ministers, Alfredo Arce-Carpio (interior) and Mario Vargas-Salinas (labor), and Roberto Suárez (Rodas 1996, 165). Arce-Crespo had earlier been accused of having received $200,000 from Suárez for the 1985 campaign of National Democratic Action (ADN), Banzer's party. The Nationalist Revolutionary Movement (MNR), Víctor Paz-Estenssoro's party, was confronting similar accusations (p. 165). The political situation became more complicated when pictures of Jaime Paz-Zamora, of the Revolutionary Left Movement (MIR), hugging his old friend and drug

[19]Coca had been a close friend of Arce-Gómez and in 1981 had been sought after by the DEA as a drug trafficking suspect (Gamarra 1994, 49).

trafficker Isaac "Oso" Chavarría, were made public. With these, the three main political parties' ended up accused of having links to the illegal drug industry.

These revelations led to a heated debate about the nature of the relationships between political leaders and the illicit industry. Some argued that the evidence presented was old, from a period before the accused narcos had become traffickers. Other arguments portrayed the traffickers as entrepreneurs who provided transportation and other legitimate paid services to the politicians involved. In mid-June 1988, Congress met explicitly to investigate these accusations, a process that ended in a political agreement among the three large parties (ADN, MIR, and MNR) to close down the investigation and not to bring up the "narco-links" in the upcoming 1989 election campaign.

President Jaime Paz-Zamora took over in August 1989. During the first year and a half of his presidency, he extradited General Arce-Gómez, and in September 1990 he captured Carmelo (Meco) Domínguez, the main Bolivian trafficker at that time. The eradication goals were also met (Gamarra 1994, 115–16). All these achievements improved Bolivia's relationship with the United States. Then, on February 25, 1991, Paz-Zamora appointed retired colonel Faustino Rico-Toro to head the Special Force Against Drug Trafficking (FELCN). "During the corrupt García-Meza's government Rico-Toro had headed the infamous armed intelligence unit (G-2). He had been suspected of having provided protection to drug traffickers and had been frequently linked with Klaus Barbie" (Gamarra 1994, 118). This appointment led to a strong American reaction, and $100 million in military aid was canceled. The political fallout forced Rico-Toro to step down quietly on March 4.

The incidence did not end there as U.S. ambassador Robert Gelbard perceived Rico-Toro's appointment as a reflection of the penetration of the drug industry in the Bolivian government and went after interior minister Guillermo Capobianco, who had approved the appointment and according to American sources also had suspect relations and appeared to have enriched himself in unexplained fashion (Hargreaves 1992, 167). These pressures forced Capobianco's resignation along with that of the police chief, Colonel Felipe Carvajal.

Paz-Zamora defended his appointment on the grounds that Rico-Toro was a meritorious man who had experienced a radical life change (Gamarra 1994, 118). Nevertheless, it is difficult to understand why Paz-Zamora appointed Rico-Toro, and Gamarra was frustrated in his research by the lack of cooperation by politicians and former government officials he interviewed about it (p. 118). Hargreaves (1992, 164–65) offered two possible explanations besides the growing influence of the illicit industry on political actors. One was simply that Bolivians were fed up by U.S. involvement in what they perceived as their internal affairs. The other was a more mundane one: Rico-Toro had a beautiful daughter who had been a finalist in the Miss Universe contest, and Paz-Zamora had fallen for her.

President Gonzalo Sánchez-de-Losada, elected in 1993, was a very different Bolivian politician. He was the scion of a traditional wealthy family, had lived most his life abroad, and was almost a foreigner in his own country. He chose an Indian for vice president, the first time a Native American had reached such a high position in government. In the first year of his administration, a congressional investigation unearthed the close relationship between Paz-Zamora and drug traffickers, particularly Issac "Oso" Chavarría (Del Granado 1994). This tarnished the image of the former president and led to the cancellation of Paz-Zamora's U.S. visa.

All these cases illustrate the pervasive effect of the illegal drug industry on the Bolivian polity. Indeed, it could not be otherwise. In a country with a small population and a very small elite, the illegal drug industry must penetrate the power structures to operate. Unfortunately, in spite of the many documented narco-link incidents, there are many unresolved questions about the way the illegal industry and the Bolivian elite are linked. The evolution of the thirty-five trafficking organizations recognized in all reports and studies from the early 1990s is not known. Have they simply stopped trafficking, and have their members been assimilated by the formal economy? If so, how have they laundered their capital and where have they invested it? Does this mean that old traffickers and politicians who benefited from the illegal industry from the early 1970s through the mid-1990s became satisfied with the wealth they accumulated and dropped out of the illegal activity? If so, why have they not been replaced by new drug entrepreneurs? From 1990 through 1997, coca hectareage remained relatively stable. If Bolivians were dropping out of the illegal business, what happened to that coca? Is it true, as U.S. ambassador Donna Hrinak asserted, that all large trafficking organizations disbanded and that the illegal industry became one of only mom-and-pop operations (see chapter 4)?

These questions suggest that the link between Bolivian traffickers and the government elite persist, albeit with a very low profile, that drug traffickers in Bolivia have become camouflaged within society, and that they have learned how to operate without attracting too much international attention. Such a process would have been helped by the 1994 dramatic shift in the U.S. focus away from Bolivia and toward Colombia, and by its more recent focus on Mexico.

Other Effects

The development of the illegal drug industry in Bolivia had other important effects. One of them was to provide a stage for the latent confrontation between the army and the police. As was noted above, the 1952 revolution dissolved the army, which was replaced by militias (Rodas 1996, 37). The army was reconstituted a year later under pressure from the United States, which made its help conditional on that development (Gamarra 1994, 1). The army official corps had always been chosen from the traditional landowning and mining elite, and the reconstituted army became an authoritarian arm of the developing bourgeoisie (Rodas 1996, 37).

Indeed, as was mentioned above, for 30 years after the 1952 revolution, the army was in power most of the time. During the early years, the police were in charge of the "war on drugs," and a special police branch (UMOPAR) was created for that purpose. After failing to make significant advances in this war, the United States compelled Bolivia to militarize the fight against the illegal industry. This created an open conflict between the two institutions, which have a mutual deep historical distrust. As has been shown, the army has had very close relations with the illegal industry, and many officers have been corrupted by drug money or have participated in the industry themselves. The police have also been corrupted and have provided protection to traffickers.

The conflict between the two institutions has been an obstacle to the coordination of many antidrug activities, and it has resulted in a lack of shared intelligence and even on occasion in open, violent confrontations. One can only wonder if conflicts between the army and the police would not have grown even in the absence of their historical animosity, simply because both had competing interests in benefiting from their participation in the war on drugs.

Another important effect of the illegal industry has been the strengthening of the rural *sindicatos*. The expansion of coca plantings forced the government and foreign donors to focus on coca-growing peasants.

Governments had to concentrate rural expenditures in coca-growing areas, where *sindicatos* were the main mediators between the peasantry and the state. This way, the *sindicatos* became actors that governments and foreign donors had to deal with.

Bolivian alternative development programs were first conceived in the early 1970s, but their implementation actually began in the mid-1980s (see chapter 11). The first programs were designed and implemented with little or no peasant participation. The *sindicatos* were instrumental in obtaining international technical assistance to improve peasants' negotiating capabilities (ILDIS 1993). Today, the *sindicatos* have increased their sophistication, and alternative development programs, compensation for coca eradication, and infrastructure projects (e.g., highways, schools, and health centers) have to be discussed and negotiated with them. They also have the capacity to organize marches of large numbers of peasants, block highways, and pressure the government. There is no question that rural *sindicatos* are important political actors and that their leaders have gained national and international notoriety.

Effects in Peru

As was noted above, the effects of the illegal industry have been milder in Peru than in the other two main drug-producing Andean countries. Several factors have contributed to this result. The illegal industry is located in the hinterland, far away from the main economic centers. Most benefits are believed to be distributed in small amounts among a large number of peasants. Peruvian elites have not become major players in the industry, and Peruvians have not developed large international trafficking organizations.

Yet the impact of the illegal drug industry on Peru depends on the degree of Peruvian participation in the smuggling and marketing parts of the business. For instance, if Peruvians managed to refine into cocaine and themselves export 10 percent of their total output, that alone would double the Peruvian coca-cocaine value-added estimates.

As was explained in chapter 4, forty to fifty Peruvian "families" have organized coca leaf collection and processing and sell to foreigners. These families are believed to be relatively poor, compared with the Colombian syndicates. For example, when Demetrio Chávez-Peñaherrera ("Vaticano"), the most prominent Peruvian trafficker, was captured in Cali in January 1994, his visible wealth was not impressive compared with that of Colombian traffickers.

To summarize, the coca-cocaine industry in Peru is a large employer of rural workers and generates significant amounts of foreign exchange which were particularly valuable during the periods of macroeconomic crises, but it is not perceived as an overly large industry that threatens the economic or political power structures of the country. Thus, Peruvians do not perceive large social costs to be associated with the industry. Furthermore, because there is a widespread perception that the Shining Path, the MRTA, and the military have profited or profit from the industry, most analysts do not want to research the issue for fear of reprisal. One possible effect of this situation is that the influence of the illegal drug industry on society can grow undetected. Still, it is possible to identify and analyze a few important effects.

As was noted in chapter 8, Shining Path and MRTA, the two main guerrilla organizations, obtained significant funds by taxing the illegal drug industry. Indeed, their move from their original highlands regions to the Upper Huallaga was influenced by the opportunity to capture those funds. During the 1980s, these two guerrilla organizations followed a strong terrorist strategy in Peru. There is no doubt that the illegal industry helped fund a substantial part of it.

Perhaps the most important social effect that the illicit industry has had in Peru has been the corruption it has generated in the armed forces. This issue clouded Fujimori's administration, though it was not discussed openly by most analysts. As was noted in chapter 4, after Fujimori's election, his main goal in the coca-growing areas was to eliminate the guerrillas' control.

To achieve this goal, it was necessary to gain the support of the peasant communities. Coca eradication was stopped, and the military's involvement in the anti-guerrilla war in the heart of the coca- and cocaine-producing region made it very vulnerable to corruption from the illegal industry (Dreyfus 1999, 387–88). This problem became aggravated after Fujimori closed Congress in 1992 and promoted and passed constitutional reform in 1993. All these changes required strong military support, which limited Fujimori's capacity to control some illicit behaviors within that institution.

"Before 1993, there were cases of corruption because the military was operating in a drug-producing area. Junior officers were paid off for protection against the police. From 1993 on, the problem of corruption escalated" (Dreyfus 1999, 388). Dreyfus attaches great importance to low military pay as a cause of military corruption.

In 1993, about 15 trafficking organizations began to pay army personnel the "taxes" formerly collected by Shining Path. Most of the evidence was uncovered because Vaticano's testimony led to a congressional investigation.[20] More than 100 Army officers were implicated in several crimes, besides receiving bribes to let traffickers operate. These included drug trafficking, the assassination of traffickers to steal their cocaine base, the release of detained accused traffickers, and even the construction of a landing strip for trafficking planes (Labrousse 1995, 107–8).

Even though the more than 100 military officers linked to drug trafficking were tried, expelled from the armed forces, and sentenced, several of the highest-ranking officers linked to trafficking were not indicted or tried. Unfortunately, there were many questions about a possible nexus of people close to Fujimori with the illegal drug industry. The most notorious case was that of Vladimiro Montesinos, one of Fujimori's closest and most controversial advisers. Montesinos was "expelled from the Army in 1977, studied Law and became a defense lawyer for Colombian and Peruvian traffickers. Besides defending them in the courts, he made arrangements to 'disappear' their case files" (Labrousse 1995, 109). It has also been argued by respected journalists that Montesinos played an important role in the 1992 self-coup and that one of his main motives for participating was to be able to "disappear" some files from the Ministry of Justice (p. 109).

As was noted above, much of the evidence for corruption in Peru is journalistic and is unlikely to meet the rigor of serious academe. However, there is no question that the actions of the Peruvian armed forces in the coca-growing and drug-trafficking areas have put them at risk and that some relatively high-ranking members have become corrupted by them. Similarly, Fujimori's dependence on the armed forces likely made him more tolerant of their links to the illicit industry.

The collapse of the Fujimori regime and the current movement toward a more transparent political system opens the door to needed research to clarify the role and effects that the illegal drug industry has had on Peruvian Society.

---

[20]"Vaticano" sold substantial amounts drugs to the Cali cartel. Journalistic reports indicate that he was probably turned in by the Cali syndicate because he had started to develop his own international marketing networks, bypassing the Cali organization.

Part III

Country Vulnerability to Illegal Drugs

9

Illegal Drugs, Violence, and Social Differences

The model presented in chapter 3 shows that the likelihood that a society will develop a competitive advantage in illegal economic activities depends on three types of restrictions on individual behavior. First, there are restrictions imposed by the state, which in turn are determined by its ability to enforce its own laws over a national territory. Second, there are restrictions generated by social institutions. These are expressed in social encouragement for or sanctions on particular activities. Third, there are behavioral restrictions, or constraints, internalized by individual people.

Variations in these three types of restrictions would explain why the illegal drug industry has been significantly different in each Andean country—that is, the peculiar geographical distribution of the various processes of the illegal industry and its evolution described in chapters 4 through 8. In particular, the variations would explain why until the 1990s the industry in Bolivia and Peru concentrated on coca growing and coca paste production and why traffickers in these two countries only recently began to develop organizations independent of the Colombian ones. The variations would also explain why the industry in Colombia has concentrated on the manufacturing and international trafficking stages of the business and why coca and poppy cultivation has exploded in that country during the past decade.

During the twentieth century, all the Andean countries experienced modernization processes that changed their societies. In all countries, urbanization proceeded at a fast pace, and such welfare indicators as educational attainment, quality of nutrition, life expectancy, and health increased. Women's role in society changed drastically. The doors to education and employment outside the home opened to them, and their labor force participation rates jumped. Suffrage rights expanded and became universal. Infrastructure and communications grew dramatically (electricity, water and sewage, telephones, highways, plane travel, etc.). This is only a partial list of the changes that have affected those societies. Although the list is similar for all Andean countries, the effects of these modernizing changes and external influences have varied substantially from country to country, depending on their social institutions and behavioral controls. It can be expected that some of these changes and pressures will make societies more vulnerable to the development of illegal economic activities. This is why it is important to identify the institutional differences among the Andean countries that can play important roles in altering behavioral constraints.

To identify these differences, it is necessary to compare the three societies by examining the main characteristics of their states, social structures, and behavioral controls. Because the credible threat of violence is an important component of a country's competitive advantage in the drug industry, comparisons of the ways in which the Andean societies handle conflicts and cope with violent behaviors are also undertaken. It is expected that these comparisons will show the reader why Colombian society was a lot more vulnerable to the development of criminal economic activities and that other Andean countries had stronger states and social controls.[1] They will also show that other societies experiencing modernization

---

[1]This is a very challenging and controversial task. Others who have tackled similar challenges (e.g., Putnam 1993) have been very cautious in their conclusions. The social problems of the Andean countries, especially those of Colombia, are so grave that despite the difficulties in finding absolute proofs, the interpretation of their realities requires the exploration of new, albeit unconventional approaches.

processes similar to Colombia's will be vulnerable to the development of criminal organizations.

Unfortunately, in-depth studies of the contribution of various institutions and social capital to the tolerance of illegal economic behaviors and the development of the illegal drug industry in the Andes do not exist. Indeed, these studies are likely to be undertaken only when the presence of the illegal industry generates a serious crisis. Thus, it is not surprising that the literature on these issues is more extensive for Colombia than for the other Andean countries.[2] The paucity of literature for other Andean countries precludes social capital comparisons and compels the use of more qualitative information and indirect data and examples.

Mestizaje, Community Strength, and Individualism in the Three Countries

The social and racial composition of Colombia is very different from that of Bolivia and Peru. Colombia is a "mestizo" country. The Indian population at the time of the Spanish conquest of what is now Colombia was estimated at between 3 and 5 million. The "demographic catastrophe of America"—brought about by a combination of factors, mainly imported illnesses, wars, and hard labor—reduced this population dramatically, so that by the beginning of the seventeenth century there were only approximately 300,000 Indians (Jaramillo-Uribe 1989, 145).

Most native communities in what is today Colombia were relatively weak and disappeared soon after the Spanish conquest. Indians lost their institutions, and most of them were assimilated into the mestizo society. Slaves were imported to other countries and became the main source of labor in some regions of the country. Racial mixing was generalized, and most Colombians today are of mixed race. Peasants have been mainly poor individuals of mixed race who do not form part of traditional communities. Indeed, "the Indian contribution to the formation of Colombian soci-

[2]Sudarsky (1999) attempted to measure some indicators of social capital in Colombia. Unfortunately, there are no international comparisons with the other Andean countries, although he concluded that there is little social capital in Colombia. It should be reminded that as was indicated in chapter 3, these empirical studies measure the organizations that can generate social capital but not the social trust and sense of belonging that are the expressions of social capital. For example, the number of nongovernmental organizations (NGOs) as an indicator of social capital might be misleading if people join NGOs simply because they are a channel to gain access to international assistance.

ety and culture was weak compared to countries like Mexico, Peru, Bolivia and Guatemala that had large native populations and strong pre-Hispanic cultures" (Jaramillo-Uribe 1989, 146). The surviving native communities are not very populous and are mainly made up of those who lived in the tropical jungles of the Amazon and the Pacific coast, along with some on lands at the southwestern border with Ecuador that were part of the Inca Empire and a few on the Guajira peninsula in the north.

In contrast to Colombia, Bolivia and Peru had strong and large Indian communities that were also decimated but maintained their identities and many of their rituals and institutions. Most Bolivian and Peruvian peasants are Indians and are members of organized communities that shun violence and impose strong controls on individual behavior. Their language is either Quechua or Aymara, and many do not speak Spanish.

Cooperation among the members of these societies is widespread and has strong cultural roots. Indeed, "reciprocity" based exchanges of goods and services is common in the Andean peasant communities. Researchers have defined reciprocity as the "normative and continuous exchange of goods and services among persons who know each other such that first, the exchange is not simultaneous. There is a lapse of time between one transfer and a compensatory one. Second, the negotiation between the parties is not an open bargaining process, but rather, a covert one concealed by ceremonial behaviors. Finally, the parties involved can be either individuals or institutions" (Alberti and Mayer 1974, 21).

Figueroa (1981, 121) measured peasants' total real income and found that about 50 percent of it was the result of selling their products on the cash market and the rest was made up of reciprocal transactions, transfers from relatives who had migrated, and consumption of their own products. Reciprocal exchanges, which have played an important role in traditional Andean societies, are trust based and have taken diverse forms (Alberti and Mayer 1974; Mayer 1974; Fonseca 1974; Mayer and Zamalloa 1974). They are more frequent within extended families, but they also involve neighbors and other members of the community (Isbell 1974). It is interesting to note that they are also present in urban areas were rural migrants live.[3]

---

[3]This is true even outside Peru and Bolivia. I found reciprocal exchanges among Peruvian immigrants in the Washington, D.C., area. E.g., in one case, each member of a group of maids and blue-collar workers contributed $100 to a common fund every month. They drew lots, and the winner got to borrow the whole amount of approximately $2,000, to be repaid at a prescribed time. This rotating fund worked well because everybody paid on time without any written documents.

The importance of Andean culture as a source of behavioral controls should not be underestimated because it has influenced values not only within Indian communities but also outside them. One important Indian cultural trait is the respect for both nature and humans. Recent work on the high-altitude shepherds who live on the Bolivian–Peruvian border (Bolin 1998) is very illustrative of this point. Residents of these communities perhaps most closely reflect ancestral Indian values because they have been highly isolated. For them, respect has played a key role as a survival strategy. Their need for solidarity and cooperation to survive in a hostile environment has required respect for nature and each other. The importance of respect is explained this way by Bolin:

> Respect is the essence of life, and like the life force itself, it knows no boundaries. Respect is owed to other human beings, to animals, to the deities—to Pachamama, the Earth Mother; to the Apus, the mountain abode of ancestral protective spirits; to Illapa, the powerful god of thunder; and to all sacred places, including rocks, springs, lakes, and meadows. Respect is the moral code that permeates all thought and action.... [Furthermore, the] respect for others so consistently reinforced in all rituals, carries over to everyday life. The people of Chillihuani are aware of the tremendous importance of respect, without which they feel society cannot be sustained. Respect is at the very root of their social relations. (Bolin 1998, xiii)

This respect for all living and inert things is rooted in traditional Inca and Aymara religion:

> The notion of religious forces, for us in the Andes, derives from the notion of natural forces, and the former and the latter cannot be divided in irrational and rational. We feel that the so-called unanimated bodies are moved by intelligence, the same as the humans, even though contemporary science still refuses to acknowledge this fact. In Andean religion there is no supernatural: everything is natural ... [Furthermore,] Andean religion is not interested in saving the *runa's* soul, but it offers them the total support of the *ayllu* through the *ayni* system to help them achieve a full and harmonious life. (Milla-Villena 1996, 283, 286)[4]

[4]*Ayllu*: kin group, lineage or indigenous community with a territorial base and members who share a common focus. *Ayni*: balanced reciprocity, aid to be reciprocated in kind. *Runa*: human being, refers to an indigenous Andean person (Bolin 1998, glossary).

It is not surprising that people holding these religious values rely on trust, shun violence, and try to avoid confrontation. These characteristics of Bolivian and Peruvian societies are frequently mentioned by most observers (e.g., Spedding 1997a, Morales 1989, Sanabria 1997, Bolin 1998, and Rodas 1996).

Notably, white and/or mestizo societies in Bolivia and Peru are still very traditional. It appears that the existence of strong Indian communities induced the other social groups that confronted them to also develop strong identities and communities. There is no question that in the non-Indian Andean environment it has been important to show that one is not Indian. These social groups might be racist and discriminate against Indians, but they also have many social controls on individual behavior. In these societies, there is strong distrust among ethnic groups, which is hidden behind a polite facade, but the level of trust and sense of belonging inside each group are high.[5] Seeing through Colombian eyes, these two countries look rather primitive and traditional. In them, family name, shame, and polite behavior, for example, are substantially more important than in Colombia.

In contrast, a recent Colombian public opinion analysis shows that for 72 percent of those surveyed, the main desire is to be respected. "The high priority given by Colombians to being respected shows that this is the most important missing element in Colombian human relations" (Lemoine 2000, 26). Urban surveys show, in addition, that many Colombians think that violence is functional; "23 percent think that it is necessary to take justice into one's hands, 14 percent believe that violence can accomplish positive changes, and 6 percent says that violence pays" (p. 44).

The effects of modernization have been extreme in Colombia. In a way, Colombian society was very ill prepared for the changes that it experienced. Jaramillo-Vélez (1998) has attempted to explain what he calls "postponed modernity" as the result of the extreme isolation of most settled regions during the nineteenth century, which led the government to attempt to protect the country from evil foreign influences and to reproduce the seventeenth-century Catholic premodern state model.[6] According to this researcher, the 1886 Constitution and the subsequent Concordat with the Holy See are examples of this attempt.

---

[5]E.g., as is seen below, Shining Path (Sendero Luminoso) was an urban-based movement whose members, as with most non-Indian Peruvian society, disdained Indians who felt treated like children (Coronel 1996, 90–91).

[6]A few other Colombian writers have been concerned with the modernization problems in Colombia. E.g., see the book edited by Viviescas and Giraldo (1991).

The Colombian case presents fascinating challenges for both researchers and policymakers. A number of leading Colombian intellectuals set out recently to identify the "deep core" (*almendrón*) of the Colombian conundrum and concluded that it is rooted in the Colombians' behavior, which shows a very strong and practical individual streak that results in a vicious collective logic.[7] Colombian society has not been able to provide the most fundamental public goods, such as protection of life and property and conflict resolution systems:

The "deep core" is a form of social organization in which "public rationality" is quite weak and in which there is a preponderance of private rationality. This is the national secret: the individual creativity, diversity, imagination, "*rebusque*," and tenacity of the Colombians. But also their difficulty to organize themselves, to forge collective projects, and to solve essential public problems. (Gómez-Buendía 1999a, 19)[8]

The Colombian ethic appears to value creativity and individual success on the one hand, and local loyalties on the other. "The winner, the crafty and even the sly who can achieve without scruples are applauded—and envied—but loyalty to family, friends, bosses and even accomplices are also applauded" (Gómez-Buendía 1999a, 19).[9] This behavior is only apparently

---

[7]This is the conclusion of a multidisciplinary group convened by Colciencias, the official research supporting institution, to analyze the main problems of the country and to produce a diagnosis of the main causes of the paradoxical Colombian situation. The group, of which I was privileged to be part, included political scientists, historians, sociologists, economists (trained in different schools of thought), environmentalists, geographers, and other social scientists. Their conclusion was surprisingly unanimous despite their wide differences in background. A book edited by Hernando Gómez-Buendía (1999b), the project coordinator, published the results of this research. In the following paragraphs, I borrow liberally from his summary chapter (Gómez-Buendía 1999a).

[8]Gómez-Buendía uses the word *rebusque*, a peculiar Colombian expression that describes a particular ability to search for informal—legal or illegal—ways to make a living.

[9]Nobel Prize winner Gabriel García-Márquez, vaccine developer Elkin Patarroyo, car racer Juan Pablo Montoya, and several international soccer players and bicycle racers are revered national figures. Even the first Colombian woman to pose for *Playboy* magazine became national news and an example of a successful Colombian a few years back.

contradictory. When the individual cannot trust institutions or unknown people, it is imperative to develop a trust network to succeed. Furthermore, given the great uncertainty of social life, Colombians' "psychology has to focus on developing ways to handle it. In Colombia, as Maria Teresa Uribe [1997] asserts, 'coping with disorder is the functional logic.' Precarious interpersonal and public norms compel everyone to figure out how to establish reliable and trustful relationships" (p. 19).

Colombia has been known as a country of laws but, "impersonal norms exist and are recognized: it is 'only' that they are not taken very seriously, that the threshold beyond which they are broken is low. It is just that the exceptional nature of 'my case' compels me to avoid or evade the norm. This type of exceptionality constitutes a kind of democracy: we are all equal because we all have the right to evade or avoid the law" (Gómez-Buendía 1999a, 19). The net result of all this is the high frequency of antisocial behaviors and the prevalence of individual over collective rationality.

This deep core does not imply that most or all Colombians are willing to break or disregard most laws. Indeed, most people live most of the time within the law. The deep core means simply that the anomie present in Colombia is high relative to that found in other systems of social organization (Gómez-Buendía 1999a, 20). It must be stressed that this does not make most Colombians criminals. However, a society in which a relatively small number of people (say 3 to 5 percent) does not feel constrained by laws and social norms and is willing to continuously break them, in which the state cannot effectively enforce its own laws, and in which other social institutions do not enforce strong behavioral constraints will sooner or later have to confront the growth of illegal economic activities.

Moreover, once the law is frequently broken without obvious negative consequences for those who do it, everyone is tempted to do so. Indeed, in Colombia every person is compelled to draw his or her personal line to discriminate among the illegal activities that he or she will engage in from those that he or she will not. Most people, for example, will drive through red lights, purchase smuggled cigarettes and electric appliances used in drug money laundering, and evade taxes but will not be willing to smuggle cocaine or heroin. These behaviors result in a generalized disdain for many social and state norms and regulations. At the same time, they produce a very fluid society with significant upward and downward social mobility.

The Roles of the Central Government, Political Parties, and the Military

Central governments in all Andean countries have been weak and unaccountable to the citizenry at large. Bolivia and Peru have had a long history of authoritarian and military regimes. But such regimes have been the exception in Colombia, which has a long tradition of elected governments. Even Colombia's only military regime during the twentieth century was atypical of Latin America. When General Gustavo Rojas-Pinilla overthrew the elected government in 1953, he did it with overwhelming public support. His coup was perceived as a way to end La Violencia (see below) and was popularly referred to as an "opinion coup." Yet most Colombians characterize their society as authoritarian and feel that this trait is incompatible with the human respect they long for (Lemoine 2000, 26).

State weakness, while general, varies across countries. History and geography have played key roles in generating these differences; for example, these two factors have determined the level and type of international trade, the taxes on which for centuries provided most funds for the central government. Lima, a port, concentrated power and population in Peru, and today it is home to more than a third of the country's people. La Paz also developed as a location through which silver mined in Potosí had to go on the way to the River Plate and Buenos Aires and then to Europe. Colombia, in contrast, has four large cities of more than 2 million people and a couple of dozen of more than a quarter-million. Bogotá is located in the center of the country, and none of the main Colombian exports have ever been shipped through it.

During most of its history, the largest part of what is today Colombia was isolated from the rest of the world. The country developed as a collection of regions, each of which had a main city, with very few links among them. For centuries, international trade was small relative to the country's size and population, and the central government remained extremely poor because tariffs were the main source of government funding. Geography has been important because the lack of physical integration has been a great obstacle for government attempts to establish a presence in the lives of most citizens. Colombia thus has had the greatest need for a government capable of funding the country's transportation and communications infrastructure, and yet it has had one of the poorest budgets.[10]

However, the Colombian state has been one of the strongest ones in Latin America in some aspects. It developed very notable institutions to manage the economy. Its Central Bank, National Planning Department, and several ministries that influence economic activity became very modern by the late 1960s. Since then, they have been staffed by *técnicos*, many of who are economists with doctoral and master's degrees. These institutions are responsible of the continuity and stability of economic policy that the country has enjoyed for decades. As was noted above, Colombia was the only Latin American country that did not suffer from the external debt crisis of the early 1980s. Peru, however, until at least 1990, had weaker economic institutions and a very unstable economy.[11] The Bolivian state has been even weaker in that respect, and thus it was not surprising that its economy was also extremely unstable until the mid-1980s.

In contrast to its strong economic policy formulation and implementation capabilities, the Colombian state has been extremely weak with regard to its ability to control the national territory and provide an effective policing, legal, and judiciary system to protect property rights and solve conflicts. This weakness has expressed itself is several forms. One is the small amount of resources devoted to police activities. Rubio (1999, 182) used data from Ospina (1996) and estimated that in 1993 Colombia had 1,670 policemen per million inhabitants. This figure compared with 7,600 in Uruguay, 4,700 in Malaysia, about 3,500 in Austria, France, and Peru, 2,500 in the United States and Australia, and a few more than 2,000 in Canada, Sweden, and Switzerland. One should wonder why a country with such a clear need for police services has so few police officers. The state's

---

[10]E.g., Palmer (1980, 28) estimated the value of international trade and total population of each Latin American country circa 1800. Using these figures to estimate per capita trade, one finds that Colombia had the lowest figure per person, 0.85 pesos. Paraguay was the next lowest, with 1.84 pesos. Other export countries were Bolivia (2.55 pesos), Ecuador (3.70 pesos), and Chile (3.84 pesos). These figures compare with 6.63 pesos for Peru, 4.34 pesos for Mexico, and more than 17 pesos for Argentina. The weakness in Colombian trade and infrastructure persisted after independence. As is elaborated elsewhere "Ocampo shows that in 1913 Colombia's per capita exports were only U.S. $34, above only those of Haiti ($31) and Honduras ($27) in Latin America, and just 10 percent of those of Cuba and Argentina. In 1920 the railroad mileage per capita was only 20 percent of the Latin American average, and higher only than the Haitian figure" (Thoumi 1995d, 18).

[11]Thorp (1991) compared these two in detail in her excellent book.

weakness is also reflected in its spotty presence on the country's borders,[12] in sparsely populated areas with a very poor internal transportation network where peasants have settled during the past 50 years.

If one had a set of maps showing the areas where people actually lived in Colombia during every decade of the twentieth century, one would see that at the beginning of the century there were many small towns and cities and that the countryside around each of them was inhabited, but that most of the country was empty and that there were no links between the settled nodes. As the century advanced, there was a dramatic expansion of the lived-in area. This differed from other Andean countries, whose Indian populations had been settled for a long time in large portions of the land. The great expansion of the rural frontier took place with very feeble state presence (e.g.: Molano 1987, 1990; Mora 1989; C. Leal 1995).[13]

The weakness of the Colombian State is also reflected in its judicial system. Rubio (1999, 139–45) has shown that for as long as statistics have been available, beginning in the 1940s, criminal cases have grown at about 7 percent per year while the judicial system's capacity has grown at 1 percent. In 1940, there were 30,000 penal cases open, and the system had the capability to process 10,000. By 1964, there were 150,000 cases and a capability for 15,000. Obviously, the system became overloaded. The solution was to shift the focus of the penal system from the most important cases to the ones easiest to solve to maximize the number of cases processed. A 1971 reform ordered the courts to try those cases for which there was a known accused perpetrator. This resulted in the resolution of the simpler criminal cases that did not require government investigations.

Furthermore, if a presumed culprit is not identified within 60 days of a crime report, the case is closed. The effects of these developments have been vicious. First, during the past three decades the state has transferred to the private sector the responsibility to find evidence to solve criminal cases in order for them to be tried. Second, they have increased the incentives for people to solve conflicts by themselves through the use of vio-

[12]E.g., Molano (1990) documented the total isolation experienced by soldiers and corporals serving in the posts of the eastern borders with Venezuela and Brazil. During the 1980s, salary payments were erratic, and the military personnel had almost no contact with headquarters and were left virtually unsupervised. Their Venezuelan and Brazilian counterparts always had better equipment and frequently loaned food and other supplies to the Colombians.

[13]As is shown below, this allowed the guerrillas to substitute for the state in many newly settled regions.

lence. Third, in Rubio's words, they have in fact given a "privateering license" to organized criminal organizations (1999, 143).

The very rapid population growth and La Violencia contributed substantially to the increase in penal cases, while the government focused on "economic development" programs and simply disregarded the pressing need to support its penal system. One wonders if investments in the justice system were not seen simply as a waste of resources!

The importance of a central city in Bolivia and Peru permitted the development of a strong military, which played a key political role in both countries' histories. Military governments have been frequent in both countries, and former military leaders have been elected president. Military professions have high social status and attract the sons of the elite. All three Andean countries in question have suffered territorial losses. Peru lost its war against Chile, and Bolivia its Pacific coast. In both countries, these losses translated into a larger military budget and stronger military participation in social and political life.[14] Furthermore, in both countries, the military has been continuously keen to protect the borders and have a presence across the national territories. Colombia lost Panama, which became an independent country through U.S. intervention. In contrast to the losses of Bolivia and Peru, the area lost did not become a part of an existing state that could be recovered without annexing the whole country.

Later on, Colombia negotiated with the United States and received monetary compensation for the loss of Panama. Colombia and Peru had a short-lived war in 1931 over part of the Amazon jungle that was solved through negotiations. That episode is only vaguely remembered in Colombia, whereas in Peru there is still a lively memory of it. In Colombia, the military has been less powerful, has supported civilian rule, has remained distant from politics, and has had a corps not drawn significantly from the elite. The Colombian military has not been prone to military coups like its counterparts in Bolivia and Peru, but it has also been less capable (perhaps incapable) of controlling the country's territory and subversive organizations.

Because of these differences, both active and retired members of the military have been among the largest drug entrepreneurs in Bolivia. In Peru, many such military members have helped in trafficking, and (as was

---

[14]E.g., at a U.S. government–sponsored conference in February 2000 in Miami, a member of the American armed forces disappointedly reported that only one of 256 Colombian members of Congress had any military background.

noted in chapter 8) a significant number have been indicted on trafficking charges or as collaborators with the illegal industry. In Colombia, most members of trafficking organization have been civilians.

A comparison of political parties highlights other important differences among the countries in question. The concentration of economic activities and population in one or a few centers in Bolivia and Peru facilitated the development of political parties with a centralized structure and political ideologies. In both countries, the old Liberal and Conservative Parties of the mid–nineteenth century gave way to a diversity of new parties that covered a wide political spectrum.

The ideologies of some of these new parties were clearly left of center, and even though most leaders came from the higher social strata, they represented some lower-class interests. In both countries, left-leaning parties obtained power, at least on occasion, and implemented substantial reforms, particularly in rural areas. The 1952 Bolivian revolution produced substantial land reform in 1953. The 1968 military coup in Peru also led to important land reform. Both countries have had populist governments that mismanaged the countries' economies in their attempts at social reform. In both cases, this led to periods of economic depression and hyperinflation. Yet these episodes weakened the traditional landholding and mining elite, opened up political space, and allowed the political systems to handle some of the most pressing claims for political participation made by large segments of the population.

In contrast, the two Colombian political parties have always been very decentralized. In the nineteenth century, their ideologies reflected the concerns of the time. The Conservatives were mainly rural based centralists who promoted the power of the Catholic Church, whereas the Liberals were more urban based, federalists, and secular. These parties have been fairly loose associations of regional leaders, who have been and are quite independent from the central organization. It is interesting that the weak presence of the central state in many areas and the decentralized parties with strong local leaders allowed the parties to substitute for and assume some of the state's roles in many regions and to gain the loyalty that citizens normally give to the nation (F. Leal 1989a; Leal and Dávila 1990).

Colombian parties are multiclassist. Beginning in the mid-1940s through at least the mid-1950s,[15] Colombia experienced what is known as La Violencia, a political conflict, led by the two traditional parties, in

[15]Some researchers extend La Violencia through 1964.

which peasants from both sides provided the cannon fodder. As the country became more educated and urban and agricultural activities lost their economic predominance, the ideological differences between the two parties became more and more irrelevant. The elite of both parties realized that the future lay in manufacturing, modern agriculture, and services and not in traditional haciendas and peasant economies.

The National Front (1958–72) agreement that ended La Violencia allowed the two parties to share power and co-govern the country. This agreement eliminated the traditional party confrontation but also destroyed party ideologies and depoliticized the parties and politics (F. Leal 1989a, 1989b) and turned the two parties into clientelistic electoral machines focused on distributing government spoils. It also excluded other political organizations from both the left and the right. The National Front was indeed a very successful "cartel" that monopolized power. Clientelism allowed the "political class" to mediate between the state and the citizenry for the provision of state services. In this sense, the two traditional parties also substituted for the community institutions that play this role in other countries.

Colombia is the only Latin American country in which the traditional parties and elite neutralized all political reform efforts.[16] Indeed, it is the only country that never had a reform government that threatened the power structure and offered the possibility of social change without violence. The policy changes and reforms implemented had to do with the modernization of state institutions that dealt with the country's economy, but there were never reforms that challenged the power structure and weakened its control over society. This does not mean that there has not been social mobility. Indeed, there have been significant movements, but those who climb are co-opted and end up reproducing the exclusionary behaviors that many criticized before. For those who refuse to be co-opted, the guerrillas offer a viable alternative.[17]

[16]The only possible exception may be Guatemala; even there, significant political change has given native communities a degree of autonomy.

[17]E.g., in 1970 I was forced to resign from the faculty of the National University after university president Mario Latorre froze my salary payments while I was investigated in response to a student's group claim that I was an agent of the U.S. Central Intelligence Agency. One of the student leaders was Guillermo León Saénz, a.k.a. "Alfonso Cano," the intellectual leader of the Colombian Revolutionary Armed Forces (FARC). One of the other two has been a university president and a clientelistic senator. The other has been the manager of a large bank and a well-known government adviser.

In the 1960s, there was a lukewarm attempt at land reform that led to a few compensated expropriations and that focused more on expanding the rural frontier into unsettled lands than on land redistribution. Colombia never had a populist government, which no doubt contributed to the country's economic stability (Urrutia 1991), but it also failed to mediate the main social conflicts. The two parties retained political control and co-opted dissidents but prevented social change and participation. The parties' depoliticization and their focus on clientelism separated them from the country's economic management and allowed highly trained economists to manage the Colombian economy. This resulted in stable (although not spectacular) growth and remarkable macroeconomic stability.

The Colombian system worked well for a fairly long time. But in its essence, it hid the seeds for violent political upheaval and for the delegitimization of the state. The pattern of political exclusion and the state's failure to respond to people's demands have been the main cause of subversion and paramilitary activities in Colombia, not poverty or inequality. It is likely that the institutional deficiencies prevented the government from responding to people's needs. The depoliticization of politics led to a predatory political system, in which the state became a bounty. The deadweight of the political system and the government's increased inability to protect human rights and property grew over time and became severe barriers to economic growth.

Urbanization and Migratory Differences

During the twentieth century, urbanization proceeded at a very fast pace throughout the Andes. Yet there are important differences among the countries of the region. Colombia and Peru are more urbanized than Bolivia. The World Bank (1995, 222) estimated that in 1993, 72 percent of Colombians were urban dwellers, a figure almost identical to Peru's (71 percent). In 1970, this figure was 57 percent in both countries. Bolivia, the least urbanized country, had 41 percent of its population in urban areas in 1970 and 59 percent in 1993.

The similarity in the rate of rural–urban migration conceals significant differences. Many migrants in Bolivia and Peru maintain ties to their original rural communities, visit them periodically, and send them funds. In Colombia, these ties are much weaker. Very large numbers of people who have been displaced by violence have no communities to go back to.[18] Others maintain ties to their families that belong to communities with weaker structures than the Bolivian and Peruvian ones. Migration in Peru has been concentrated in Lima and in Bolivia in La Paz, Cochabamba, and Santa Cruz. In Colombia, migration has been much more dispersed due to the country's large number of cities. This has made it more likely for the family ties of those displaced by violence to be dissolved. In Colombian cities, the evidence of the rural origins of a large proportion of its citizens is hidden from the layperson, whereas in Peru and Bolivia it is startling.[19]

All throughout the Andes, there have been significant migration flows into the countryside. Most of it has been rural–rural in nature. In Peru and Bolivia, this migration has been encouraged by population growth in rural areas, particularly in those of prevalent *minifundia*, or by regional economic problems. Peasants have migrated mainly in search of land and economic opportunities.

In Colombia, a significant share of rural–rural migration has been induced by rural violence. Migrants have been expelled from their original lands more than attracted by their destinations. Many of these migrants have been armed for protection. Because at least some of La Violencia had been associated with the state and some of its institutions (e.g., as the police), many migrants were running away from the state. They settled as individuals, not as communities, in distant and isolated areas where the state was not present. Indeed, the police and the army had been active actors during La Violencia and had committed atrocities. Many migrant peasants considered these state institutions their enemy (Molano 1988, 143, 167, 270). Because of this experience, they were deeply suspicious of any armed state presence. In contrast, in Bolivia and Peru, many new peasant settlements were along important highways, and settlers sought the state's presence to provide social and physical infrastructure.

---

[18]The number of displaced or internal refugees is the subject of speculation, but there is no doubt that Colombia has the largest number of internal refugees in the Western Hemisphere and one of the largest in the world. Obregón and Stavropoulou (1998, 399) estimated that "more than a million people were displaced between 1985 and 1998, and they have little hope of resolving their situation in the future."

[19]This is just an impression, but it reflects the weak community roots of many recent Colombian migrants.

A Comparison of the Incidence of Rural Violence

Any social comparison among Bolivia, Colombia, and Peru must first highlight the high level of violence in Colombia relative to the rest of the region and indeed, the world. Violence is a reflection of the weakness of the three types of constraints posited by the model: the weak internalized individual and social behavioral constraints and the state's inability to enforce its own laws. Therefore, following the argument developed in chapter 3, violence and illegal drug production are symptomatic of the same social problems and reflect each society's institutional structure and development. At the same time, because violence plays important roles within organized crime, the propensity to use it in solving conflicts is an important contributor to the concentration of the illicit drug industry in a country.

Violence in Colombia

During the past 55 years, Colombia has been characterized by an inordinate amount of violence. As was noted, during the mid–twentieth century, Colombia experienced La Violencia, which resulted in the violent death of about 2 percent of the population,[20] almost exclusively in the countryside and small towns, and forced large mass migrations to cities and unsettled vacant lands (*terrenos baldíos*). At that time as noted above (page 200), violent deaths apparently peaked in 1958, at 51.5 per 100,000 inhabitants and declined from then on until about 1970 (Thoumi 1995d, 72). Rubio's (1999, 36–38) detailed and rigorous study showed that by 1970 the violent death rate had fallen to about 20 per 100,000. From that year on, it increased steadily to about 40 per 100,000 by 1980, a level that remained relatively stable for a few years.

After 1985, there was a dramatic increase in violent deaths, reaching 85 per 100,000 inhabitants in 1990. where it remained until the late 1990s. Recent reports indicate a decline in 1998 and 1999 to about 60 per 100,000. Still, 44 percent of urban residents surveyed know someone who was assassinated in the previous 5 years (Lemoine 2000, 44). Throughout this period, Colombia has experienced guerrilla activity, compounded by the development of paramilitary groups during the past 15 years.

---

[20]Estimates vary between 200,000 and 300,000 people killed, depending on the source and period covered. The population of Colombia at that time was about 10 million.

Other Latin American countries where violence has been a problem—such as Brazil, Mexico, and Venezuela—have shown violent death rates of between 15 and 25 percent of the Colombian one (Rubio 1999, 38). In 1998, the Colombian rate was more than ten times higher than that of the United States, the most violent industrial country. "These figures show clearly that we are dealing with a country at war. No contemporary society, or community for which there is statistical evidence, has had similar violence levels during peaceful times" (Rubio 1999, 39).[21] This war, however, does not fit into traditional classifications. and some are beginning to refer to it as the Ambiguous War.[22]

Colombian violence began to be studied in earnest in the mid-1980s when President Virgilio Barco funded a commission for that purpose. Since then, it has been accepted that the direct conflict is not responsible for more that 20 percent of all violent deaths. Rubio (1999) has challenged this assertion. First, he found that violent deaths are concentrated in areas were violent actors operate (guerrillas and paramilitary and drug-trafficking organizations). The differences among departments are impressive; in 1996, the ten most violent departments had 124 violent deaths per 100,000 inhabitants whereas the ten least violent had only 24. This figure is, of course, still very high by international standards and comparable to that for the violent countries mentioned above.

Second, Rubio found that "during the decade when Colombian violence became explosive, data on personal injury reports made to the police show a continuous decline" (Rubio 1999, 58). Third, he found that the dramatic increase in violent deaths coincided with the development of the illegal drug industry and the strengthening of the various guerrilla and paramilitary groups. These findings led Rubio to cautiously conclude that a large proportion of Colombians have become less prone to appeal to violence to solve conflicts or force their will on others but that a significant group of "violent actors" have become more and more aggressive and are responsible for the bulk of violent deaths.

Violent deaths are the most glaring, but not the only, expression of social violence. Kidnappings and extortion are other important ones. Unfortunately, data on these crimes are weaker and harder to collect

---

[21]In the late 1990s, El Salvador reached comparable levels. It is also possible that a similar situation has developed in recent years in some African countries.

[22]Two recent conferences on Colombia at the U.S. Army War College in Carlisle, Pennsylvania, have characterized the Colombian situation that way.

because many victims do not make a report. Yet these crimes have become commonplace in Colombia. Throughout the 1990s, reported kidnappings were in the range of 3,000 to 4,000 a year. The existence of a special anti-kidnapping and anti-extortion national police group (Gaula) is symptomatic of the importance of these crimes. A recent survey in twenty cities shows that 35 percent of urban residents know a relative, coworker, or friend who has been kidnapped (Lemoine 2000, 49). The victims of kidnapping tend to be concentrated in particular families. Indeed, once a family has been victimized, it has a 50 percent probability of again becoming a victim. Furthermore, kidnapping intimidates a very large segment of the population because 49 percent of the population feel that they or a close relative may be kidnapped (Lemoine 2000, 48).

It is interesting to note that whereas 71 percent of those surveyed think kidnappers should be sentenced to death or life in prison, in the view of some of the main violent actors, kidnapping and extortion are simply justified fund-raising activities. For example, in a remarkable letter to *Semana* magazine, Nicolás Rodríguez-Bautista[23] (1999), the leader of the National Liberation Army (ELN), rebuked an earlier *Semana* article that asserted that ELN benefits from the drug trade. He stressed that ELN is "one of the few Colombian groups that can take pride in the fact that they don't have anything to do with illegal drugs." He also emphasized that ELN has always been ready to accept responsibilities for controversial actions such as "financial detentions" (the euphemism used for kidnappings) and attacks to the oil industry's infrastructure. It is clear that according to ELN ethics, growing coca and producing and trafficking in cocaine are morally worse than kidnapping and extorting civilians!

Rubio (1999, chap. 3) concluded that the "violent actors" play an important role in what the conventional wisdom perceives as violent deaths unrelated to insurrection and the illegal drug industry. Once a violent actor settles in a region, it introduces both the equipment to kill (arms) and the technology to do so (know-how). It also trains people in the use of arms and violence. Furthermore, in many cases it also appeals to violence to solve conflicts or to sanction traitors or those who want to leave the organization. All these factors contribute to widespread violence.

Colombian violence has also produced another important phenomenon: the *sicario* or assassin for hire. *Sicarios* are not found exclusively in Colombia, but they have flourished there as an accepted industry among

[23]A.k.a. "Gabino."

some segments of the population (Salazar 1990; Rubio 1999). These groups of young people in their late teens and early twenties have become integral to organized crime.[24]

The proportion of violent deaths that are the direct result of organized crime, insurgency, and counterinsurgency is impossible to determine because of the very low proportion of homicide cases resolved within the justice system (about 5 percent). This is particularly important in the most violent regions, where it is more difficult to find a suspect so that the case can be actively maintained and tried (Rubio 1999, chap. 3).

These findings are consistent with the model posited in chapter 3. As modernization and economic development advanced in the midst of a violent environment, both social and state controls on behavior collapsed. This meant that everyone was free to determine independently what behaviors were acceptable. Furthermore, armed organizations rationalized the use of force as part of a fight against a corrupt system of imperialism. Given the law of large numbers, there will always be a group that will be willing to use violence indiscriminately. That particular group is likely to represent a small proportion of the country's population, but it has a great capacity to disrupt the lives of the great majority who act individually and cannot be protected by the weak state or other social institutions.

Violent crimes, kidnapping, and other crimes against the individual have created a human rights crisis. Indeed, a comparative survey of 60 countries showed that Colombia had the highest percentage (65) of respondents who believed that human rights were not respected (Lemoine 2000, 46).

Colombian Violence and Rural–Rural Migration

La Violencia was mostly rural and occurred in many recently settled areas, such as the Old Caldas Department and the Tolima and Valle Departments. These were all regions in which settlement had been carried out by individuals two or three generations previously and strong communities had not had enough time to develop. There is no question that the hunger for land was one of the main motivating factors behind La Violencia. Many peasants were compelled to sell their land at low prices;

---

[24]Guerrillas also use very young soldiers, boys and girls, some as young as 12 years of age. The use of underage fighters has become an important human rights issue in Colombia's ambiguous war.

others were simply forced to abandon their plots or were killed.[25] Population displacements and migrations were massive in some areas, and the population of many regions changed substantially. Guerrillas who were members of the Liberal or Conservative parties—the latter frequently aided by the police or the army—sought to force out every member of the opposite party from the regions they controlled.

At the end of La Violencia, few peasants returned to the areas from where they had been expelled. Most ended up in urban areas, but a significant number sought lands in unsettled areas. From the mid-1950s to the mid-1960s, successive governments decreed amnesties. As was mentioned above, many guerrillas perceived the police and the army as their enemies and harbored a profound distrust of state institutions. But some guerrilla groups, particularly those associated with the Communist Party, did not turn in their arms. Instead, they sought refuge in distant, out-of-the-way, unsettled regions in the middle of the jungle, where they established armed communities.[26]

Most migrants were not guerrillas but were displaced by violence, were attracted by the availability of vacant land, and settled in various locations in the eastern half of the country. Many of these were also armed for protection from marauders and wild animals. They were not necessarily antagonistic toward the state and actually hoped that it would provide such basic services as education, police, and legal conflict resolution systems (C. Leal 1995). In all these areas, the state's presence was extremely weak and violence was widespread (C. Leal 1995; Molano 1990).

State authorities were isolated from their supervisors and were not accountable. Their abuses of power for individual benefit were frequent and created fierce resentment.[27] Indeed, the police and the army were frequently perceived as enemies (Molano 1988, 143, 167, 170).

A collection of testimonies from settlers in one location near the Venezuelan and Brazilian borders is very revealing (Molano 1990). Payments to the couple of border police officers were greatly delayed and sporadic. These officers had to find ways to support themselves "using their authority." Brazilian and Venezuelan border presence was substan-

[25]The bibliography on La Violencia is quite long. E.g., see Molano (1988, 1989), Alape (1985), González-Arias and Marulanda-Alvarez (1990), and Sánchez and Meertens (1983).

[26]Alape (1985) and Molano (1988, 1989) provided a good description of these processes.

[27]E.g., see Molano (1988, 93, 105, 120).

tially stronger. The lack of trust among settlers was generalized to the point that one wisely asserted that "trust is a lot more valuable than capital" (p. 48). When the "boys" (guerrillas) arrived, they imposed a very authoritarian order that was based on their armed power.[28] In these regions, there has been significant violence associated with the lack of trust and uncertain property rights. The guerrillas' authoritarian government allowed businesses to extend credit to peasants and miners because it guaranteed a system of debt collection (p. 53).

Another negative effect of La Violencia was to eliminate individual responsibility. Any action, no matter how violent and inhumane, was justified as a reaction to what had been suffered.[29] In this situation, the thrill of power is for some the main driving force. "They did not form a band to assassinate or rob, they did it to give orders" (Molano 1988, 85). "It is an extraordinary feeling to hold someone's life in the palm of your hand. When the lives of other men depend on the movement of a single finger, that gives you great self-assurance" (Molano 1988, 182).

To summarize, La Violencia weakened and destroyed many incipient community organizations and generated a large number of displaced peasants. This process was armed and violent. Settlers in faraway vacant lands had weak or nonexistent property rights over their lands and very lax community ties. The state's presence was at best weak and sporadic, and officials frequently abused their power for personal benefit. Once guerrillas arrived, they substituted for the state and imposed their authoritarian order.

One likely reason that guerrillas were welcomed in many locations was because, though harsh and undemocratic, it was not clear that they were profiting as individuals. Civil society was at best incipient in these regions and left a vacuum filled by guerrillas. It is well acknowledged that guerrillas substituted for the state in many isolated Colombian regions. It is interesting that they also substituted for civil society and other institutions, and today authoritarian guerrilla organizations are a main obstacle to the development of these institutions.

---

[28]Curiously, their regulations included strict limits on alcohol consumption and an outright prohibition on prostitution. These measures were not taken out of concern for the women involved but to prevent businesses from "exploiting" peasants and miners. Women were only merchandise used in the exploitation of the workers! (Molano 1990, 86).

[29]E.g., see the testimonies in Molano (1988, 165, 179).

Peruvian Rural Violence and Guerrillas in the 1980s

In the early 1980s, the guerrilla group Shining Path (Sendero Luminoso, or SL) became an important violent actor in Peru. Many peasants were caught in the middle of the struggle between SL and the government. Fortunately, their traditional organizations were quite sophisticated and allowed them to overcome that violence and to come out of it in much better social shape than the Colombian peasants. The rural structures of Peru are no doubt very different from those in Colombia:

> As a surviving social structure of the Inca Empire, Peru is made up of traditional communities, whose social organization, in many ways, still defies the influence of the modern Western world. The traditional community presents three clear characteristics: agrarian, social and economic. From the agrarian point of view, the traditional community is an indissoluble unit where man is an agent of both continuity and change. Socially, the community has governmental and legislative systems based on free election of its individual members or *comuneros* and on a rigorous scheme of norms and sanctions imposed by tradition. From an economic standpoint, Indian communities are indivisible work units with socialistic and collective characteristics, that is, units whose members have equal access to communal property." (Morales 1989, 2)

Figueroa's (1981) study of eight Peruvian South Sierra communities showed that the nuclear family is the productive unit but has strong community links. When couples get married, they receive substantial community help to build their house, and the family exchanges a significant amount of services within the community through reciprocal exchanges, barter, and trade. It also has access to communal lands. It is clear that "peasants' families are not isolated from the rest of the community" (Figueroa, 72). Temporary and permanent migrations are common. The Sierra communities are net receptors of monetary transfers from community members who have migrated (p. 76). Most young people migrate, but many return after a year or more (nonseasonal migration). Prevalent reasons for returning include parents' deaths or incapacity (49 percent), *por la chacra* (to recover or protect property) (13 percent), illness (13 percent), misadaptation to urban life (8 percent), loss of a job (8 percent), low income (4 percent), and other reasons (5 percent) (p. 121). Thus at least 83 percent return for reasons related to having a community in the Sierra and only 12 percent return for economic reasons.

From 1980 to 1993, the Peruvian Sierra was the scene of the SL uprising against the Peruvian state. Peasants were trapped in the middle of a
war between alien powers. SL had an urban base and a strong pro-urban
bias. Many of its members were middle class and educated, and very few
spoke Quechua (Coronel 1996, 43). Their socialist discourse found limited acceptance within the rural population. Educated peasant youth tended
to accept it more than the older, less educated generation. However, "the
Andean cultural codes were not known by Shining Path militants" (p. 46).
Indeed, SL with its emphasis on orthodox Maoist ideology had a profound
disdain for Indian culture. According to Maoist theory, any culture is only
the ideological reflection of political and economic realities. Therefore,
all Andean cultural manifestations represent a reflection of the past that
has to be destroyed (Degregori 1996b, 210). It was not surprising that
SL did not acknowledge and actually tried to supplant traditional Indian
authorities.

SL arrived with a vision that required the destruction of the old system
before a new and just one could be created. From its point of view, authoritarianism and terrorism were justified by their "correct" goals. These
beliefs were used to justify the massacre of 80 peasants in Ayacucho, for
example (Degregori 1996b, 297). Following Mao's teachings, SL also
wanted to eliminate the state and other authorities from the rural areas.

Many of the orders of the SL were simply incomprehensible to pragmatic, risk-averse peasants. SL wanted, for example, to promote a city
blockade to starve city dwellers. When peasants asked to whom they
would sell their products, the answer was simple: The party would decide.
Peasants simply did not understand why after they had produced something they were not allowed to benefit from their own work (Del Pino
1996, 132).

In another case, SL organized communal production and peasants co-
operated. But at the time of the harvest, SL left peasants only with products for their subsistence and the rest was kept for the party (Degregori
1996, 195). SL also engaged in a campaign to eliminate all state presence
from rural areas. This included schools, health posts, and physical infrastructure projects. All these actions generated a strong peasant reaction
against SL. Furthermore, in many regions SL had little to offer the peasantry, who had already benefited from the land reform that had broken
down the haciendas (Coronel 1996, 79).

SL activities in the Sierra generated a strong government reaction. First,
the Marine Infantry was sent to confront the subversion. Like SL, these

Marines came from urban areas, felt profound disdain for Indian culture, and in their zeal to squelch the insurgency, attacked and killed peasants—indeed, "they acted as a foreign occupation force" (Coronel 1996, 49). For these city-based marines, it was frequently impossible to distinguish between a common peasant and an SL member, which led to many incidents of aggression against innocent peasants.

Fortunately, the government realized that keeping the marines involved was a guarantee for failure and brought in the army to substitute for them. This was a wise move because the army had a significant number of conscripts from the Sierra, many of Indian origin. Army officers were more respectful of the Indians and encouraged the formation of civil self-defense committees (CDCs), also known as peasant *rondas campesinas*, which were patterned on similar organizations that had traditionally existed in the Northern Sierra in Cajamarca. The *rondas* traditionally had protected communities against criminals, mainly rustlers. They became a very successful instrument against SL and eventually forced it out of many regions. At the end of the war, many social institutions had survived, and in some regions they actually came out stronger. The following paragraphs summarize the experience of several communities in this process.

Degregori explained that SL entered Ayacucho in the early 1980s, forced the police out the region, used violence, and weakened the social fabric (Degregori 1996a, 18–21). However, "there were many cases in which communities and extended families proved their resiliency and flexibility to adapt to a war environment. New feminine organizations sprouted: mothers' clubs, glass of milk committees. These formed the Ayacucho Departmental Mothers' Clubs Federation" (p. 18). They were strong enough so that they even held a congress. One reason they survived was that the conflict actors did not see women as dangerous. Evangelical churches had grown substantially, and they became the center of community activities, along with the Ronderos. The army had regained a strong presence. These two institutions formed a new power focus. "The visitor finds today an extremely poor and devastated region with its meager infrastructure destroyed, and with very few development opportunities within the current macroeconomic model. It does not find, however, a defeated, depressed and hopeless population. Instead, he finds one full with awesome vitality in the midst of its own ruins" (p. 21).

Many peasants from Ayacucho were displaced, but about a third returned. Most of those displaced acquired urban experience. Perhaps half will remain in the cities, but the rest will live with one foot in the city and one in the countryside. The ones who come back want to develop the countryside. They insist on having village maps, on building an urban infrastructure, and on providing public utilities (Degregori 1996a, 22–23).

Many CDCs were organized by the army, but they are not army puppets. "These actors have their own will and goals and are capable of making their own decisions even in the most adverse conditions" (Degregori 1996a, 27). "Rondas make the difference between hopelessness and social vitality" (p. 24). In Peru, as the conflict lost intensity, the *rondas* tended to drift away from their defensive role and developed other social functions.

Coronel (1996) focuses on the experience of several communities in Huanta:

> [In Culluchaca,] the nuclear and extended family and the community constituted the most important organizational and identity generating social elements. The community was also a key ideological transmitter through its authority system, communal tasks, assemblies, and festivities … Until 1980 the *varayoccs* system constituted the axis of community social life. Productive activity, social relations and religious festivities were organized by it. The *llacta vara* or main *vara* organized the rotating planting cycles, communal tasks, religious festivities, presided the assemblies and solved internal conflicts. The *campos* took care of the natural resources (grazing lands and trees) and plantings. They guarded against and sanctioned the "damages" caused by animals and the cases of rustling. The *regents* were in charge of enforcing the orders of the main *vara* and *campos*. Finally, the *alfacires*, two from each of the community's barrios, implemented the tasks for which the main *vara* was responsible. Many times they also did errands for the national authorities. (Degregori 1996a, 69)

This was a hierarchical and ritualized society. SL ignored this working structure, imposed its own authority, and executed several *varayoccs* and others community leaders. Although it was weakened, the community was not destroyed. *Varas* stopped functioning, but CDCs substituted for them. CDC *comandos* assumed the roles of the old *alfacires*. "The war did not destroy the cultural references. Myths, beliefs, costumes, were revalued in the midst of the uprooting of the changing life conditions" (Degregori 1996a, 75). Thus the community survived, though weakened.

In Ocana, SL had problems. Their activists arrived in 1977 and promised victory following their *"pensamiento* Gonzalo." However, SL had little to offer because peasants had already benefitted from land reform and the SL had not developed strong grassroots support (Degregori 1996a, 79). In 1983, the Marine infantry arrived. Peasants were caught in the crossfire as the Marines attacked many peasants as SL members and SL attacked peasants as Marine supporters and informers. The community, seeking to be neutral, formed CDCs that became generalized and a main instrument for community survival. In Ocana, there was no significant forced migration, and the culture maintained its dynamism. Traditional offerings to their gods increased, as well as traditional religious festivities, including those to the Virgin and other Catholic saints (pp. 82–83, 85).

Cangari was a weak community in the early 1980s (Degregori 1996a, 89–91). There was no state presence, but there were community organizations. SL's political discourse reflected the Peruvian country–city conflict and showed disrespect for peasants, who were treated as children. SL did not have anything to offer except—if it got power—better prices for peasants' products. SL opposed some development projects that peasants wanted, such as a small dam. In 1983, the Marines came in, attacked the peasants, and generated significant out-migration. In 1985, the Army substituted for the Marines, and the peasants' conditions improved. CDCs were organized with Army support and began to fight SL. After CDCs became widespread, they succeeded against SL. By 1993,

Cangari peasants that before had very few interrelations among them, concentrated themselves within a semi-urban area within a fort that they constructed and shared with the Viru-Viru residents. In this environment they established frequent assemblies to discuss their common problems and generated a new collectivity characterized by:

1. Practice of solidarity levels previously non-existent. If someone gets sick, his or her care is a communal responsibility. Differences regarding access to the "wilds" to collect firewood and cochineal are quickly resolved; as are the settlement of compensations for "damages" caused by the livestock to plantings. Nobody, absolutely nobody is exempted from taking his and her turn guarding the fort, even at night. There are no special privileges.

2. Everybody is involved in maintaining social cohesion under a known leadership and the distribution of productive tasks among community members. This is based on the acknowledgement that security is everybody's job. Failure of an individual to fulfill his responsibilities is socially sanctioned.

3. Elements of Andean culture like music and traditional festivities are highly valued after so many years of hardship and have gained strength. (Degregori 1996a 98–99)

Del Pino (1996) summarized the experience of the Apurimac Valley. In this region, Evangelical churches had grown substantially before SL came in. The Pentecostals were particularly important. The Catholic hierarchy's traditional treatment of peasants fluctuated between paternalism and marginalization. Pentecostal gringos called peasants "brothers," shook their hands, and told them about equality. To be a Pentecostal pastor did not require previous high status or a profession but only to be devoted entirely to God. The Catholic Church was associated with the elite, the city, and the invasion of the Indian lands. The Pentecostals had an apocalyptic message that offered hope in the midst of famine and suffering that was very attractive to native communities (Del Pino 1996, 130–31).

CDCs appeared in the mid-1980s, and 836 communities were organized around them (Del Pino 1996, 118–19, 132, 137–38). In this region, SL found another organization that had a comparably strong ideology as the SL. Indeed, Evangelicals demonized SL. This region was also producing coca, and some peasants established alliances with drug traffickers in exchange for arms and resources to defeat SL and keep the area clean of the police and the military. In the early 1980s, the Apurimac River Valley Peasant Federation had up to 106 *sindicatos*. It marketed peasants' products and had begun to cooperate in building medical posts and schools. SL arrived with its vision of destroying the whole system and creating a new one. Their Evangelical beliefs put peasants in a quandary, and they did not comply with SL demands. SL then massacred peasants, which led to a holy war of the SL against the Evangelical peasants. In 1985, the army arrived—an event that helped the morale of the CDCs, which then eliminated SL from the region. CDCs have sophisticated structures. "The traditional organizational capacity of the Chungui communities made possible such response." They organized in *montoneras* (bands of civilian fighters), the same way that they had done in earlier generations against the Chilean army in Huanta in 1883 and against landlords' abuses in 1923.

There is no question that CDCs obtained military power through their links to drug trafficking. At the end of the war, the CDCs were stronger, and the *ronda*–coca–narco alliance had increased their independence from the state and the military (Del Pino 1996, 167, 177).

Starn (1996) studied the Cangari and Viru-Viru communities in the South-Central Sierra. In this region, the army organized *rondas* and also ordered peasants to move their homes to form clusters easier to patrol and protect. The army led "an aggressive campaign to organize the 56,000 rural inhabitants against Shining Path" (p. 232). The *rondas'* counterrevolution was an important social movement against foreign invaders. "The thoroughly ideologized Senderistas, willing to kill and be killed for their project, did not know and did not respect the Andean codes" (p. 249). It is interesting that *rondas* have contributed to a surprising rebirth of civil society, a fact recognized even by their critics. Today there is widespread participation in communal tasks and protection systems. "In most cases, this participation is not due to military intimidation but to the peasants' collective conviction that *rondas* are something desirable" (p. 254).

A Comparison of Coca-Growing Regions

A comparison of what has happened in the main coca-growing regions of the three countries—Chapare in Bolivia, Alto Huallaga in Peru, and Guaviare in Colombia—is also very illustrative of the differences discussed above. The Bolivian government sponsored many Chapare settlements while others developed spontaneously. The state was always present in this endeavor. Large infrastructure projects were partially financed by multilateral and bilateral lending agencies. Government investment in Chapare has been significant, with the result that today it has the best infrastructure (electricity, education, health services, communications, transportation, etc.) of any Bolivian rural region.

Civil society groups have also participated actively in this process, with peasant *sindicatos* playing a key role (as was already noted in chapter 4). These are institutions peculiar to Bolivia. *Sindicatos'* membership is determined by residence. Each *sindicato* covers a particular area, and each family that settles on a parcel of land within its jurisdiction becomes a *sindicato* member. *Sindicatos* require their members' presence at periodic meetings, where many of the community's problems are vented. They have developed communal conflict resolution systems, the decisions of which are enforced by the community. They "possess the authority, legitimacy, and power to establish private land boundaries for new colonists, to influence transport fares, and to manage and tax coca-leaf markets in the towns of the Chapare, with the funds so raised to be used for local, small-scale public works programs" (Healy 1991, 89).

The *sindicatos* are grouped in federations, which form confederations. These organizations provide coca growers with political representation by acting as mediators among peasants, the state, and such foreign donors as the United Nations Drug Control Program and the U.S. Agency for International Development. A few *sindicato* leaders are members of the Bolivian Congress.

Sindicatos were originally organized after the 1952 revolution in the peasant Sierra communities, the home of most migrants to Chapare. Their cohesion reflects the strong community infrastructure among Bolivian peasants. Although each peasant's decision to move was made individually, migration to the Chapare was communal. Sierra peasants from a particular village migrated to the same Chapare area, so that many Sierra *sindicato* members are also members of a parallel *sindicato* in Chapare.[30] It may be argued that the peasants migrated with their institutions on their backs—indeed, most Chapare migrants did not sever their links to their original Sierra communities. Indeed, many migrants have been seasonal and return to their original regions, where they invest most their savings.

Illegal coca has been grown in Peru primarily in the "Selva's Eyebrow" (Ceja de Selva), the recently settled mountainous jungle on the east side of the Andes that remained almost totally unpopulated for centuries. Settling and colonizing this region was an old goal of Peruvian governments and the elite. Government policy during the 1960s contributed to the jungle's colonization, integrating that region with Peru's coastal markets, particularly that of Lima. In 1966, the Inter-American Development Bank financed a settlement project in the Upper Huallaga Valley (Tarazona-Sevillano and Reuter 1990, 101). This region was targeted to become the breadbasket of Peru. Policies changed substantially after the 1968 coup by General Juan Velasco that implemented land reform on the coast and in the High Sierra; promoted cooperatives in the Huallaga; and increased the pro-urban-policy bias of its overall policies, which led to declining rural incomes (Cotler 1996).

---

[30]Sanabria (1993) has provided an excellent anthropological analysis of this process and the nexus that has developed between Sierra and Chapare communities.

Velasco's forced cooperative organization in the valley resulted in lower outputs because that form of organization was alien to peasants and the jungle's low soil fertility resulted in quickly declining crop yields (Tarazona-Sevillano and Reuter 1990, 104–7). In this process, coca substituted for legal traditional crops in places like the Upper Huallaga Valley. Contrary to other crops, coca is perhaps the most environmentally friendly crop for these types of soils and grows for a long time.

Most migrants to the Selva's Eyebrow came from the Sierra, and as in Bolivia, they belonged to structured communities. Because of these settlers' characteristics, the colonization was pacific, as it was in Bolivia.

Coca growers' income became an attractive possible source of funding for Shining Path, which tried to infiltrate and control peasant communities. The coca growers in the Huallaga organized themselves first against government eradication and later on against Shining Path. The guerrilla group at first protected the peasants against traffickers and government policy, but its strong Maoist ideology led it to indoctrinate peasants and force them to undertake many actions that the communities rejected (Obando 1993, 92). The lack of army actions against drug trafficking also contributed to the peasants' disenchantment with the guerrillas. Besides, in 1991, "Fujimori eliminated coca cultivation from the penal code" (Jones 1999, 45). This move left coca plantings in a legal limbo, but it was equivalent to a de facto decriminalization of coca growers, who thus no longer needed the protection of Shining Path.

The peasants developed 175 committees organized in the Defense Front Against Coca Eradication in the Upper Huallaga (FEDECAH) and a smaller Agrarian Federation of the Selva Maestra (FASMA), which had the support of the National Agrarian Confederation (CAN). Many of these groups were armed and organized peasant self-defense groups (*rondas campesinas*) to fight Shining Path (Jones 1999, 45). This was a broadly based development that transcended the Huallaga Valley. Indeed, the most important *rondas* developed in areas where Shining Path had a strong presence and had massacred peasants several times, particularly in Ayacucho Department. The government took advantage of these conditions and encouraged the creation of the *rondas*, which played an important role in weakening Shining Path.[31]

---

[31]E.g., see Degregori et al. (1996). Gorriti (1990) is the classic history of Shining Path.

The settlement of the Guaviare and other coca-growing areas of Colombia was very violent. Many settlers were people who had been displaced by violence. Some were part of organized guerrilla marches, whereas others migrated as individuals. There were also peasants who came in search of land and those who came from urban areas, either in search of adventure or to escape the law (Molano 1987). The government's presence was very weak, and frequently, when a state institution was present, the lack of accountability of local government officials led to power abuse and the delegitimization of the state. The settlement of that region was very violent and most peasants were armed. The cultivation of illegal crops led to a large increase in violence. Reports of homicides to steal illegal crop proceeds and to "solve" property-line conflicts were common, and the avoidance of payments to illegal laboratory workers and stealing of coca by-products were daily events. Atrocities were also common. These crimes frequently involved law enforcers (Molano 1987; C. Leal 1995).

Guerrilla organizations took advantage of that situation and established order by force in the Guaviare. At the same time, they began to charge "taxes," which were used to support subversive actions and also to provide social services. They provided a justice system, made sure that classes were taught at schools, and provided police and security for the region. Their law was arbitrary, authoritarian, imposed from above, and undemocratic. Still, it was welcome by most residents, who longed for order and stability in their lives (Molano 1987).

The contrasts among the three coca-growing regions highlight the extreme difficulty that Colombians have in nurturing communal institutions that contribute to conflict solution and to social order and also their propensity to appeal to violence. The contrasts also show the strength of traditional social organization in Bolivia and Peru.

It is not surprising, then, that in Bolivia and Peru the illegal drug industry tended to concentrate on the coca-growing stage, which was based on a tradition of coca cultivation and use. In both countries' discourse, there are frequent statements like "coca is not cocaine." Indeed, in Indian culture it is incomprehensible that a plant could be declared illegal if Pachamama, Mother Earth, gave it to them. In both countries, the illegal industry started with a traditional agricultural product and expanded slowly into manufacturing. Neither country has produced traffickers of the caliber of the large Colombian ones. In both countries, drug trafficking is related to shame. It is interesting that the trafficking Bolivian firms have used "gentlemen's agreements" to divide the coca sources and avoid conflicts (Rodas 1996). The various "lines" or "firms" have almost exclusively been family affairs and have respected other families' illegal businesses. There have been cases in which violence has been used, but these have been relatively few compared with Colombia.

In Colombia, the illegal industry started with the manufacturing and smuggling processes. The agricultural part of the industry developed as a backward linkage to the manufacturing stage. Colombians have also developed new products (crack cocaine and heroin) and have used widespread violence to eliminate competition and to intimidate law enforcement officials and society at large. This attitude has given Colombian traffickers the upper hand over Bolivian and Peruvian ones. The latter have began to advance in the manufacturing and smuggling stages of the industry only since the main Colombian trafficking organizations have been disrupted and most of their key members have been jailed.

Part IV

Antidrug Policies

10

The Nature of the Drug Policy Problem

This book shows that illegal drug production and trafficking in the Andes is not just the response to poverty, inequality, economic crisis, corruption, or illegal demand. No doubt these are elements that influence the illegal drug industry, but they can be at best triggering causes of the illegal industry's development. The industry grew in the Andes not just because it was a profitable business; it also grew because the institutions of Andean societies made them vulnerable to its development. Indeed, illegal drugs could be a lucrative business for all countries, but only a handful participate in that trade.

During the past 30 years, the United States, Andean, and some European countries, and several multilateral agencies all have tried to deal with a worsening Andean "drug problem," which has become more and more complex and intractable, by implementing a set of antidrug policies in the Andean countries that have focused on supply control. "Going to the source" has been a frequently used motto to promote these policies. The most important policies have focused on

1. Eradication of coca and poppy plantings.
2. "Crop-substitution" programs that aimed to find alternative sources of income, mainly through other crops, for peasants engaged in coca and poppy cultivation. These programs had little success and evolved over time into "alternative development" programs that go well beyond the search for possible crop alternatives into such other aspects of economic development as transportation infrastructure, energy, education, health, and marketing.
3. Interdiction efforts and controls on chemical inputs ("precursors") used in the process of refining cocaine and heroin.
4. Laboratory seizure and destruction and domestic interdiction of illegal coca- and poppy-based products, marijuana, and synthetic drugs.
5. Interdiction and seizure of the same products outside the Andean countries.
6. Extradition of the main Andean traffickers to the United States.
7. Strengthening the Andean justice and law enforcement systems to improve efficiency and to prevent the corruption of justice officials and police and military personnel; to change and enact new laws to increase minimum sentences for drug-trafficking crimes; to make money laundering a crime; and to facilitate the seizure, confiscation, and expropriation of assets bought with drug money.
8. Training police and armed forces to improve their antidrug performance.

These policies incorporate carrot-and-stick elements, but on the whole they are heavily biased toward the stick side. Indeed, the main thrust of these policies is repressive. Alternative development policies constitute the main carrot side, but they also contain repressive elements inasmuch as they force eradication. Independent of the repressive policy bias, all these policies are formulated to make illegal drugs less profitable. Some aim to make them absolutely less profitable, that is, to lower returns. Others, like alternative development, aim to lower the illegal industry's relative profitability by making other activities more attractive.

Andean antidrug policies have been designed and implemented through significant bilateral and multilateral cooperation programs. The U.S. Agency for International Development and the United Nations Drug Control Program have been the main external actors, but several European countries have also contributed funds and other forms of assistance. These can also be considered a carrot for Andean governments, which get extra funds and/or other resources and foreign exchange for their antidrug efforts.

One important characteristic of all antidrug policies is that they are formulated without first spelling out the underlining causality of drug production and trafficking. It is as if the pressure to confront a social problem leads pragmatic individuals to attack it before fully understanding it. It appears that policymakers believe they understand the "drug problem" and proceed accordingly. However, they do not bother to empirically test their beliefs or to spell them out explicitly before acting.

Antidrug policies in the Andes have had some successes. But on the whole, the balance has been negative. Most leading Colombian traffickers were captured or killed in the mid-1990s, and the main drug "cartels" were dismembered. Through 2001, about fifty Colombian and a couple of Bolivian traffickers had been extradited to the United States. Coca production has declined in a few regions, but antidrug policies have not achieved their main goal of reducing illicit drug production and supply.

If anything, antidrug policies have failed.[1] Total cocaine output today is at least eight times larger that in the early 1980s when President Ronald Reagan renewed the "war on drugs." As has been extensively noted above, new cocaine-based products have been developed, new production technologies have increased yields and purity levels, and the industry has opened new markets in Europe, Japan, and in other parts of the world. During the 1990s, Colombia became a poppy grower and a major heroin supplier to the United States. New actors and trafficking routes have appeared. Mexicans are now important cocaine intermediaries and have developed substantial trafficking networks in Mexico and the United States. Colombian and Bolivian drug-trafficking organizations have developed links to international criminal syndicates in Europe and the former Soviet Union. Drug money has been a main source of revenue for Colombian insurgency and counterinsurgency guerrillas and has been a main factor in bringing that country to the brink of a political and economic collapse.

In the United States, the numbers of drug arrests and inmates serving drug-related prison sentences have skyrocketed. In the early 1990s, the United States had about 1.35 million prisoners, two-thirds of whom had se-

---

[1]This has been recognized by many analysts, including Mathea Falco (1996), who was the first undersecretary of state for narcotics when the office was created during the Jimmy Carter administration.

rious drug habits (Falco 1994). By 2000, the inmate population had risen to about 2 million, 800,000 of whom were imprisoned on drug-related charges. Drug prices in the United States and Europe are excellent indicators of policy performance because they reflect drug availability and market risks. Cocaine prices in the United States have declined about 75 percent since 1983 and purity has increased. A similar decline occurred in European markets during the 1990s. The price trends for heroin are similar.

As was shown in chapter 2, it has been very difficult to have a sensible antidrug policy debate. The discussions tend to be of two types: those among people who share ideas and reinforce each other's positions; and those that degenerate into dialogues among the deaf, in which everyone wants to state a case but not listen to or respond to someone else's arguments. The former type is common among government and multilateral agency officials who promote current policies, and among academics who support a common policy approach to the drug issue. The latter type is common between "legalizers" and "criminalizers." Unfortunately, there are many reasons why it is very difficult to have various actors agree on the terms of a policy debate or evaluation.

A key element in the failure of dialogues is the expectation that the "drug problem" can be "solved" through policy. As was argued in chapter 3, the reasons why people produce drugs are very complex and depend not only on profitability but also on social institutions and the stock and nature of social capital. In the United States, academics have acknowledged government policy limitations and have warned against having expectations that policies can "solve" the "drug problem."

For example, after an in-depth comparison of American and European drug use, addiction, and policies, Reuter (1997, 263) concluded that "the severity of health and crime consequences of dependence may all be much more shaped by factors other than policy" and "most of the relevant differences appear to be rooted in broader features of society." These findings led him to argue that "if policy is only moderately important in controlling drug use, then perhaps we can mitigate the harshness of our policies with little risk of being seen an expansion of drug use and related problems" (p. 263).

Why Are Antidrug Policies Difficult to Debate and Evaluate?

To evaluate antidrug policies, it is important to start by stating a trivial but fundamental point. To explain why a particular policy succeeds or fails it is necessary to explain why drugs are produced and consumed. In other words, if policies are formulated under the wrong assumptions about production and consumption causality, chances are that they will fail; and if they succeed, they will do so because of sheer luck.

There are several reasons why antidrug policies are difficult to debate and evaluate. First are the differences in what people conceive as the "drug problem" and perceptions about its causes and effects. Indeed, there is a need to construct an agreement about demand and supply causalities. Drug policies have been influenced by some of the deepest American cultural fears and prejudices, and have peculiar characteristics. As was extensively discussed in chapter 2, there are profound differences in how Andean and American societies perceive drug phenomena. There is no doubt that when many of the American-driven policies are looked through an Andean prism, they are seen as an attempt to impose on them a particularly American vision of the problem, and many Andean citizens consider these policies a foreign, imperialistic intervention in their societies.

Furthermore, given the Andean history of foreign exploitation, it is not surprising that many in the Andean world would be suspicious of the alleged reasons behind U.S. policy formulation. High levels of distrust characterize all Andean societies, and people have learned not to take statements at face value. Thus, they "know" that Americans have hidden reasons for their actions. From the American angle, there is the conviction that "good people" all over the world share fundamental values and that they should validate these "good" American policies. Indeed, even serious scholars such as Condoleezza Rice are convinced that "American values are Universal" (Rice 2000, 49) and thus that the interests of the United States coincide with world welfare.

The American attempt to impose drug policies on the Andean countries is rooted in the depths of the American ethos and thus should not be considered a traditional imperialistic action. Rather, it is an attempt at "policy conversion." Americans do not want to gain territory, access to raw materials, or cheap labor.[2] They only want to convert the rest of the world to their way of dealing with psychoactive drugs; after all, any reasonable human would like to be like an American. The history of the Spanish efforts

---

[2]Notice that nineteenth-century "Manifest Destiny" beliefs led to the westward expansion of the United States into mostly sparsely populated lands rather than into the Caribbean and Central America. This contrasted with European empire-building policies.

to force traditional Andean societies to adopt Catholicism suggests that policy conversion efforts will at best find lukewarm support in the Andes. In any case, the differences in the way the United States and Latin America look at psychoactive drugs are a main obstacle to a meaningful policy debate.

As was noted in chapter 2, many American policymakers and Latin American policy critics arrive at their positions from within closed philosophical systems. From the point of view of the American war on drugs, the goal is to eliminate the drug enemy. This makes it difficult to evaluate policies and to debate other policy goals. When goals are not achieved, antidrug policy enforcers attribute the policy failure to immorality, corruption, or human failure and conclude that it is necessary to continue the same policies with more zeal.[3] Indeed, following this logic, it is not possible to evaluate the negative effects of some drug policies; if those policies happen to have some unpleasant effects, they should be attributed to illegal drug activities that must be eliminated at any cost.

Looking at drug policies through the prism of the dependency-theory model used by many Latin Americans leads to a similar debate deadlock. Americans promote prohibitionist policies because they benefit from them. Furthermore, policies are not supposed to end the illegal drug business, because that would hurt American capitalists (mainly the banking industry) that make money from it. This fact is so obvious that there is no need to even evaluate the gains of the banking system, which are known to be enormous. Here again, there is nothing to evaluate. The policies themselves are just incidental to the real intentions behind them.

Another reason why antidrug policies are difficult to evaluate is simply that they are frequently formulated using politically appealing phrases or slogans that set totally unrealistic goals. Policies are frequently defined with such slogans as "zero tolerance," a favorite during the Reagan administration. If this were taken literally, it would imply the establishment of an authoritarian regime in the United States that would not respect most rights guaranteed by its Constitution. A zero-tolerance goal did not take into account the U.S. government's physical and legal inability to achieve

---

[3] An excellent example of this view is that of a high-ranking official of the U.S. Drug Enforcement Administration who was interviewed by the author in 1994. His view was simply that the "war on drugs" was akin to the war against smallpox, which had taken about four centuries to eradicate. Following this parallelism, it was necessary to fight drugs independent of current policy failures, because they were just part of the normal processes of fighting "social viruses."

it. Expressing goals through slogans and catch phrases was useful to attract the public's attention and establish large minimum sentences for drug trafficking and possession, but then it was quietly dropped.

Other policy goals have given the appearance of having been better defined, but they have not been. For example, the George H. W. Bush administration set as a goal a 15 percent decline in drugs entering the United States. The problem with such a policy is simply that the volume of drugs that actually enters the United States is not known with certainty. Furthermore, because drug-smuggling estimates are frequently based on drug seizures, a cynic might argue that a drug seizure decline of 15 percent would satisfy the policy goal.[4] In Latin America, there are also unrealistic policy goal examples. President Gonzalo Sánchez-de-Losada used the slogan "zero option" to set the goal of eradicating all illegal coca from Bolivia. But widespread political disturbances in Chapare, coca growers' marches on La Paz, and opposition from important parties dissuaded him from carrying on his program.

Chapter 11 examines in detail two international cooperation experiences: Alternative development programs in Bolivia and the Special Cooperation Program in Colombia funded by the international community after the assassination of presidential candidate Luis Carlos Galán in 1989. These experiences highlight the glaring lack of coordination between donor and recipient countries, the lack of participation of beneficiaries in program formulation and implementation, the great expectation differences between donors and beneficiaries, the project implementation difficulties, the frequent political opportunism of project promoters, and the great coordination difficulties among various project agencies.

Drug policy evaluation problems transcend the Latin American–United States differences in perceptions and cultures. Within the United States, one finds similar difficulties rooted in basic philosophical concepts. MacCoun and Reuter (2001) have argued that drug policy positions can be based either on consequentialist or deontological arguments. The former arise from the utilitarian tradition, which evaluates each act according to empirical (observable) consequences. The latter arguments, "most closely associated with Immanuel Kant, ... assert that certain moral obligations hold irrespective of their empirical consequences" (MacCoun and Reuter

---

[4]This policy also reinforces the views of those in Latin America who argue that U.S. drug policies are just another form of protectionism against primary products (Del Olmo 1988; Quiroga 1990.)

2001, 56). Moreover, "only two positions—legal moralism and extreme libertarianism—are purely deontological and hence impervious to research evidence or policy analysis" (p. 71).

Most individuals take positions in between these two extremes. Still, within the consequentialist group, there are great differences about what should be the limits to individual choice and policy effects' evaluation and interpretation. Yet MacCoun and Reuter express the hope that within this broad group, empirical evidence and research may lead people to shift some of their positions and get closer to a policy agreement.

Policy Goals and Implementation Difficulties

The discussion in chapter 3 highlights the complexity of the causality problem in illicit drug markets. It shows that morally based positions or simplistic catch phrases—such as "drugs are an evil to be extirpated from society," "drugs are a good business," and "when there is demand there is supply"—cannot explain the structure of production or the international trade and consumption patterns for illegal drugs.

As is shown in chapter 3, policy success depends on economic, social, political, cultural, moral, public health, and environmental factors. The information and knowledge about how these factors interact are weak, and policy formulation and implementation are based partially on knowledge and partially on beliefs and questionable data. Unfortunately, many policymakers do not see the need for better data and analysis. Indeed "drug enforcement has become a crusade, and crusaders scarcely need a map, let alone evaluation" (Reuter 1997, 273).

Antidrug policies have faced many types of implementation difficulties in the Andes, and many factors contribute to the ineffectiveness of drug policy. One reason is the extreme cultural and power differences within Andean societies and among the governments of the Andean countries, the United States, and other industrial nations involved. These differences lead to mutual distrust and a feeling among the Andean countries that the United States and Europe impose policies on them. The other side of the coin is the United States and European governments' veiled but widespread lack of trust of the Andean governments, which are seen as unreliable, corrupt, and vulnerable to political, financial, and other pressures. Most of the literature that criticizes drug policies in the Andes provides examples of this type of policy implementation difficulty (Malamud-Goti 1994; Tokatlian 1997; Clawson and Lee 1996; Rodas 1996).

The heavy influence of puritan American values in drug policy formulation is another obstacle to policy implementation in the Andes. In every country, policies are influenced by cultural traits, and every culture produces some policy "quirks"; that is, policies that cannot be fully explained by simple economic or power motivations. In some countries, for example, stores are not allowed to open during certain religious days; in others, like firearms markets in the United States, regulations are uncommonly weak, and for a powerful segment of the population the right to bear arms has become akin to a fundamental human right. And in some countries, people have developed a profound distrust for the ability of market mechanisms to determine the price of some or most goods and services.

Indeed, in many Andean regions, market transactions and the price mechanism are *not* perceived as helping people obtain the goods and services they want but as part of a power struggle or of zero-sum games in which someone gains and others must lose.[5] In some oil-rich countries, like Ecuador and Venezuela, people feel entitled to have a very low price for gasoline and oil products and demand strict price controls. This is a way in which people feel they get their share of the country's natural resource endowment.[6] In these cases, the idea that local prices should be equal to international prices minus transportation costs, which is implicit in a smoothly functioning globalized market, is alien to large groups of the population. Many of these policies look peculiar to outsiders because their logic is hidden in the unspoken values and principles of the culture that are behind each country's political economy (Thoumi 1990).

The great power inequality between the United States and the other hemispheric countries involved in the drug trade is another factor that makes policy formulation and agreement very difficult. Most if not all antidrug policies have been formulated or implicitly vetoed by the United States, and most Andean countries' policies have been reactive to either U.S. policies and pressures or to the violence associated with the illegal trade (Lee 1989; Tokatlian 1990; Rodas 1996). The Andean countries' citizenry and governments share a widespread belief that they simply do

[5]This trait has its roots in the Spanish conquest and colonial periods, and it persists today. These beliefs, which are based on the conviction that wealth is not created but captured or taken away from others, are a source of property rights illegitimacy in the region (see Thoumi 1995a, 1996).

[6]Ironically, on a per capita basis the high-energy-consuming upper class is the main beneficiary of these policies.

not have the power to design and formulate their own drug policies, which instead are imposed by the international community (Quiroga 1990; Orjuela 1990; Blanes and Mansilla 1994). Within this framework, there is no room for a meaningful international policy dialogue. The United States has a lot to say about Andean countries' policies, but the Andean countries' opinions about U.S. policies are largely irrelevant, particularly for those issues related to demand reduction in the United States.[7] This power inequality partly undermines any policy conversion efforts.

Because the illegal drug industry's participation and addiction problems vary among countries, it is not surprising that every country involved has a "drug problem" that appears to be different at different points in time and also different from that of other countries. Very frequently, it is not clear what the problem actually is. For instance, for the countries involved, and at different times, the "drug problem" could essentially consist of, among others, seven possible realities: (1) the large number of drug users; (2) the number of drug addicts; (3) drug entrepreneurs who have made large amounts of money and threaten to take over a country's political system and corrupt its government institutions; (4) the fact that drug-generated funds finance guerrilla movements; (5) the fact that if drugs are wiped out, a country will experience a deep economic recession, large unemployment, and currency devaluation;[8] (6) the fact that illegal drugs make a country vulnerable to external pressures; and (7) a combination of some or all of the above.

Coordination problems among agencies are another important problem. In each country, many government agencies are involved in drug policy formulation and implementation. In many instances, their roles are not clear and their functions overlap. The interests of these agencies are very different. For some of them, fighting drugs is their main activity. But for others, it is marginal. For others, the war on drugs has become a way of life and a source of funds (see below on the Colombian experience with foreign assistance). Reuter's study of the antidrug budget in the United States concluded that independent uncoordinated decisions are made by many agencies at the federal, state, and local levels. Their funds are not transferable; the decisions are independent and respond to a variety of factors. Summarizing, he noted that the antidrug "budget is a misleading myth. That budget is not an appropriated budget, decided on by the

[7]Perl (1994) gave an excellent summary of these issues.
[8]Bolivia experienced some of these effects in 2000 and 2001.

Administration or Congress, but is instead a complex, after-the-fact cal-culation of what agencies claim to be spending on drug control" (Reuter 1994, 148).

In the Andean countries, there are conflicting interests among country governments. A similar conflict of interests and goals arises among at least the government agencies in charge of eradication, the promoters of alter-native development, the military and police, and prosecutors and in-the-field law enforcers. Coordination problems also arise between foreign relations ministries and agencies in charge of seeking foreign funds and implementing foreign-funded projects.

In Colombia, the Alternative Development Agency (PLANTE) has not been able to coordinate with the police and military, so frequently PLANTE makes an agreement with a peasant community and a few days later the military sprays coca and other crops in the region. In these cases, peasants believe that the government has deceived them. The frequency of these events creates great distrust of government actions within the peas-antry and makes it very difficult to implement alternative development policies.[9]

The case of the Andean military involvement in the war on drugs is also illustrative. The United States has pressed the Latin American countries to involve their military forces in their antidrug efforts. This has created sub-stantial conflicts within the military, who see themselves as having other priorities like fighting insurrections and foreign enemies, or who fear the risk of corruption by drug money. Problems between the military and other government agencies are also frequent—mainly with the police, who see military forces' antidrug efforts as an encroachment on their turf. This problem has been present in Colombia and Peru, but it has been particu-larly acute in Bolivia (Rodas 1996; Malamud-Goti 1994). As was noted in chapter 9, the Bolivian army has identified with the traditional seigniorial landholding class, and the police have identified with a more modernizing capitalist group that overthrew the government in 1952 and disbanded the army. The army was reestablished a few years later, but the distrust between the two institutions has remained deep.

Coordination problems among various government agencies in charge of formulating and implementing drug policies has led governments to cre-ate special agencies in charge of such coordination. In the United States,

---

[9]This is based on an author's interview with PLANTE director Juan Carlos Palau in Bogotá in February 1998.

the Office of National Drug Control Policy has this function. The Dirección Nacional de Estupefacientes in Colombia, CONTRADROGAS in Peru (which was reorganized and its name changed to DEVIDA), and CONALID in Bolivia are all in charge of antidrug policy coordination. In all countries, these agencies have struggled to coordinate policies.

As was noted in earlier chapters, there is great diversity in the economic structure of the illegal drug industry, and in its social and economic effects in the various countries involved. These differences create a variety of conflicting interests that are at the root of policy goal differences. One important reason is that the costs and benefits generated by illegal drug use and the policies designed to attack drug production and marketing are distributed very unevenly among countries. Costs are concentrated in Colombia and the United States, whereas Bolivia and Peru are affected in a comparatively lesser way (Thoumi 1995b, 1995c). Economic benefits are distributed among the four countries. Although the United States and European countries take the lion's share, it is a very small proportion of their gross domestic product. In the Andes, Colombia gets most economic benefits, but because of its small economy, Bolivia is the country most dependent on the drug economy.

Costs and benefits also change over time. When the illicit drug industry starts up in a country, many can see it as beneficial. Indeed, this happened in Colombia during the 1970s and early 1980s. Only when the industry generates violence or develops a symbiotic relationship with parts of the state or other social institutions like guerrilla and paramilitary groups do people become aware that it can generate large social costs.

The model developed in chapter 3 points to other important obstacles to antidrug policy success. These may be called institutional, and they arise from the complex nature of psychoactive drug demand and supply. As has been noted, antidrug policy formulation has not paid enough attention to the causality of supply and demand. That is, policies have not been based on an in-depth analysis of the reasons that people and societies consume and produce drugs. They have simply been based on the conviction that it is good to eliminate or at least lower illicit drug production and consumption. To achieve this goal, policies that have been considered reasonable by law enforcement agents and public health officials have been formulated and implemented.

The model shows that drug policy coherence requires policies to be designed while keeping in mind that drug phenomena are multidimensional and have at least criminal, moral, public health, economic, social, political, and environmental aspects. In democratic societies, the success of government policies designed to alter or control consensual behaviors, including those related to illegal drugs, depend on (1) whether they are consistent with the mores of society, that is, whether social values, civil institutions, and government policies reinforce each other; (2) whether they are politically acceptable, that is, whether the political system can build a consensus around those policies to facilitate their implementation; and (3) whether they are consistent with the market system.

Policies that are based on market incentives are more likely to succeed than policies that try to force changes in market results, that is, that fight the market. In the short run, a government can frequently "break" the laws of demand and supply by controlling prices and quantities and thus going against market forces. But in the long run, this is extremely difficult to do. When some of these aspects are disregarded, policies tend to have negative effects on the neglected dimensions. In other words, a policy based only on moral grounds that disregards social mores and political and economic realities will frequently fail to achieve its goals.

One fundamental problem with antidrug policies has been the weak input of the social sciences in their formulation. This problem has been present in the United States and in multilateral agencies.[10] It is interesting that some authors acknowledge the multidimensionality of drug policy issues but refer to these negative effects as "unintended consequences" (Tullis 1995). I am afraid that they are just the result of bad policies formulated under partial approaches about the nature of the problem that they are supposed to solve. In other words, it cannot be argued that a policy based on moral grounds but disregarding its economic, social, political, and environmental effects produces "unintended consequences." It is simply a bad policy unless it justifies those consequences because of the moral benefits it achieves.

Caulkins and Reuter (1997) have argued that in the United States policy goals have emphasized lowering the number of drug users (occasional and addicts) over harm reduction. They also have shown that the specific choice of a goal determines whether a policy evaluation is positive or

---

[10]As an example, the 1995 members of the United Nations International Narcotics Control Board (INCB) were two pharmacists, one pharmacist-biologist, two medical doctors, one psychiatrist, one chemist, four lawyers, and an expert in drug enforcement administration (INCB 1995). The absence of social scientists is obvious. Only in 1999 was Sergio Uribe, a political scientist with hands-on experience with illegal crops, appointed to the INCB. In 2001, Uribe was not reappointed.

negative. For example, if the goal is to lower the number of total users, a particular policy may achieve that result while total drug consumption or social harm might increase.

They have also argued that the probability of policy success is enhanced if goals are objectively defensible, integrative, politically feasible, inspirational, and relevant to policy decisions. Objectively defensible goals are those that can be associated with social welfare. Integrative goals "unite people in a common struggle" (Caulkins and Reuter 1997, 1148). Politically feasible goals are those that are not "blocked by another agency or level of government" (p. 1148). Inspirational goals can motivate people, and goals that are relevant to policy decisions are such "that the responsible individuals and agencies can affect the extent to which the goals are attained" (p. 1148). Caulkins and Reuter conclude that harm-reduction goals are better on these counts than use-reduction goals.

Applying these criteria to the antidrug goals followed in Latin American policies, it is easy to see why goals have not been achieved. Antidrug policies in Latin America have had several goals, some of which conflict with each other. But more important, all fail to meet the Caulkins-Reuter criteria for goal attainability. These goals have been (1) to lower illegal drug output; (2) to minimize traffickers' illicit revenues; (3) to punish traffickers, preferably large ones; and (4) to maximize cocaine, marijuana, and heroin retail prices.

To achieve these goals, polices have to fight market forces in fundamental ways because increases in the price of any finished product tend to increase the prices for its raw materials and intermediate products. Successes in increasing street-level prices increase production incentives, and lower farm gate prices create consumption incentives. To neutralize these market incentives, it is necessary to repress markets all along the way between the farm and the final street drug markets. Furthermore, repressive measures must be maintained as long as it is desirable to seek the policy goals. This is so because these policies do not tackle the causes of drug supply and demand, but just attempt to repress them.

Chapter 11 analyses in detail two case studies in Bolivia and Colombia that illustrate many of the policy problems described above. Chapter 12 surveys antidrug policies in the Andes and presents conclusions.

11

Policy Case Studies of Alternative Development in Bolivia and International Cooperation in Colombia

This chapter focuses on two specific antidrug policy issues and aims to illustrate in detail some of the main problems faced in policy formulation and implementation. The first section presents a short summary of alternative development policy issues and of 25 years of crop-substitution and alternative development experiences in Bolivia. The second section presents a detailed study of the foreign assistance program developed in Colombia after the assassinations of Luis Carlos Galán and other presidential candidates in 1989.

Alternative Development

This section first looks at the programs and issues related to alternative development in the Andes. Then it focuses on Bolivia, which has had the region's most extensive experience with alternative development programs.

The Programs and the Issues

In the antidrug policy arsenal, alternative development has been the main carrot for coca- and poppy-producing peasants and countries. These programs have attempted to provide licit income-generating alternatives for peasants, and international cooperation has provided a substantial part of the funds. Alternative development has also been the main weapon in the antidrug agenda of the United Nations.

Alternative development started with crop-substitution programs almost 30 years ago (see chapter 12 for more on this).[1] The lack of success of these earlier attempts led policymakers to argue for the need to develop coca- and poppy-growing regions. The reasoning behind this was simply that it was not enough to find alternative crops but was also necessary to provide education, infrastructure, and health services to make sure that coca- and poppy-growing regions would attract and support other economic activities.

Experience with these more comprehensive programs induced policymakers to focus on broader development problems, particularly in those regions that supplied migrants to illicit crop areas. This evolution has been toward a gradual increase in the scope of antidrug policies and programs from crop substitution to regional development and finally into alternative development (Lee and Clawson 1993).

Coca-growing countries have expected foreign donors to foot a substantial part of the alternative development bill, which they have done. This development has allowed foreign donor countries and multilateral agencies to have a strong say in key economic development strategies, particularly in Bolivia.

Alternative development programs are an offspring of failed crop-substitution efforts. The failure of alternative development to achieve its goals has motivated its expansion to include employment generation programs in regions from which peasants migrate to illicit coca- and poppy-growing areas (see chapter 12 for more on this). This poses an interesting question: Would the next step be to make all national

[1] One of the earlier crop-substitution programs began in Thailand in 1971 (Agricultural Research Service 1993).

development plans and strategies focus primarily on eliminating illicit crops?[2] Such development would raise further questions about the role of bilateral and multilateral agencies, such as the U.S. Agency for International Development (USAID), the Organization of American States's Inter-American Commission for Drug Abuse Control (Comisión Interamericana para el Control del Abuso de Drogas, or CICAD), and the United Nations Drug Control Program (UNDCP) in formulating country development policies and programs.

Lee and Clawson (1993) have described area development programs as including five types of activities: crop substitution, the development of markets for legal agricultural products, the industrialization of agricultural products to add value in rural areas, the provision of social infrastructure, and organizational development in the communities involved. Alternative development includes these five types plus development activities in nonillicit crop-producing regions that expel migrants to coca- and poppy-growing areas.

It is important to understand what each of these activities entails. Let us begin with crop substitution. The first step is to find substitute crops that can generate reasonable peasant income. Substitute crops are not easy to find. In most coca- and poppy-growing regions, a very limited number of other agricultural crops have been tried and peasants are already familiar with them. The idea then is to find some new crops or to improve on existing ones to achieve higher yields. This process begins with a list of possible products, from which some are selected for experimental farming to identify the best crops. The Agricultural Research Service (1993) explained that it began in 1971 in Thailand by looking at 1,080 possible substitutes, which were "screened to 250 crops which would undergo more extensive review."

Once the experimental farms are established, several cultivation methods are tried to find the best farming practices. At this stage, it is also necessary to test the plants against plagues to make sure that they will not be unexpectedly wiped out. This is particularly important because almost any crop considered is alien to the tropical forest and can be vulnerable to pests. These pilot studies also have to evaluate the danger that new plants may pose to the alien environment.

Some of the lands currently used for coca and poppy growing are very fragile and are not likely to sustain any agricultural or livestock

---

[2]Of course, such programs would be consistent with a "holy war" approach to dealing with psychoactive drug production, trafficking, and consumption.

development. High tropical forests destroyed to grow poppies play a key role in the region's water supply. These considerations raise important issues about having crop substitution in situ. It is then necessary to consider the possibility of moving peasants to areas more conducive to traditional agricultural activities.

Most illegal crops in the Andes are planted in areas that until recently had virgin tropical forests. Illicit crop expansion normally brings in substantial primary forest destruction. In some of these areas, mechanized agriculture cannot be used because it would destroy the fragile soils. To prevent this from happening in coca- and poppy-growing regions, alternative development programs have to test ways to exploit the forest without destroying it. Thus, forest management pilot programs have been funded. These allow for the selective cutting of tropical trees and the exploitation of tropical plants used as foods and inputs in the pharmaceutical and chemical industries.

Once a set of substitute crops has been identified, it is necessary to convince peasants to switch to them. This is not easy. Andean peasants have profound distrust (justified) of the government and strangers. Besides, peasants tend to be risk averse and resistant to change. To gain the peasants' trust, it is important to show them that crop failure will not occur and that there are secure markets for the proposed products. This presents several problems. Many coca- and poppy-growing regions are simply very far from markets.[3] To eliminate this bottleneck, highways must be built and maintained.[4] Many of the new products require special handling. Collection centers must be established for some products; others might require refrigeration or special packing facilities; and still others have to be graded before packing and shipping.

Most products face another disadvantage when compared with coca or poppies: Their initial cash outlay is substantially higher. Comparisons of coca with bananas, pineapple, hearts of palm, and a few other products in Chapare show that coca has the highest internal rate of return, uses the most family labor that does not have to be paid, and has a much better cash flow. Lanza and Caro (1998, 3) showed that the negative cash flow per hectare during the first year is $249 for coca, $511 for bananas, $5,068 for pineapple, and $1,482 for hearts of palm. From then on, all have positive cash

---

[3]In the Andean region, this is a particularly grave problem in Colombia.

[4]The lack of maintenance and deterioration of the highway linking the Upper Huallaga with Lima was a contributing factor to coca expansion in the 1970s and 1980s.

flow. In an economic environment where most people do not have savings and credit is very difficult to obtain, this is a great advantage for coca, particularly when other crops are subject to plagues that make them risky.[5]

A standard economist's solution to the credit problem is to make peasants credit subjects. The first step in this direction is to title their properties so that they can be mortgaged. This is a useful step, but one cannot expect great results from it. Most coca plantings are deep in the forest in areas very far from highways and other infrastructure on lands that have little value. Indeed, their value as collateral for a loan would be minimal unless they are used to grow coca. Besides, in Bolivia and Colombia illegal drugs are widely planted in national parks or nature preserves where plots cannot be legally titled to peasants.[6]

From a marketing viewpoint, coca and opium poppies are also a lot more attractive than alternative products. First, their products are homogeneous and do not require sophisticated packing or handling. Many of the important markets for pineapples, bananas, and other alternative development products require the use of strict quality-control techniques that peasants are not used to caring about. Second, coca and poppies do not face competition from many other regions or countries. In today's increasingly globalized economy, all alternative development products face many competitors and could encounter unexpected competition when other countries increase their production, devalue their currencies, have economic crises, and the like. As was noted in chapter 3, many countries produce legal crop products but illegal crops are found only in a few.

Furthermore, in any of the Andean countries, coca- and poppy-growing areas are not the best locations for substitute crops. In other words, if one were interested in developing banana, pineapple, or heart of palm plantations in Bolivia, Colombia, or Peru, one would not choose Chapare, Caguán, and the Upper Huallaga Valley. These alternative development investments are made only because of illegal crops, not because they are efficient. There is no question that there is an element of political bribery in them.

Agribusiness development programs should accompany crop substitution to generate higher-paying jobs in the region and to lower crop losses.

---

[5]Lanza and Caro (1998, 30) also showed that the cost of protecting a banana plantation against the black *sigatoka* that was spreading in Chapare was equal to a year's profits, de facto wiping out profitability.

[6]By the way, marijuana farmers in the United States also plant in national parks to prevent law enforcement agents from going after the farm owners if they discover the illicit crop.

Many crops rot easily and require dehydration plants. Milk has to be processed before shipment, and fruit should be canned and/or have its juices extracted. Commercial agriculture is particularly important for types of fruit that have very low ratios of value to weight and to volume and otherwise face very high transportation costs. Other types of rural industrial development should also be considered. Silkworm and fish farming have been used for these purposes.

The processes described above are facilitated by the existence of cooperatives and other communal organizations that "can aggregate products for sale to processors, intermediaries or consumers and that can deliver government services to scattered peasant households" (Lee and Clawson 1993, 9). As has been shown in earlier chapters, community organizations are relatively strong among Bolivian peasants, but "projects in Colombia must build such organizations virtually from scratch" (p. 9).

Other development projects such as schools, electricity, water and sewage systems, health posts, social centers, sports facilities, highways, and the like are also part of alternative development programs. Here the idea is that if the state and foreign donors improve the peasants' quality of life, they are more likely to stay away from illicit crops. These projects, unfortunately, can have both positive and perverse effects because they benefit licit and illicit products simultaneously. A confidential report by the World Bank (1996, 19) is very explicit on this point.[7] It notes that alternative development projects

> provide infrastructure that facilitates coca production and makes life attractive in those regions so that farmers move there and plant more coca. In Bolivia the development of schools and clinics in the Chapare may make it a more attractive region in which to settle, thereby discouraging out-migration to the Cochabamba highlands, the Santa Cruz area, or other regions that could absorb labor. Second, USAID and other agencies provide technical assistance, such as training in how to use fertilizer or pesticides, which can be used by coca growers just as

[7]The World Bank was contemplating the possibility of funding alternative development programs and had some of its staff members do a paper on the Andean drug industry. The results were very discouraging, and the study was not published to avoid problems with potential borrowing countries and bilateral and multilateral agencies that had funded alternative development. I secured the report through a former World Bank consultant who had kept a copy.

well as by legal farmers. Third, roads facilitate transport and (in the Chapare) also serve as traffickers' airstrips, help coca producers as well as other residents. The [Inter-American Development Bank]–financed Cochabamba–Santa Cruz highway, as well as smaller road networks in the Chapare financed by USAID, have probably facilitated movement of essential chemicals to cocaine processing sites as well as exports of cocaine paste and base from the region. However, these roads could also facilitate greater enforcement/eradication efforts.

To these perverse effects, one may add that alternative development creates a strong link between illicit crops and government infrastructure investment. This is an incentive for other people in other regions to grow illicit crops, particularly when other rural support activities, such as integrated rural development programs, have been cut off.

Policies to prevent migration to coca- and poppy-growing regions are also quite complex and are based on assumptions that may prove wrong. First, these policies assume that if employment increases in a migration source region, migration to coca- and poppy-growing areas would not come from other areas. USAID has funded substantial research in Bolivia and Peru aimed at identifying what factors determine migration to coca-growing regions (Rasnake and Painter 1989; M. Painter 1990; Painter and Bedoya 1991; Perez-Crespo 1991; Jones 1991) that is based on this assumption. In Colombia, where coca- and poppy-growing regions have been under the influence of guerrilla groups and where violence has created many internal refugees who have migrated to those regions, similar research has been lacking. If the incentives to migrate are strong, it is likely that in due course migrants will come from regions that have less social links with current coca and poppy growers.

Second, policies to prevent migration to coca- and poppy-growing regions assume that the lack of economic opportunities in population-expelling regions can be solved with a few employment-generating projects. As has been seen in all Andean countries, migration to coca-growing regions and the development of the illicit industry has frequently been triggered by a national or sectoral crisis that was rooted in bad macroeconomic management or in changes in international commodity markets. In these cases, alternative development programs are likely to achieve little.

If alternative development succeeds in one region, governments should make sure that illegal plantings are not simply displaced to other regions.

This "balloon effect" would confront governments with a development challenge, because they would have to make sure that every region suitable for illegal crops gets developed. In the best possible scenario, the most that one government can do is to make sure that illicit plantings are not displaced within its own territory. This in itself is quite a task because, to begin with, government policies did not prevent the original plantings. All Andean countries have large, sparsely populated regions where the state has little presence and where illicit plantings can flourish. Controlling displacement to other countries of course falls outside the realm of the country undertaking alternative development programs.

To conclude, alternative development faces many obstacles and it is unlikely to achieve much. There is no question that alternative development can have positive effects on regions and communities where it is implemented, but it is a policy that cannot contribute significantly to illicit crop reduction:

> In some micro-areas, there have been instances of a reduction in coca production. In the Ponanza Valley, for instance, the impact of a road improvement and a bridge over the Huallaga River connecting the valley to the main highway resulted in a 30 percent reduction in coca production between 1992 and 1993. However, the reduction in area in absolute terms was only 647 hectares, while the bridge alone cost $50 million to construct. Overall coca production in the Upper Huallaga has increased, and legal crops have actually fallen in total area. Compared to 1987, the area of coca cultivation is 78% higher, while legal crops are down 30 percent. A ministry of Agriculture spokesman notes that coca accounted for 78.4% of the [gross domestic product] of the Upper Huallaga Valley as a whole in 1993. Since 1990, there has been a slight decrease in the area of coca cultivation. However, as a December 1994 USAID report notes, the major causative factor was probably the *fusarium* blight which has the effect of sharply shortening the productive life of the plants. (World Bank 1996, 26–27)

Alternative development programs have been used to help peasants after forced eradication programs have been implemented, as was the case in Bolivia during 1998 and 1999. In these situations, the causality between alternative development and diminished illicit crops is backward: The crop decline produces a government reaction that generates alternative development programs.

It must be noted that alternative development faces more obstacles in Colombia than in any other Andean country because illicit crops grow very far from any market, in areas that are not even connected by roads to the main cities. In these regions, soils are extremely fragile and road building faces great geographical obstacles. Besides, many of them are under guerrilla control. The following section on the Bolivian experience provides insights about how alternative development has actually been implemented.

The Bolivian Experience

The Bolivian experience is important because Bolivia has had the largest and longest-running alternative development programs in the Andes and because the social and geographical environments in Bolivia are more favorable to alternative development than in other Andean countries, for three main reasons. First, the major rural highway traverses Chapare, the primary illicit coca-growing area. Once produce reaches this highway, trucking it to Cochabamba takes 4 to 5 hours and to Santa Cruz 5 to 6 hours. From this city, truckers make it to the large Buenos Aires market in a 30-hour run.

Second, the social organization in Chapare is strong and coca-grower *sindicatos* and federations facilitate negotiations and debates about policies and policy implementation. Third, Bolivians are very peaceful. They tend to avoid violence and to seek to solve conflicts in peaceful ways. These factors facilitate the implementation of alternative development programs. There is no question that they have a much better chance to succeed in Bolivia than in other Andean countries.

The origins of alternative development programs in Bolivia go back to 1974, when the U.S. secretary of state committed $5 million to then-dictator Hugo Banzer for studies to identify crop-substitution products for Yungas and Chapare. This grant funded the Chapare-Yungas Development Project (PRODES), which began work in 1975 (Antesana 1992, 13).[8] More than 4$^1/_2$ years later, toward the end of 1979, the project report was completed. It included a development project for Chapare and several policy recommendations for Yungas. After some discussions with the U.S. government, which was expected to fund the project, PRODES became a victim of political events. General Luis García-Meza's coup led to a

[8]M. Painter (1990, 2) claimed that actual research began only in 1977.

breakdown of diplomatic relations between the United States and Bolivia in 1980.

After the Garcia-Meza regime fell in August 1981, the U.S. and Bolivian governments resumed relations and interest in alternative development revived. By 1983, the Chapare Regional Development Project (CRDP) was funded. This new project faced many obstacles, which made it impossible for the Bolivian government to implement it. "The period of military control of the Bolivian government had permitted an enormous expansion of drug-related activities in the Chapare. Even after the [Popular Democratic Unity] government came to power in late 1982, the newly installed civilian regime could not assert its authority in the area and by the end of the year had effectively lost control of the Chapare to the narcotics traffickers" (Rasnake and Painter 1989, 14).

The external debt crisis and the macroeconomic policies of the Hernán Siles-Zuazo regime combined to produce an economic depression and hyperinflation that encouraged large migrations to Chapare and that became severe obstacles to project implementation. The project could not begin before August 1984, when the government sent troops to the Chapare to regain state control of the area. However, the extent of coca cultivation and the penetration of trafficking structures on Chapare were so great that some of the early CRDP efforts had significant unintended negative consequences. For instance:

> When the gathered officials questioned the local inhabitants whether or not the road was well constructed, one replied that, indeed, it was so well constructed that the previous evening, before the arrival of the dignitaries, a small airplane had landed on it. This exemplary case of cocaine traders' use of project benefits which were intended for tropical settlers led USAID officials to terminate most project activities in the field. (Rasnake and Painter 1989, 15)

By 1986, it was clear to many analysts that to prevent further coca expansion in Chapare it was necessary to provide employment opportunities in other regions that supplied migrants (Pool et al. 1986). They concluded that push factors in many Sierra communities were more important than attracting factors in Chapare and that coca was not the main determinant of migration into Chapare. This realization led to the addition of an Associated High Valleys component to the CRDP (M. Painter 1990, 3) and the creation of a new program, the

Triennial Plan, by the Victor Paz-Estenssoro administration in November 1986.

This new plan gave peasants the alternative to eradicate coca voluntarily during a 12-month period and receive $2,000 compensation per eradicated hectare. After that period had elapsed, coca was to be eradicated by force and without compensation. The United States provided the compensation funds. Simultaneously, the CRDP continued as part of the new plan.

Peasants' bitter complaints about their lack of representation in this alternative development program formulation and implementation and the Triennial Plan implementation difficulties led to the formulation of the Plan Integral de Desarrollo y Sustitución de Cultivos (PIDYS) by mid-1987 (CERID 1994a, 21–22).[9] The lack of peasant participation has been a source of continuous complaints by peasants, who feel that all government policies come from the top down without taking them into account. These complaints still go on today. This is not surprising in a country whose history has been marked by a strong authoritarian bent and whose society is segmented along racial and cultural lines.

The implementation of PIDYS required the execution and coordination of many different activities. New agencies were created with that purpose.[10] To do this, the government established an interministerial council (CONALID) "charged with coordinating Bolivian government anti-narcotics activities, including policies regarding development, interdiction, repression, prevention, and rehabilitation activities outlined in the PIDYS" (M. Painter 1990, 8). A deputy ministry for alternative development, the Subsecretaría de Desarrollo Alternativo y Sustitución de Cultivos (SUBDESAL), was created to act as the executive secretariat of CONALID. The role of SUBDESAL was complex, and its capacity was overestimated. It became "intimately involved in a wide range of foreign and domestic policy issues, the politics of which created acute short-term pressures that were often inimical to achieving the medium- to long-term development objectives embodied in the PIDYS" (M. Painter 1990, 9).

[9]This short book on alternative development was published under Centro de Estudios de las Relaciones Internacionales y el Desarrollo (CERID) authorship, and its publication was funded by UNDCP. The actual author was Fernando Salazar-Paredes, CERID's executive director.

[10]M. Painter (1990) surveyed all the agencies involved and illustrated many of the conflicts encountered among them. CEDIB (1993) also presented the list of actors, describing the role that each played.

PIDYS was formulated with strong participation of the Chapare peasant federations that were fearful of the effects of Law 1008, which required the gradual eradication of coca (Healy 1997, 234). This plan

> contained the standard "integrated rural development" elements for a tropical colonization zone of this type. These included infrastructure for potable water and electricity, agricultural credit, technical assistance in tropical agriculture, road infrastructure, and agricultural research and extension services. One of the cornerstones of the PIDYS was to max-imize peasant participation in decision-making through representation by the Chapare federations and other trade union leaders in the planning and execution of this rural development program. (Healy 1997, 234)

Unfortunately, peasant participation did not materialize, which led to peas-ant strikes and protests.

To implement PIDYS, in late 1989 the government created the National Alternative Development Commission (CONADAL), Alternative Development Regional Committees (COREDAL), and Alternative Development Local Committees (COLODAL), and it placed SUBDESAL under the Ministry of Peasant Issues and Agriculture (MACA) and limited its function to planning and implementing alternative development programs. SUBDESAL was not involved in policy formulation or interpretation (M. Painter 1990, 9). CONADAL was expected to offer a venue for peasant participation.

Program implementation requires coordination of activities with the Bolivian Institute of Agricultural and Animal Husbandry Technologies (IBTA), the School of Agricultural Technologies (ETSA), the Association of Rural Artisans (ASAR), foreign technical assistance organizations like USAID and CARE, the National Roads Service (SNC), the National Colonization Institute (INC), and several local and foreign nongovern-mental organizations. All evaluations indicate that the coordination of the many activities required and the large number of organizations involved were deficient and became a main problem of CRDP (M. Painter 1990; Painter and Bedoya 1991; Jones 1991).

Many of the agencies were created as a result of the CRDP's establish-ment, but their functions were not always clear and their structures were weak. Their actions overlapped with each other, and their implementation capacity was questionable. Besides, "the institutional framework was based on the premise that participation of coca leaf producers is absolutely necessary in all phases of alternative development planning and execution" (M. Painter 1990, 9).

It needs to be noted that coordination problems also extended to agencies that were not concerned with alternative development. The Direccion de Reconversión Agrícola (DIRECO) was charged with administering the eradication compensation program. The special anti-narcotics police (UMOPAR) was charged with interdiction and laboratory destruction. These agencies operated in alternative development areas, and their actions had to be coordinated with those of alternative development agencies for policies to succeed. When the carrot and stick branches of antidrug policies are not coordinated, they are likely to fail.

The CRDP's problems were compounded by the presence of other foreign actors in Chapare. European organizations and the United Nations were also working in the region. Some of the criteria used by these groups differed from the USAID-inspired ones applied by the CRDP. Particularly, for these actors the link between alternative development and eradication was not direct, as it was for USAID. In some cases, their actions appeared to be benevolent and paternalistic but were greatly misguided.

Perhaps the best example of such misguided actions was the infamous milk-processing plant (MILKA) built in Chapare with a contribution from the Swedish government through a Protestant church. The plant had been used in Sweden, where a more modern one replaced it. MILKA was greatly oversized given the possible milk production in Chapare. Besides, it was installed in a zone known for banana production that was far from cattle grazing areas. Since its installation, it has been considered a white elephant and a great example of poor planning and lack of project coordination.

In other cases, well-intentioned projects failed because they were based on bad data and questionable technologies. A peasant's description of the experience with a solar banana-drying plant is very enlightening (ILDIS 1993, 104–6). The drying plant was conceived to take care of the great proportion of the banana crop that is wasted, but it was designed and installed on a set of mistaken assumptions. The actual banana hectareage in the zone was a quarter of the estimated one, the construction estimates grossly underestimated labor costs, and the days of sunlight were overestimated. Besides, a plant of that type had never been used in Bolivia.

Indeed, this project was an experiment that proved to have significant technical difficulties. In the end, annual production was about 45 tons a year while capacity was 200 tons. With a capacity utilization of about 22.5 percent, the plant was simply not profitable. Later experiments have shown that plants of this type operate well in Cochabamba and Santa Cruz but not in Chapare (Lanza and Caro 1998, 23). Social issues complicate matters more. The plant was given to the Association of Banana Producers, which has 60 members. The *sindicato* in that zone had 120 members, which were left out of the project. The association members were very reluctant to dry nonmembers' produce, which created a division within the community.

Agribusiness development promoted by alternative development programs in Chapare has been a failure. Lanza reported on a 1997 survey of fourteen plants that had been established to process yucca, palm oil, tea, and milk in Chapare. Only two of the fourteen were operating, one processing tea and the other milk (MILKA; see above). The tea producer was working at 30 percent capacity and its prices were not competitive. MILKA was processing 7,000 liters a day, or 14 percent of its capacity. Neither one was profitable.[11] There is no doubt that Bolivian authorities and foreign donors have learned from these experiences, but the projects have left a sour taste in peasants' mouths and have increased their distrust of outsiders' interventions on their turf.

As was discussed in chapter 4, Law 1008 of 1988 established a system to compensate peasants for eradicated "surplus" coca, mainly in Chapare. This compensation was to be paid by foreign donors, a reason why most local politicians supported it. Compensation was established at $2,000 per eradicated hectare, a figure that was increased in some cases to about $2,500 when it was accompanied by technical assistance.

This measure has had at least six very interesting effects. First, it has created a de facto coca price support. Peasants know that the worst-case scenario they would face would be to cut down coca fields and collect the compensation, particularly when they have old coca fields.[12] With this in mind, the original law limited compensation to plantings already existing in selective regions. Subsequent negotiations have extended this benefit to some "new coca," which indicated to peasant leaders that this is a negotiable issue and raised compensation expectations among the peasantry.

---

[11]This is based on Gregorio Lanza's presentation at a seminar organized by Corporacióon Observatorio para la Paz in Bogotá, December 10–12, 1997. Lanza is a well-known UNDCP consultant in Bolivia.

[12]"Although *cocales* have a long life, eventually production in aging fields decreases and fewer and fewer plants come back after *pillu* (a periodic radical pruning). Trading in unproductive older cocales for $2000 a hectare makes far more sense to the growers than uprooting coca fields at their productive height" (Léons 1997, 148).

Second, the program was justified as part of an international "shared responsibility" approach to fighting illegal drugs. Independent of the ethical issues related to paying citizens not to break a law,[13] coca compensation raises an important question about shared responsibility: It implies that main consumer countries are responsible for the addiction of their citizens but that major producer countries are not. In other words, the consumer has to compensate the producer to stop producing an addictive product.[14]

Third, compensation encourages the "balloon effect." It creates incentives for the eradication of old, low-yielding coca fields to be replaced by new fields deeper into Chapare, which apparently is what happened.[15]

Fourth, compensation has created corruption incentives for authorities administering the programs. Léons (1997, 147) reported instances in which government officials charged with measuring the peasants' plots to determine the compensation level charged peasants a considerable fee to do their job. In other cases, peasants complained that DIRECO officials "rarely if ever left them with a copy of the survey they had undertaken" (Sanabria 1997, 179) and peasants were convinced that they had been deceived and that DIRECO officials had pocketed part of what the peasants were entitled to. Other rumors generated further peasant distrust. One, for example, asserted that "gringos" were paying $7,000 per eradicated hectare and DIRECO and UMOPAR personnel were making a lot of money keeping the difference (p. 178).

Fifth, peasants also cheated. In some cases they cut down their coca plants but did not uproot them. "They were gambling that the agents would return before the coca resprouted or would not return at all" (Léons 1997, 148), which was frequently the case in hard-to-reach fields. In other instances, they "stuck upright in an old coca field bushes which had been cut off in the pro-

[13]This is a reason why such a program would have been unconstitutional in most modern democracies.

[14]I raised this issue at a seminar on drug policies in Cochabamba in September 1997 and cited the example of the heavy fines against the tobacco industry that had recently been imposed in the United States as a precedent that requires producer responsibility. These comments were not well received, and a couple of Bolivian members of Congress rebutted my point on the grounds that the drug cartels were the responsible parties, not the Bolivian government or people. However, they did not have any qualms about funds received from governments and multilateral agencies instead of trafficking organizations.

[15]The author's interviews with Bolivian coca growers' representatives on several occasions support this point.

cess of *pillu*[16] elsewhere. The plant tops were then discarded as they withered and before the field was rechecked and validated as eradicated" (p. 148).

Sixth, the compensation provided by Law 1008 was to individual coca growers and requires the beneficiaries to sign a document committing themselves not to plant coca again in the same plots. This might make sense within an individualist capitalist framework. It is likely that it would have been more effective to establish a system of compensation for families or communities that negotiated eradication. Spedding (1997b, 134) has explained that in the cultural context of Bolivian peasantry a man may have title to his land but his rights are restrained by social mores that extend rights to others who currently or potentially may benefit from the property, such as his children. Thus, "people who received eradication money were viewed as having made a personal profit through selling something (rights over future land use) which didn't really belong to them" (p. 134). In the eyes of the community, this was an unenforceable contract. Peasant compensation in Chapare has also had indirect effects in Colombia because the guerrilla organizations that controlled coca-growing areas have asked $6,000 per eradicated hectare.

The peasants' vision of alternative development programs is interesting and very different from that of foreign donors and government officials. To understand their position, it is necessary to put it in the context of social conflicts within Bolivian society. Capital accumulation in Bolivia has been associated with the exploitation of natural resources and labor. Indians have been exploited and have been victims of governments' arbitrary law enforcement for centuries. Indeed, until the 1952 revolution, the laws of Bolivia were just a set of rules imposed on them by the country's elite. Within this context, for Bolivian peasants the idea that something is illegal does not mean that it is socially bad or undesirable. It is simply something that those in power want to be illegal for their own purposes. This idea is quite different from that held in advanced industrial societies.

A June 1992 seminar that brought together many peasants illustrates some of these views (ILDIS 1993). They all had a sense that the government and USAID had attempted to impose the Triennial Plan from the top down without peasant participation. They argued that PIDYS was the result of their own proposal to the government, which had been trying to impose a United States–inspired program.

---

[16]As was stated in footnote 12, this is a periodic radical pruning of the coca plant.

Peasants defended coca cultivation, claimed that they were not criminals, and maintained that they were fighting against the United States for their right to grow coca (ILDIS 1993, 22). There is no question that they benefited from coca and that coca was part of an illegal network, but to peasants with strong Indian roots the idea that a plant given by nature could be illegal seemed totally alien. It is not clear that they understood the difference between a plant that in itself is legal and its cultivation for illicit, illegal purposes. Besides, article 61 of the 1961 United Nations convention—which committed Bolivia and Peru to declare coca chewing illegal within 25 years—has been interpreted by many coca-grower supporters as a commitment to eliminate coca from Earth in 25 years' time, providing an argument that made this distinction irrelevant. The 1988 convention eliminated this commitment and formally recognizes traditional uses of coca as legitimate, a fact that is played down or denied by coca growers and their supporters.

Peasants also expected external solutions to many of their problems and were conscious that coca cultivation brought them foreign aid and credit—very good reasons to continue growing coca. "We cannot continue tolerating a policy that requires coca eradication as a condition to receive credit"; "peasants must grow coca to protect themselves" (ILDIS 1993, 37, 76).

Coca growers expressed profound distrust of government actions and U.S. intervention: "We are aware that Bolivian government policies, dictated by the United States, do not give peasants a real say in (alternative) development plan formulation and implementation. This is only a cover up to legitimize the real goal to eradicate coca" (ILDIS 1993, 36). Somehow, they appear to miss a simple point: The United States would not foot the bill for alternative development programs unless they contributed to its eradication goals.

Chapare electrification had presented a particularly thorny issue. USAID had initially opposed it on the grounds that it would facilitate cocaine base and cocaine production and would encourage further migration to Chapare. Even though USAID had later consented to that project and by the time of the seminar Chapare already had electricity, peasants strongly decried this foreign intervention (ILDIS 1993, 65).

It was also quite clear that there was a substantial difference between what peasants considered and expected alternative development programs to achieve and what the government and foreign donors had in mind. It is not surprising that peasants' expectations were frustrated. They argued that a few unrelated projects do not result in alternative development and expected somehow to have the government and foreign donors develop Chapare in exchange for eradicating coca. Because they distrust the government and foreigners, they also demanded that development should take place before eradication.

One specific complaint was that they claimed a need for 1,500 kilometers of highways but there were resources for only 160 (ILDIS 1993, 86). There were also complaints about a lack of facilities to process tea, bananas, oranges, yucca, and other products. There were also several references to the infamous MILKA fiasco.

The gap between perceived needs and actual resources concerned some peasant leaders, who thought that the government and foreign donors were using small projects in particular regions to divide their movement (ILDIS 1993, 53, 87). "The politicians' friends get the roads built by their properties" (p. 88). This problem was highlighted by the presence of a few peasants who had benefited from alternative development and were satisfied with it. "I decided to organize my zone. First, I established a civic committee in my small town. I was elected union leader and we made a plan to get the things we needed. The first step was to get potable water for my zone, which we now have. We saw that alternative development does work with those who volunteer and show interest" (p. 55).

The peasants were also concerned about government corruption and the very high costs of the alternative development projects that were implemented. They were particularly concerned about the high costs of building roads, which they themselves could build at about 20 percent of what the alternative development project was paying (ILDIS 1993, 87).

Cultural clashes presented further difficulties. Some peasants were worried that, through alternative development, Aymaras and Quechuas were losing their native values and were being victimized by strange cultures as their ways of life were being forced to change (ILDIS 1993, 74). They also failed to understand why they had to pay interest on loans devoted to growing crops during the time the plants were growing and were not productive. In other words, why should they pay interest during the years the macadamia, ginger, or pepper crops were growing and not yielding anything?

Some alternative development credits had been extended to business-people from outside Chapare who had the know-how to develop a few agro-industries, such as a chicken farm (ILDIS 1993, 77). This was also the subject of strong peasant criticism. Somehow, they felt entitled to all alternative development benefits. If Chapare was to be developed, they felt that they should be the only ones to benefit from it and criticized credits to outsiders, even though they contributed to the region's economy.

A similar problem is generated by the difference in living standards between peasants and project workers. Peasants feel that bureaucrats make a very good living out of funds that should go to them. Project workers, however, feel that they are entitled to their high salaries (Léons 1997, 155). These differences raise questions about project success when there is no empathy among the actors.

Peasants vehemently opposed Law 1008 on the grounds that it made coca growing illegal and turned peasants into criminals, even though the law provided for cash compensation for eradication. For them, eradication is something that should be done only after development takes place, and they were convinced that the government had not lived up to the bargain they had made. Thus, they felt that they were under no obligation to eradicate (Léons 1997, 149). Indeed, all rigorous studies of Yungas and Chapare find strong peasant resentment against eradication efforts and deny the existence of voluntary eradication (Léons 1997; Sanabria 1993, 1997; Spedding 1997b).[17]

Peasants were advised by a group of academics and intellectuals that, to put it mildly, seemed to be somewhat unrealistic. One of them referred to the programs and projects in question as "alternative underdevelopment" and argued vehemently for coca industrialization (ILDIS 1993, 44–45). This adviser argued that cocaine legalization was imminent and praised coca as representing the dignity of Andean culture opposed to U.S. imperialism (ILDIS 1993, 97, 98).

Another peculiar belief strongly expressed by the advisers was the geopolitical importance of Bolivia. The argument was simply that Bolivia, being at the center of South America, had a strategic location for the control of the continent. The attempts by the United States to militarize the fight against drugs were just an excuse to control the continent.[18] Realities

---

[17]The author's interviews with coca growers' representatives in several occasions in La Paz, Cochabamaba, and Chapare support this position.

[18]This peculiar belief appears to be common among coca growers. In a trip to La Paz in April 1999, I interviewed a coca growers' leader and asked him a simple question: Did he think that Bolivia was more important to the United States than the United States to Bolivia or vice versa? Without hesitation, he answered that it was clear that Bolivia was more important to the United States.

like the powerful obstacles to integration represented by the Andes and the Amazon jungle, Bolivia's great isolation from most of South America, and the great importance of sea transportation for international trade were facts that the Bolivian experts apparently were not aware of or dismissed as irrelevant.

The attitudes of the peasants contrast with those of others who see significant successes in alternative development. Villarroel (1994) argued that there has been significant development in Chapare. He claimed correctly that Chapare had been electrified and that health services were increasingly available to peasants. An issue he did not deal with is the effect of these improvements in living standards on coca cultivation.

The expectations of Bolivian politicians and foreign donors about alternative development also differ. For foreign donors, the main issue is to eradicate coca directly or indirectly. Bolivians see alternative development as something more complex:

> This strategy not only aims to substitute the drugs' raw material, the approach to alternative development should be multi-sectoral and lead to integrated development ... Integral development is a substantial, real and sustained improvement in the quality of life of the inhabitants of a region. It requires improvements in education, health and nutrition, poverty elimination through stable employment under an equal opportunities regime and a high degree of individual freedom within a democratic framework. It also envisions a complete, productive and progressive cultural life within an improved and sustainable environment. (CERID 1994b, 17)

One can only wish that this description of what alternative development was expected to achieve resembled Bolivian society outside Chapare and Yungas. Their expectations did not end here. Alternative development should also be expected "to develop an alternative economic structure to replace the employment, income and foreign exchange generated by coca" (CERID 1994b, 17). [19]

The Jaime Paz-Zamora administration was the first one after Law 1008 was enacted and "surpassed all predecessors in playing the coca-cocaine

---

[19]It is difficult for the outsider not to think that Bolivian politicians were looking at alternative development as an instrument to get the international community to solve many of their country's economic problems.

card in bilateral politics for larger resource transfers from the U.S. government" (Healy 1997, 237). His slogan, "Coca for Development," drew widespread support in the country and supported peasants' aspirations. The coca for development program was predicated by minister of planning Samuel Doria-Medina on the premise that peasant poverty was the main reason that illicit crops were grown in Bolivia.

To eliminate poverty required a large infusion of foreign aid, and Paz-Zamora commissioned a study showing that the value added of Bolivia's illegal drug industry was $490 million and that the indirect value added generated was $449 million.[20] With these estimates, he went to the Cartagena Drug Summit to request similar compensation to eliminate the drug industry (Healy 1997, 237). As was discussed in chapter 8, Paz-Zamora had close friends and supporters involved in drug trafficking. However, at the time of the Cartagena summit these had not been uncovered and he still had international credibility.

The Gonzalo Sánchez-de-Losada administration came to power in mid-1993. "Gony," as González-de-Lozada is known, had spent most of his life abroad, spoke with an accent, and included an Indian candidate for vice president on his ticket. For this international man, laws should be enforced, and he tried to do so with Law 1008. He proceeded with alternative development, but his plan of action—"Zero Option"—required the eradication of all surplus coca, as mandated by Law 1008. His actions produced massive peasant protests and marches toward La Paz, and eventually he had to accept political realities and stop eradication.

After many years, the economic complexity of alternative development projects in Chapare continues to be a great obstacle to their success. A description of what is considered a possibly successful model based on an actual Chapare pilot project visited by the author in September 1997 illustrates this point. To begin, a peasant family cuts down the forest and proceeds to slash and burn to clean the field. Curiously, until 2000 they could bring the trees down but were not allowed to cut the good-quality wood trees after they have fallen to take them to the closest road and sell them.[21] After this is done, they plant rice and get one good crop. However, the soil chemicals required by rice are exhausted after one

---

[20]A team from the Harvard Institute for International Development did this study and produced several academic papers, such as De Franco and Godoy (1992) and Gibson and Godoy (1993).

[21]The American expert who accompanied me estimated that as much good wood was burnt out as taken out of Chapare.

crop. This compels the peasants to switch to pineapple, which produces good crops for 3 or 4 years, after which the soil is not good for that crop either.[22]

Because of this time limitation, right after the first rice crop, the peasants have to begin acting on what they will harvest 5 years down the road. Several alternatives are open to them—including hearts of palm, citrus, and pepper trees. Each of these will produce for a few years and also exhaust the soil. Therefore, the peasants also need to think about what they will be doing 8 and 10 years hence and simultaneously plant rubber and fast-growing poplar trees that they can begin harvesting at that point. (In these projects, bananas and coffee were ruled out because of the black sigatoka and broca blights, respectively.)

Most of the crops listed are new to the region, and peasants do not have know-how about them. Indeed, many of them are the result of pilot farm projects directed by agronomists. Cultivation techniques vary from crop to crop and have to be transmitted to peasants. The amount of technical assistance required is quite large. The prices of all these products fluctuate in domestic and international markets, which make these crops quite risky. The storing, processing, marketing infrastructure, and production technical assistance required for success are very complex and sophisticated. Furthermore, a project like this requires peasants to have a very long-term horizon and be committed to full-time life in Chapare. From their point of view, doesn't coca look awfully appealing?

In 1998, another alternative development study commissioned by UNDCP–La Paz (Lanza and Caro, 1998) surveyed previous studies and researched the current price and production conditions. This study concluded that under ideal circumstances it might be possible to find suitable alternatives to coca, but it was very skeptical about the possibilities. All the obstacles to alternative development listed above were confirmed by this study, which added a new twist: Sustainable development in Chapare is viable only if it is based on agro-forestry development, that is, if it is eco-development.

A UNDCP–La Paz staff member has argued that the main achievements of alternative development in Chapare have been infrastructure development (roads, water, and electricity), health services, and the establishment of more than 100,00 hectares cultivated with banana, pineapple, passion

---

[22]Pineapple also requires the intensive use of fertilizers and preventive anti-plague measures.

fruit, hearts of palm, citrus fruit, and grazing land. His goal is to slowly wean peasants from coca.[23]

There is no question that alternative development has had some achievements. It is also clear that it has been a means by which peasants who have been forgotten and abandoned by their governments for decades and centuries finally get their governments' and the international community's attention and receive assistance from them. This is the main achievement of alternative development. It is only a shame that peasants could not be helped unless they grow illegal crops.

Bolivian bureaucracies have also benefited from alternative development. Their definition of shared responsibility allows them to claim international funds but, as was discussed above, it is a very peculiar definition, in which the consumer has to subsidize the producer of a seriously addictive good. Some Bolivian governments have managed this argument successfully. In reality, it boils down to having the international community pay to solve the inequities of Bolivian society. It is as if the international community accepted dependency theory, according to which the structure of unjust Bolivian society is totally the responsibility of external forces.

In conclusion, there is no question that alternative development plays an important political role. The question is whether it makes economic sense, and the economist's answer is a simple no.[24]

From 1990 through 1997, Bolivian coca plantings did not expand, which lowered external pressures on the Paz-Zamora and Sánchez-de-Lozada governments. This lack of expansion was due to external forces, mainly the breakup of the Medellín and Cali "cartels" and the large coca expansion in Colombia. In mid-1997, General Banzer was elected president as part of a coalition that includes a vice president, Jorge Quiroga, who was committed to eliminating coca from Bolivia. A new program, "For (the country's) Dignity!" (¡Por la Dignidad!) was put in place in 1998 (República de Bolivia 1998). The plan is based on alternative development, eradication, interdiction, and drug use prevention and rehabilitation.

---

[23]This is based on Gregory Minick's presentation at a seminar organized by Corporación Observatorio para la Paz in Bogotá, December 10–12, 1997.

[24]I mentioned to Peter Reuter—the economist who has done the most work on illegal drug markets in the United States—that I was writing this section for my book. He reacted by telling me first that it was a waste of time because alternative development was a dead horse that did not need to be beaten anymore. On second thought, he encouraged me to do so because he realized that alternative development is a Phoenix that you can burn to ashes but always comes back.

This particular plan assumes that there are no significant criminal organizations in Bolivia exporting drugs and that the industry is made up a large number of small traffickers. Referring to the 1970s, it explains that "during those years the absence of State policies to combat the drug-trafficking related illicit activities created an adequate environment for them to grow and to generate economic, social and political effects that could have compromised the nation" (República de Bolivia 1998, 5). It curiously fails to mention that this occurred during Banzer's dictatorship (1971–78). In practice, the government has proceeded to eradicate by force and appears to have done it successfully. The emphasis on involuntary eradication confirms the futility of alternative development as an economic instrument to reduce illicit crops and its usefulness as a political instrument to appease and help peasants.

The Special Cooperation Program in Colombia

As was elaborated in chapter 7, in the late 1980s the Medellín cartel under the leadership of Pablo Escobar declared an all-out war on the Colombian government. During this war, many judges, police officers, prosecutors, journalists, politicians, and private citizens lost their lives. The most dramatic event of this terrorist campaign was the assassination of presidential candidate Luis Carlos Galán on August 18, 1989.

Until the mid-1980s, most Colombians perceived mainly the positive economic effects of the illicit industry and discounted the negative ones. Foreigners had a similar view of what was going on in Colombia. The Medellín cartel's war against the Colombian government produced a change in international and domestic perceptions about the effects of the illegal drug industry on the country, which was seen more and more as not just a beneficiary of an illegal export boom but also as a victim of the illegal industry.

The Colombian government felt overwhelmed by a "drug problem" that it could not solve alone and sought ways to have the international community recognize its global nature and the need for a global solution.[25] Immediately after Galán's assassination, President Virgilio Barco sought

[25]The Andean countries always claim that the "drug problem" is global—i.e., because it involves all the world's countries, they are not more responsible for it than are the rest. Though drugs are a problem in many countries, however, in many countries they are not a big issue. There is no question that the "drug problem" is multilateral, but referring to it as "global" is an interesting exculpatory strategy.

international economic assistance as an expression of international support and shared responsibility in fighting drugs. Foreign donors were also shaken by the political violence inflicted by drug traffickers on Colombia and were willing to cooperate. The government then proceeded to elaborate the Special Cooperation Program (PEC),[26] which was funded by bilateral and multilateral aid, to help Colombia in its fight against drugs.

This section summarizes the results of an unpublished PEC evaluation done at the Center for International Studies of the Universidad de Los Andes 5 years later.[27] The PEC involved several Colombian government and foreign agencies. The main actors within the Colombian government were the Special Division for International Cooperation (DECTI) of the National Planning Department and the Office of the President's Adviser on Foreign Matters (Consejería de Asuntos Internacionales). The international actors were donor-country embassies and aid agencies, the United Nations Development Program, and UNDCP. The evaluation was based on DECTI files, interviews with Colombian professionals who participated in PEC's creation and implementation, members of the foreign donor community involved, and a questionnaire sent to all project-implementing organizations.

Characteristics of the Program, Its Projects, and Funding

The first challenge for the research team was to identify the PEC projects. By late 1994, when many PEC projects were supposed to have been completed or in the process of implementation, the institutional memory about PEC was at best cloudy and in most cases nonexistent. The Consejería at the Presidency and DECTI, the two government offices overseeing PEC, disagreed about what projects were actually included in PEC. Besides, each office had its own filing system, the project identification codes did not coincide, and institutional memory had been lost

---

[26]This is after the Spanish Programa Especial de Cooperación.

[27]I had the supervisory responsibility for the research team coordinated by Alexandra Guáqueta. Other team members were Nicoleta Danieli, Fernando García, Giancarlo Romano, and Juan David Torres. The study was commissioned by the National Planning Department's (DNP) Special Division for International Technical Cooperation (DECTI), in response to a request for a PEC evaluation by the German GTZ. DECTI was hoping for a positive evaluation to allow it to request more funds. This research project encountered several obstacles and difficulties, and the drafts submitted to DECTI did not satisfy their expectations. This led to DNP's rejection of the project report and cancellation of the project.

due to personnel turnover.[28] Among the foreign entities, only the French and Italian embassies and the German foreign aid agency Deutsche Gesellschaft für Technische Zusammenarbeit (GTZ) knew about the existence of PEC. The embassies of Belgium, Germany, Holland, Japan, and the United Kingdom and USAID did not have any recollection of the program.

The lack of PEC coordination was glaring. The roles of the Consejería and DECTIC were not clearly defined, and both agencies found themselves competing and failing to cooperate in an adequate manner. At one point, the officer hired at the Consejería under the PEC budget to work on it was clearly diverted to other tasks. And the international actors did not coordinate their efforts. There was no real coordinating committee or agency, and each donor tended to follow its own path. There was no discussion or agreement about the policy parameters for the projects to be funded or about how the drug problem was to be tackled.

The research team put together a list of 112 PEC projects for which the Colombian government had requested foreign financing. The type of projects and percentages of funds solicited are distributed as follows. Thirteen projects were to promote exports (12 percent). Fifty were for industrial and agro-industrial development (45 percent). Ten were crop substitution projects (9 percent). Fourteen were part of the National Rehabilitation Plan (12 percent).[29] Two projects were for rural development (2 percent). Eight were designed to improve the justice system (7 percent). One was to fund a freedom-of-the-press program (1 percent). Nine were for youth development programs (8 percent). Five were designed to improve Colombia's image abroad (4 percent).

---

[28]The cooperation of these two offices with the research team was at best lukewarm. DECTI did not provided full access to PEC records on the grounds that the new personnel themselves were not aware of their existence. I suspect that they were just concerned that the evaluation results would bring up many of the PEC deficiencies and would make it very difficult to request more funds from donors. To access the DECTI files, the research team located a former DECTI officer, who provided the needed computer file names, and a team member illegally sneaked into the DECTI office during lunch time and copied the files. Such is the life of illicit drug researchers in the tropics!

[29]This program aimed to promote community participation in the formulation and implementation of local investment programs funded by the government. The PNR focused on rural areas that were far from most markets and where guerrilla presence was common. In some of these regions, there were illegal drug crops. The PNR sought to develop community–state links, to show that the state actually delivered public services and to weaken community support for guerrilla groups. The PNR was more a political than an economic development program.

The list of PEC projects covers a wide range and includes an odd mix of projects, some of which were related to illegal drug issues and some which were quite far off the field. The projects to strengthen the justice system were designed to improve the government's ability to apply punitive measures on drug traffickers. Crop-substitution, rural development, and national rehabilitation plan projects were concentrated in coca-growing areas and were also related to illegal drug issues. Youth oriented programs were aimed at limiting domestic drug consumption.

However, most foreign trade, industrial, and agro-industrial projects were at best indirectly related to drug issues. The best that can be said of some of them is that increased development and employment opportunities may have indirect positive effects on the incentives for people to participate in illegal drug activities. The efforts to improve Colombia's image were justified as an attempt to make the world aware of the magnitude of Colombian sacrifices in the "war on drugs" and increase foreign aid to the country. However, some of the uses of these funds were highly questionable.[30]

The amount of funds committed by the international community could not be established with certainty. The Consejería in the president's staff and a preliminary DECTI estimate produced similar figures ($319.6 million and $314.3 million, respectively), but the distribution among donors varied. The Consejería's figures included data from several European countries and Australia contributed through UNDCP. These sums were not included in DECTI's figures. Conversely, DECTI had a United Kingdom contribution that was not part of the Consejería's list.

A further consolidated estimate by DECTI produced a somewhat higher figure: $346.6 million, distributed as follows: the United States, $200 million; the European Union, $75.6 million; Luxembourg, $20 million; Germany, $15 million; and UNDCP, $36 million. It appears that these commitments were made in haste in response to narcoterrorism attacks and were cut later on, particularly after 1991. DECTI estimated that the United States cut $80 million; Italy, $20 million; Holland, $10 million; and Canada, $5 million (contributed through UNDCP). It was not possible to determine the reasons for the cuts, and one can only speculate about them.

It should also be pointed out that there was significant disagreement among the donor countries about the appropriate ways to help Colombia.

---

[30]E.g., they were used to send popular Colombian singer Carlos Vives and his band to perform at an international book fair in Guadalajara, Mexico.

The disagreement was based on differences in European and American attitudes toward the "drug problem" and drug policies, in donor-country interests in Colombia, and in donor-country size.

France supported Colombian antidrug efforts but disagreed about the effectiveness of several antidrug polices. Specifically, the French government did not contribute to alternative development programs because it believed that they were not likely to succeed, that they ran the risk to become politicized, and that they were too broad in scope and difficult to implement.

Furthermore, the French believed that alternative development programs should not be implemented through bilateral aid systems. France's technical cooperation package has focused on law enforcement and scholarship and fellowship programs to encourage applied research, mainly in basic and natural sciences. Behind France's programs there is also an acknowledged goal of promoting knowledge and understanding of French culture. Because of these factors, several French-funded projects appear to have little antidrug content.

The United Kingdom is also skeptical about the effectiveness of some antidrug policies, but its economic interests in Colombia are large and influence its policies toward the country. BP (formerly British Petroleum) is one of the largest oil investors in Colombia. Its investments are located in guerrilla-controlled areas, where its oil pipeline is a continuous victim of terrorist bombings. There is no question that the United Kingdom has an interest in collaborating with the Colombian government's antidrug effort, but it considered alternative development projects as based on flawed economic analyses and found the American influence on PEC too strong for its taste. It has funded a few projects outside PEC to strengthen public administration and to contribute to rural and mineral development in areas were it has large investments.

The German contribution to PEC was channeled through GTZ, a semiofficial technical cooperation agency. As was noted, the German embassy itself was not aware of PEC, but GTZ was a main contributor and followed PEC very closely. GTZ funded seven PEC projects related to illegal drugs, including alternative development, justice and police improvement, and drug addiction. However, by 1995 only four projects had been started, and three were in the pipeline. German cooperation emphasizes attempts to help solve social problems and does not demand policy conditionality.

The European Union contributed funds to PEC through UNDCP and granted Colombia tariff preferences usually reserved for the least developed countries for a 10-year period. These complemented the U.S. Initiative of the Americas and became known as the Trade PEC, an accomplishment which was a source of pride among Colombian officials. The antidrug impact of these preferences was not questioned, even though even a superficial economic analysis suggests that it is likely to be insignificant.

USAID had left Colombia in the mid-1970s at the request of then-president Alfonso López-Michelsen (1974–78), who considered USAID involvement in Colombian domestic affairs as unjustified. This expression of independence from the United States was partly allowed by a coffee boom, which was followed by the Colombian marijuana boom. Indeed, during the López-Michelsen administration, for the first time in 20 years Colombia enjoyed an ample foreign exchange supply. The PEC program offered an opportunity for the return of USAID to fund several of PEC's most important alternative development programs.

The United States granted trade preferences to Colombia under the Initiative of the Americas and supported several programs outside PEC. These included programs to help the Colombian police and armed forces fight drugs and strengthen the country's justice administration system; to modernize the General Prosecutor's Office (Fiscalía); to develop the Presidential Advisory Office on Medellín (Consejería de Medellín), the city where drug traffickers had done the most damage; to protect the environment; and to support Colombia's economic liberalization effort, which had started during the Barco administration (1986–90). Programs funded within PEC include alternative development, rural and industrial development, and justice system strengthening.

Although the United States has been the main PEC contributor, one should question whether the creation of PEC itself had an impact on the total amount of U.S. aid to Colombia. Most interviews suggest that PEC was a useful instrument for channeling some funds but did not influence the size of the total U.S. aid contribution.

When PEC was put together, Italy offered a $50 million contribution. At the time, Italian technical cooperation programs were being questioned domestically, which led to a funding delay. Negotiations between Colombia and Italy concerning PEC programs were started only in 1991, but they were suspended because Italy was in the process of changing its international technical assistance laws. The new legislation, approved in 1993, required Italian assistance to focus on social-sector projects. Finally, in October 1993, Italy started a technical cooperation program concentrated on education, health, and agricultural development. However Italy's contribution to PEC has been small, limited to $2 million contributed through UNDCP.

Other countries also made small contributions to PEC. In 1989, Australia was one of the countries interested in promoting integration programs in the Pacific Basin. Colombia had expressed an interest in joining these programs, and Australia was interested in showing that it was concerned about the issue of illegal drugs. In 1990, Australia made a token contribution (about $100,000) to a drug prevention program in Colombia under PEC.

Results

As of 1995, only 33 of 112 (29 percent) PEC projects were either finished or in progress. Another 17 (15 percent) were being studied, and 62 (56 percent) had not gone beyond the formulation stage or had been discarded.

Among the projects completed or in process there were twelve related to international trade and industrial development issues. The project to promote the production of natural silk was directly related to illicit drugs because this was an attempt to develop the silkworm industry in illegal crop regions of Cauca Department. The rest were only indirectly related at best. These included a program to modernize the Colombian Foreign Trade Institute and streamline export procedures; programs for technology development, adaptation, and innovation in several industries; technical assistance to improve the quality of apples produced in the country; and programs to control foot-and-mouth disease. Also included were programs to improve product quality and facilitate exports, particularly of plastic, rubber, and leather products.

Some of the programs implemented were similar to past efforts that apparently had not achieved success. For example, the Colombian leather industry has had leather quality problems for ages. Furthermore, public funding for these projects is highly questionable because the lion's share of any possible benefits is captured by the private sector. It may be argued that leather is a product of the cattle-ranching industry in coca-growing areas, but on the one hand, the possibility of substituting extensive ranching for coca is rather weak, and on the other, the increase in the total value of a head of cattle brought about by better-quality leather is quite small.

There were five crop-substitution programs and three more related to the National Rehabilitation Plan (PNR) in coca-growing areas that had been or were being implemented. A project to support the General Legal Medicine Department also was under way. These projects were either related to illegal drug production or to narcoterrorism. Nine other projects dealt with various aspects of youth drug addiction and youth gangs. These were also related to illicit drugs.

Finally, three projects to improve the image of Colombia abroad included one to define a policy toward the Colombian image, a fund to support a Colombian presence in international events, and the coordination of PEC itself. As was noted above, it is questionable whether these can be included as part of the antidrug effort.

In 1995, there were under study five crop-substitution and three justice-support projects that were related to drug issues. Other projects under consideration were in international trade and industrial development fields, some of which (e.g., coconut development in Urabá, rubber development, and farm fishing support) could affect illegal crop or drug contraband areas. Others—such as a project to create an institute to provide technical support to the soldering industry—could be good development projects but ones for which it would be difficult to find an antidrug link.

Forty-two of the 62 projects that had been rejected or not considered were in trade and industry fields. There were also 15 crop-substitution, PNR, rural development, and justice projects. It is likely that one reason for international funding cuts in PEC was the inclusion of many projects that were hard to justify on drug-fighting grounds.

Case Studies

The research team studied a few projects implemented under PEC in detail. The choice of case studies was determined by the availability of data that, fortunately, existed for some of the most relevant projects.

Crop-Substitution and Alternative Development Projects

The first attempt to substitute illicit drug crops in Colombia dates from 1985 in southern Cauca Department. After the development of this type of project around the world, its labeling evolved from crop substitution to alternative development. The government's alternative development institute (PLANTE) was established in late 1992 to assume responsibility for alternative development in Colombia. PLANTE is part of the office of the president, and it is linked to the PNR.

As was noted above, by 1995 there had been four crop-substitution and alternative development projects funded under PEC. At the time, six more were under funding consideration. Alternative development projects include development programs and expenditures that transcend crop substitution. In Colombia, some of these were separated from PLANTE and made part of PNR projects. Within this scheme, PNR would be in charge of regional infrastructure investments, such as highway construction, land improvement (irrigation and similar investments), and community education and social projects. When PEC was formed in late 1989, the PNR was in financial difficulty. It is likely that the separation of programs between PEC and PNR was done as a way to refinance PNR. It is also possible that Colombian officials bet that a larger number of projects would increase total external funding and included several PNR projects in the original PEC list.

The first project studied was in the southern Cauca and northern Nariño Departments. As was noted, crop-substitution efforts had begun several years earlier in that region. The goal of the PEC project was to eliminate 3,700 hectares of coca and to develop plantings of coffee, bananas, yucca, sugarcane, beans, and fruit. The total project cost was $7.3 million, of which $4.1 million were from foreign sources. Funds were to be disbursed annually.

The project achieved a high degree of community participation and also the cooperation of such regional agencies as the Integrated Rural Development Fund (DRI). The project built slaughterhouses, coffee- and sugarcane-processing centers, and localities where produce could be bought and warehoused for further marketing. The project also developed pilot farms and promoted pork raising and fish farming. Several formal agreements were signed with municipal governments to strengthen the Municipal Agricultural and Husbandry Technical Assistance Teams (UMATAS). Booklets illustrating environmentally protective farming methods were distributed among the peasantry, and a health center was built.

Coca eradication has been significant. DECTI files indicate that 75 percent of the eradication goals have been achieved. This was a rather successful project in a relatively easy region to work in. Indian communities are well established and felt threatened by illegal crop development, markets are relatively accessible, and the land is of high quality when compared with other alternative development projects.

The second project studied was in Caquetá Department. The main project goals were to eradicate 6,527 coca hectares and to promote cattle raising, cocoa, and rubber. The total project budget was $62.6 million, of which $34.7 million had external funding.

The project, under the responsibility of the Colombia Land Reform Institute (INCORA), was delayed a year and started in March 1991. Implementation through INCORA was not advancing satisfactorily, and a year later it was transferred to the United Nations Office of Special Projects (UNOPS). By late 1994, project reports indicated that approximately 600 hectares of coca had been eradicated. The project that finally was approved covered a smaller area than planned, and its eradication goal had been lowered to 4,000 hectares. A UNDCP official provided a project report to the research team, in which it was claimed that 25 percent of the eradication goal had been achieved.

The actual project was a lot smaller than originally planned. Its total costs came up to about $3.4 million in external and $1 million in domestic resources. According to those interviewed, one of the main implementation problems was political clientelism. The project had to be scaled down and delayed to protect it from becoming just a clientelistic bounty. It appears that in Caquetá local government officials, coca growers, and others involved in the illegal industry were not interested in a serious alternative development project that would lead to coca eradication. This is one of the regions "vacated" by the government of President Andrés Pastrana and left under guerrilla control in late 1998.

The third project was in Putumayo Department. Its goal was to eliminate 3,869 coca hectares and to promote cattle raising, farm fishing, sugarcane, and bean crops, to recover the forest and plant timber trees, and to develop an artisan leather industry. The project costs were $37.1 million, of which $20.6 came from external funds.

Administrative and external funding difficulties delayed this project, which also started a year late. As with the second project, the eradication goal was lowered, to 2,500 hectares in this case. In 1992, UNOPS also assumed implementation responsibilities. The foreign donor contribution for the actual project was $4.5 million, much lower than planned.

The project had some achievements. It helped develop rubber forests, and sugarcane, Amazonian wheat, and *chontaduro* plantings. A plant to produce fruit concentrates was built, as were several school cafeterias and a health center. Community Boards (Juntas de Acción Comunal) participated actively in the project, which benefited more than 3,000 families. Unfortunately, the antidrug results of the project were dismal: as of 1995, it had eradicated only 200 hectares.

The fourth and last alternative development project analyzed was in Guaviare Department, another of the areas of the "distension zone." The project goal was to eliminate 3,821 hectares of coca, one for each of the families to benefit from the project. The original estimated total cost was $36.7 million, of which $20.3 million was to be a foreign contribution. Coca plantings were to be replaced by pork and cattle, rubber, cocoa, and farm fishing.

As with the previous two projects, there were starting delays and the project administration, originally assumed by PNR, had to be taken over by UNOPS. The project goal was scaled down to eradicate 2,100 hectares, and the external donor contribution was lowered to $4 million.

The project had several social achievements, which are highlighted by its promoters. Several schools were built; a cattle-ranching fund was established, as well as the so-called Guaviarences funds for regional development. The project also developed links to and obtained support from local governments and the UMATAS. Unfortunately, in this case coca eradication was almost nil. During the first 3 years of the project, only 120 hectares were eradicated, and by 1995 the project reported only a 10.4 percent eradication success.

The four projects analyzed illustrate several of the implementation problems encountered by alternative development projects in Colombia. The local implementation ability and/or will was quite limited, and three of the four projects had management failures and required the involvement of UNOPS. The interviews also indicated that the relations between PNR and UNOPS were not smooth and cordial and that once UNOPS assumed the projects' responsibilities, it proceeded on its own, frustrating PNR officials. Several Colombians interviewed expressed dismay about the high costs of UNOPS services, which were reported at 35 percent of total project costs. Colombians complained that UNOPS not only consumed a very large share of donors' contributions, but also that it was in its interest to perpetuate the current foreign assistance system because it lives off it.

There is no question that at least some of these projects had significant positive effects on the communities they served, but besides the administrative problems and bureaucratic conflicts they encountered, their eradication record was very poor. Independently of whether one thinks that alternative development projects should eradicate by force or not, the point is simply that foreign donors would not contribute funds to these projects if in the medium and long runs if they do not lead to smaller illegal crops. Eradication was significant in only one of the four projects studied. This was the case of the southern Cauca and northern Nariño project, where native communities have a significant social capital stock and collaborated in the eradication. At the other sites, eradication was not just dismal, but in hindsight, the projects could have simply been a total waste because in those regions coca plantings increased dramatically all throughout the 1990s.

Apple Production and Marketing

The apple production and marketing project was designed to improve the quality of apples produced in Colombia and to organize their domestic and international marketing. This project was funded by USAID, its total costs were only $1.5 million, it was based at the Universidad de Caldas, and it appears to have been successful.

The project did not have the implementation and bureaucratic problems encountered by the alternative development projects surveyed. The project identified several apple varieties that can grow well in Colombia and established a network to transmit the relevant technology to farmers. Colombia has a market for apples that is supplied mainly by Chile, where local producers could compete. It is not clear however, that Colombia could or should compete internationally by exporting apples to the European Union, as was suggested in the project's document.

There is no question that this was a valid development project and that it may have been successful. But its relevance within an antidrug program is highly questionable. To begin with, apples in Colombia grow in regions that are not adequate for coca or poppies and are not important suppliers of migrants to the coca- and poppy-growing zones.

Support for the Legal Medicine Institute

The Legal Medicine Institute support project aimed to strengthen the forensic medicine capabilities of the government, a necessary step in improving justice administration. The project provided funds to train experts abroad, to purchase material and equipment, and to establish quality-control standards in forensic medicine laboratories in seven Colombian cities.

This was a successful project for which GTZ provided about $3.4 million. The project filled a strongly felt need, and a meeting of donors' and recipients' minds facilitated its implementation. Once the project was approved, it developed smoothly. Investments were made and funds were disbursed on time. It appears that the need for the project was identified after PEC started, which explains why the project started in 1994. By the time the evaluation was done, all participants were satisfied, but not enough time had gone by to assure that this situation would prevail in the long run.

Conclusions

The evaluation of PEC highlights many failures and few successes of international antidrug cooperation. Seven points bear mentioning. First, the diversity of interests and goals among the various donors and beneficiaries was an obstacle to the success of many projects. When there was a coincidence of interests, the chances of success were indeed much higher.

Second, on the Colombian side, it was clear that the dramatic series of political assassinations that culminated in that of Luis Carlos Galán provided an opportunity for the Colombian bureaucracy to stake a claim for international funds. The PEC projects were put together more as an attempt to obtain a larger quantity of international financial assistance more rapidly than as a coherent antidrug program. Indeed, many of the PEC projects had at best marginal links to illegal drug issues.

Third, on one hand, Colombian aid recipient agencies realized that the actual foreign grants had to be negotiated and inflated the original request. On the other, donor countries cut down their commitments after projects had been approved. As a result, the projects as actually implemented had much smaller funding than had been requested and approved.

Fourth, external PEC funding was also used symbolically to legitimize and support Colombia's claim that the illegal drug problem was a global one for which national solutions were inadequate.

Fifth, from the donor country side, it was clear that they were shocked by the spate of Colombian violence and wanted to be seen as helping the Colombian government. However, the donors' varying interests and their own foreign assistance regulations made it difficult to respond rapidly and effectively to Colombian needs.

Sixth, the life of domestic and international bureaucracies involved in international technical cooperation depends on continuous international assistance flows. This driving force prevails over project quality.[31]

---

[31]This was probably a factor in the DNP's cancellation of this evaluation. The two drafts submitted were critical of PEC, and it was likely that the final report could have become an obstacle for the Colombian bureaucracy's request for more international funds.

Seventh, the structural deficiencies implicit in many antidrug policies are glaring and make long-term project success very unlikely. In the case of alternative development projects, even when they succeeded in the short run, their success was not maintained in the long run.

12

A Short Survey of Antidrug Policies in
the Andes and Policy Conclusions

This chapter focuses broadly on the antidrug policies followed by the Andean countries. It examines the policies listed in the first section of chapter 10. The chapter summarizes the main antidrug policies followed by the Andean countries; their results are evaluated, and a few policy conclusions are derived. This review does not provide much hope for antidrug policy success unless significant changes are made to the policy approach followed until now.

Policies to Eradicate Illegal Drugs

To start, let us look at eradication. Many antidrug programs have sought to eradicate coca and poppies. The goal set by these programs has always been a number of hectares eradicated. Of course, there could be other policy goals that would result in different policy strategies and evaluations.

For example, a goal could be a decline in the number of cultivated hectares. The policy strategy would of course be very different in cases where peasants eradicate old unproductive coca bushes and plant new ones. A further and more sophisticated goal could be to lower the actual total cocaine and heroin production potential of the illegal plantings. In this case, if some coca is eradicated but productivity increases (as it has) because of improved seeds and agricultural techniques and practices, the evaluation of the policy would produce very different results.

Eradication can be forced or voluntarily. Forced eradication programs can be done using various means. They can force peasants to do the eradicating themselves, they can use an outside force (hired workers, police, army) to do it, or they can use aerial spraying. Voluntary eradication requires convincing peasants that they should cut down their trees or plants. Asking peasants to eradicate on the grounds that it contributes to the national welfare is not persuasive, and it has not worked anywhere. To get peasants to eradicate the plantings voluntarily, it is necessary to use a credible threat or bribe (compensation). Indeed, peasants are painfully aware that their illegal plants provide their only real leverage on the government and are very reluctant to eradicate unless they are pushed to do it. In these cases, eradication becomes "voluntary."

Openly forced eradication is a very socially divisive policy. If it is manual, it confronts those doing the eradication (army, police, other government officials, or hired hands) and the growers. If it is aerial, the confrontation is impersonal but can be worse because aerial spraying would also affect other crops and have greater environmental effects. To avoid confrontation, governments such as the Bolivian one complemented their forced eradication program with alternative development programs to appease the peasantry.

Eradication in the Andes has worked only in Bolivia since 1998. It has been done forcibly, with strong armed forces' support, and still it is not clear that it is sustainable in the long run. Furthermore, it does not seem to have had a significant effect on cocaine prices in the main retail markets, and it appears to have displaced production to other locations. As was noted in chapter 4, the decline in Peruvian coca output was due to a combination of factors, and most coca bushes were abandoned rather than eradicated.

In Colombia, a strong aerial fumigation campaign has displaced plantings but has not been able to stop a huge expansion in illegal crops. This campaign has produced a significant peasant reaction, which has been supported by nongovernmental organizations and other civil society organizations, both in Colombia and abroad. Aerial spraying is a complicated policy. First, it is implemented only because the government does not have control over the territory and cannot eradicate manually.

Second, the defoliants used are chosen because they are not supposed to affect people or to have long-term effects on the environment. Unfortunately, such defoliants are chemically formulated to be sprayed from close distances instead of the relatively high altitudes required for the protection of the spraying planes. Many critics argue that to achieve their goals, the defoliants have to be mixed with other damaging substances and that what is sprayed in Colombia differs substantially from the products approved for domestic use in the United States and Europe.

Third, aerial spraying is not as accurate as manual eradication. It hurts other plants, it might not kill all the illegal plants, and peasants may use protective methods such as spraying the coca plants with diluted molasses when they fear spraying. Because of these problems, aerial spraying is illegal in all Andean countries except Colombia. The fact that it is legal in Colombia is a reflection of the government's weak territorial control.

Eradication reduces illegal drug supply only if plantings are not displaced to other locations. This "balloon effect," which was discussed in the previous chapter, is not given sufficient attention in eradication programs that focus only in particular areas. The eradication advocates argue that planting expansion would occur even if there were no eradication and that therefore an eradicated hectare is always a contribution to lower supply. This is an empirical issue that could be clarified looking at the evidence.

Policies to Promote Crop Substitution and Alternative Development

Policymakers realized early in the "war on drugs" that most peasants involved in illicit drug production were poor and extremely dependent on illicit crops. In response to this, purely criminal repression policies began to be complemented in the hemisphere by "crop-substitution" programs since the late 1970s.[1] These programs sought to identify and promote other crops that could provide income to growers.

---

[1]Alternative development programs in general, and the Bolivian experience in particular, are discussed in detail in chapter 11. Beginning in the early 1970s, crop-substitution programs were tried in Asia. In the Andean region, these experiments began in the late 1970s (CICAD 1986; UNDCP 1993).

The premise underlining crop-substitution programs was that peasants were inherently good people who grew illegal crops because they could not survive otherwise. They would rather live within the law, and if they were provided with alternative ways to make a living legally they would pursue them. This was a very naive and somewhat paternalistic way to look at the reasons that peasants get involved in illegal drugs and at possible solutions. As was shown in the previous chapter, this approach was flawed on four grounds. First, it is very difficult to find crops or other rural activities that would generate the same income level as illicit drugs.

Second, illegal crops have a ready and secure market at the farm gate. Marketing of legal market products tends to be difficult to organize, and market prices are frequently subject to large fluctuations. Marketing peasant farm products has been a problem all throughout Latin America. Almost everywhere, the peasantry complains that intermediaries make large profits and that peasants get shortchanged. Many coca- and poppy-growing areas are distant from the main possible markets, and transportation costs are high. Some possible products require refrigeration and other special handling. Coca, coca paste, and opium are comparatively a lot easier to market.

Third, if a crop that yields the same income as illegal crops is found, traffickers can increase the illegal crop price several-fold and continue making very large profits. As was shown in chapter 5, coca costs account for less than 1 percent of the cocaine street price in the United States and Europe. Doubling or trebling coca prices would have an insignificant effect on street prices and traffickers' profits.

Fourth, if eradication and crop substitution succeed, illegal coca and opium prices would go up and generate incentives to expand illegal crops elsewhere. This is the well-known "balloon effect."

By the mid-1980s, it was clear that crop substitution alone was not successful and that other "factors should be incorporated to future crop substitution programs' planning and implementation" (CICAD 1986). At this time, CICAD argued for multisector development programs, and emphasized the importance for the governments and institutions involved to meet their commitments to gain the trust of the population, and the need of complementary education programs.

CICAD's early multisector approach was supported by experiences outside the region: "From about 1985 onward there was consensus as to the need for a strategy based on massive integrated rural development as a means to achieve eventually the level of development necessary to put an end to illicit drug production. This strategy presupposes, of course, parallel action in the areas of prevention and control of demand" (UNDCP 1993, 15).

Alternative development programs include the search for other crops; technical assistance programs to process and market those crops; exploiting the natural forest without destroying it; infrastructure development, including highways, electricity, schools, hospitals, and water supply systems in coca- and poppy-growing regions; and community development programs to improve family quality of life and promote stable community organizations. The need to prevent migration to illicit-crop regions led to the incorporation into alternative development programs of employment-generating initiatives in areas that are a migrant source for illegal-crop-producing areas.

During the 1990s, traditional agriculture in the Andean countries was one of the hardest hit sectors by globalization and the opening of the Andean economies. Moreover, the elimination of many government rural subsidies and integrated rural development programs and the support of alternative development programs created some very perverse incentives. This policy combination sent a very strong message to the peasantry: If you want to get the attention of the government and the international community, you have to plant coca or poppies.[2]

Alternative development programs in the Andean countries have focused almost exclusively on coca eradication and substitution. In a few small Colombian cases, these programs have targeted poppy-growing areas. In these areas, one should expect particular difficulties arising from the short season of the crop, around 4 months, which makes any crop-substitution advances very vulnerable to a reversal.

Alternative development programs are supposed to substitute a new economic base for illegal crops and must counteract strong market forces. These two challenges are very difficult to overcome, and usually are not. As was shown in detail in the previous chapter, they require investments in regions where investors normally would not invest, and if they succeed in cutting the hectareage devoted to illegal crops in a particular region, strong measures are required to avoid illegal crop growth somewhere else (the well-known "balloon effect").

---

[2] An author's interview with coca growers' leaders in Cochabamba in October 1997 confirmed that they had encouraged farmers to plant coca to be able to request alternative development funds from foreign donors.

There is no question that alternative development programs can raise the quality of life in the affected regions. For instance, the foreign visitor in Bolivia's Chapare may be struck by the widespread peasant poverty, but an expert's eye will be impressed by the infrastructure of the place. There is no question that among all rural Bolivian regions, Chapare enjoys by far the best infrastructure. One can also wonder if making Chapare more attractive than other non-coca-producing regions would not attract more migrants who would end up producing coca (a point of concern among U.S. embassy officials in La Paz).

As was explained in detail above, alternative development may also achieve some coca and poppy production declines in those communities, but the incentives these programs create are not conducive to overall declines in illegal crops. The consensus among analysts is that alternative development programs do not contribute to lower drug production but that they are necessary and politically useful (Joel 1999; Lee and Clawson 1993).

Policies to Promote Interdiction and to Control Chemical Inputs

The interdiction of precursors for the production of cocaine and heroin presents particular problems. To begin with, cocaine and heroin can be refined using several processes and inputs, and every precursor can be substituted for. Furthermore, many precursors are common products produced by many firms and have widespread uses within an economy. Therefore, to limit traffickers' access it is necessary to focus on

1. Those precursors that have a few producers or that because of high weight or volume are difficult to transport, and that have local markets that can be monitored.
2. Access controls to the cocaine- and heroin-producing regions. Highway checkpoints and searches of people coming in and out drug-producing regions.
3. International trade controls. Requiring exporters to know their trade partners and to keep strict records on sales and forms of payment.
4. Controls on domestic precursor producers similar to those of international producers.

As was noted above, in some cases (perhaps exceptional ones) it is also possible to trace precursors using satellites to locate laboratory sites, as with the well-known Tranquilandia case in Colombia in the early 1980s. In spite of such successes, the record of precursor controls and interdiction is not encouraging. The nature of drug production processes (the "production function" in economics jargon) makes it unrealistic to eliminate drug production through precursor interdiction. The fact that there are several ways to produce cocaine and heroin and that every chemical input used can be substituted is a main problem. Furthermore, precursor interdiction has a small effect on cocaine and heroin production costs. As was seen in chapter 5, cocaine-manufacturing costs are about $1,000 a kilogram, or approximately 1 percent of American street prices and less of European ones. And a significant amount of these costs are rewards for risk taking and payments to chemists, guards, and other labor costs.

Let us assume that there is a very important precursor that accounts for 20 percent of manufacturing costs (very unlikely), that is, for $200, and that a successful interdiction campaign increases its cost five times, to $1,000 (also very unlikely). This increases total manufacturing costs by 80 percent to $1,800, but it increases costs as a percentage of retail prices by only 0.8 percent. Furthermore, this figure should be considered a ceiling because traffickers would seek alternative, relatively cheaper precursors. Unfortunately, one frequent negative effect of a search for new precursors is to bring new actors into the illegal industry. When one precursor is controlled, traffickers find substitutes that come from different sources and incorporate new players into the illegal industry. These shifts increase costs to the trafficker, and these funds are revenues to the producers of the substitute precursor.

Another effect is to force traffickers to shift from the technically superior to other precursors. For example, controlling lime in Colombia induced traffickers to use cement. A by-product of this shift has been increased environmental damage, because cement is used only for its lime content and leaves substantial residues that are dumped on the ground. As was noted in chapters 6 and 7, the environmental damage resulting from attempts to hide controlled substances can also be high, as in the example of toxic chemicals kept submerged in rivers to avoid detection.

In summary, precursor control can increase costs for traffickers and can bring new actors into the illegal industry. But it is unlikely to have a significant long-term effect on traffickers' profits and on the drug supply.

Policies to Destroy Laboratories and Domestically Interdict Coca and Poppy By-Products

The destruction of laboratories and the domestic interdiction of coca and poppy by-products are carried out in drug-producing countries by the army and police with the support of intelligence services and other government agencies. They frequently also have the support of foreign advisers, mainly from the United States.

Laboratory destruction has gone on for more than two decades. Unfortunately, as was discussed in chapter 4, laboratories are primitive operations, require little machinery and equipment (fixed capital), and are very mobile and easily replaced. Lab destruction provides a type of body count in the war on drugs and makes for good evening news, but it does not have a significant effect on the drug supply. Furthermore, lab seizure operations capture mainly very-low-level workers or no one at all. Furthermore, in most lab destructions, there are no or very few drug seizures.

Domestic drug interdiction in Andean countries focuses on ports, airports, and drug warehouses. Some of these efforts have produced significant seizures, but the average drug volume seized in each case tends to be small, particularly at airports where many "mules" are captured. There are frequent reports of traffickers who tip the authorities about one of their own "mules," who carry a small amount of a drug to divert the attention of customs officials while a large shipment goes by (Molano 1997).

Interdiction and lab destruction place local authorities at high risk for corruption and offer possibilities for drug traffickers to tip off authorities about abandoned labs that they can destroy to show successes (Rodas 1996). When authorities seize drugs, there is always the temptation to keep at least part of the catch to be resold on the underground market. Furthermore, when illegal drugs are seized and labs destroyed, money is almost never found, which suggests that corruption does occur.

Policies to Promote Downstream Interdiction

Downstream interdiction is done in international waters, at entry points, and inside drug-importing countries. Drug seizures allow law-enforcing agencies to keep a scorecard and are also good news material. In spite of frequent large seizures, the challenges to interdiction are overwhelming. In a globalized economy, searching for illegal drugs is frequently like searching for a needle in a haystack.

For example, after estimating the volume and weight of all drugs that enter the United States in a year, Falco (1996, 128) concluded that "three DC-3A or five Cessna Caravan turboprop planes could carry the nation's annual heroin supply, while three Boeing 747 or 12 trailer trucks could carry could transport the necessary cocaine." When one considers that more than 20 million containers and trailers enter the United States every year, the magnitude of the challenge and the difficulty of expecting much from interdiction become quite clear.

Indeed, Riley's (1995) detailed econometric study concluded that traffickers treat interdiction seizures simply as a cost of doing business, but that seizures have not had a significant long-term effect on supply. They have learned that a proportion of their shipments are seized, and those costs are built into their profit estimates. This is one reason why large drug "cartels" subcontract transportation services. If a shipment is seized, those captured can provide little or no useful information to the authorities about high-ranking traffickers. In spite of these weaknesses, interdiction is strongly supported in the U.S. Congress, where many viewed attempts by the Bill Clinton administration to shift funds from interdiction to demand-side programs as "going soft on drugs" (Falco 1996).

Policies to Extradite Principal Andean Traffickers

The United States has insisted that the Andean countries extradite drug traffickers to be tried in the United States. This policy has been very controversial in Latin America. Bolivia extradited only a couple of politicians accused of drug trafficking during the dictatorship of Luis García-Meza. They were "whisked away in a D.E.A. plane in the middle of the night," just after their capture, without complying with the country's legal procedures. During the 1980s Colombia has extradited fewer than fifty traffickers,[3] some of whom had never set foot in the United States.

Extradition was implemented reluctantly by President Belisario Betancur only after Justice Minister Rodrigo Lara Bonilla's assassination in 1984. President Virgilio Barco, who succeed Betancur, supported extradition. Extradition was also applied during the César Gaviria administration, but the 1991 Constitution banned it. Since then, the United States pressured

---

[3]Three of them were actually sent back to Colombia because the evidence against them in the United States had not been collected following all legally required procedures and did not hold up in court!

successive Colombian governments to change the country's constitution, a feat that was achieved in 1997. Still, the United States was unsatisfied because extradition is not retroactive and applies only to crimes committed after the constitutional amendment. In late 1999, Colombia resumed extraditing drug traffickers.

The arguments for extradition are simple: First, some crimes transcend the jurisdiction where they are committed. Many technological and economic changes have shrunk the world. As a result, issues that were of domestic, or national, concern are now "intermestic." Events can take place in a particular country, but their effects are felt in others. Because of these changes, an intermestic crime can be tried in a different country from the one where it took place.

Second, the legitimacy of states and their ability to enforce their laws varies substantially. The strong emphasis on drug trafficker extradition implies that either a particular state does not have appropriate legislation or that it cannot enforce its laws and punish lawbreakers. Because of these deficiencies, other affected states should take over, enforce their laws, and punish criminals.

Extradition has also been justified as a way to go after the head of trafficking organizations. This justification has been based on the need to punish traffickers and to behead, disorganize, and disband trafficking organizations. This assumes that eliminating the cartel heads would have a significant effect on drug supply.[4] As was explained in earlier chapters, this questionable assumption is valid under the right conditions only in the short run. After a criminal organization is beheaded, it takes only a few months for the organization to reshape itself. Jailing cartel heads has taught a lesson to all other industry leaders, many of whom have opted for a low-key approach in their relations with the rest of society, have shied from the limelight, and have built smaller, harder-to-identify, trafficking organizations, which constitute today's industry core. This industry adaptation has neutralized the possible effects of the destruction of the large cocaine cartel on the illicit drug's supply.

Extradition is a very complex and costly procedure that requires excellent coordination and cooperation among the justice systems and many law enforcement agencies of several countries. This limits its application to a few, selective cases, mainly cartel heads and their closest associates. On a practical level, extradition punishes few traffickers, but to achieve any ef-

---

[4]This argument was justified to implement the U.S. "kingpin" strategy in the 1980s.

fect on the illegal drug supply, the illegal drug market and criminal organizations must meet two conditions. First, it is necessary for criminal organizations to have a centralized structure, so that eliminating a big trafficker destroys the organization. Second, after such an event, the industry cannot reorganize itself. The evidence on the structure of the Andean criminal industry discussed in chapter 4 shows that neither of these conditions holds and that there is no evidence that extradition lowers illicit drug supply. Its value is mainly punitive.

Extradition as a legal weapon raises important legal issues. Extradited suspects are judged by individuals from cultures, traditions, languages, races, religions, and nationalities different from theirs. There is no question that they cannot be judged by their peers. Most legal systems consider these limitations as severe obstacles to achieving justice. In fact, this was the main argument of President Betancur when he procrastinated on the implementation of the extradition treaty before his justice minister was assassinated.

Drug trafficker extradition is different from other extradition experiences. Most other cases of extradition deal with individuals who have committed a crime in the country requesting the extradition, but not in the country from where they are extradited. Drug trafficker extradition is also an implicit recognition that a state simply cannot do the job. There is no question about the weak legitimacy of many states and their inability to enforce their laws, but openly recognizing such is politically costly. Many citizens of the Andean countries see extradition as a severe loss of sovereignty. The only cases of extradition of country nationals are related to illegal drugs and are seen as forcing a country to implement the policy of a foreign power.

Extradition has been a pebble in the shoe of Andean–U.S. relations. It has been a continuous irritant that frequently flares up. Within the Andean countries, it has been very divisive, particularly in Bolivia and Colombia. Extradition in Bolivia has been used frequently by political opponents to highlight the government's weaknesses and the country's loss of sovereignty. In Colombia, it was the main reason why drug traffickers unleashed a terrorist campaign against the government in the late 1980s.

Furthermore, drug trafficker extradition is a bilateral attempt to impart justice in cases of intermestic crimes that are frequently multilateral. Other affected countries may agree with the treatment and sentencing of extradited traffickers, but they do not participate in it and have little or nothing to say about it. Intermestic tribunals and prisons are an alternative to extradition that is worth exploring. To do so, it is necessary to agree on fundamental goals. Intermestic procedures should provide transparent and equitable trials, sentences should be proportional to crimes committed, and prisons should meet minimum health, comfort, and human dignity standards. Prisoners should be well treated, but they should not be allowed to operate their illegal business from prison, and the probability of them escaping should be very low or zero.

These conditions can be achieved by a multilateral tribunal and prison system. The establishment of such a system would be recognition by the international community that intermestic crimes should be tried and sentenced intermestically. A specific alternative would be to establish an international tribunal to try Colombian traffickers, who would serve their sentences in a newly built prison in Colombia, administered by a multinational force or the United Nations. Foreign countries would contribute a share of the costs. A multinational force of prison administrators and guards, medical doctors and nurses, and other personnel would run the prison and would be rotated periodically to minimize the possibility of corruption. The prison would meet all United Nations humanitarian standards. Every prisoner would have clean cells and beds, access to sunlight, education programs, television, gym facilities, medical services, nutritious food, and other goods and services to provide for their basic needs, including periodic visits by family and close friends. Indeed, such a place could be quite similar to Pablo Escobar's famous "Cathedral," except that it would be run by a qualified, difficult to corrupt team.

A second, and perhaps more controversial, step would be the establishment of an intermestic court system with prosecutors, defense lawyers, and judges from several countries. Such a court would be located outside Colombia to safeguard it against terrorism. This would increase the probability that sentences would be proportional to the crimes committed and would make court corruption difficult. The establishment of such a court would be more complex that the intermestic prison suggested. It would require negotiating agreements about what laws to apply. The possibilities are ample in this respect. There are the laws of countries where the crimes originate, those of other countries affected, possibly new intermestic legislation, or a combination of the above. Financing this court would also require complex international negotiations.

These two proposals may be dismissed as impractical. But the growing importance of transnational organized crime would eventually require systems like these. Indeed, they could be extended to cover crimes other than drug crimes.[5] They can also be attacked because they require all countries involved to sacrifice a degree of sovereignty. At the same time, they would simply recognize the realities of diminished national sovereignty in a more and more complex, globally interdependent system.

Policies to Strengthen the Andean Justice and Law Enforcement Systems

Policies to strengthen the Andean justice and law enforcement systems are implemented with external financial and technical assistance and include an ample set of programs. A nonexhaustive list includes (1) technical cooperation programs to train police officers, detectives, judges, and other Justice Ministry, attorney general, comptroller, and Prosecutor's Office personnel, to ensure that everyone dealing with drug-related offenses has the necessary know-how an equipment; (2) programs to improve the government's capabilities to build legal cases that would stand up in trials,[6] and to improve the salaries and other working conditions of law-enforcing personnel; (3) reforms and training programs in government institutions in charge of auditing and overseeing banks and other financial institutions where money laundering can take place (establishing financial intelligence units is particularly important); (4) similar programs for institutions in charge of managing and disposing of seized traffickers' assets; (5) cooperation programs with military and police units to train personnel, supply equipment, and share intelligence; and (6) assistance in legal reform programs, including model law formats to criminalize money laundering, to facilitate asset seizure and expropriation, and to establish minimum sentence guidelines.

All these programs aim at improving the governments' abilities to repress illicit drugs. There have been significant advances on some fronts. For example, CICAD and UNODCCP have helped countries adopt compatible legislation packages that have made drug money laundering a crime.

---

[5]It is worth noting that I discussed these ideas with Senator Charles Grassley of Iowa, a well-known drug hawk, at a seminar in the Heritage Foundation in 1996. His response was that they were worth considering but Colombians would not accept them. A year later, I discussed the same proposal with former interior minister, presidential candidate and Liberal Party head Horacio Serpa, who also thought they were worth pursuing but, conversely, believed that the Americans would not accept them.

[6]One example is support for forensic medicine labs, which was discussed in the previous chapter.

These are important necessary steps that have to be complemented with actions to achieve practical results. Unfortunately, these have been frequently lacking. For example, among the Andean countries, Colombia has the biggest money-laundering problem and advanced anti-money-laundering legislation. Many traffickers' assets have been seized, but most of them have been returned after the seizure has been challenged in court and virtually no traffickers' assets have been expropriated. The government has been able to use some seized buildings and cars, but by mid-1999 it had not been able to formally expropriate and sell any assets.[7] One basic problem faced by any potential purchaser of seized assets is how to protect his life and that of his close relatives from the violent retaliation of the trafficking organizations. This has been a large obstacle for the government to distribute land seized from traffickers. The following paragraph summarizes some of the specific problems encountered with seized assets in Colombia.

One of the main tasks of Colombia's National Drug Control Agency (Dirección Nacional de Estupefacientes, or DNE) is to manage seized property.[8] The expropriation trials have been frustratingly slow, and there are no assurances that they will be decided in the government's favor. DNE has found it very difficult to find tenants willing to rent the seized properties because of fear of retaliation by former owners. Indeed, in some cases, mainly in Cali, it had been necessary to hire the same companies that had managed the seized properties before. These were the only ones able to get tenants. This arrangement was accepted, in spite of the fact that those companies were suspected to have close links to the traffickers who had owned the real estate. Another problem facing DNE was the lack of cash to fix damaged properties. In most real estate seizure cases, police forces caused great damage to buildings at the time of seizure while searching for drugs and hideouts (*caletas*). Fixing these damages requires large expenses before the property can be used.

Fear among possible buyers is another great obstacle to the possible disposal of seized property. To deal with this problem, DNE was considering in early 1999 the creation of a trust fund where real estate sales proceeds

[7]E.g., *El Tiempo*, on its August 25, 1999, first page, reported that interior minister Néstor Humberto Martínez, speaking to Congress, indicated that the government was about to submit a bill to modify the expropriation law because 3 years after it had been enacted, not a single asset had been expropriated.

[8]This is based on an author's interview with Rubén Olarte, head of Colombia's National Drug Control Agency (Dirección Nacional de Estupefacientes), Bogotá, February 1999.

were to be placed. This fund was to be used to pay the former owners in case the courts at a future date revert the property ownership to them. This system would hopefully discourage previous owners from retaliating directly against the new buyers.

One of the most interesting cases of properties controlled by DNE at the time was the Chinauta Resort Hotel, in Girardot, a well-known resort town with a hot climate about $2^{1}/_{2}$ hours drive from Bogotá. This property had been seized from Pastor Perafán, a well-known Cali cartel member. The resort had been operated at a loss; it was overstaffed and many workers did not have specific functions. It is likely that it had been used to pay drug industry workers and to launder money. As soon as the property was seized, the employees formed a labor union, which made the government shy away from firing excess workers. Besides, the suspicion that some of these employees had been involved in criminal cartel activities discouraged the DNE from trying to fire anyone, for fear of retaliation. The DNE has been losing money on this property since they have had control of it. They had even offered to give it free to the union, which refused to take it. One solution they were contemplating was to turn it into a resort club for a government agency so that at least it would be used.

Policies to Train Police and Armed Forces to Improve Their Antidrug Performance

Programs to train police and armed forces to improve their antidrug performance involve foreign assistance, mainly from the United States, and frequently are controversial and raise many political and social questions. Here we will touch on only four. First, Andean police and armed forces have a poor human rights record. Is antidrug training going to exacerbate this problem?

Second, would the United States, which provides most of this training, use it for purposes other than antidrug trafficking? Are the trainees going to use their training to fight domestic political dissidents?[9] Some analysts

---

[9]Unfortunately, the long history of U.S. military support for totalitarian regimes in Latin America has generated widespread distrust in the region. The shadow of the School of the Americas in Panama and Fort Benning, where many of the worst Latin American human rights abusers were trained, still weighs heavily, in the opinion of many Latin Americans. This is in spite of the fact that the United States during the past few years has been a strong promoter of human rights in Latin America and that the school has introduced a human rights curriculum.

argue that United States army supports Andean police and armies not because it really believes in antidrug policies but simply because it needs a job. According to this view, technical assistance is just an attempt of the U.S. military to find alternative employment after the end of the Cold War.[10]

Third, involving the military in antidrug activity creates conflicts with other domestic agencies, mainly the police.[11] Indeed, should the armed forces—whose responsibility is to protect a country against external enemies—assume anticriminal roles, basically a police function?[12] To what extent does involving the army in the drug-trafficking war divert it from its proper roles?

Fourth, would involving the army in antidrug activities make it vulnerable to drug money corruption, which would weaken it in the medium and long run?[13] This is not a trivial issue because Andean armed forces' members have been active in the illegal industry. As was argued in chapters 7 and 8, the Andean military has had links to drug trafficking. These have been particularly important in Bolivia, less so in Peru, and have also been present to a lesser degree in Colombia.

These general issues and concerns are valid. But beyond them, the real question is, How effective can the police and military be fighting illegal drugs? Their roles are always in support of the policies listed above; as has been shown, they are in themselves not very effective. It is true that the Andean police and armed forces can do a better job than what they have done, but even the best done job is limited by the structural limitations of the policies themselves. Because of these limitations, it is expected that the armed forces and police can achieve some or even many battle victories, but it is highly doubtful that they would win the drug war.

[10]The assertions that the United States has had an unprecedented economic boom, that it has enjoyed full employment for several years, and that its armed forces are having great difficulties finding enough volunteer soldiers do not sound very convincing to many Latin Americans.

[11]As was shown in chapter 8, American support for the antidrug efforts of Bolivian armed forces and police has been an important source of friction between the institutions.

[12]In no modern democracy would the armed forces be allowed to take on internal police functions. In the United States, even the National Guard interventions to protect civil rights during the 1960s raised substantial constitutional issues.

[13]This has been why high-ranking Pentagon officials have frequently opposed the U.S. armed forces' involvement in the drug war.

Policy Conclusions

Antidrug policies have proven to have marginal success. The war on drugs has been waged for 30 years, and the problem has not gone away. There are those who argue that policies have been appropriately thought out and formulated but they have not succeeded only because they have not been applied the way they should. In other words, the problem does not lie in expecting policies to achieve what they cannot but in lack of coordination, failure to implement, lack of political will, and the like.[14] According to this view, there is no need to find another solution; what is needed is to apply all the tried policies simultaneously and with great zeal.

The short survey of supply control policies presented in this and the last two chapters supports a different position, with five dimensions. First, repressive policies like forced eradication and extradition can have some deterrent effects on some would-be coca and poppy growers and traffickers, but they do not have a significant overall effect on the drug supply. One basic problem these policies have is that their success does not depend on punishing some people in some place, but they should establish a credible threat for all potential industry members in all possible locations; otherwise the most they achieve is a short-term decline in production and trafficking and a displacement of the industry's location.

Second, policies advocating such measures as alternative development and laboratory destruction and other interdiction efforts are based on implausible assumptions about the economics of the illegal industry and the behavior of industry actors. At best, they have small effects on the illicit drug supply and retail prices.

Third, different polices have effects that tend to cancel each other out. For example, jailing and extraditing traffickers create promotion and entry opportunities for others; coca eradication increases coca prices and induces others to begin producing. Another example is aerial spraying, which weakens whatever loyalty peasants have to the state. The state's presence in fumigation simply delegitimizes the state.

Fourth, it may be argued that to eliminate drugs, current policies need to be aggressively enforced simultaneously. But to do this, the state and a society in coca-cocaine-, poppy-, and heroin-producing countries must have great repressive capabilities and social controls on individual

---

[14]To my knowledge, this view is not formulated in the academic literature, but it is frequently expressed in seminars and discussions by government and multilateral agency officials and individuals working in law enforcement.

behavior. If that kind of society existed in the Andean countries, it would not be growing illegal crops and producing illegal drugs in the first place.

Fifth, because this type of society does not exist, the only other way to succeed is to make antidrug goals the indisputable main government policies, to which all other considerations are sacrificed. This antidrug crusade certainly would be welcomed by a powerful group of Americans but would not have the backing of most Andean or, for that matter, U.S. and European citizens.

As was argued in chapter 3, and following the main thesis of this volume, illegal drugs' production, marketing, and consumption are symptomatic of deeper social institutions and values. Current antidrug policies skirt these problems and pretend they are not relevant. One can then match on the supply side Reuter's (1997) conclusion on the demand side: Antidrug policies have small effects, and the expectation that antidrug policies will get rid of drugs is unfounded.

As has been noted, Caulkins and Reuter (1997) have identified goal characteristics that increase a policy's probability of success and have argued that domestic U.S. policy goals fail to meet those conditions. This failure in the Andean countries is more accentuated than in the United States. Antidrug goals are not objectively defensible, not simply because policies can only achieve marginal results; the problem is not just that the goals do not fit together, but that policies have created deep cleavages in Andean societies and are not politically feasible, for three reasons. First, government agencies that implement policies do not have common goals or cannot force their employees to try to achieve them.

Second, in coca-growing regions like Chapare, growers' unions are a political power that can block government efforts to achieve antidrug goals. Third, in other regions, where the state presence is minimal or worse, there is another de facto violent state that prevents goal achievement. In Guaviare, Caguán, and Putumayo, Colombian guerrillas act as local governments. Antidrug goals are certainly not inspirational. Coca eradication cannot inspire most Colombian or Peruvian citizens, who have grown up in urban areas and have had little or no contact with drug problems. This is why people tend to rally against the drug industry only when there is a terrorist or external threat. Policy goals are relevant to policy decisions in the sense that a policy can try to accomplish an eradication target, but not in the sense that policy decisions can find ways to eliminate illicit crops and trafficking.

Illegal drug policies in the Andes are based on the assumption that profits are a necessary and sufficient condition for illegal drug production, and thus focus on lowering their absolute and relative profit levels. Absolute profit levels are lowered by policies that affect profits in three ways: first, by increasing peasants and traffickers' costs and risks; second, by lowering returns; and third, by making it difficult for traffickers to enjoy and use the proceeds of their activities. Relative profits are lowered by policies that make other crops and activities more profitable and less risky. Current antidrug policies seek institutional changes only marginally and do not confront the root causes of the drug trade.

It is not surprising that expectations for antidrug policy success are unrealistic because, again, the "drug problem" is not a policy but an institutional one, in the sense that illegal drug production, trafficking, and consumption arise in societies with deep social problems and institutions that provide appropriate environments for the development of those illegal behaviors. If profits determined the location of illegal drug production, it would be widely spread around the world instead of being concentrated in a few countries. Illegal drugs are produced mainly in countries in which the state does not control the territory, where there are widespread internal armed conflicts, where some sectors of the population have been excluded from political participation and from mainstream society, where social values and institutions condone illegal economic behaviors, or where for any of many possible reasons the social fabric has broken down. This is not an exhaustive list of the institutional causes of the illegal drug industry, but it simply illustrates some of the most common ones.

For example, Colombia does not produce drugs because they are profitable; it produces them because they are illegal! In other words, Colombia does not concentrate on illegal drug production because it has the natural resources and labor skills and the know-how necessary to grow coca and poppies and manufacture cocaine and heroin; it produces drugs because it has the skills to produce them illegally. Thus, the Colombian state and society are unable to prevent illegal plantings and clandestine cocaine and heroin manufacturing from flourishing because they cannot eliminate the illegal distribution networks that use contraband to smuggle drugs out of the country and to bring in weapons and other goods, such as cigarettes and electrical appliances, to launder the illegal external revenues, and the government cannot expropriate the investments of the illegal drug traffickers. Successful antidrug strategies must recognize that profits are an important factor, but also that the competitive advantage in illegal drugs is based on a weak state and tolerant institutions.

The solution to the "drug problem" can be found only in the long term and requires institutional changes in all Andean countries. This does not mean that all current antidrug policies must be dropped. Some could be useful under some circumstances, but they alone cannot achieve their posited goals. Furthermore, some antidrug policies might achieve results that counter the long-run solution of the "illegal drug problem."

Thus, there are no reasons to be optimistic about "solving" the "drug problem." In the meantime, the Andean countries will continue to struggle with an evolving illegal drug industry that has permeated their societies and their political agendas; that has become more and more complex; and that has acted as a catalyst in a social process that is fascinating and unpredictable but that has made life in those societies, particularly Colombia, more and more unpleasant. In other words, the dynamics generated by the illegal drug industry can easily become perverse; if the root causes of the illegal drug industry are not dealt with early in the industry's development, illegal drugs are likely to become the catalyst for a process of social breakdown with serious grave domestic and international consequences.

Antidrug strategies should also recognize the complex, multidisciplinary nature of the problem. This means that sensible antidrug strategies and policies must be formulated by experts and policymakers who acknowledge their limitations and promote a policy dialogue across disciplines. For instance, economists must recognize that political scientists have something valid to say and vice versa. People trained in statistics and econometricians should be used to interpreting empirical results, and a similar use of other disciplines should be made. In other words, those able to understand the moral, public health, economic, social, political, and environmental aspects of illegal drug phenomena should be brought together in a strategy formulation effort. In the past, antidrug policies have been formulated following a narrow disciplinary approach that disregards the contribution other disciplines can make. It has been as if economists, political scientists, sociologists, and others where enemies of good antidrug policies and their views were not worth being taken into account.

A good antidrug strategy in the Andean countries must acknowledge that the reasons each society produces drugs and participates in the different aspects of the illegal industry are complex and are related to each of those societies' institutions and history. The strategy should be based in the understanding of each society's weaknesses and strengths and should have a long time horizon. This means that antidrug policies should not seek a short-term solution to the "drug problem" but that they should cope with it.

Coping with illegal drugs in the Andean countries requires an acknowledgment that they have been and will be with us for the long haul. It also means that the antidrug strategy should not just focus on fighting illegal drugs but also on the characteristics of the Andean societies—such as political and social exclusion, political power abuse, lack of local and central government accountability, and, in general, poor governance—that make illegal activities in those countries attractive and socially acceptable. There is no question that this is a tall order and that it would be much easier to simply follow repressive policies that would just punish the bad guys, if only they worked.

References

Agricultural Research Service. 1993. Crop Substitution Activities in Thailand, 1973–Present. Paper presented at the International Technical Seminar on Illicit Poppy Cultivation in Latin America, Bogotá, May.

Aguiló, Federico. 1992. *Narcotráfico y Violencia*. Cochabamba: CEDIB-IESE.

Alape, Arturo. 1985. *La Paz, La Violencia: Testigos de Excepción*. Bogotá: Editorial Planeta.

———. 1998. *Las Vidas de Pedro Antonio Marín, Manuel Marulanda Vélez, Tirofijo*. Bogotá: Editorial Planeta.

Alberti, Giorgio, and Enrique Mayer. 1974. Reciprocidad Andina: Ayer y Hoy. In *Reciprocidad e Intercambio en los Andes Peruanos*, ed. G. Alberti and E. Mayer. Lima: Instituto de Estudios Peruanos.

Alvarez, Elena. 1992. Coca Production in Peru. In *Drug Policy in the Americas*, ed. P. H. Smith Boulder, Colo.: Westview Press.

———. 1993. The Political Economy of Coca Production in Bolivia and Peru: Economic Importance and Political Implications. Center for Policy Research, University of Albany, State University of New York. Photocopy.

———. 1995. Economic Development, Restructuring, and the Illicit Drug Sector in Bolivia and Peru: Issues. *Journal of Interamerican Studies and World Affairs* 37, no. 3: 125–49.

———. 1998. Economic Effects of the Illicit Drug Sector in Peru. In *Fujimori's Peru*, ed. J. Crabtree and J. Thomas. London: University of London.

Alvarez, Elena, and Associates. 1996. Economic Structure, Size and Economic Implications of Illicit Drugs in Peru. United Nations Development Program, New York. Photocopy.

Alvarez, Elena, and F. Joel Cervantes. 1996. The Economic Consequences of the "Peruvian Disease." In *The Peruvian Economy and Structural Adjustment: Past, Present, and Future*, ed. E. Gonzales-de-Olarte. Coral Gables, Fla.: North–South Center of University of Miami.

Andvig, Jens Christopher, and Karl O. Moene. 1990. How Corruption May Corrupt. *Journal of Economic Behavior and Organization* 13, no. 1: 63–76.

ANIF (Asociación Nacional de Instituciones Financieras). 1995. Implicaciones Económicas del Desmonte del Cartel de Cali. *Carta Financiera* (Bogotá), October.

Antesana, Oswaldo. 1992. Evaluación de los Programas de Desarrollo Alternativo. In *Impacto de los Programas de Desarrollo Alternativo*. Drogas el Debate Boliviano No. 4. La Paz: Sistema Educativo Antidrogas y de Movilización Social.

Antezana, Oscar. 1995. Bolivia's Coca-Cocaine Sub-Economy in 1994: A Computer Model. U.S. Agency for International Development, La Paz. Photocopy.

Arango, Mario. 1988. *Impacto del Narcotráfico en Antioquia*, 3d ed. Medellín: J. M. Arango.

Arango, Mario, and Jorge Child. 1987. *Narcotráfico: Imperio de la Cocaína*. Mexico City: Editorial Diana.

Astete, Inés, and David Tejada. 1988. Elementos para una Economía Política de la Coca en el Alto Huallaga. United Nations Development Program, Lima. Photocopy.

Ayala, Victor Hugo. 1999. La Economía de la Hoja de Coca. In *Drogas Ilícitas en Bolivia*, ed. E. Gamarra and F. E. Thoumi. Prepared for United Nations Development Program, La Paz, 1999. Unpublished.

Balakar, James B., and Lester Grinspoon. 1984. *Drug Control in a Free Society*. New York: Cambridge University Press.

Banco de la República. 1994. Comments to the Document Colombian Economic Reform: The Impact of Drug Money Laundering within the Colombian Economy, published by the Intelligence Division of the United States Drug Enforcement Agency [*sic*] (DEA). Banco de la República, Bogotá. Photocopy.

Bardhan, Pranab. 1997. Corruption and Development: A Review of the Issues. *Journal of Economic Literature* 35: 1320–346.

Bascopé Aspiazu, René. 1993. *La Veta Blanca: Coca y Cocaína en Bolivia*, 3d ed. La Paz: Ediciones Gráficas E.G.

Baum, Dan. 1996. *Smoke and Mirrors: The War on Drugs and the Politics of Failure*. Boston: Little, Brown.

Becker, Gary. 1968. Crime and Punishment: An Economic Approach. *Journal of Political Economy* 76, no. 2: 169–217.

———. 1976. *The Economic Approach to Human Behavior*. Chicago: University of Chicago Press.

Bedoya, E. 1990. Las Causas de la Deforestación en la Amazonía Peruana: Un Problema Estructural. Clark University and Institute for Development Anthropology, Binghamton, N.Y. Photocopy.

Bedregal, Guillermo, and Ruddy Viscarra. 1989. *La Lucha Boliviana Contra la Agresión del Narcotráfico*. La Paz: Los Amigos del Libro.

Bejarano, Jesús Antonio, Camilo Echandía-Castilla, Rodolfo Escobedo, and Enrique León Queruz. 1997. *Colombia: Inseguridad, Violencia y Desempeño Económico en las Areas Rurales*. Bogotá: FONADE and Universidad Externado de Colombia.

Bejarano, Jorge. 1947. El Cocaísmo en Colombia. Paper presented to the National Academy of Medicine, Bogotá.

Bertram, Eva, Morris Blachman, Kenneth Sharpe, and Peter Andreas. 1996. *Drug War Politics: The Price of Denial*. Berkeley: University of California Press.

Betancourt, Darío, and Martha L. García. 1994. *Contrabandistas, Marimberos y Mafiosos: Historia Social de la Mafia Colombiana (1965–1992)*. Bogotá: Tercer Mundo Editores.

Blanes, José, and H. C. F. Mansilla. 1994. *La Percepción Social y los Hechos Reales del Complejo Coca/Cocaína: Implicaciones para la Formulación de una Política Nacional*. Investigación para el Debate No. 9. La Paz: Sistema Educativo Antidrogas y de Movilización Social.

Bolin, Inge. 1998. *Rituals of Respect: The Secret of Survival in the High Peruvian Andes*. Austin: University of Texas Press.

Bonilla, Adrián. 1991. Ecuador: Actor Internacional en la Guerra de las Drogas. In *La Economía Política del Narcotráfico: El Caso Ecuatoriano*, ed. B. Bagley, A. Bonilla, and A. Páez. Quito: FLACSO and North–South Center of University of Miami.

Caballero, Antonio. 1996. El Costo de dos Visas. *Semana* 744.

——. 1999a. Los Verdaderos Criminales. *Semana* 888 (May 10).

——. 1999b. Sólo Somos Tres. *Semana* 873 (January 25).

Caballero, Carlos A. 1988. La Economía de la Cocaína: Algunos Estimativos para 1988. *Coyuntura Económica* 18, no. 3: 179–84.

Cabieses, Hugo. 1998. Nuevas Tendencias sobre la Coca y el Narcotráfico en el Perú. *Debate Agrario*, March.

Camacho, Alvaro. 1988. *Droga y Sociedad en Colombia: el Poder y el Estigma*. Bogotá: CIDCE-CEREC.

Camacho, Alvaro, and Andrés López. 1999. Perspectivas Críticas sobre los Cultivos Ilícitos en Colombia. In *Las Drogas: Una Guerra Fallida*, ed. A. Camacho, A. López, and F. Thoumi. Visiones Críticas. Bogotá: Tercer Mundo Editores–IEPRI (UN).

Camino, Alejandro. 1989. Coca: Del Uso Tradicional al Narcotráfico. In *Coca, Cocaína y Narcotráfico: Laberinto en los Andes*, ed. D. García-Sayán. Lima: Comisión Andina de Juristas.

Canelas, Amado, and Juan Carlos Canelas. 1983. *Bolivia: Coca Cocaína*. La Paz: Los Amigos del Libro.

Cano-Isaza, Alfonso. 1997. De la Doble Moral y la Extradición. *El Espectador*, March 9: 2-A.

Carter, William E., and Mauricio Mamani. 1986. *Coca en Bolivia*. La Paz: Libreria Editorial Juventud.

Castillo, Fabio. 1991. *La Coca Nostra*. Bogotá: Editorial Documentos Periodísticos.

——. 1996. *Los Nuevos Jinetes de la Cocaína*. Bogotá: Oveja Negra.

Caulkins, Jonathan P., and Peter Reuter. 1997. Setting Goals for Drug Policy: Harm Reduction or Use Reduction? *Addiction* 92, no. 9: 1143–50.

CEDIB (Centro de Documentación e Investigación Bolivia). 1993. La Absurda Guerra de la Coca. In *Violencias Encubiertas en Bolivia*, ed. Xavier Albó and Raúl Barrios. La Paz: CIPCA-ARUWIYIRI.

Cepeda, Fernando. 1994a. Agradecimientos. In *La Corrupción Administrativa en Colombia: Diagnóstico y Recomendaciones Para Combatirla*, ed. F. Cepeda Bogotá: Tercer Mundo Editores.

————, ed. 1994b. *La Corrupción Administrativa en Colombia: Diagnóstico y Recomendaciones para Combatirla*. Bogotá: Tercer Mundo Editores, Contraloría General de la República, and FEDESARROLLO.

————. 1997. Presentación: La Convivencia Política Propicia la Corrupción. In *La Corrupción en Colombia*, ed. F. Cepeda. Bogotá: Tercer Mundo Editores, FEDESARROLLO, and Facultad de Administración, Universidad de Los Andes.

CERID (Centro de Estudios de las Relaciones Internacionales y el Desarrollo). 1994a. *Desarrollo Alternativo: Diagnóstico de la Comunicación Social*. La Paz: Ediciones CERID–United Nations Drug Control Program.

————. 1994b. *Desarrollo Alternativo: Partidos Políticos*. La Paz: Ediciones CERID–United Nations Drug Control Program.

CICAD (Comisión Interamericana para el Control del Abuso de Drogas). 1986. *Estudios Socio-Económicos para la Conferencia Especializada Interamericana sobre Marcotráfico*. Rio de Janeiro: CICAD.

Clague, Christopher. 1973. Legal Strategies for Dealing with Heroin Addiction. *American Economic Review* 63, no. 2: 263–69.

Clawson, Patrick L., and Rensselaer W. Lee III. 1996. *The Andean Cocaine Industry*. New York: St. Martin's Press.

Coleman, James. 1990. *Foundations of Social Theory*. Cambridge, Mass.: Harvard University Press.

Comité Coordinador de las Cinco Federaciones del Trópico de Cochabamba. 1996. *Mujeres Cocaleras: Marchando por Una Vida sin Violencia*. Cochabamba: Comité Coordinador de las Cinco Federaciones del Trópico de Cochabamba.

Coronel, José. 1996. Violencia Política y Respuestas Campesinas en Huanta. In *Las Rondas Campesinas y la Derrota de Sendero Luminoso*, ed. Carlos I. Degregori, José Coronel, Ponciano del Pino, and Orin Starn. Lima: Instituto de Estudios Peruanos.

Correa, Patricia. 1984. Determinantes de la Cuenta de Servicios de la Balanza Cambiaria. *Ensayos sobre Política Económica* 6: 47–125.

Cortez, Róger. 1992. *La Guerra de la Coca: Una Sombra sobre los Andes*. La Paz: FLACSO-CID.

Cotler, Julio. 1996. Coca Sociedad y Estado en el Perú. PNUD, Lima. Photocopy.

———. 1999. *Drogas y Política en el Peru: La Conexión Norteamericana.* Lima: Instituto de Estudios Peruanos.

Cotler, Julio, and Patricia Zárate. 1993. Political Conditions of the Drug Problem in Peru. U.S. Agency for International Development, Lima. Photocopy.

Craig, Richard B. 1981. Colombian Narcotics and United States–Colombian Relations. *Journal of Interamerican Studies and World Affairs* 23, no. 3: 243–70.

Cruz-Saco, M., J. Revilla, and B. Seminario. 1994. ¿Es Relevante la Coca? *Apuntes* 35.

CUÁNTO S.A. 1993. Impacto de la Coca en la Economía Peruana: Perú 1980–1992. U.S. Agency for International Development, Lima. Photocopy.

Dallek, Robert. 1983. *The American Style of Foreign Policy: Cultural Politics and Foreign Affairs.* New York: Alfred A. Knopf.

DEA (U.S. Drug Enforcement Administration). 1994. Colombian Economic Reform: The Impact on Drug Money Laundering within the Colombian Economy. Drug Intelligence Report, DEA, Washington, D.C. Photocopy.

De Franco, Mario, and Ricardo Godoy. 1992. The Economic Consequences of Cocaine Production in Bolivia: Historical, Local and Macroeconomic Perspectives. *Journal of Latin American Studies* 24: 375–406.

Degregori, Carlos I. 1996a. Ayacucho Después de la Violencia. In *Las Rondas Campesinas y la Derrota de Sendero Luminoso*, ed. Carlos I. Degregori, José Coronel, Ponciano del Pino, and Orin Starn. Lima: Instituto de Estudios Peruanos.

———. 1996b. Cosechando Tempestades: Las Rondas Campesinas y la Derrota del Sendero Luminoso en Ayacucho. In *Las Rondas Campesinas y la Derrota de Sendero Luminoso*, ed. Carlos I. Degregori, José Coronel, Ponciano del Pino, and Orin Starn. Lima: Instituto de Estudios Peruanos.

Degregori, Carlos I., José Coronel, Ponciano del Pino, and Orin Starn. 1996. *Las Rondas Campesinas y la Derrota de Sendero Luminoso.* Lima: Instituto de Estudios Peruanos.

Del Granado, Juan. 1994. *Contra la Corrupción y la Impunidad: Caso Narcovínculos.* La Paz: Movimiento Bolivia Libre.

Del Olmo, Rosa. 1988. *La Cara Oculta de la Droga.* Monografías Jurídicas 58. Bogotá: Editorial Temis.

————. 1992. *¿Prohibir o Domesticar? Políticas de Drogas en América Latina*. Caracas: Editorial Nueva Sociedad.

Del Pino, Ponciano. 1996. Tiempos de Guerra y de Dioses: Ronderos, Evangélicos y Senderistas en el Valle del Río Apurímac. In *Las Rondas Campesinas y la Derrota de Sendero Luminoso*, ed. Carlos I. Degregori, José Coronel, Ponciano del Pino, and Orin Starn. Lima: Instituto de Estudios Peruanos.

De Rementería, Ibán. 1995. *La Elección de las Drogas: Exámen de las Políticas de Control*, Lima: Fundación Friedrich Ebert.

De Roux, Rodolfo R. 1990. *Dos Mundos Enfrentados*. Bogotá: CINEP.

De Soto, Hernando. 1986. *El Otro Sendero: La Revolución Informal*. Lima: Editorial El Barranco.

DiIulio, John J. 1996. Help Wanted: Economists, Crime, and Public Policy. *Journal of Economic Perspectives* 10, no. 1: 3–24.

Dombois, Rainer. 1990. ¿Por que Florece la Economía de la Cocaína Justamente en Colombia? In *Economía y Política del Narcotráfico*, ed. J. Tokatlian and B. Bagley. Bogotá: Ediciones Uniandes.

Doria-Medina, Samuel. 1986. *La Economía Informal en Bolivia*. La Paz: Samuel Doria-Medina.

Dourojeanni, M. 1989. Impactos Ambientales del Cultivo de Coca y la Producción de Cocaína en la Amazonía Peruana. In *Pasta Básica de Cocaína*, ed. F. León and R. Castro de la Mata. Lima: Centro de Información y Educación para la Prevención del Abuso de Drogas.

Dreyfus, Pablo G. 1999. When All the Evils Come Together: Cocaine, Corruption, and Shining Path in Peru's Upper Huallaga Valley, 1980 to 1995. *Journal of Contemporary Criminal Justice* 15, no. 4: 370–96.

Echandía-Castilla, Camilo. 1995. Colombie: L'accroissement récent de la production de pavot. *Pròblemes d'Amerique Latine* 18, new series (July–September): 41–71.

Ehrlich, Isaac. 1996. Crime, Punishment, and the Market for Offenses. *Journal of Economic Perspectives* 10, no. 1: 43–67.

Evans, Rod L., and Irwin M. Berent. 1992. *Drug Legalization: For and Against*. La Salle, Ill.: Open Court.

Fajardo, Humberto. 1993. *La Herencia de la Coca: Pasado y Presente de la Cocaína*. Santa Cruz: Imprenta Landívar S.R. L.

Falco, Mathea. 1994. *The Making of a Drug-Free America: Programs That Work*. New York: Times Books.

————. 1996. U.S. Drug Policy: Addicted to Failure. *Foreign Policy* 102 (spring): 120–34.

Falco, Mathea, et al. 1997. *Rethinking International Drug Control: New Directions for U.S. Policy*. Task Force Reports. New York: Council on Foreign Relations.

Farthing, Linda. 1997. Social Impacts Associated with Antidrug Law 1008. In *Coca, Cocaine, and the Bolivian Reality*, ed. M. B. Léons and H. Sanabria. Albany: State University of New York Press.

Fierro-Carrión, Luis. 1992. *Los Grupos Financieros en el Ecuador*. Quito: Centro de Educación Popular.

Figueroa, Adolfo. 1981. *La Economía Campesina de la Sierra del Perú*. Lima: Pontificia Universidad Católica del Perú.

Figueroa, Adolfo, and Farid Matuk. 1989. Fuerza Laboral y Mercado de Trabajo en el Valle del Alto Huallaga. U.S. Agency for International Development, Lima. Photocopy.

Fonseca, Cesar. 1974. Modalidades de la Minka. In *Reciprocidad e intercambio en los Andes peruanos*, ed. G. Alberti and E. Mayer. Lima: Instituto de Estudios Peruanos.

Freeman, Richard B. 1996. Why Do So Many American Men Commit Crimes and What Might We Do About It? *Journal of Economic Perspectives* 10, no. 1: 25–42.

Freemantle, Brian. 1986. *The Fix: Inside the World Drug Trade*. New York: TOR Books.

Fukuyama, Francis. 1995. *Trust: The Social Virtues and the Creation of Prosperity*. New York: Free Press.

Gaitán-Daza, Fernando. 1996. Una Indagación sobre las Causas de la Violencia en Colombia. In *Dos Ensayos Especulativos Sobre la Violencia en Colombia*, ed. M. Deas and F. Gaitán-Daza. Bogotá: FONADE and Departamento Nacional de Planeación.

Gamarra, Eduardo A. 1994. *Entre la Droga y la Democracia: La Cooperación entre Estados Unidos-Bolivia y la Lucha Contra el Narcotráfico*. La Paz: Instituto Latinoamericano de Investigaciones Sociales.

——. 1999. La Guerra Contra las Drogas en Bolivia: Donde los Instrumentos de la Guerra Fría Siguen Vigentes. In *Drogas Ilícitas en Bolivia*, ed. E. Gamarra and F. E. Thoumi. Prepared for United Nations Development Program, La Paz. Unpublished.

Gamarra, Eduardo, and Francisco E. Thoumi, eds. 1999. *Drogas Ilícitas en Bolivia*. Prepared for United Nations Development Program, La Paz. Unpublished.

García-Márquez, Gabriel. 1998. *News of a Kidnapping*. New York: Penguin Books.

Garzón, Edgar. 1997. Estudios sobre Aspectos Legales y Praxis del Narcotráfico y Lavado de Dinero en Colombia. In *Drogas Ilícitas en Colombia: Su Impacto Económico, Político y Social*, ed. F. Thoumi. Dirección Nacional de Estupefacientes and United Nations Development Program. Bogotá: Editorial Planeta.

Gately, William, and Yvette Fernández. 1994. *Dead Ringer*. New York: Donald I. Fine.

Gibson, Bill, and Ricardo Godoy. 1993. Alternatives to Coca Production in Bolivia: A Computable General Equilibrium Approach. *World Development* 21, no. 6.

Giraldo, Fabio. 1990. Narcotráfico y Construcción. *Economía Colombiana* 226–27: 38–49.

Gómez, Hernando J. 1985. Colombian Illegal Economy: Size, Evolution and Economic Impact. Brookings Institution, Washington, D.C. Photocopy.

——. 1988. La Economía Ilegal en Colombia: Tamaño, Evolución e Impacto Económico. *Coyuntura Económica* 18, no. 3: 93–113.

——. 1990. El Tamaño del Narcotráfico y Su Impacto Económico. *Economía Colombiana* 226–27: 8–17.

Goméz, Hernando J., and M. Santa María. 1994. La Economía Subterránea en Colombia. In *Gran Enciclopedia Temática de Colombia, Vol. 8*. Bogotá: Círculo de Lectores.

Gómez-Buendía, Hernando. 1999a. La Hipótesis del Almendrón. In *¿Para Dónde Va Colombia?* ed. H. Gómez-Buendía. Bogotá: Tercer Mundo Editores–Colciencias.

——, ed. 1999b. *¿Para Dónde Va Colombia?* Bogotá: Tercer Mundo Editores—Colciencias.

González, Fernán E. 1997. *Poderes Enfrentados: Iglesia y Estado en Colombia*. Bogotá: CINEP.

González-Arias, José Jairo. 1998. Cultivos Ilícitos, Colonización y Revuelta de Raspachines. *Revista Foro* 35: 43–54.

González-Arias, José Jairo, and Elsy Marulanda-Alvarez. 1990. *Historias de Frontera: Colonización y Guerras en el Sumapaz*. Bogotá: CINEP.

Gonzales-Manrique, José E. 1989. Perú: Sendero Luminoso en el Valle de la Coca. In *Coca, Cocaína y Narcotráfico: Laberinto en los Andes*, ed. Comisión Andina de Juristas. Lima: Comisión Andina de Juristas.

Gorriti, Gustavo. 1990. *Sendero: Historia de una Guerra Milenaria*. Lima: Editorial Apoyo.

Gossaín, Juan. 1985. *La Mala Hierba*. Bogotá: Editorial La Oveja Negra.

Guerrero, Rodrigo. 1996. Epidemiología de la Violencia en la Región de las Américas: El Caso de Colombia. Paper presented at Second World Bank Conference for Latin American and Caribbean Development, Bogotá, June 30–July 2.

Gugliotta, Guy. 1992. The Colombian Cartels and How to Stop Them. In *Drug Policy in the Americas*, ed. Peter H. Smith. Boulder, Colo.: Westview Press.

Gugliotta, Guy, and Jeff Leen. 1990. *Kings of Cocaine*. New York: Harper Collins.

Guissarri, Adrián. 1988. *La Argentina Informal: Realidad de la Vida Económica*. Buenos Aires: Emecé Editores.

Hargreaves, Clare. 1992. *Snow Fields: The War on Cocaine in the Andes*. New York: Holmes & Meier Publishers.

Heale, Michael J. 1990. *American Anticommunism: Combating the Enemy Within, 1830–1970*. Baltimore: Johns Hopkins University Press.

Healy, Kevin. 1991. Political Ascent of Bolivia's Peasant Coca Leaf Producers. *Journal of Interamerican Studies and World Affairs* 33, no. 1: 87–121.

——. 1997. The Coca-Cocaine Issue in Bolivia: A Political Resource for All Seasons. In *Coca, Cocaine, and the Bolivian Reality*, ed. M. B. Léons and H. Sanabria. Albany: State University of New York Press.

Heath, Dwight B. 1992. U.S. Drug Control Policy: A Cultural Perspective. *Daedalus* 121, no. 3: 269–91.

Henman, Anthony. 1978. *Mama Coca*. London: Hassle Free Press.

Hernández, Manuel. 1997. Comportamientos y Búsquedas Alrededor del Narcotráfico. In *Drogas Ilícitas en Colombia: Su Impacto Económico, Político y Social*, ed. F. Thoumi. Dirección Nacional de Estupefacientes and United Nations Development Program. Bogotá: Editorial Planeta.

Herrán, María Teresa. 1987. *La Sociedad de la Mentira*, 2d ed. Bogotá: Fondo Editorial CEREC–Editorial la Oveja Negra.

Hurtado, Osvaldo. 1986. *Political Power in Ecuador*. Boulder, Colo.: Westview Press.

Husak, Douglas N. 1992. *Drugs and Rights*. New York: Cambridge University Press.

Husch, Jerri A. 1992. Culture and U.S. Drug Policy: Toward a New Conceptual Framework. *Daedalus* 121, no. 3: 293–304.

Hyde, Henry. 1995. *Forfeiting Our Property Rights: Is Your Property Safe from Seizure?* Washington, D.C.: Cato Institute.

ILDIS (Instituto Latinoamericano de Investigaciones Sociales). 1993. *Desarrollo Alternativo: Utopias y Realidades* La Paz: ILDIS.

Im, Donald. 1994. The Columbian [*sic*] Economic Reform: The Impact of Drug Money Laundering within the Columbian [*sic*] Economy. Conference Report: Economics of the Narcotics Industry, Bureau of Intelligence and Research, U.S. Department of State and Central Intelligence Agency, Washington, D.C. Photocopy.

INCB (United Nations International Narcotics Control Board). 1995. *Report of the International Narcotics Control Board for 1994.* Vienna: United Nations.

Irusta, Gerardo. 1992. *Narcotráfico: Hablan los Arrepentidos, Personajes y Hechos Reales.* La Paz: Gerardo Irusta.

Isbell, Billie Jean. 1974. Parentesco Andino y Reciprocidad. Kukaq: Los que Nos Aman. In *Reciprocidad e Intercambio en los Andes Peruanos,* ed. G. Alberti and E. Mayer. Lima: Instituto de Estudios Peruanos.

Jaramillo, Jaime E., Leonidas Mora, and Fernando Cubides, eds. 1989. *Colonización, Coca y Guerrilla,* 3d ed. Bogotá: Alianza Editorial Colombiana.

Jaramillo-Uribe, Jaime. 1989. *Ensayos de Historia Social, Tomo I: La Sociedad Neogranadina.* Bogotá: Tercer Mundo Editores–Ediciones Uniandes.

Jaramillo-Vélez, Rubén. 1998. *Colombia: La Modernidad Postergada,* 2d ed. Bogotá: Argumentos.

Joel, Clark. 1999. Tamaño y Efecto Macroeconómico de la Industria de la Coca/Cocaína en la Economía Boliviana. In *Drogas Ilícitas en Bolivia,* ed. E. Gamarra and F. E. Thoumi. Prepared for United Nations Development Program, La Paz. Unpublished.

Jones, James. 1991. *Farmer Persperctives on the Economics and Sociology of Coca Production in the Chapare.* Working Paper 77. Binghamton, N.Y.: Institute for Development Anthropology.

———. 1999. La Experiencia del PNUFID. In *Desarrollo Alternativo y Desarrollo Rural: Debate sobre sus Límites y Posibilidades,* ed. H. Cabieses and E. Musso. Lima: Centro Regional Andino and IICA.

Junguito, Roberto, and Carlos Caballero. 1979. La Otra Economía. *Coyuntura Económica* 7, no. 4: 103–39.

Kalmanovitz, Salomón. 1989. *La Encrucijada de la Sinrazón y otros Ensayos.* Bogotá: Tercer Mundo Editores.

———. 1990. La Economía del Narcotráfico en Colombia. *Economía Colombiana* 226–27: 18–28.

———. 2001. *Las Instituciones y el Desarrollo Económico en Colombia.* Bogotá: Grupo Editorial Norma.

Kalmanovitz, Salomón, and Rafael H. Bernal. 1994. Análisis Macroeconómico del Narcotráfico en la Economía Colombiana. In *Drogas, Poder y Región en Colombia,* vol. 1, ed. R. Vargas. Bogotá: CINEP.

Kirsch, Henry, ed. 1985. *Drug Lessons and Education Programs in Developing Countries.* New Brunswick, N.J.: Transaction Publishers.

Krauthausen, Ciro. 1998. *Padrinos y Mercaderes: Crimen Organizado en Italia y Colombia.* Bogotá: Planeta Colombiana Editorial.

Krauthausen, Ciro, and Luis F. Sarmiento. 1991. *Cocaína & Co.: Un Mercado Ilegal por Dentro.* Bogotá: Tercer Mundo Editores.

Labrousse, Alain. 1995. Pérou: enjeux politico-militaires de la production et du trafic des drogues. *Problèmes d'Amérique Latine,* new series 18: 101–11.

———. 1996. Colombie-Pèrou: violence politique et logique criminelle. In *Economie des guerres civiles,* ed. François Jean, and Jean-Christophe Rufin. Paris: Hachette.

Lamas, Luis. 1995. *Estudio sobre Aspectos Legales y Praxis Penal del Control del Lavado de Dinero en el Perú.* Lima: United Nations Development Program.

Lanza, Gregorio, and Sergio Caro. 1998. Mercados de la Hoja de Coca y de los Productos Alternativos. United Nations Drug Control Program, La Paz. Photocopy.

La Rotta, Jesús E. 1996. *Las Finanzas de la Subversion Colombiana: Una Forma de Explotar la Nación.* Bogotá: Ediciones los Ultimos Patriotas.

Laserna, Roberto. 1996. *20 Juicios y Prejuicios sobre Coca-Cocaína.* La Paz: Clave Consultores S.R.L.

Laserna, Roberto, Gonzalo Vargas, and Juan Torrico. 1999. La Estructura Industrial del Narcotráfico en Cochabamba. In *Drogas Ilícitas en Bolivia,* ed. E. Gamarra and F. E. Thoumi. Prepared for United Nations Development Program, La Paz. Unpublished.

Lavaud, Jean-Pierre. 1998. *El Embrollo Boliviano: Turbulencias Sociales y Desplazamientos Políticos: 1952–1982.* La Paz: IFEA-CESU-Hisbol.

Leal, Claudia. 1995. *A la Buena de Dios: Colonización en la Macarena, Rios Duda y Guayabero.* Bogotá: CEREC-FESCOL.

Leal, Francisco. 1989a. *Estado y Política en Colombia*, 2d ed. Bogotá: Siglo Veintiuno Editores y CEREC.

———. 1989b. El Sistema Político del Clientelismo. *Análisis Político* 8: 8–32.

——— 1996. *Tras las Huellas de la Crisis Política*. Bogotá: Tercer Mundo Editores–FESCOL–IEPRI.

Leal, Francisco, and Andrés Dávila. 1990. *Clientelismo: El Sistema Político y Su Expresión Regional*. Bogotá: Tercer Mundo Editores and IEPRI.

Lee, Rensselaer W., III. 1989. *The White Labyrinth*. New Brunswick, N.J.: Transaction Publishers.

———. 1998. Colombia: Insurgency, Inc. Prepared for Internal Conflict 1998–2025. Science Applications International Corporation. Office of the Assistant Secretary of Defense, Washington, D.C. Photocopy.

Lee, Rensselaer W., III, and Patrick Clawson. 1993. *Crop Substitution in the Andes*. Washington, D.C.: Office of National Drug Policy Control.

Lee, Rensselaer W., III, and Francisco E. Thoumi. 1999. The Criminal–Political Nexus in Colombia. *Trends in Organized Crime* 5, no. 2: 59–84.

Lema, Ana María. 1997. The Coca Debate and Yungas Landowners during the First Half of the 20th Century. In *Coca, Cocaine, and the Bolivian Reality*, ed. M. B. Léons and H. Sanabria. Albany: State University of New York Press.

Lemoine, Carlos. 2000. *Nosotros los Colombianos del Milenio*. Bogotá: Tercer Mundo Editores–Cambio.

Léons, Madelaine Barbara. 1997. After the Boom: Income Decline, Eradication and Alternative Development in the Yungas. In *Coca, Cocaine, and the Bolivian Reality*, ed. M. B. Léons and H. Sanabria. Albany: State University of New York Press.

Léons, Madelaine Barbara, and Harry Sanabria. 1997. Coca and Cocaine in Bolivia: Reality and Policy Illusion. In *Coca, Cocaine, and the Bolivian Reality*, ed. M. B. Léons and H. Sanabria. Albany: State University of New York Press.

Lerner, Roberto, and Delicia Ferrando. 1989. El Consumo de Drogas en Occidente y Su Impacto en el Peru. In *Coca, Cocaína y Narcotráfico: Laberinto en los Andes*, ed. D. García-Sayán. Lima: Comisión Andina de Juristas.

Levine, Michael. 1991. *Deep Cover: The Inside Story of How DEA Infighting, Incompetence, and Subterfuge Lost Us the Biggest Battle of the Drug War*. New York: Dell Publishing.

López, Andrés. 1997. Costos para el Gobierno Colombiano del Combate a la Producción, la Comercialización y el Consumo de Drogas y a la Violencia Generada por el Narcotráfico. In *Drogas Ilícitas en Colombia: Su Impacto Económico, Político y Social*, ed. F. Thoumi, with Olga Lucía González. Dirección Nacional de Estupefacientes and United Nations Development Program. Bogotá: Editorial Planeta.

López-Caballero, Juan Manuel. 1997. *La Conspiración: El Libro Blanco del Juicio al Presidente Samper*. Bogotá: Editorial Planeta.

López-Michelsen, Alfonso. 2001. *Palabras Pendientes: Conversaciones con Enrique Santos Calderón*. Bogotá: El Ancora Editores.

López-Toro, Alvaro. 1970. *Migración y Cambio Social en Antioquia Durante el Siglo Diez y Nueve*. Bogotá: Centro de Estudios sobre Desarrollo Económico, Universidad de Los Andes.

Lusane, Clarence. 1991. *Pipe Dream Blues: Racism and the War on Drugs*. Boston: South End Press.

McClintock, Cynthia. 1988. The War on Drugs: The Peruvian Case. *Journal of Interamerican Studies and World Affairs* 30, nos. 2–3: 127–42.

MacCoun, Robert J., and Peter Reuter. 2001. *Drug War Heresies: Learning from Other Vices, Times, and Places*. New York: Cambridge University Press.

MacDonald, Scott B. 1988. *Dancing on a Volcano: The Latin American Drug Trade*. New York: Praeger.

Machicado, Flavio. 1992. Coca Production in Bolivia. In *Drug Policy in the Americas*, ed. P. H. Smith. Boulder, Colo.: Westview Press.

MACROCONSULT S.A. 1990. Impacto Económico del Narcotráfico en el Perú. MACROCONSULT S.A., Lima. Photocopy.

McWilliams, Peter. 1996. *Ain't Nobody's Business If You Do: The Absurdity of Consensual Crimes in Our Free Country*. Los Angeles: Prelude Press.

Malamut-Goti, Jaime. 1994. *Humo y Espejos: La Paradoja de la Guerra Contra las Drogas*. Buenos Aires: Editores del Puerto.

Mansilla, H. C. Felipe. 1991. Los Enfoques Teóricos para la Explicación de la Economía Informal y Sus Implicaciones Socio-Políticas. In *Economía Informal y Narcotráfico*, ed. H. C. F. Mansilla and C.

Toranzo. La Paz: Instituto Latinoamericano de Investigaciones Sociales.

———. 1994. *Repercusiones Ecologicas y Eticas del Complejo Coca/Cocaina*. Investigación para el Debate No 7. La Paz: Sistema Educativo Antidrogas y de Movilización Social.

Marceló, B. 1987. Víctimas del Narcotráfico. *Medio Ambiente* 23.

Mayer, Enrique. 1974. Las Reglas de Juego en la Reciprocidad Andina. In *Reciprocidad e Intercambio en los Andes Peruanos*, ed. G. Alberti and E. Mayer. Lima: Instituto de Estudios Peruanos.

Mayer, Enrique, and Cesar Zamalloa. 1974. Reciprocidad en las Relaciones de Produccion. In *Reciprocidad e Intercambio en los Andes Peruanos*, ed. G. Alberti and E. Mayer. Lima: Instituto de Estudios Peruanos.

Medina, Javier. 1995. *El Trueno Sobre los Cocales: Coca, Cultura y Democracia Participativa Municipal*. La Paz: HISBOL.

Meier, Kenneth J. 1994. *The Politics of Sin: Drug, Alcohol, and Public Policy*. New York: M. E. Sharpe.

Méndez-Bernal, Rafael. 1996. *Grandes Escándalos en la Historia de Colombia*. Bogotá: Planeta Colombiana Editorial.

Mendoza, William R. 1993. *Los Mercaderes de la Muerte*. Buenos Aires: Marymar Ediciones.

Milla-Villena, Carlos. 1996. Religión Andina. In *Cosmovisión Andina*, ed. Centro de Cultura, Arquitectura y Arte Taipinquiri. La Paz: Taipinquiri.

Mishan, E. J. 1990. Narcotics: The Problem and the Solution. *Political Quarterly* 61, no. 4: 441–62.

Molano, Alfredo. 1987. *Selva Adentro: Una Historia Oral de la Colonización del Guaviare*. Bogotá: El Ancora Editores.

———. 1988. *Los Años del Tropel: Crónicas de la Violencia*, 2d ed. Bogotá: CEREC–El Ancora Editores.

———. 1989. *Siguiendo el Corte: Relatos de Querras y de Tierras*. Bogotá: El Ancora Editores.

———. 1990. *Aguas Arriba: Entre la Coca y el Oro*. Bogotá: El Ancora Editores.

———. 1997. *Rebusque Mayor: Relatos de Mulas, Traquetos y Embarques*. Bogotá: El Ancora Editores.

Mora, Leonidas. 1989. Las Condiciones Económicas del Medio y Bajo Caguán. In *Colonización, Coca y Guerrilla*, 3d edition, ed. J. E. Jaramillo, L. Mora, and F. Cubides. Bogotá: Alianza Editorial Colombiana.

Morales, Edmundo. 1989. *Cocaine: White Gold Rush in Peru.* Tucson: University of Arizona Press.

Mora de Tovar, Gilma. 1988. *Aguardiente y Conflictos Sociales en la Nueva Granada Siglo XVIII.* Bogotá: Universidad Nacional de Colombia.

Mosquera-Chaux, Víctor. 1989. Las Relaciones entre Colombia y los Estados Unidos y el Narcotráfico Internacional de Drogas. Paper presented at a symposium on Colombia–United States relations, School of Advanced International Studies, Johns Hopkins University, Washington, D.C., March 6.

Musto, David F. 1992. Patterns in U.S. Drug Abuse and Response. In *Drug Policy in the Americas*, ed. P. H. Smith. Boulder, Colo.: Westview Press.

———. 1999. *The American Disease: Origins of Narcotics Control*, 3d ed. New York: Oxford University Press.

Nadelmann, Ethan A. 1993. *Cops across Borders: The Internationalization of U.S. Criminal Law Enforcement.* University Park: Pennsylvania State University Press.

Obando, Enrique. 1993. El Narcotráfico en el Perú: Una Aproximación Histórica. *Análisis Internacional* 2: 80–100.

Obregón, Liliana, and Maria Stavropoulou. 1998. In Search of Hope: The Plight of Displaced Colombians. In *The Forsaken People: Case Studies of the Internationally Displaced*, ed. Roberta Cohen and Francis M. Deng. Washington, D.C.: Brookings Institution Press.

Observatoire Géopolitique des Drogues. 1996. *Atlas Mondial des Drogues.* Paris: Observatoire Géopolitique des Drogues.

———. 1998. *Geopolitical Drug Dispatch* 87.

O'Byrne, Andrés, and Mauricio Reina. 1993. Flujos de Capital y Diferencial de Intereses en Colombia: ¿Cuál es la Causalidad? In *Macroeconomía de los Flujos de Capital en Colombia y América Latina*, ed. M. Cárdenas and L. J. Garay. Bogotá: Tercer Mundo Editores–FEDESARROLLO–FESCOL.

Orjuela, Luis J. 1990. Narcotráfico y Política en la Década de los Ochenta: Entre la Represión y el Diálogo. In *Narcotráfico en Colombia: Dimensiones Políticas, Económicas, Jurídicas e Internacionales*, ed. Carlos G. Arrieta et al. Bogotá: Tercer Mundo Editores-Ediciones Uniandes.

Ospina, Paula. 1996. Gasto Público y Privado en Seguridad. B.A. thesis, Universidad Javeriana, Bogotá.

Painter, James. 1994. *Bolivia and Coca: A Study in Dependency*. Boulder, Colo.: Lynne Rienner.

Painter, Michael. 1990. *Institutional Analysis of the Chapare Regional Development Project (CRDP)*. Working Paper 59, Binghamton, N.Y.: Institute for Development Anthropology.

Painter, Michael, and Eduardo Bedoya. 1991. *Socioeconomic Issues in Agricultural Settlement and Production in Bolivia's Chapare Region*. Working Paper 70. Binghamton, N.Y.: Institute for Development Anthropology.

Palmer, David Scott. 1980. *Peru: The Authoritarian Tradition*. New York: Praeger Publishers.

Pax Christi Netherlands. 2001. *The Kidnap Industry in Colombia: Our Business?* Utrecht: Pax Christi Netherlands.

Peele, Stanton. 1989. *The Diseasing of America: Addiction Treatment Out of Control*. Lexington, Mass.: Lexington Books.

Pérez-Crespo, Carlos A. 1991. *Why Do People Migrate? Internal Migration and the Pattern of Capital Accumulation in Bolivia*. Working Paper 74. Binghamton, N.Y.: Institute for Development Anthropology.

Perl, Raphael F. 1994. *Drugs and Foreign Policy: A Critical Review*. Boulder, Colo.: Westview Press.

Policía Nacional de Colombia, Dirección Antinarcóticos. 1993. Amapola: Producción, Procesamiento y Canales de Distribución. Paper presented at the International Technical Seminar on Illicit Poppy Cultivation in Latin America, United Nations Development Program, Bogotá, May.

Pool, D. J., C. Adams, C. Boonstra, and G. L. Morris. 1986. *Evaluation of the Chapare Regional Development Project*. Gainsville, Fla.: Tropical Research and Development, Inc.

Putnam, Robert D. 1993. *Making Democracy Work: Civic Traditions in Modern Italy*. Princeton, N.J.: Princeton University Press.

——. 2000. *Bowling Alone: The Collapse and Revival of the American Community*. New York: Simon & Schuster.

Quiroga, Jorge. 1990. *Coca/Cocaína: Una Visión Boliviana*. La Paz: AIPE-PROCOM-CEDLA-CID.

Ramírez, María Constanza. 1993. El Cultivo de la Amapola en Colombia. Paper presented at the International Technical Seminar on Illicit Poppy Cultivation in Latin America, United Nations Drug Control Program, Bogotá, May.

——. 1998. Conflicto Agrario y Medio Ambiente. *Revista Foro* 35: 5–27.

Rasmussen, David W., and Bruce L. Benson. 1994. *The Economic Anatomy of a Drug War: Criminal Justice in the Commons.* Lanham, Md.: Rowman & Littlefield.

Rasnake, Roger N., and Michael Painter. 1989. *Rural Development and Crop Substitution in Bolivia: The U.S. Agency for International Development and the Chapare Regional Development Project.* Working Paper 45. Binghamton, N.Y.: Institute for Development Anthropology.

Reina, Mauricio. 1996. La Mano Invisible: Narcotráfico, Economía y Crisis. In *Tras las Huellas de la Crisis Política*, ed. Francisco Leal-Buitrago. Bogotá: Tercer Mundo Editores–FESCOL–IEPRI.

República de Bolivia. 1998. *¡Por la Dignidad! Estrategia Boliviana de la Lucha Contra el Narcotráfico, 1998–2002.* La Paz: Ministerio de Gobierno.

Restrepo, María Isabel. 1994. Planteamiento Teórico: Corrupción Política. In *La Corrupción Administrativa en Colombia: Diagnóstico y Recomendaciones Para Combatirla*, ed. F. Cepeda. Bogotá: Tercer Mundo Editores.

———. 1997. Conceptualización de la Corrupción Política. In *La Corrupción en Colombia*, ed. F. Cepeda. Bogotá: Tercer Mundo Editores, FEDESARROLLO, and Facultad de Administración, Universidad de Los Andes.

Reuter, Peter. 1994. Setting Priorities: Budget and Program Choices for Drug Control. *University of Chicago Legal Forum*: 63–80.

———. 1996. The Mismeasurement of Illegal Drug Markets: The Implications of Its Irrelevance. In *Exploring the Underground Economy*, ed. S. Pozo. Kalamazoo, Mich.: W. E. Upjohn Institute.

———. 1997. Why Can't We Make Prohibition Work Better? Some Consequences of Ignoring the Unattractive. *Proceedings of the American Philosophical Society* 141, no. 3: 262–75.

Reyes, Alejandro. 1997. La Compra de Tierras por Narcotraficantes en Colombia. In *Drogas Ilícitas en Colombia: Su Impacto Económico, Político y Social*, ed. F. Thoumi with Ana Lucía Gómez-Mejía. Dirección Nacional de Estupefacientes and United Nations Development Program. Bogotá: Editorial Planeta.

Rice, Condoleezza. 2000. Promoting the National Interest. *Foreign Affairs* 79, no. 1: 45–62.

Riley, Kevin Jack. 1995. *Snow Job? The War against International Drug Trafficking.* New Brunswick, N.J.: Transaction Publishers.

Robertson, James Oliver. 1980. *American Myth, American Reality*. New York: Hill and Wang.

Rocha, Ricardo. 1997. Aspectos Económicos de las Drogas Ilegales en Colombia. In *Drogas Ilícitas en Colombia: Su Impacto Económico, Político y Social*, ed. F. Thoumi. Dirección Nacional de Estupefacientes and United Nations Development Program. Bogotá: Editorial Planeta.

———. 1999. *La Economía Colombiana tras 25 Años de Narcotráfico*. Bogotá: United Nations Drug Control Program and Siglo del Hombre Editores.

Rodas, Hugo. 1996. *Huanchaca: Modelo Político Empresarial de la Cocaína en Bolivia*. La Paz: Plural Editores.

Rodríguez-Bautista, Nicolás. 1999. Del ELN. *Semana* 908, September 27–October 4.

Rojas, Fernando, Germán Burgos, and Mauricio Sanabria. 1993. El Narcotráfico en Colombia: Del Discurso a la Realidad. In *Economía Política de las Drogas: Lecturas Latinoamericanas*, ed. Roberto Laserna. Cochabamba: CERES.

Roldós-Aguilera, León. 1986. *Los Abusos del Poder: Los Decretos-Leyes Económicos Urgentes Aprobados por el Gobierno del Ing. León Febres Cordero*. Quito: Editorial El Conejo.

Ronken, Theo, and Associates. 1999. *The Drug War in the Skies. The U.S. "Air Bridge Denial" Strategy: The Success of a Failure*. Acción Andina, Transnational Institute, Cochabamba.

Rose-Ackerman, Susan. 1997. The Political Economy of Corruption. In *Corruption and the Global Economy*, ed. K. A. Elliot. Washington, D.C.: Institute for International Economics.

Rubio, Mauricio. 1996a. Crimen y Crecimiento en Colombia. In *Hacia un Enfoque Integrado del Desarrollo: Ética, Violencia y Seguridad Ciudadana, Encuentro de Reflexión*. Washington, D.C.: Inter-American Development Bank.

———. 1996b. Reglas del Juego y Costos de Transacción en Colombia. Documento CEDE 96-08. Centro de Estudios sobre Desarrollo Económico (CEDE), Universidad de Los Andes, Bogotá. Photocopy.

———. 1997. Perverse Social Capital: Some Evidence from Colombia. *Journal of Economic Issues* 31, no. 3: 805–16.

———. 1999. *Crimen e Impunidad: Precisiones Sobre la Violencia*. Bogotá: Tercer Mundo Editores and Centro de Estudios sobre Desarrollo Económico, Universidad de Los Andes.

Ruiz-Hernández, Hernando. 1979. Implicaciones Sociales y Económicas de la Producción de la Marihuana. In *Marihuana: Legalización o Represión*, ed. Asociación Nacional de Instituciones Financieras. Bogotá: Biblioteca Asociación Nacional de Instituciones Financieras de Economía.

Salazar, Alonso. 1990. *No Nacimos Pa' Semilla*. Bogotá: Corporación Región and CINEP.

Salazar, Alonso, and Ana María Jaramillo. 1992. *Medellín: Las Subculturas del Marcotráfico*. Bogotá: CINEP.

Salm, Hans, and Máximo Liberman. 1997. Environmental Problems of Coca Cultivation. In *Coca, Cocaine, and the Bolivian Reality*, ed. M. B. Léons and H. Sanabria. Albany: State University of New York Press.

Sanabria, Harry. 1993. *The Coca Boom and Rural Social Change in Bolivia*. Ann Arbor: University of Michigan Press.

———. 1997. The Discourse and Practice of Repression and Resistance in the Chapare. In *Coca, Cocaine, and the Bolivian Reality*, ed. M. B. Léons and H. Sanabria. Albany: State University of New York Press.

Sánchez, Gonzalo, and Donny Meertens. 1983. *Bandoleros, Gamonales y Campesinos: El Caso del a Violencia en Colombia*. Bogotá: El Ancora Editores.

Santos-Calderón, Enrique. 1989. *Fuego Cruzado: Guerrilla, Narcotráfico y Paramilitares en la Colombia de los Ochenta*. Bogotá: CEREC.

Sarmiento, Eduardo. 1990. Economía del Narcotráfico. In *Narcotráfico en Colombia: Dimensiones Políticas, Económicas, Jurídicas e Internacionales*, ed. C. G. Arrieta et al. Tercer Mundo Editores–Ediciones Uniandes.

Sarmiento, Libardo. 1996. *Utopía y Sociedad: Una Propuesta para el Próximo Milenio*. Bogotá: FESCOL.

Scott, Peter Dale, and Jonathan Marshall. 1991. *Cocaine Politics: Drugs, Armies and the CIA in Central America*. Berkeley: University of California Press.

SEAMOS (Sistema Educativo Antidrogas y de Movilización Social). 1993. *Primera Aproximación al Impacto Social y Económico de la Coca-Cocaína en el Departamento de Tarija*. Drogas: Investigación para el Debate, No. 6. La Paz: SEAMOS.

Shelley, Louise I. 1995. Transnational Organized Crime: An Imminent Threat to the Nation-State? *Journal of International Affairs* 48, no. 2: 463–89.

Siegel, Ronald K. 1989. *Intoxication: Life in Pursuit of Artificial Paradise*. New York: E. P. Dutton.

Soux, María Luisa. 1993. *La Coca Liberal: Producción y Circulación a Principios del Siglo XX*. La Paz: Centro de Información para el Desarrollo.

Spedding, Alison L. 1997a. The Coca Field as a Total Social Fact. In *Coca, Cocaine, and the Bolivian Reality*, ed. M. B. Léons and H. Sanabria. Albany: State University of New York Press.

———. 1997b. Cocataki, Taki-Coca: Trade, Traffic and Organized Resistance in the Yungas of La Paz. In *Coca, Cocaine, and the Bolivian Reality*, ed. M. B. Léons and H. Sanabria. Albany: State University of New York Press.

Starn, Orin. 1996. Senderos, Inesperados: Las Rondas Campesinas de las Sierra sur Central. In *Las Rondas Campesinas y la Derrota de Sendero Luminoso*, ed. Carlos I. Degregori, José Coronel, Ponciano del Pino, and Orin Starn. Lima: Instituto de Estudios Peruanos.

Steiner, Roberto. 1997. *Los Dólares del Narcotráfico*. Cuadernos de FEDESARROLLO 2. Bogotá: Tercer Mundo Editores.

Sudarsky, John. 1999. *El Capital Social en Colombia: La Medición con el BARCAS*. Series Archivos de Macroeconomía, Nos. 122, 123, 124, 125, and 126. Bogotá: Departamento Nacional de Planeación.

Szasz, Thomas. 1992. *Our Right to Drugs: The Case for a Free Market*. Westport, Conn.: Praeger.

Tarazona-Sevillano, Gabriela, with John B. Reuter. 1990. *Sendero Luminoso and the Threat of Narcoterrorism*. New York: Praeger Publishers.

Thornton, Mark. 1991. *The Economics of Prohibition*. Salt Lake City: University of Utah Press.

Thorp, Rosemary. 1991. *Economic Management and Economic Development in Peru and Colombia*. Pittsburgh: University of Pittsburgh Press.

Thoumi, Francisco E. 1987. Some Implications of the Growth of the Underground Economy in Colombia. *Journal of Interamerican Studies and World Affairs* 29, no. 2: 35–53.

———. 1990. The Hidden Logic of "Irrational" Economic Policies in Ecuador. *Journal of Interamerican Studies and World Affairs* 32, no. 2: 43–68.

———. 1991. Privatization in the Dominican Republic and Trinidad and Tobago. In *Privatization of Public Enterprises in Latin America*, ed.

William Glade. San Francisco: International Center for Economic Growth.

———. 1992. Why the Illegal Psychoactive Drugs Industry Grew in Colombia. *Journal of Interamerican Studies and World Affairs* 34, no. 3: 37–63.

———. 1993. *The Size of the Illegal Drug Industry in Colombia.* North–South Agenda 3. Coral Gables, Fla.: North–South Center of University of Miami.

———. 1995a. *Derechos de Propiedad en Colombia: Debilidad, Ilegitimidad y Algunas Implicaciones Económicas.* Documentos Ocasionales 38. Bogotá: CEI-Uniandes.

———. 1995b. Los Efectos Económicos de las Drogas Ilegales y las Agendas de Política en Bolivia, Colombia y Perú. *Colombia Internacional,* 29: 7–17.

———. 1995c. Pays Andins: l'échec des politiques anti-drogue. *Problèmes d'Amérique Latine,* new series 18: 3–19.

———. 1995d. *Political Economy and Illegal Drugs in Colombia.* Boulder, Colo.: Lynne Rienner.

———. 1996. Legitimidad, Lavado de Activos y Divisas, Drogas Ilegales y Corrupción en Colombia. *Ensayo y Error* 1, no. 1: 22–45.

———, ed. 1997a. *Drogas Ilícitas en Colombia: Su Impacto Económico, Político y Social.* Dirección Nacional de Estupefacientes y PNUD. Bogotá: Editorial Planeta.

———. 1997b. U.S.–Colombia Struggle over Drugs, Dirty Money. *Forum for Applied Research and Public Policy* 12, no. 1: 91–97.

———. 1999. Las Drogas Ilegales y las Relaciones Exteriores de Colombia: Una Visión desde el Exterior. In *Las Drogas: Una Guerra Fallida: Visiones Críticas,* ed. A. Camacho, A. López, and F. Thoumi. Bogotá: Tercer Mundo Editores–IEPRI (UN).

———. 2002. Illegal Drugs in Colombia: From Illegal Economic Boom to Social Crisis. *Annals of the American Academy of Political and Social Science*: 102–16.

Tokatlian, Juan. 1990. La Política Exterior de Colombia hacia Estados Unidos, 1978–1990: El Asunto de las Drogas y Su Lugar en las Relaciones entre Bogotá y Washington. In *Narcotráfico en Colombia: Dimensiones Políticas, Económicas, Jurídicas e Internacionales,* ed. C. G. Arrieta et al. Bogotá, Tercer Mundo Editores–Ediciones Uniandes.

———. 1995. *Drogas, Dilemas y Dogmas: Estados Unidos y la Narcocriminalidad Organizada en Colombia.* Bogotá: Tercer Mundo Editores–CEI.

———. 1997. La Política Pública contra las Drogas de la Administración del Presidente César Gaviria (1990–1994) y las Relaciones entre Colombia y los Estados Unidos: Los Límites de la Autonomía y los Dictados del Prohibicionismo. In *Drogas Ilícitas en Colombia: Su Impacto Económico, Político y Social,* ed. F. Thoumi. Dirección Nacional de Estupefacientes and United Nations Development Program. Bogotá: Editorial Planeta.

Tokman, Victor, ed. 1992. *Beyond Regulation: The Informal Economy in Latin America.* Boulder, Colo.: Lynne Rienner.

Tovar, Hermes. 1994. La Economía de la Coca en América Latina: El Paradigma Colombiano. *Nueva Sociedad* 130: 86–111.

Trebach, Arnold S. 1982. *The Heroin Solution.* New Haven, Conn.: Yale University Press.

Trebach, Arnold S., and James A. Inciardi. 1993. *Legalize It? Debating American Drug Policy.* Washington, D.C.: American University Press.

Tullis, LaMond. 1995. *Unintended Consequences: Illegal Drugs and Policies in Nine Countries.* Boulder, Colo.: Lynne Rienner.

Twinam, Ann. 1980. From Jew to Basque: Ethnic Myths and Antioqueño Entrepreneurship. *Journal of Interamerican Studies and World Affairs* 22, no. 1: 81–107.

UNDCP (United Nations Drug Control Program). 1993. Alternative Development as an Instrument of Drug Abuse Control. Bogotá: UNDCP.

———. 1997. *World Drug Report.* New York: Oxford University Press.

United Nations Office of Drug Control and Crime Prevention. 1998. *Financial Havens, Banking Secrecy and Money-Laundering.* New York: United Nations.

Uribe, María Teresa. 1997. La Negociación de los Conflictos en el Ámbito de Viejas y Nuevas Socialidades. In *Conflicto y Contexto,* ed. F. Gutiérrez et al. Bogotá: Tercer Mundo Editores.

Uribe, Sergio. 1997. Los Cultivos Ilícitos en Colombia: Evaluación— Extensión, Técnicas y Tecnologías para la Producción y Rendimientos y Magnitud de la Industria. In *Drogas Ilícitas en Colombia: Su Impacto Económico, Político y Social,* ed. F. Thoumi. Dirección Nacional de Estupefacientes y PNUD. Bogotá: Editorial Planeta.

Urrutia, Miguel. 1991. On the Absence of Economic Populism in Colombia. In *The Macroeconomics of Populism in Latin America*, ed. Rudiger Dornbush and Sebastián Edwards. Chicago: University of Chicago Press.

Urrutia, Miguel, and Adriana Pontón. 1993. Entrada de Capitales, Diferenciales de Interés y Narcotráfico. In *Macroeconomía de los Flujos de Capital en Colombia y América Latina*, ed. M. Cárdenas and L. J. Garay. Bogotá: Tercer Mundo Editores–FEDESARROLLO–FES-COL.

U.S. Department of State, Bureau of International Narcotics and Law Enforcement Affairs. 1995. *International Narcotics Control Strategy Report*. Washington, D. C.: U.S. Government Printing Office.

———. 1998. *International Narcotics Control Strategy Report*. Washington, D.C.: U.S. Government Printing Office.

———. 1999. *International Narcotics Control Strategy Report*. Washington, D.C.: U.S. Government Printing Office.

U.S. Department of State, Bureau of International Narcotics Matters. 1990. *International Narcotics Control Strategy Report*. Washington, D.C.: U.S. Government Printing Office.

———. 1992. *International Narcotics Control Strategy Report*. Washington, D.C.: U.S. Government Printing Office.

Vargas, Mauricio, Jorge Lesmes, and Edgar Téllez. 1996. *El Presidente que se Iba a Caer*. Bogotá: Editorial Planeta.

Vargas, Ricardo. 1994. La Bonanza de la Marimba Empezó Aquí. In *La Verdad del '93: Paz, Derechos Humanos y Violencia*. Bogotá: CINEP.

———. 1999. *Drogas Máscaras y Juegos: Narcotráfico y Conflicto Armado en Colombia*. Bogotá: Tercer Mundo Editores–TNI–Acción Andina.

Vargas, Ricardo, and Jacqueline Barragán. 1995. Amapola en Colombia: Economía Ilegal, Violencias e Impacto Regional. In *Drogas Poder y Región en Colombia*, vol. 2, ed. R. Vargas. Bogotá: CINEP.

Vega, J., and Rufino Cebrecos. 1991. *La Enfermedad Holandesa y la Economía Peruana*. Lima: Instituto de Estudios Económicos y Mineros.

Verdú, Vicente. 1996. *El Planeta Americano*. Barcelona: Editorial Anagrama.

Vidart, Daniel. 1991. *Coca, Cocales y Coqueros en América Latina*. Bogotá: Editorial Nueva América.

Villamarín, Lius Alberto. 1996. *El Cartel de las FARC*. Bogotá: Ediciones El Faraón.

Villarroel, Gilberto. 1994. Desarrollo Alternativo. In *Desarrollo Alternativo: Opiniones para Debate*, ed. CERID–United Nations Drug Control Program. La Paz: Ediciones CERID–United Nations Drug Control Program.

Viviescas, Fernando, and Fabio Giraldo, eds. 1991. *Colombia: El Despertar de la Modernidad*. Bogotá: Foro Nacional por Colombia.

Walker, William O., III. 1991. *Opium and Foreign Policy: The Anglo-American Search for Order in Asia, 1912–1954*. Chapel Hill: University of North Carolina Press.

Weinschelbaum, Federico. 1998. El Triángulo de la Corrupción. In *Corrupción, Crimen y Justicia: Una Perspectiva Económica*, ed. M. Cárdenas and R. Steiner. Bogotá: Tercer Mundo Editores–FEDESAR-ROLLO–LACEA–COLCIENCIAS.

Whynes, David K. 1992. The Colombian Cocaine Trade and the "War on Drugs." In *The Colombian Economy: Issues of Trade and Development*, ed. A. Cohen and F. R. Gunter. Boulder, Colo.: Westview Press.

World Bank. 1995. *World Development Report 1995: The Challenge of Development*. New York: Oxford University Press.

———. 1996. Illegal Drugs in the Andean Countries: Impact and Policy Options. Report 15004, Latin America and Caribbean Confidential Draft. World Bank, Washington, D.C. Photocopy.

———. 1997. Helping Countries Combat Corruption: The Role of the World Bank. Poverty Reduction and Economic Management Network, World Bank, Washington, D.C. Photocopy.

Yrigoyen, Raquel, and Ricardo Soberón. 1994. Narcotráfico y Control Penal. In *Drogas y Control Penal en los Andes: Deseos, Utopías y Efectos Perversos*, ed. Comisión Andina de Juristas. Lima: Comisión Andina de Juristas.

Zabludoff, Sid. 1997. Colombian Narcotics Organizations as Business Enterprises. *Transnational Organized Crime* 3, no. 2.

Index

absorptive capacity, Bolivia, 240–41
academic disciplines, 4
accountability, 176–77, 177n
addiction: early US, 18–19, 21;
    medical treatment, 21–22
aerial fumigation: Bolivia, 115;
    dangers, 354; economic results,
    11; environmental effects, 197,
    199; forced eradication, 353;
    peasant loyalty to state, 368; Peru
    and Bolivia, 246; Plan Colombia,
    230, 231; protests, 103, 103n,
    193; Putumayo, 91; *raspachines*
    protesting, 89; Sierra Nevada
    marijuana, 82
Africa, 98
agribusiness, 319–20, 328, 332–33
agricultural economics departments,
    4n
agriculture: credit problem, 319, 331;
    marketing obstacles, 355;
    neoliberal policies affecting, 356;
    Peru prices, 138n; pineapple, 336;
    productive capacity, 52; rice
    crops, 335–36
agronomists, 336
alcohol abuse, Colombia, 35n

alcohol consumption, prohibition, 23–24
alternative development: activities
    categories, 317; British view, 342;
    cash flow compared to coca,
    318–19; controlling supply, 302;
    crop substitution link, 316;
    economist's view, 337; favorable
    conditions, 323; foreign donors,
    316–17; forest management, 318;
    French view, 342; high cost, 332;
    infrastructure benefits, 320–21;
    issues, 315–23; limitations, 322;
    peasants benefiting, 332; peasant
    view, 330–34; Peru, 130–31;
    perverse effects, 320–21; policies
    recommended, 356–57;
    unintended consequences, 324
alternative development, Bolivia,
    323–38; achievements argued,
    336–37; Chapare benefits, 334;
    foreign donors, 114; government
    agencies, 325, 326; history, 259;
    origins, 323; summarized, 307
alternative development, Colombia,
    196n, 346–49; Amazon jungle,
    198; deficiencies summarized,
    307; obstacles, 323; PLANTE

alternative development (*Continued*)
  program, 215, 311, 345–46;
  strategy, 188
Ambiguous War, 282
American moralistic model:
  demonization, 46–47; economic
  crime model, 77, 78
amnesties, 285
Andean nations: distrust, 308; policies
  imposed, 308, 309–10; view of
  drug problem, 338n
ANIF (Colombian Financial
  Institutions Association), 44
anomie, Colombia, 272
anti-coca movements: of 1940s,
  34–35; colonial, 30–31, 33
antidrug policies: assessed, 303–4,
  368–72; attainability criteria, 314;
  Bolivia, 248; causality ignored,
  303; coherence, 312–13;
  conclusions, 368–72; cultural
  influences, 309; culturally
  specific, 17; debate positions,
  304; effectiveness analyzed, 77;
  environmental damage, 169;
  environmental effects, 248;
  evaluation problems, 304–8;
  goals, 306, 308–14;
  implementation difficulties,
  308–14; international agencies,
  302; Mexico, 101; models
  surveyed, 17–18; Plan Colombia,
  231; policy change vs. social
  change, 77; political clout, 51;
  profits vs. illegality, 369–71;
  programs summarized, 9–10;
  repressive bias, 302; social
  scientists, 313; successes, 303;
  summarized, 9–10; supply
  control, 301–2; views, 27–28,
  28n; who benefits, 51
Antioquia, 42–43, 42n, 84–85
apple production and marketing, 349
apuntada, 96
Apurimac Valley, 292
Arce Gómez, Luis, 121

Arciniegas Huby, Alberto, 133
armed forces: Andean nations, 311;
  antidrug policies, 302; antidrug
  spending, 194, 195; Bolivia, 120,
  251–54, 258; compared, 276;
  corruption, 260; drug trade, 108;
  effectiveness, 367; Fujimori coup,
  135; Peru, 131, 135, 260; Peru
  and Bolivia, 250; Plan Colombia,
  231; police rivalry, 311; policies
  recommended, 366–67; Shining
  Path, 288–89, 290, 291, 292, 293;
  social status, 276; territorial
  losses, 276; trafficker-
  paramilitary links, 211, 218
art objects, 164
Aruba, 167n
Asociación para una Colombia
  Moderna, 224–225
assassinations, 195, 350
assassins-for-hire (*sicarios*), 102–3,
  283–84
asset forfeiture/seizure, 206, 207, 359,
  365–66
asset and income laundering, 163–68
asset laundering, 164–165
assumptions, 2
attitudes: Bolivia and Peru, 296–97;
  Colombia, 202, 203n
Australia, 344
authoritarian traditions, 8; behavioral
  control, 64; Bolivia, 248, 251;
  Colombia, 273; compared, 273;
  corruption, 175–77, 178;
  guerrilla, 286, 288; peasant input,
  325; US military support, 366–67,
  366n
Avella, Juan Manuel, 216n
Ayacucho, 289
Aymara religion, 269

backward-linkage effects: Bolivia,
  239; Colombia, 297; Peru,
  157–58, 239
balloon effect: alternative
  development, 321–22, 356;

compensation creating, 329;
eradication, 354; price effect, 355
banana-drying plant, 327–28
banking system, 188, 189, 306
Banzer, Hugo, 119, 125, 251–53, 337
Barbie, Klaus, 254, 256
Barco, Virgilio, 206, 282, 338–39
Barranquilla, 192
Becerra, Manuel Francisco, 216n
Bedoya, Harold, 40, 40n
behavioral constraints, 62–64;
external, 68–71; internalized,
67–68
Belaúnde Terry, Fernando, 128
Beni Department, Bolivia, 114, 117,
119, 120, 251
Betancur, Belisario, 82, 204, 209, 222,
360, 362
biases, 2
biodiversity, Colombia, 197
Bolivia: backward-linkage effects,
239; coca production, 7;
Colombia confused with, 42–43,
43n; dependency theorists, 36;
drug industry, 106–26; drug trade
in 1990s, 121–26; economic
crises, 37, 50; economy, 152–53;
employment, 154–55; "evil
foreigner" model, 242;
extradition, 360, 362; foreign aid
requests, 146, 146n; foreign
donors, 316; military-police
rivalry, 311; new coca, 111–16;
size estimates, 152–55; traditional
coca, 109–11
bombing campaign, 205, 207, 222–23
bonds, foreign debt, 184
book, plan of, 5–10
border areas, remoteness, 285–86
boss chargé, 129, 130
Botero Zea, Fernando, 212, 212n,
224, 225
BP (formerly British Petroleum), 342
bribery, 171, 172, 174, 226. *See also*
corruption
Bush, George H. W., 307

Caballero, Antonio, 39–40, 39n, 40nn
Caguán region, 85, 86, 92, 151
Cali cartel, 97, 99; alliances, 211;
clientelism, 211; control of
market, 99; election funds, 202n;
growth, 99; leadership, 98, 204;
negotiations, 217; Peru impact,
135–36; Peruvian connection,
261n; political strategy, 208;
recent trends, 99; Samper's
campaign, 223–25, 226; social
cleansing, 208; support for, 208
Cambas, 116, 117–18, 119, 244
campaign financing, 211–14, 219, 222;
collusion with traffickers, 219;
extent (size), 219; intermediary
system, 221; local level, 220–21;
Pastrana, Andrés, 213n, 223;
presidential campaigns, 222.
See also Samper, Ernesto
Cangari, 291, 293
Cano Isaza, Alfonso, 39
capital flight, 184
capital inflows, 188, 189–90
capital investment, 8
Caquetá Department, 346–47
Caribbean, 98, 101
Cartagena drug summit, 335
cartels: concept challenged, 95, 95n;
concept of, 6n; creation, 94–95;
dismembered, 303; extradition,
361, 362; history, 6; managerial
core, 151; Peru, 135–36; transport
subcontracted, 360.
See also Cali cartel; Medellín
cartel
Catholic church, 30, 292
Cauca Department, 82, 345–46
causes and effects, 159
Ceja de Selva, 127–28, 134, 294–95
central governments, 273–79
Central Intelligence Agency (CIA):
allegations in Colombia, 278n;
cartel links, 102; Huanchaca case,
255
Cepeda, Fernando, 173n

Chapare region: alternative development, 323–25, 334; Cochabamba studied, 124; *Collas,* 116; compared, 293–94; electrification, 331; environmental issues, 245, 246, 247; forced eradication, 125, 325; history, 111; living conditions, 113; migration, 49, 113–14; perverse incentives, 357; pilot project, 335–36; population groups, 113–14; recent conditions, 124; schools and clinics, 320–21; state links, 293; structural adjustment related, 236; technical assistance, 320–21. *See also* Bolivia

Chapare Regional Development Project (CRDP), 324, 326

Chapare-Yungas Development Project (PRODES), 323–24

Chávez Peñaherrera, Demetrio ("Vaticano"), 259, 261

chemical inputs, 90, 94; Bolivia, 118; Chapare, 124; controlling supply, 302; data issues, 142–43; environmental hazards, 168–69, 246; highways, 321; interdiction effects, 358; policies recommended, 357–58; pollution, 197; substitution, 357

chichipatos, 89

child soldiers, 284n

Chile, 177–78

China, 19

Chinauta Resort Hotel (Girardot), 366

CIA. *See* Central Intelligence Agency

CICAD, 355

civic virtue, 65

civil rights movements, 17, 24

civil self-defense committees (CDCs), 289, 290, 291, 292, 293

civil society: Bolivia, 293; social capital, 67

clientelism, 208; Cali cartel, 211; drug trade, 219; eradication, 347;

National Front, 278; political system, 43, 44

Coca, Ariel, 251, 254–55

coca: Bolivia, recent, 242; Bolivia acreage, 111–16, 153; Bolivian traditional, 109–11; cash flow compared, 318–19; Chapare acreage, 113; concentration, 9; data issues, 142; ecological impact, 169; economic aspects, 33; employment, 151–52; environmental damage, 198; geopolitical location, 53; Guaviare, 296; hectareage estimates, 113, 147, 148; history, 29–35; Inca Empire, 29–30; Marxist critics, 40–41; nontraditional growing areas, 53n; Peru, 99, 134, 155, 322; processing, 53; production in Bolivia, 116–19; production trends, 86–88; pruning, 328n; recent trends, 88, 90–91; regions compared, 293–97; sacredness, 31–32; Samper era, 215; social role, 31–32; Spanish conquest, 30–31; terracing, 110–11; traditional, and environment, 246–47; traditional consumption, 79; traditional regions recognized, 109; types of plantings, 87; Yungas vs. Chapare, 111

coca chewing, 16

Coca-Cola, 126n

coca for development program, 335

cocaine: background of industry, 45; beautiful people, 25; Colombia estimates, 147, 147t; data issues, 142; early black use, 22–23; early epidemic, 18–19; early US use, 18; economic model, 59; history, 79; market trends, 91; output, 303; prices, 59, 59n, 304; production process, 84, 87, 93–94; recent trends, 98; social

class, 25; wholesale prices, 94n;
yields studied, 87
cocaleros (coca growing peasants), 129
Cochabamba, 124, 244
Cold War, 29, 367
Collas, 116, 244
Colombia: advantages, 42; Bolivia
confused with, 42–43, 43n;
Bolivian drug trade, 123; costs
and benefits, 312; costs of war
on drugs, 193–96; criminal-
political nexus, 216–19;
dependency theory, 37; domestic
drug sales, 149; drug industry, 38,
80–108; drug industry actors, 38,
42–45; drug problem viewed,
338; drug trade effects, 181–82;
economic effects, 182–90;
electoral politics, 219–27;
environmental effects, 196–99;
estimates of drug industry,
146–52; estimates of GNP, 142;
history, 85–86; mestizos/
mestizaje, 267–68; organized
crime, 44–45; Pastrana
administration, 227–31; regional
and sectoral effects, 192–93;
social capital, 66; social and
political effects, 199–216;
structural effects, 190–92;
violence, 281–84
Colombian Foreign Trade Institute
(INCOMEX), 344
Colombian immigrants: data issues,
144; distribution networks, 96
colonial era: anti-coca, 30–31; coca
use, 33
commercial agriculture. *See*
agribusiness
Committee of Notables, 217
common good, 174
communism, 26
communities, indigenous. *See* Indians
comparative advantage, 43, 46, 55
competition, 319
competitive advantage, 55, 265, 266

CONALID (Bolivia), 312, 325
conflict resolution, 250, 274
conglomerates, 59, 184–85, 185n, 190;
campaign finances, 221; vote
buying, 220
consequentialist arguments, 20n, 307
Conservative Party, 277
conspicuous consumption, 164
Constitution of 1991, 188; analyzed,
209–10; campaign financing, 212;
crisis origins, 209; drug money,
222–23; electoral reform, 219;
extradition, 195; US pressure,
360–61
consumption: estimates, 144; money
laundering, 160
contraband, 42, 43, 44, 90;
acceptability, 174; cigarettes,
167n; goods, types of, 166–67;
money laundering, 183; money
laundering related, 167–68;
"technical," 166, 167; technical,
183
contract enforcement, 184
CONTRADROGAS (Peru), 312
cooperation, 268
cooperatives, 320
La Corporación, 118, 118n
corruption: alternative development,
332; Andean studies, 173–74;
ANIF view, 59n; armed forces,
260; authoritarian traditions,
175–77, 178; Bolivia, 258;
common good, 174; costs and
benefits, 174; cultural differences,
175–77; defining, 170, 174; degree
of centralization, 179;
drug magnitude, 179; drug
production related, 50–51;
Ecuador, 59, 59n; eradication
officials, 329; factors promoting,
177; illegal drugs related, 170–77;
impunity alleged, 59n; informal
sector, 174; interdiction and lab
destruction, 359; judicial system,
203, 203n; military, 367;

corruption *(Continued)*
  nature, 171–77; necessity debated,
  174; organized crime, 202–203;
  Peru, 260–61; political, 179,
  225–26; private sector, 171–72;
  propensity, 177–79; public sector,
  171–73, 175, 203; rankings,
  51; Samper era, 173n; social
  networks, 8; typology, 178. *See
  also* bribery
Corruption Perceptions Index, 51
cost-benefit analysis, 58; distribution,
  312
"crack" cocaine, 25
crime: economic crime model, 71–74;
  moralistic approach, 20;
  segmented societies, 67; variables
  associated, 61, 75
criminal activities, economic model,
  57–71
criminal organizations: Bolivia, 338;
  Colombian modus operandi, 80;
  extradition, 361, 362; gangs, 60;
  political nexus, 216–19;
  privateering licenses, 276;
  structural shifts, 99
criticism of drug policies: policies
  recommended, 352–72;
  summarized, 27
crop substitution: Bolivia, 114, 115,
  323; Colombia, 344–46;
  controlling supply, 302;
  described, 317; Peru, 130;
  policies recommended, 354–55
Cuba, 102
Cuban criminal organizations, 96

data issues, biases, 148–49
DEA. *See* Drug Enforcement
  Administration
death rates, 281–82
debt crisis: Bolivia, 8, 324; Bolivia and
  Peru, 233; Colombia, 187;
  Colombia compared, 274; impact,
  234; Peru, 8, 235
decertification, 214–16, 227

decriminalization: Andean nations, 35;
  early recommendations, 25;
  policy critics on, 28n
defoliants, 354. *See also* aerial
  fumigation; eradication
deforestation, 168–70; Chapare, 247;
  Colombia, 196, 198; crop
  substitution, 317–18; Peru, 249;
  Shining Path, 249
de Greiff, Gustavo, 218, 218n
de la Calle, Humberto, 213, 216n
delegation system, 132
delegitimation process, 191
demand control, Colombia, 195
demand side explanation, 38–40
demand side perspective, 369
demonization: American moralistic
  model, 46–47; dependency-theory
  model, 46–47
deontological arguments, 20n, 307–8
Departamento Nacional de Seguridad
  (DAS), 207
dependency-theory model, 5, 35–38,
  40–41; alternative development,
  337; demonization, 46–47; drug
  policies, 306; economic crime
  model, 77–78
depoliticization of politics, 279
De Soto, Hernando, 133
deterrent policy effect, 75n
deviant behaviors, 62
DEVIDA (Peru), 312
dialogue short-circuit, 5
dictators, 176–77
Diodato, Marino, 125, 253
Dirección de Reconversión Agrícola
  (DIRECO), 327, 329
Dirección Nacional de Estupefacientes
  (DNE, Colombia), 312, 365
direct foreign investment, 188
dishonesty trap, 71, 74, 178n
distension zone, 108, 228
distribution networks: Peru, 137; US,
  96
domestic value added, 149
Dominican Republic, 176

Doria Medina, Samuel, 36, 36n, 335
downstream interdiction, 359–60
drug consumer profile, 25
drug consumption, Colombia, 79, 84
drug criminalization, early US, 22
drug economy, estimates, 142. *See also*
    economic effects; economic
    features
Drug Enforcement Administration
    (DEA): Huanchaca case, 255;
    liberalization effects, 188–89,
    190; Tranquilandia, 90n
drug governments, 253–54
drug industry: Bolivia in 1990s,
    121–26; Bolivia, 106–26, 116;
    Bolivia, importance, 123–24;
    Colombia, 38, 80–108;
    Colombian angle, 41–42;
    explanation, 38–39; industry-
    specific tasks, 56; Peru, 45–46,
    126–33; size, 141–46;
    structural changes (data), 148
drug problem: Andean nations on,
    338n; Colombia on, 338; differing
    perceptions, 305; foreign donors'
    views, 341–44; possibilities of,
    310; solving, 304; structural
    reasons listed, 370
drug revenues: Bolivia, 240–41; uses
    of, 192
drug traffickers: anti-law enforcement
    activities, 202; Bolivia, 118–21,
    123, 124, 125, 155, 251–59, 338;
    campaign contributions, 225–26;
    corruption, 179–80; estimated
    effects on Bolivia, 240–43;
    extradition, 205; FARC not,
    228–29; guerrilla goals, 107; land
    purchases, 186; leadership
    structure, 204; links to military-
    paramilitary, 211, 218; military,
    276–77; negotiated surrender,
    210, 217; negotiations, 217–18;
    paramilitary links, 226; Peru, 130,
    135–37, 259; political nexus,
    216–19; political values, 200;

recent trends, 54; "repented
    ones," 122
drug use: Colombian consumption, 79;
    productive capacity, 52–53; use
    and abuse debated, 15–18;
    US history, 18–28

Echavarría, Erlan, 121
economic analyses, 3–4
economic booms, 8
economic crime model, 71–74;
    causality of illegal drugs, 75–78
economic crises: Bolivia, 50; drug
    production related, 49–50; Peru,
    50; poppy crops, 92; as triggering
    factors, 77
economic development, foreign
    donors, 317
economic effects, 160–68; Bolivia,
    232–36, 240–43; Colombia,
    182–90; Peru, 232–39
economic features: coca use, 33;
    Colombia, 187–90; competitive
    advantage, 55–57; criminal
    activities modeled, 57–71;
    dependency theory, 36;
    geographical distribution of
    illegal drugs, 53; peasant poverty,
    41; US drug policies, 36
economic growth: Colombia, 191–92;
    violence and corruption, 57
economic liberalization, 187
economic model of crime, antidrug
    policies summarized, 10–11
economic policy formulation, 274, 279
economic theory of crime, 5–6
economy: Bolivia, 242; Peru, 235–36,
    236–39; Samper crisis, 213;
    structural effects, 190–92
electoral politics: drug money, 202n,
    219–27; drug trade as issue, 208;
    influencing, 202n. *See also*
    campaign financing
electrification, 331
elites, coca use, 33
El Salvador, 282n

emerald underground, 107
employment: alternative development, 316; Bolivia, 154–55, 236, 243, 324; Chapare, 124; economic effects, 160; estimating, 150–52; hourglass structure, 161, 161n; incentives to migrate, 321; issues, 103; peasants, 103, 161, 161n; Peru, 157, 158, 243, 260; Peru and Bolivia, 250; regional effects, 193; rural, 151–52
environmental effects, 168–70; Bolivia, 248; Bolivia and Peru, 245–49; Colombia, 196–99, 346; interdiction of precursors, 358; Peru, 248–49; Plan Colombia, 231
eradication, 197–98; alternative development, 322; balloon effect, 354; Bolivia, 125–26, 138, 155, 256, 259, 307, 327–30, 353; Bolivian peasants on, 331; Chapare, 325; Colombia, 82, 346–49, 353–54; controlling supply, 302; environmental damage, 169; evaluated, 353; expenditures, 194; foreign aid request, 146; indigenous communities, 92; involuntary, 338, 353; manual, 231; marijuana, 82–83; Mexican marijuana, 81; peasant compensation, 328–30; peasant opposition, 333; Peru, 130; Peruvian reaction, 134–35; policy goals, 369; policy recommendations, 352–54; Samper era, 215; as state presence, 231; unintended consequences, 248; voluntary, 353; zero option, 335
Escobar, Pablo, 99, 100, 195; bounty on policemen, 211; death, 210–11; electoral politics, 222–23; failure to arrest, 203n; political career, 203–4; prison, 210, 226; terms of surrender, 210

ethnicity, Peru, 129
Europe: Bolivian cocaine, 122; cocaine prices, 145; Colombian marijuana, 84; criminal links, 7; demand growing, 98; distrust of, 308; wholesale cocaine prices, 59
European economics, 4n
European Union, 342–43
evangelical churches, Peru, 289, 292
exclusion, political, 279
exports: Bolivia, 153, 154; drug revenues compared, 150; Peru, 238
export syndicates: creation, 94–96; listed, 97
expropriation, land, 186, 187
external constraints, 68–71
extraditables, 206, 220
extradition, 7, 195, 204–5; arguments for, 361; Barco, 206, 207; Betancur, 204; Bolivia, 360, 362; Colombian administrations, 360; complexity and cost, 361–62; controlling supply policies, 302; Escobar campaign, 100; legal issues, 362; low-level actors, 220; non-extraditables, 220; policies recommended, 360–64; political costs, 362; public opinion, 223; trafficker influence, 201; trends, 303; US pressure, 360–61

family, Peru, 287
FARC (Fuerzas Armadas Revolucionarias de Colombia): army allegations, 104; coca and coca paste, 107; demilitarized zone, 90, 106; distension zone, 228; drug use, 40n; Pastrana negotiations, 227–28, 227n, 229; revenues estimated, 105; Samper era, 214n
feminist movement, 24
fiscal decentralization, 176, 188, 209, 210
food prices, 238–39
footloose industries, 52

foreign aid: alternative development, 337; assessing Colombian, 350–51; Colombia, 342–44; peasants on, 331; politicians, 334–35; poverty in Bolivia, 335; vested interests in, 146

foreign debt bonds, 184

foreign donors: alternative development, 316–17, 331–32; Bolivian politicians vs., 334; drug problem viewed, 341–42; PEC amounts, 341, 350; trafficker violence, 339

foreign exchange: economic effects, 160, 187; liberalization, 187; parallel vs. official, 183, 183n; Peru, 236–37

forensic medicine, 349–50

France, 342

front men (*testaferros*), 96; real estate, 185–86

Fujimori, Alberto, 133; coup by, 135; flights interdicted, 98, 99; foreign exchange, 237; military corruption, 260–61; Montesinos drug link, 261; structural adjustment, 235–36

"Fujimori doctrine," 133–34

funding, antidrug budget, 310–11

fungus ("El gringo"), 99, 135, 136

fusarium blight, 322

Galán, Luis Carlos, assassination, 206, 338

game-theory model, 172

gangs, 60, 345

Garavito, Rodrigo, 216n

García, Alan, 131–33, 156

García Meza, Luis, 120–21, 251, 253–54; alternative development, 323–24; extradition, 360

Gaviria, César, 199, 208

Germany: forensic medicine, 349–50; GTZ (foreign aid agency), 340, 342–43, 349–50

globalization: drug seizures, 359–60; extradition, 361

glysophate, 169, 199

GNP: Bolivia, 153, 154; drug revenues compared, 150

government agencies: Bolivia, 325, 326; Colombia, 339–43; coordination, 310–12; foreign aid, 350; policy goals, 369

government expenditures, Colombia, 193–96

government policies, 6; behavioral controls, 63; crime and punishment, 70; Ecuador compared, 59; goals and success, 369; illegal skills, 57; innovation in drug industry, 97; structural flaws, 59

Guaviare, 86, 89; alternative development, 348; employment, 151; opium, 92; violent settlement, 296

guerrillas: antidrug goals, 369; drug trade, 80; drug trade link, 106–7; early Colombian, 285; Guaviare, 296; kidnapping and extortion, 102, 104, 106; marijuana, 83; motivations, 286; narco-guerrilla concept dubbed, 101–3; peasant support, 103; Peru, 131, 287–93; property rights, 286; recent trends, 98; regional networks, 201; research on role, 88; revenues, 103, 104–6, 105; Samper era, 214; substitute for state, 286; trafficking attempts, 106. *See also* FARC; National Liberation Army (ELN); Shining Path; Tupac Amaru Revolutionary Movement (MRTA)

haciendas, 109, 110

Harrison Act (1914), 22

hashish, 83

health professions, 21

hegemony (US): dependency theorists, 36; drug war vs. Cold War, 29; Latin American strategy, 28

herbicides and fertilizers, 168. *See also individual products*

heroin, 6, 91; Colombia estimates, 147, 147t; comparative advantage, 93n; criminal organizations, 100; prices, 59–60, 304; production estimates, 93; Vietnam War, 24–25

history: geography and, 273; of illegal drug industry, 6; marijuana, 81

Huanchaca region, 254–55

Huanta, 290

human rights, crisis in Colombia, 284

hyperinflation: Bolivia, 233; Bolivia and Peru, 236

"identification" problem, 61

illegal activity skills, 56–57

illicit enrichment legislation, 182

image of Colombia abroad, 341, 345

immigrant communities, drug distribution, 85

immigration, 22–23

imperialism, 305

impunity, 191

Inca Empire, 29–30

incarceration: Colombians, 149; extradition, 363

incarceration rates: antidrug policy critics, 27; drug users, 25, 25n; United States, 303–4

Inca religion, 269

income distribution: Bolivia, 242; Colombia, 8; illegal drug activity related, 49; Peru, 245; Peru and Bolivia, 250; rising expectations, 50; sharp declines, 50

INCORA (Colombian Land Reform Institute), 347

Indians: coca use, 29; Colombian eradication, 346; Colombian surviving, 268; conflict resolution, 250; cooperation, 268;

degeneration alleged, 127, 127n; opium poppies, 92; Peru, 287; pre-Columbian, 267; respect, 269–70; Shining Path, 288; traditional worldview, 296; values, 268–70

individualism, success, 271

individualist behaviors, 9

individual rights, 368–69

industrial development, 344

information about illegal drugs, 2

institutional environment, illegal skills, 57

institutional structure, economic crime model, 76

insurance, "revolution and kidnapping," 184

Integrated Rural Development Fund (DRI), 346

Inter-American Commission for Drug Abuse Control (CICAD), 182n

internalized constraints, 67–68

international division of labor, 3, 4

international organizations: alternative development, 316–17, 327–28; development policies, 317. *See also* foreign donors

Italy, 65, 343–44

Jamaica, 81

Joel, Clark, 240, 240n

joint ventures, 99

judicial system: antidrug policies, 302; corruption, 203, 203n; crisis, 208–9; multilateral court and prison proposal, 362–63; policies recommended, 363–66; trends, 275–76

kidnappings, Colombia, 200n, 282–83

laboratory destruction, 359

labor force, coca use, 33–34

labor market, liberalization, 188

labor shortages, Peru, 156

land reform, 110; Bolivia, 251, 277; Colombia, 279, 284–85, 347;

Peru, 128, 277; policy to prevent migration, 169; programs, 120; La Violencia, 284
land use, Colombia, 275
Law 1008 of 1988, 109, 111n; compensated eradication, 248; compensation paid, 328–29; described, 115; effects listed, 328–30; peasant opposition, 333; PIDYS creation, 326; U.S. influence, 115, 115n
League of Nations, 109–10, 110n
leather industry, 344
legalization view, Caballero, 39–40, 40n
Legal Medicine Department (Colombia), 345, 349–50
legislation: Colombia, 165; Peru, 165
Lehder, Carlos, 94, 94n, 204
leisure consumption, 16
León Saénz, Guillermo (Alfonso Cano), 278n
Levine, Michael, 118, 118n
Liberal Party, 277
liquid marijuana, 83
living standards, 333, 334
location, geopolitical, 42, 42n, 44; coca, 53; production and consumption, 54; profitability issue, 52–54
López, Felipe, 216n
López Michelsen, Alfonso, 222, 343
Low, Enrique, 205, 205n

M-19 guerrilla organization, 102, 103
macroeconomic effects: Bolivia and Peru, 232–36; Colombia, 187–90
manual eradication campaign, 7
Maoism, 288
Marginal Jungle Highway, 128, 128n
marijuana, 80–84; area planted (hect.), 83; Colombia estimates, 147, 147t; Mexico, 144
market system: advantages of illegal drugs, 319; distrust of, 37, 309; production and consumption

patterns, 314; supply and demand, 312, 313
Medellín, 42, 42n, 192
Medellín cartel: alliances, 211; Bolivia, 122; crackdown target, 206–7; electoral politics, 222–23; export syndicates, 97; guerrilla-drug link hypothesis, 102; leadership, 204; narco-terrorism, 204–5, 338; negotiations, 217; Panama meeting, 217–18; rural land, 192, 204; war on, 97
Medina, Santiago, 216n, 224–25
mestizos/mestizaje, 267–68, 270
methadone treatment programs, 25
Mexico, 81; Bolivian connections, 98, 123; certification, 215, 215n; cocaine networks, 100–1; importance, 303; marijuana, 144; payment system, 100–1; smuggling, 6–7, 148–49
migration, 113–14; Ayacucho, 289–90; Bolivia, 245, 247, 324; debt crisis, 324; environmental impact, 198; peasants, 169; Peru, 134, 287, 289–90; policies to prevent, 321; rural-rural, 280; time horizon, 248; urban-rural, 279
military assistance programs, 194
milk-processing plant, 327, 328, 332
M (individual internal constraints), 64, 70, 71–75
model for criminal activities, 57–71; applications of model, 71–74; behavior restraints, 62–64; modified model, 64–71; moral values, 60–62
modernization, 63; Andean nations, 266; Colombia compared, 9; effects on Colombia, 270
money laundering, 8, 44, 96; biases in data, 149; Bolivia, 153, 240–41; Colombia, 182–87; Colombian balance of payments, 145–46; constraints, 162–68; controlling,

364–65; definitions, 162; dollarization, 236; domestic impact, 149–50; estimates, 142, 142n; history, 85, 186–87; investment channels, 184; large sums, 201; legislation, 165; Peru, 238; political corruption, 179; small sums, 201; smurfs, 151; social support networks, 201; steps, 166; subcontractors, 100
monopolies, 184–85
Montesinos, Vladimiro, 137n, 261
moral decay, early US attitudes, 19
Morales, Evo, 112, 112n
Morales Bermúdez, Francisco, 127
moralistic American model, 5, 19–21; policy implications, 26–27
moral values: behavioral restraints, 62–64; changes over time, 61; economic model, 60–62; measurement difficulties, 60–61
Mormon Church, 19
morphine, 18, 19, 93
mortality rates, 281–82
mules, 69, 85, 94; as diversionary tactic, 359; Peru, 130; small traffickers, 97
multilateral banks, 112
Municipal Agricultural and Animal Husbandry Technical Assistance Teams (UMATAS), 346, 348
mushrooms, psychoactive, 81

narco-governments, 120–21
narco-guerrilla theory, 101–3
narco-terrorism, 204–7, 338; effects, 211; extradition, 362; Gaviria, 210
narco-videos, 255–56
National Alternative Development Commission (CONADAL), 326
National Coca Enterprise (ENACO), 127
National Commission on Marijuana and Drug Abuse, 25
National Front, 278
national identity, 2, 2n

National Liberation Army (ELN): funding sources, 283; paramilitary groups, 229; revenues, 105
National Planning Department (DNP, Colombia), 339
National Rehabilitation Plan (PNR, Colombia), 340, 341
national security, 195; foreign enemy targets, 25–26
NB (net benefits of the action), 64, 68–69; policy implication, 75
negotiated surrender (*sometimiento*) policy, 210, 217, 223, 226
neoliberal economic policies, 37
neoliberalism, 187–90
Nicaragua, 102
Nixon, Richard, 25
non-extraditables, 220
nongovernmental organizations (NGOs), 67, 267n
norms: internalized, 67–68; role of, 62
North Valley cartel, 100
Notables, 217
Nueva Cajamarca, 245, 249

OAS (Organization of American States), 182n
Observatoire Géopolitique des Drogues, 54
Ocana, 291
Office of National Drug Control Policy, 70n, 312
offshore banking, 166
oil companies, 105, 342
opiate production, 91–93
opium, 91–93; aerial spraying, 199; data issues, 142; deforestation, 169; early epidemic, 18–19; environmental damage, 198; geographical distribution, 53; Peru, 156; Peru and Bolivia, 246; processing, 53; production, 93; Samper era, 215
opportunity cost of the time devoted to crime, 69

organized crime, 80; cocaine business, 94; Colombia, 44–45; European links, 98; extradition, 363; multilateral courts and prisons, 363–64; political nexus, 216–19; as political threat, 202–3; violence, role of, 281. *See also* criminal organizations; drug traffickers

Pacific Basin, 344
Padre Abad, 249
paisa, 43, 43n
Panama, 102, 276
parachuters, 90
paramilitary groups, 8; creation, 102, 107, 204; drug lord promotion, 192; drug trade, 80, 107–8; lauded, 226; Pastrana era, 229; peasants, 103n; recent trends, 98; revenues, 103; role, 226–27; rural real estate, 186; Samper era, 214; trafficker-military links, 211, 218
paraquat, 81, 92, 92n, 197
Pastrana, Andrés, 90, 106, 227–31; campaign financing, 213n, 223; effects of drugs, 231; insinuations about, 173n
patent medicine industry, 18
Patriotic Union (UP), 205, 207–8, 217
patriotism, 24
payment system, Mexicans, 100–1
payoff cones, 179
Paz Estenssoro, Victor, 325
Paz Zamora, Jaime, 255–57, 334–35
Peace Corps, 81
peace negotiations, 90; drug issue, 106; obstacles, 200; Pastrana, 227–28, 227n, 229
peasants: on alternative development, 330–34; Bolivia, 155; bribery, 172; Chapare migration, 247–48; coca paste, 117, 122; ooperatives, 320; credit problem, 319; crop

substitution, 318; dependency theory, 41; distrust of government, 311, 332; employment, 103, 161, 161n; ethnicity, 267–68; guerrilla support, 103; health hazards, 197; Law 1008 of 1988, 115; marijuana growing, 81; migration, 113–14, 169; organizations in Peru, 131; paramilitary risk, 229; Peru, 129, 259, 287; planning input, 325, 326, 328, 331; poverty, 38–39, 39n, 49; protests, 193; real income sources, 268; role in production, 122–23; three types, 89; Yungas vs. Chapare, 248
peasant unions, 114; antidrug goals, 369; bananas, 328; Bolivia, 112–13, 258–59, 293–94, 328; migration, 347; Peru, 292; social cohesion, 294
PEC. *See* Special Cooperation Program
Pedro Abad District, 245
Perafán, Pastor, 366
Peru: backward-linkage effects, 239; cocaine output, 89; coca production, 7; deforestation, 249; drug industry, 45–46, 126–33; economy, 50, 156–57; effects of drug trade, 259–61; employment, 157, 158; environmental effects, 248–49; estimates, 155–58; new markets, 99; opium, 99; production networks, 129–30; regional impact, 244–45; rural violence, 287–93; traditional coca, 126–27
perverse effects: alternative development, 320–21, 356; quality of life, 357
perverse social capital, 66
Philip Morris Co., 167n
PIDYS. *See* Plan Integral de Desarrollo y Sustitución de Cultivos
pineapple, 336
Pizarro, William "Pato," 118

Plan Colombia: authorship, 229–30; drug rationale, 229, 230–31; effects, 231; lauded, 231; military aid, 230

Plan Dignidad, 125, 155, 337

Plan Integral de Desarrollo y Sustitución de Cultivos (PIDYS), 325–26, 330

PLANTE program (Colombia), 215, 311, 345–46

PNR. *See* National Rehabilitation Plan

point of reference, 1

police: antidrug expenditures, 194; antidrug policies, 302; Bolivia, 258, 327, 329; Colombia-U.S. relations, 215; effectiveness, 367; military rivalry, 311; policies recommended, 366–67; resources compared, 274–75

policy conversion efforts, 305–6, 310

policy effectiveness, growth of drug industry, 77

policy goals, implementation problems, 9–10, 308–14

political economy, 4n

political parties, 201; Bolivia, 255–56; Colombian described, 277; compared, 277; influence buying, 202; leftist, 277

political reform, 209; Colombia, 278–79

political systems, 8

politicians, alternative development, 334–35

Ponanza Valley, 322

Popayán, 31

poppy. *See* opium

Popular Liberation Army (EPL), revenues, 105

population, Colombia trends, 85–86

poverty: Bolivia, 335; drug production related, 48–49; Indians, 127n; as latent cause, 76; peasants, 38–39, 39n; Peru, 128, 129, 238; weakening constraints, 76–77

power inequality, 5, 308, 309–10

precursors, interdiction of, 357–8. *See also* chemical inputs

Presidential Advisory Board on Medellín, 194

President's Adviser on Foreign Matters (Consejería de Asuntos Internacioneles), 339, 340

price controls (commodities), 309

prices: Andean goods and services, 309; Bolivian eradication, 125; cocaine in Peru, 135–36, 137, 138; coca in Peru, 134; coca price supports, 328; Colombian value added, 144–45; manufacturing costs, 358; supply side, 358

prisons, 303–4. *See also* incarceration; incarceration rates

privatization, 37n, 188, 189

production function, 55; illegal activity skills, 56–57

productivity, 16

profitability, 52; antidrug policy goals vs., 369–71; cocaine price structure, 145; early cocaine trade, 85; factors in crime, 61; noneconomic factors, 5; organized crime, 94

profit motive, 3

prohibition, 22, 23, 34

property rights: Bolivian peasants, 330; guerrillas, 286; state weakness, 274

protectionism: effects on agriculture, 38, 307n; repressive policies, 51

psychoactive drugs: responses to, 62–63; traditional drug use, 29; use and abuse, 15–18

public health: colonial coca use, 33; Peru, 249

public health model: Andean nations, 35; history, 21–22; policy implications, 26–27

public-sector salaries, 175

Puka Llacta ("Red City"), 131

punishment: external constraints, 69–71; government, 69–70;

modified model, 64; moralistic approach, 20–21; political backlash, 11; social, 70
punitive policies, 11
puritan values, 309
Putumayo, 86, 107; employment, 151; eradication, 347; peasant expulsion, 90–91; struggle for control, 108

quaaludes, 82
"queen base," 136
Quito, 30–31

race, 22
raspachines, 89
Reagan, Ronald, 303, 306
real estate, 8, 164; urban, 185–86, 186
reciprocal exchanges, 268, 268n
refugees, internal, 279, 280n
regional effects, 160; Bolivia and Peru, 243–45
regions, Peru, 238
religion, 19, 63. *See also* Catholic church; evangelical churches
remittances, 183
research sources and techniques, 2
respect, 269–70
retirement funds, 188
rice crops, 335–36
Rico Toro, Faustino, 256
risk management, 96
river contamination, 249
Roca Suárez, Jorge ("Techo de Paja"), 121
Rodríguez Bautista, Nicolás, 283
Rodríguez Gacha, Gonzalo, 218
Rodríguez Orejuela, Gilberto, 203n, 204
Rojas Pinilla, Gustavo, 273
ronda-coca-narco alliance, 293
rondas campesinas, 134, 289, 290, 291, 292, 295
Roundup, 169
routes, trafficking, 100
rule of law, 272

rural real estate, 186, 192–93; Medellín cartel, 204; Middle Magdalena, 192
rural-rural migration, 280
rural-urban migration, 86, 285; compared, 279–80
rural violence: Colombia, 280, 281–86; compared, 280, 281; Peru, 287–93; La Violencia, 284–85

Samper, Ernesto, 40, 40n; campaign financing, 211–14, 219, 222, 223–25, 226, 227; corruption, 173n; social pact, 214
Samper Pizano, Ernesto, shooting, 205
Sánchez de Losada, Gonzalo (Gony), 257, 307, 335
Santa Cruz: Camba impact, 244; drug trade, 116, 117; elite families, 252; land to powerful, 251; military officers, 120; ranches searched, 252; traffickers, 119, 252
Santos Calderón, Enrique, 39n
satellite photography, 143–44
School of the Americas, 366n
securitization, 237–38
security costs, 191
September 11, terrorism in Colombia, 230
Serpa, Horacio, 216n
Serrano, Rosso José, 215
Shamboyacu, 245, 249
Shining Path (Sendero Luminoso, SL), 131; armed forces, 288–89, 290, 291, 292, 293; deforestation, 249; drug trade, 26, 132–33; evangelicals, 292; Indian attitudes, 270n; peasant Indian culture, 288
sicarios (assassins-for-hire), 102–3, 283–84
Sierra Nevada de Santa Marta, 81–82
sin semilla variety of marijuana, 82
size of drug industry: Colombia, 146–47, 147t; data issues, 141–44

skills, illegal activity, 56–57
SL. *See* Shining Path
smurfs, 151
social capital, 64–67, 170; bonding and bridging, 66–67; nongovernmental organizations (NGOs), 267n; perverse social capital, 66; research, 267, 267n
social cleansing, 208, 211
social consensus, 177
social costs, 16; alcohol prohibition, 23; Peru, 260
social fabric, 65
social institutions, 8–9
social mobility, Colombia, 272, 278
social networks, 8
social pact, 214
social and political effects, 170; Bolivia, 250–59; Bolivia and Peru, 249–50; Colombia, 199–203, 199–216; Peru, 259–61
social protest, 24
social punishments, 70
social reciprocity, 65, 268
social sciences, 27, 313, 371
social support networks, 7; money laundering, 164, 201; notoriety, 96; participants, 96; political links, 201, 203–11, 220; protection, 97; provincial narcos, 220; trust networks, 272
social welfare indicators, 266
Society of Landowners of Yungas and Inquisivi (SPY), 109–10
sovereignty, 364
Soviet Union, former, 98
Spanish-American War, 19
Spanish conquest, 30–31
Special Coca Control and Eradication Project in the Upper Huallaga (CORAH), 130, 131
Special Cooperation Program (PEC), 339–44; other programs, 346; results, 344–45, 350
Special Division for International Cooperation (DECTI), 339

Special Force Against Drug Trafficking (FELCN), 256
special interest groups, 221–22
Special Upper Huallaga Project (PEAH), 130
state presence, guerrillas vis-à-vis, 88
state weakness, 273; conflict resolution, 274; judicial system, 275–76; property rights, 274; remote territories, 274, 275
stock market, 185, 185n
strategic issues, 333
structural adjustment: balance of payments model, 233–34; Bolivia and Peru, 234–66; drug trade facilitating, 236, 238
structure of illegal drug industry, 6
Suárez, Roberto, 119, 120, 121, 122, 253, 254, 255
Subsecretaría de Desarrollo Alternativo y Sustitución de Cultivos (SUBDESAL), 325
supply control policies, 368
Sweden, 327

Tarija Department, 244
taxes, on coca, 33
tax evasion, 70, 164, 166; reforms since 1974, 182
Tebuthiuron (Spike), 133n, 199n
technical assistance: Chapare, 320–21, 336; Italian, to Colombia, 343–44
technocrats, 274
technology, embodied or disembodied, 56
tin mine workers, 113, 114
Tirofijo (Pedro Marín *aka* Manuel Marulanda Vélez), 107
Tocache, 245, 249
trade issues: Colombia, 273, 343, 344; comparative and competitive advantages, 55; compared, 274n; tax revenues, 273; unfair conditions, 38
traditional drug use, 29

trafficking organizations: Bolivia, 97; cartel concept, 95; coca-producing regions, 89; economic crises related, 49–50; history, 84–85; Peru, 97
trafficking routes, 100
Tranquilandia laboratory, 90n
transaction costs, 191
Transparency International, 51, 180
transportation costs, 190n; alternative development, 318; Chapare, 332; Colombian history, 273–74; DEA estimates, 148–49; downstream interdiction, 359–60; highways as landing strips, 324; Peru, 135, 136–37; to US, 145
traqueteros (coca collectors), 129, 136
traquetos, 89
treatment approach, 313–14, 345
Triennial Plan, 325, 330
Trujillo Molina, Rafael Leonidas, 176
trust networks and loyalty, 271–72
Tupac Amaru Revolutionary Movement (MRTA), 132, 260
Turbay, Julio César, 82, 205

UMOPAR (Bolivian police special branch), 258, 327, 329
UNDCP-La Paz study, 336
United Kingdom, 342
United Nations, alternative development, 316
United Nations ban on coca use (1961), 34–35, 79–80, 331
United Nations Convention Against Illicit Traffic in Narcotics and Psychotropic Substances, money laundering, 162
United Nations Drug Control Program: antidrug policies, 302; estimates, 142, 142n
United Nations International Narcotics Control Board (INCB), 313n

United Nations Office of Drug Control and Crime Prevention, money laundering, 182n
United Nations Office of Special Projects (UNOPS), 347, 348, 349
United States: aid to Colombia, 343; antidrug budget, 310–11; Bolivian peasants on, 330, 331; Colombian relations, 214–16; distrust of, 308; drug distribution networks, 42, 44; drug use history, 18–28; interagency coordination, 310–11, 312; market share, 101; military aid criticized, 366–67, 366n; PEC aid, 343; Plan Colombia, 229–31; School of the Americas, 366n; social capital deficiencies, 66; violence compared, 282
Upper Huallaga Valley, 128–29, 244; armed forces, 131; coca growers' response, 134; coca production, 322; development, 294; environmental damage, 249; eradication and alternative crops, 130–31; guerrillas, 260; hectareage, 155–56, 158; rivers contaminated, 249; Shining Path, 131, 132–33, 134
Urabá, 108
urbanization, 266; compared, 279–80
urban real estate, 185–86
USAID: antidrug policies, 302; apples, 349; Bolivia, 112; Chapare electrification, 331; history in Colombia, 343

Valdivieso, Alfonso, 216n
Valle, Luis F., 252–53
value judgments, 2
value systems, 5
varayoccs system, 290
Velasco, Juan, 128, 294–95
Vienna Convention (1961), 126, 331
Vienna Convention (1988), 34, 331
Vietnam War, 24

violence: alcohol abuse, 35n; among traffickers, 96; Bolivia, 243; Bolivian Indians, 114; Chapare, 114; Colombia, 43, 200n, 281–84; competitive advantage, 266; economic impact, 57; Indian societies, 250; opium poppies, 92; rural-rural migration, 280; social capital, 66; social crisis of 1990s, 209; urban surveys, 270
La Violencia, 66n, 273; characterized, 277–78; death rates, 281; individual responsibility, 286; land issues, 284–85; rural-rural migration, 280, 285; summarized, 286
violent actors, 283
violent deaths, 282, 284
Viru-Viru, 293
voting system, 219–20

war against narcoterrorism, 97, 98
"war on drugs": Andean view, 46–47; Nixon, 25; Reagan, 303
water, Colombia, 196–97
weak states: conflict resolution, 9; territorial control, 9
weapons, U.S., 309
weapons trafficking, 80, 90
women: changes in role, 266; Peruvian peasant, 289; Victorian-era morphine, 19

xenophobia, 22–23

Yungas region, 32; environmental issues, 245, 246; history, 109; La Paz vs. Vandiola, 109; water privatization, 37n

zero tolerance goal, 306–7